Agnes Heller

D1563284

AGNES HELLER

A Moralist in the Vortex of History

John Grumley

Pluto Press

LONDON • ANN ARBOR, MI

First published 2005 by
Pluto Press 345 Archway Road, London N6 5AA
and 839 Greene Street, Ann Arbor, MI 48106

www.plutobooks.com

British Library Cataloguing in Publication Data
A catalogue record for this book is available from the British Library

ISBN 0 7453 2194 1 hardback
ISBN 0 7453 2193 3 paperback

Library of Congress Cataloging in Publication Data applied for

10   9   8   7   6   5   4   3   2   1

Designed and produced for Pluto Press by
Chase Publishing Services, Fortescue, Sidmouth, EX10 9QG, England
Typeset from disk by Stanford DTP Services, Northampton, England
Printed and bound in the European Union by
Antony Rowe Ltd, Chippenham and Eastbourne, England

Contents

For Pol

Acknowledgements

It takes a long time to read all of Heller's works and it took me a great deal longer to get to the point where I felt able to offer an interpretation.

I would like to take this occasion to express my thanks to several members of the former Budapest School who have assisted this project in various ways. Foremost I thank my former teacher, György Márkus. To be the pupil of a great master is a real privilege. Since that time we have been friends and colleagues. I've learnt more about philosophy from him than I could say. It was he who arranged some of my first meetings with Agnes Heller. I would also like to thank both him and Maria Márkus for their comments on an early version of my Introduction. On my first visit to New York in 1994, Agnes Heller and Ferenc Fehér very kindly offered me the use of their New York apartment while they were away. Agnes has always been very generous with her time and a diligent e-mail correspondent for bibliographical and other queries. Mihaly Vajda took time to show Pauline and me around Budapest in 1995 and answer some biographical and theoretical queries.

I would also like to thank the editors of Thesis Eleven, who thought so highly of Heller that they published several of my earlier efforts to get her into focus, and Anthony Winder at Pluto Press for his excellent copy-editing of the final draft. Harriet Johnson often kept me amused and gave generously in the final production of the manuscript and index. Finally, I express my gratitude to Pauline Johnson, who read various versions of all the chapters, suggested many improvements and forced me to make most of them. Naturally, I take full responsibility for the final product.

Introduction:
Dark Times, the Existential
Choice and the Moral Mission

'My work is my whole life' – Agnes Heller

For almost 30 years Agnes Heller has been recognised as one of the leading thinkers to emerge from the tradition of Western Marxist critical theory. After Leszek Kolakowski, she is the best-known philosopher to emerge from the now defunct Eastern European communist regimes. Her books have been translated into most European languages and she is regarded as a public intellectual in Hungary, Germany and Italy. She has authored or co-authored more than 30 works on an amazing variety of topics and thinkers in the history of philosophy and has developed her own unique philosophical vision. She has written on ancient, Renaissance and modern philosophy. The impressive historical coverage of her work is matched by its almost unparalleled diversity. While centred in ethics and social and political philosophy, she has extended the orbit of all, introducing novel and neglected areas and topics as well as writing extensively on aesthetics and culture in an ever extending range. Despite this very considerable achievement and the adoption of English as her main language of publication since the late 1970s, her resonance in the English-speaking world has not been as great as that of other leading European contemporaries such as Jürgen Habermas and Michel Foucault. Aside from two early books by John Burnheim and Douglas Brown that focused respectively on her social philosophy and on the work of the Budapest School,[1] Simon Tormey's recent *Agnes Heller: Socialism, Autonomy and the Postmodern* is the only monograph to give an introductory presentation of her main ideas.[2] He also comments on the remarkable lack of secondary material on Heller, given 'her prodigious output, the complexity of her work and the profound changes in her outlook over the course of her long career'. To explain the relative neglect of her work we need to recall the unique circumstance of her early works.

Heller came to prominence from behind the Iron Curtain as a star pupil of the great Hungarian Marxist Georg Lukács. In collaboration with his informal group of followers (the Budapest School) she worked within his programme of 'Marx Renaissance' and initially contented herself with the role of humble interpreter of Marx. This claim has an ironical aspect, as she testifies to the fact that Marx never played a leading role in her early conception of the tasks of philosophy. Yet the first work to bring her to a wide international audience was *Marx's Theory of Needs* (1976). This was supposed to be a 'finger exercise' towards her own never completed theory of needs, which became redundant once her own interpretative effort had said exactly what she wanted to say. Even the theoretically path-breaking *Everyday Life* (published in Hungarian in 1970), which laid the foundations of her own independent paradigm, was couched in a forbidding Hegelian terminology that belied its real originality. Thus, while often breaking new theoretical ground and introducing innovative topics such as everyday life, needs, feelings and instincts into the purview of Marxism, her theoretical originality was obscured and she was later pigeon-holed within the stable of 'humanist Marxism'. This view was reinforced by Heller's own increasing political exclusion as an intellectual dissident. This was both a blessing and a curse. In the first instance, it provided *Marx's Theory of Needs* with a ready audience from a Western left craving alternative Marxist theoretical and lifestyle options and attracted by the aura of humanist dissent. However, it also meant that almost contemporaneous works that announced her break with Marxism only appeared in the West some years after they were initially written. This delay is vital in appreciating the reception of all Heller's subsequent work. By this time, many on the Western left had already succumbed to the seductive postmodern turn and arrived at the judgement that all humanism was either theoretically obsolete or should be consigned to the totalitarian camp. Typically intent on the next wave of intellectual fashion, these readers preferred to celebrate 'iconoclastic' ideas from new theorists rather than the development of new insights in authors they thought they already knew.[3] Finally, political ostracism also meant that Heller was eventually faced with the task of reconstructing her life and career in another country and language. This is an obstacle that has destroyed many intellectuals. Yet Heller's emigration to Australia in 1977 was followed by an enormous burst of theoretical productivity. Writing in another language and re-establishing her credentials in novel surroundings was just the challenge that she needed. In the next decade, she not only authored no fewer than another 15 books and migrated once again, this time to the United States (the New School, New York) but she also finally found her own mature philosophical voice. She has since developed the idiosyncratic position she calls 'reflective postmodernism' and written some of her most innovative and insightful works. But despite this formidable body of work, the high point of her popular reception amongst English-speaking readers has remained *Marx's Theory of Needs*.

The present book is a comprehensive introduction to the work of Agnes Heller, intended to shake such comfortable preconceptions. Why is this book necessary? Tormey is correct to say that Heller has produced a prodigious oeuvre of great complexity and changing outlook. But that in itself is insufficient reason to justify another in the genre of academic secondary works whose value Heller herself quite openly questions. The warrant required is the conviction that she is a thinker who really has something of importance to offer the contemporary reader. To my mind, this evaluation rests upon more than the 'diversity' and 'complexity' of Heller's output or the twists of her 'changing perspective and long career'. After all, many contemporary academic oeuvres meet these criteria but do not necessarily deserve intensive critical exposition. However, only a few thinkers today attempt to provide an almost *total* vision of the contemporary world. In scale and scope Heller's writings are comparable to those of Habermas. His theory traverses the global dynamics of modern political and sociocultural processes and its impact on the life-world and the ethical discourse of contemporary individuals, and articulates all this in the innovative conceptual paradigm of communicative rationality. In a similar way, Heller's works has gradually built into a comprehensive vision of modern '*dissatisfaction*', from the *existential leap* of the contingent individual to the fragile balance of the great social–cultural–economic–political 'pendulum of modernity'. Commencing from everyday life, she has incrementally constructed a view of the modern condition that illuminates instincts, feelings, needs, rationality, justice, ethics, history and the dynamics of modern social, political and cultural life. She, too, offers her own distinctive *paradigm of objectification* and a conceptual language of striking metaphors. But, unlike Habermas, she also wants to accompany the modern contingent individual into her everyday life. Against the modern trend to reduce philosophical ethics to questions of justice, she evokes the contemporary meaningfulness of the classical pursuit of the 'good life' and formulates general maxims of the conduct of a modern ethical life. She purports to fulfil a role in the 'care of the self' that is not unlike that which Foucault in his last interviews allocated to the wise friend. While she shares Habermas' general social-democratic vision and hopes for modernity, she is both more *sceptical* and more *utopian*. She casts an acerbic eye at the potentials of democratic culture but also retains a recessive moment of communitarian hope that resides in the belief that the modern philosopher can still be the bearer of utopia. Of course, in an age where utopian energies have been declared to be exhausted, Heller's persistence in the view that utopia is a constitutive feature of philosophy has contributed to the apparently untimely aura of some of her major works.

If Heller's work demands attention on the basis of the very scale of its philosophical vision, it has also evolved. Along with an *essential unity* that stems from a continuity of fundamental orientating values, her work is characterised by shifting perspectives and tensions. To unlock this complex constellation of continuity and rupture, an interpretative key is required. Yet to find this key is no easy task. A sense of the difficulty is evident in Tormey's path-breaking effort. He subtitles his book *Socialism, Autonomy and Postmodernism*. Certainly Heller's intellectual journey has been characterised by both evolution and discontinuity, by dazzling diversity and dogged single-mindedness. His subtitle captures this combination of stark oppositions and ethical intent: he wants to imply a field of tensions and he is undoubtedly right. What I think is missing from this gesture to the dynamic tension at the heart of Heller's work is a sense of the inner core of this field from which everything else stems. To locate this, we must find the inner pulse of her remarkably diverse and dynamic output. I want to suggest that the pulse that drives Heller's work is a profound dual imperative. All her work emanates from a deep continuity of moral vision and basic orienting values coupled to an urgent need to respond to the changing 'demands of the day'. Beilharz captures this well when he suggests that her work depends as much on intuition and experience as on insight and intellect.[4] However, this goes a little too far and leaves out of account the missing ingredient of moral vision. As we shall see, the roots of this moral vision lie in Heller's experience of the Holocaust and the ethical imperatives it imposed. At the same time, she has always been willing and able to respond quickly and surely to the rapid turn of political events and cultural trends. She has the rare capacity to illuminate the everyday. She brings philosophy to bear on the everyday while, in turn, transforming the everyday into philosophy; she is always receptive to the contingent flow of historical experience and able to absorb from diverse contemporary intellectual influences those with affinity to her own idiosyncratic perspective. This impressive synthesis of the singular and the general often provides insight not only into individual experience but also into the modern condition.

It is this combination of *scale of vision*, the *continuity of values and philosophical intention* and the *urgency to engage the present* that has enabled Heller to produce a philosophy that continues to have much to say to the contemporary reader.

This rare combination of ingredients has its sources in a quite unique meeting of biography, intellect and historical fate. Heller was born in Budapest in 1929. The year of the Great Crash was an ominous sign of the 'dark times' about to descend upon Europe. She came from a middle-class Jewish but hardly orthodox family. Her father was intellectually inclined but restless: although educated in law, he simply could not abide a single profession. Author of a science-fiction novel, he was, according to Heller, a 'hippie' before this became fashionable. A man of broad cultural interests, he counselled her against her initial preference for Schiller over Shakespeare. That Shakespeare constantly illustrates Heller's moral and political thinking, and that his philosophy is the topic of one of her most recent books, *The Time is Out of Joint* (2002),[5] testifies to the absorption of this fatherly advice. During the war her father employed his legal training and fluency in German to assist others seeking documents and travel papers. Heller remembers him even visiting internment camps to help potential deportees. Along with many thousands of other Hungarian Jews he was finally arrested, deported and died in Auschwitz only months before liberation. He had earlier refused to convert to Christianity, an option taken by many Jews in the vain belief that doing so would save their lives. He affirmed the motto of 'never desert a sinking ship'. She heard that even in Auschwitz he behaved courageously. Without any illusions, he continued to bolster the spirits of others. Her father remained for her an exemplification of goodness and moral courage that she was never to forget. By dint of luck and her own adolescent quick judgement, Heller and her mother survived several close brushes with deportation and death in the Jewish ghetto towards the end of the war.[6] Against the backdrop of this personal experience of loss and of staggering inhumanity, it is hardly surprising that ethics has occupied a central place in her philosophical oeuvre. In her autobiography, *Der Affe auf dem Fahrrad* (1999), Heller speaks of the sense of ethical duty that determined her lifelong efforts to understand these events and their implications.[7] Ethics was her philosophical first love, and at the core of her understanding of the philosophical life was a 'moral mission'.

The story of Heller's first encounter with the great Hungarian Marxist philosopher Georg Lukács is both enchanting and revealing. It tells us something vital about her personality and prefigures her commitment to the classical notion of philosophy as a unity of life and work. A young student at Budapest University studying physics and chemistry in the late 1940s, Heller, at the instigation of a friend, found herself in a crowded general lecture listening to an old, quietly spoken professor of philosophy. His lecture was both incomprehensible and mesmerising. She was immediately captivated by this tantalising vista of knowledge about the world and felt compelled to take up its challenge. That afternoon she changed her enrolment to philosophy.[8] Here we have a concrete instance of the existential leap into a calling that was much later to become the centrepiece of her theory of morals. For her, philosophy and life would be inextricably and passionately interwoven. This episode also demonstrates the confidence, resolution and undaunted commitment that have characterised Heller's prodigious philosophical output. She initially felt the lack of the appropriate pessimistic temperament for intellectual pursuits.[9] However, momentary self-doubt was immediately overtaken by her characteristic organic optimism. This latter has assisted her always to rise to existential challenges, such as surviving the Holocaust, divorce and 'political' emigration, and has also underpinned her enormous productivity.

The fortuitous crossing of paths with Lukács was the most decisive philosophical event of her life. The discovery of philosophy presented her with a calling in the Weberian sense. Within a few years she had habilitated under his supervision on the topic of the ethical views of Chernyshevski. Also during this time she married Istvan Hermann, who was a leading member of the first post-war generation of Lukács' students. This marriage, which lasted a decade and produced Heller's daughter, ended in an acrimonious divorce. After habilitation, Heller taught philosophy at the University of Budapest during 1957–58. However, after the Hungarian Revolution in 1956, Lukács was interned in Romania as punishment for his belated participation in Imre Nagy's reform government, and, as his assistant, Heller was already under suspicion. Refusing to denounce the dangerous revisionist in 1958, she was dismissed from her position and demoted to schoolteaching. She was not able to return to research until 1963. With the assistance of 'Budapest School' friends and the intervention of Andras Hegedus, who was at that time the director of the Institute of Sociology, she was appointed as a researcher in sociology. Official ostracism had not excluded the support of the small group of young friends and intellectuals that was forming around Lukács in the last decade of his life. This group included Heller's second husband, Ferenc Fehér, whom she married in 1963, her colleague in philosophy from the University of Budapest György Márkus, his wife Maria and Mihaly Vajda, her own erstwhile student. This informal group enthusiastically discussed their respective individual and joint efforts as contributions to the Lukácsian programme of a 'Renaissance of Marxism'. Yet, Heller's return to research by no means signified 'rehabilitation': she was excluded from teaching or postgraduate students. Party authorities clearly hoped she had learnt her lesson.

The slogan 'Renaissance of Marx' had a double meaning. Firstly, 'back to Marx' signified a critique of the official diamat of the Communist Party. It heralded a theoretical retrieval of Marx's own intentions and the basic ideas of his various efforts at emancipatory critical theory. Secondly, and even more fundamentally, it promised revitalisation. Now 100 years old, the original Marxian programme needed to be amended and filled out. Classical texts and ideas must address contemporary problems and develop new perspectives. This programme to rejuvenate the critical function of Marxism was not merely a theoretical endeavour. Official Marxism was viewed as a symptom of the gross distortion of socialist ideals. 'Really existing socialism' had to be confronted with the emancipatory values embodied in Marx's authentic vision of communist society. This belief (or illusion as it turned out) was accompanied by a commitment to a broad but vague vision of 'reform communism'. Only after 1968 and the Soviet invasion of Czechoslovakia did the members of the school recognise that their earlier hopes for reform were misplaced and that the regime was not capable of internal correction. They came to view their own earlier 'reformist' stand as apologetics because they had simply presupposed that this regime was reformable. From this time on, they entered a course of direct collision with the regime.

Until Lukács' death in 1971, they were partially protected by his international reputation. Soon after he died, however, the communist authorities used privately circulated writings as a pretext to remove Heller from public life for a second and final time. In 1973 some leading figures of the school were dismissed from their positions and the others resigned in solidarity. They endured several years of 'political' unemployment, official surveillance and living on translation. However, harassment and discrimination against the Márkus children at university entrance finally convinced the core group they had little alternative but to emigrate. Aside from Vajda, who also began teaching in West Germany, all found jobs in Australia. Heller and Fehér spent the next nine years in Melbourne with Heller as a reader in the Department of Sociology at La Trobe University. Their impact on the Melbourne intellectual scene was immediate and considerable. They heavily influenced the group of young intellectuals who formed what was to become the leading Australian journal of social theory, *Thesis Eleven*. However, by 1986 Fehér's continuing difficulty finding a permanent position in Australia persuaded them to take up positions offered at the New School for Social Research in New York. Soon after her arrival in New York, the New School bestowed on Heller's chair the title of Hannah Arendt Professor of Philosophy. With the collapse of Eastern European communism in 1989, Heller and Fehér frequently revisited Budapest. They were officially rehabilitated and inducted into the Hungarian Academy of Sciences. This run of good fortune was shattered by Fehér's sudden death in 1994. More than a marriage and a family, Fehér had provided Heller with a significant intellectual partnership over 30 years. As author of books on the modern novel and numerous articles on aesthetics and as co-author of a number of books with Heller and others on the French Revolution and the politics of Eastern Europe,[10] he was a significant intellectual in his own right. In their political essays it is difficult to distinguish their views. In the domains where they developed and published their ideas jointly I will occasionally cite his work in order to elucidate aspects of her standpoint. This is especially relevant to their political essays and the early theory of modernity.

During the years of emigration and since her return to live in Budapest, Heller has published many books in a wide variety of areas. The author of *Renaissance Man* is indeed a Renaissance woman. Well over seventy, she remains vital and very productive. In her recent autobiography, she announced a sort of retirement from what she has called 'systematic philosophy' and a return to the interests of her adolescence. Nevertheless, this has definitely not reduced the flow of her publications. Recent books on the historical Jesus and Shakespeare are proof enough.[11] Her proximity to unprecedented historical events of the twentieth century has even followed her into the new century. She was in New York at the time of 9/11 and it was this sudden re-emergence of terror that prompted an unanticipated return to political theory.[12] This capacity for an immediate response to current events is typical of Heller and makes it clear that her self-proclaimed retirement from work on these questions is very much conditional and dependent on the unpredictable course of historical fortune.[13] She remains a truly cosmopolitan intellectual who continues to lecture and teach all over the world and to teach for a part of the year in New York. Yet, as her writing on 'home' once made clear, Heller resides mostly in her current intellectual projects, where she is equally at home almost anywhere in the history of Western philosophy or at its junctures with popular culture, everyday life and politics.

As suggested, with Heller prodigious intellectual coverage is coupled with a rare capacity to synthesise, bridge and originate in the light of contemporary experience and events. These intellectual capacities were forged in extraordinary historical circumstances. The young

Heller lived through the Second World War, the Holocaust, the last years of Stalinism, Kádár's Hungary and 'political emigration'. She has been provided with an ample ration of those 'dark times' she has always viewed as fertile soil for the existential calling of philosophy. The result is a unique perspective tempered by the experience of a variety of cultures and regimes, times and politics and immense learning. Heller views modernity as a society of paradox. This society thrives in a precarious state of equilibrium between dynamism and chaos. Given the extraordinary parallelism between Heller's own biography and the flux of recent world history, it is not surprising that her work is a site of similar paradox. She has a remarkable talent not only for metamorphosis but also for holding opposites together in tension and turning them to philosophical account in an illuminating way. She has remained true to her moral mission and key values while urgently responding to rapidly changing circumstances and novel historical challenges. This dual imperative explains the subtitle of my book: *A Moralist in the Vortex of History*. Early in her philosophical career she believed it incumbent on Marxism to provide answers to all fundamental philosophical questions, including ethics. Her introduction of a whole new range of topics into Marxist discourse was a first instalment of this promise. With the new theoretical freedom that followed the break with Marxism this initial aim was transmogrified into a bold attempt to resurvey the entire theoretical terrain and give shape to a post-Marxist *radical philosophy*. However, within a few years even this programme quickly mutated into her mature reflective postmodernism. She willingly accepted the postmodernism signature when she realised the full implications of her left-wing radical commitment to pluralism. This shift was a realignment rather than a rupture. To give full expression to her core values she moved without hesitation on to the postmodern terrain. Yet this did not mean a capitulation to an exclusively negative critique nor a sacrifice of the orientating values of freedom and equality.

The impressive continuity of purpose remains through the twists of her thinking. At all times, Heller viewed philosophical rationality as an expression of the values of freedom and equality even if it had *to negotiate the real internal tensions between these values*. Her most recent reflective postmodern phase has been especially concerned to force these tensions out of conventional straitjackets and reconcile them with human contingency. For her, these efforts exemplify the essence of philosophy. This is an enterprise built on reconciling immanent tensions. For Heller, philosophy is founded on the miraculous sleight of hand that mediates 'is' and 'ought' and somehow holds these two in creative tension. It is a vital expression of social existence with a crucial functional and creative role to perform. Heller is a passionate philosopher because she has committed her life to this role. The philosopher ought to express all the tensions and contradictions of modern life while, at the same time, protecting the reservoir of values and intellectual tools that allows her to think through these issues. If what emerges from this endeavour is not knowledge in the sense of *episteme*, then it is at least enhanced self-understanding and self-consciousness. Heller has conceived her own role as that of providing the orientation and moral 'crutches' she is convinced most individuals will need from time to time to make their way through the difficulties of the complex and contingent modern world.

Wholehearted commitment to this very serious 'game' has allowed Heller to acknowledge and explore the tensions in her own intellectual and value commitments. The young optimist had to learn that serious contemplation was not the preserve of the pessimist. She also had to discover that the will to symmetry, system and solutions – 'to make everything click' – is a false dawn that typically only obscures the deeper problems and the ultimately contingent and paradoxical character of our times. At the same time, her understanding of philosophy as rational utopia has had to struggle with increasingly pervasive suspicion that the philosopher is no better qualified than anyone else to offer utopian insights. The devotee of European high culture has also had to come to terms with modern 'omnivorous culture' with its emphatic subjectivism and erosion of 'taste'. She struggles to hold on both to universal values and to the postmodern recognition of deep historicity and cultural pluralism. In the following pages we examine just how these and other tensions are formulated and dealt with in Heller's work. The existence of such tensions is not surprising in a thinker of Heller's rank. Nor is my interest solely confined to assessing the adequacy of her attempts to resolve them. Of course, answers to these questions are important in the ultimate assessment of any philosophy. However, we actually come much closer to the spirit of Agnes Heller's work if we view her 'solutions' as prompts that facilitate our own exploration of the many paradoxes that permeate the modern human condition. Heller says categorically that she was never interested in the 'solutions' of other philosophers for their own sake. She was much happier to take up their questions and work towards her own answers. For her, this is the task set before the true philosopher.

These paradoxical elements and creative tensions are evident in the major turns in Heller's work. While the story of her biographical displacement is not untypical of a central European Jew during the middle decades of this century, her close association with Lukács and the subsequent flowering of the Budapest School is almost a unique episode. Yet the story of Heller's own philosophy is also in large part one of the conclusions to the story of Western Marxism and the beginnings of an entirely new venture whose outcome is still rather obscure. Heller and the other members of the Budapest School soon developed serious theoretical misgivings about the fundamental theoretical direction of Lukács' last work on social ontology. In spite of this, they remained committed to the project of reviving Marx both as the exponent of the most comprehensive critical theory of bourgeois society and as a reform perspective within Eastern Europe. From a contemporary perspective her commitment to this programme could be viewed as a source of both strength and weakness.

Although Lukács himself ultimately became infected by the virus of a rigid Marxist orthodoxy that he had spent most of his Marxist career combating, his young colleagues drew their inspiration from his early founding contribution to Western Marxism: *History and Class Consciousness* (1923). Their humanist Marxism was a theoretically sophisticated attack on scientism and historical determinism and a defence of the role of consciousness, ideology and praxis in human history and politics. As we have seen, living under the somewhat milder Kádár regime of the 1960s, the group's reformist illusions were sustained longer than they might otherwise have been. Even after the suppression of the Prague Spring and the disappearance of these illusions, Heller's comprehensive reappraisal of her allegiance to Marxism was delayed by the practical difficulties of dismissal, cultural marginalisation and bans on publication. It is difficult for a contemporary reader of her early works to fully appreciate this truly impressive attempt to breathe new life into orthodoxy and to abandon all theoretically indefensible dogma while remaining within an overarching Marxist philosophy of history. I have gone to some lengths in the first two chapters to recreate this context and her attempts at innovation. But her acute sensibility for prevailing cultural breezes has never dictated her theoretical position. True to her father's moral maxim, never one to follow intellectual fashion or abandon friends, Heller worked within the humanist Marxist framework until it was absolutely clear that it could no longer be theoretically resuscitated and reconciled with emancipatory politics. Here we witness this same staunch commitment to cherished values and resistance to conformism that earlier surfaced in her refusal to denounce Lukács.

I previously mentioned Heller's initial doubts about whether she possessed the most suitable temperament for intellectual pursuits. Fortunately she was quick to recognise that pessimism does not ennoble man. Yet her early self-doubt was not completely misplaced. In retrospect, she admitted that as a young philosopher she could not avoid the spell of the system. She felt a pressing need to see 'everything click', to tic up all loose ends and allow her philosophical vision to culminate in unity, coherence and the utopian end of alienation promised by the Marxian philosophy of history as the jolly joker.[14] This discomfort with loose ends, paradox and fragmentation remained a strong residual impulse in her work into the immediate post-Marxist phase. In works like *A Radical Philosophy* and *Theory of History* she seemed, even to her former Budapest colleague Mihaly Vajda, to still be involved in the construction of a 'monumental building'.[15] On the model of classical German Idealism, each new book seemed like another stone in the construction of a philosophical system. Only when she had fully assimilated the break with Marx could she finally begin to reconcile herself fully to contingency and paradox. While Heller's philosophical character is marked by a certain systematic intent and classicist elements, these are now very much tempered by the sceptical postmodern moment of fallibility, open-endedness and paradox.

In the light of emigration and the opportunity to rethink her own commitments and the experience of the 'dictatorship over needs', she finally closed the circle and connected the Marxian philosophy of history to political substitutionalism, therefore viewing it as justifying the negation of freedom. In another light, this allegiance could seem only less original and philosophically groundbreaking to an audience that no longer associated Marxism with radicalism. Theoretical loyalty to the Lukácsian programme, along with the practical difficulties associated with being a marginalised dissident in her own country, was also responsible for the delay in finding her own unique philosophical voice. Heller writes easily and is capable of beautiful prose.[16] She has ready powers of striking formulation and real evocation. However, too often during the Marxist and immediate post-Marxist period, her prose and originality were stultified and constrained by theoretical and terminological baggage. Only in emigration did she gradually find her authentic voice and style, along with her idiosyncratic postmodern perspective.

It would be a mistake to view Heller's relation to Marxism as merely that of some form of impediment from which she was finally able to liberate herself. While it aided her systematising bent and her will for closure, she also derived things of great value from it. It provided form for her moral intent and a method that linked this impulse to an appreciation of historicity. She understood philosophy from the Marxian perspective of practical engagement. Those who wish to change the world stand before the task of making sense of the flow of contingent historical experiences. While Heller eventually came to condemn the reckless theoretical ambition that had inspired the Marxian presumption to enlighten everyday consciousness and direct politics, she has nonetheless always striven to criticise the existing from the standpoint of 'ought', to bring clarity and perspective to contemporary experience. When Marxism was no longer able to do this, she struck out on her own to fashion a conceptual armoury that would do justice both to critical ambitions and to the complex dialectics of modernity. Keeping the core values of her life experience always in sight, she was not afraid to innovate, synthesise disparate traditions and respond quickly to political events and cultural trends as they emerged. This virtuoso talent to draw philosophy from the sinews of the everyday and simultaneously bring her philosophical *instrumentarium* to bear on the analysis of the quodian is one of the outstanding features of Heller's work as a whole.

In this respect her relative silence on feminist issues may seem exceptional and even difficult for some contemporary readers to comprehend.[17] However this is not as paradoxical as it seems. Heller has acknowledged feminism as one of the greatest modern emancipatory movements. She has always considered herself a feminist even if she is critical of some of the trends and tactics within the recent US movement. Her confident entry in the late 1940s into the almost exclusively male preserve of philosophy, before the advent of second-wave feminism, is proof enough of her belief in the equality of the sexes. Yet her age also explains a great deal about Heller's attitude to modern feminism. She once remarked that although she did not choose to be female, Hungarian or Jewish, she has consciously rechosen all these determinations. To do otherwise would have been inauthentic.[18] Whatever tensions may have resulted from these multiple identities in the course of her life they remained for her personal. She has never felt the need to explore her female identity philosophically. She chose philosophy before the appearance of contemporary feminism. While this exclusive choice might be viewed as a limitation, it has allowed Heller the freedom to explore the whole philosophical terrain and its history unconstrained by a focus that can sometimes narrow the ambitions of contemporary female philosophers. Heller has made contributions across the whole spectrum of social and political philosophy as well as writing on almost every significant figure in the history of the Western tradition. One of her strongest complaints against contemporary academic feminism is the development of 'gender studies'. This she views as another form of 'kitchen' where women are confined to the study of cultural works that, with some exceptions, are of only secondary significance.[19] Though Heller has not explicitly contributed to contemporary feminist debates, her gender sensitivities have been allowed free reign in shaping her interests and perspective. I have already mentioned the appearance, for the first time within the Marxist tradition, of novel and marginalised topics, such as everyday life, needs and feelings. After reading a few pages of Heller, the reader is well aware that here is a woman speaking. Her critique of the truncation of the classical ethical agenda in contemporary moral theory is at least in part inspired by a conventional feminine concern for the whole person and the conviction that ethics cannot abandon discussion of love and happiness.

The following chapters are not intended to be a full-scale intellectual biography of Heller. This would have required a close study of the many articles and several books that only saw the light of day in Hungarian and are inaccessible to me. While such a work is needed and would undoubtedly enrich our understanding of Heller's intellectual development, especially in the 1950s and 1960s, I doubt that it would fundamentally alter our understanding of her philosophical development or of her deepest philosophical intentions. The most important of Heller's early books are now available in English or German and the early period is well, if succinctly, covered by her close friend György Márkus in his article 'The Politics of Morals'.[20] Although I treat this early Marxist period systematically rather than biographically, I have drawn on his work when necessary to fill in gaps. This monograph is primarily intended as an introduction to Heller's later oeuvre when she began herself to publish in German and English. However, it is essential to locate these works in the context of her overall development and to achieve this the analysis will fall into three parts. Part I elaborates her relation to the Lukácsian programme of the 'Renaissance of Marx'. In these works (published first in Hungary) she laid down her major philosophical interests and her own version of Western Marxism. Part II considers the intermediate group of works that registered her break with Marxism and the first outlines of an alternative vision of radical philosophy. Finally, Part III explores her turn to postmodernism and her own idiosyncratic synthesis of Enlightenment and postmodern elements called 'reflective postmodernism'. Not surprisingly, the latter two sections are more extensive insofar as they cover the larger part of her oeuvre. In the period covered in Part III, Heller finally assumes her mature and most distinctive philosophical persona and fully assimilates the lessons of her own self-critique. In this phase, she completed her comprehensive three-volume ethics and her theory of modernity, and most fully consummated her desire to engage critically with contemporary society and culture. In this part we see to best advantage the tensions and paradoxes that permeate and energise Heller's vision.

Part I
The 'Renaissance of Marxism'

1
Lukács, Ethics and Everyday Life

To understand the direction and milieu of Heller's early work we need to locate it within the broad Lukácsian 'Renaissance of Marx' programme. In the Introduction, I mentioned the talented circle of young philosophers and sociologists – the so-called 'Budapest School' – that coalesced around Lukács in the 1960s. His idea of a Marx Renaissance was unmistakably formulated in opposition to what was at that time the official orthodox Marxism of the communist regimes in the Soviet Union and the Eastern Bloc countries. This official version of Marxism – *diamat* – was a vulgar distillation of some of the key ideas from the Second International and Lenin, finally codified by Stalin in the late 1930s. The framework to this orthodoxy was Marxist philosophy – dialectical materialism – as a science of the general laws of reality, nature, society and thought. From this could be drawn the specific scientific disciplines concentrating on the actual laws of natural phenomena and systems. Dialectical materialism was philosophy rather than science; the results of the specialist sciences were synthesised into a uniform worldview and ideology. However, more than just a synthesis, this worldview also provided a set of methodological directives that allowed Stalin, for example, to make judgements within the domain of science.[1] The ideological universality of this philosophy supposedly established the cultural hegemony of the proletariat. In fact it allowed the Communist Party or its leadership, acting as the concrete representative of the workers, to usurp this position. In an analogous way, historical materialism was a science of the general laws of society and history. These operated independently of the intentions and activities of individuals and prescribed deterministically the future march of history; however, knowledge of them could be employed either to modify or to promote actions in harmony with them.

This scientistic understanding of Marx's theory of history was largely inherited from the Second International. The leading theoreticians of German social democracy had viewed Marxism as a value-free positive science capable of describing and explaining the evolution and decline not only of capitalism but also of every social structure. In this respect, Lukács' seminal early reinterpretation of Marxism, *History and Class Consciousness* (1923),[2] is vital to understanding Heller's initial orientation to orthodox *diamat*. She and the other members of the Budapest School departed from his alternative Western reading of Marx. The catastrophes of fascism, the Second World War and Stalinism and his own political marginalisation explain the almost four-decade-long interruption between Lukács' first Marxist classic and his eventual return to philosophy and formulation of the programme for a 'Marx Renaissance'. In the late 1920s the party repudiated his theoretical efforts as dangerous left deviations. Nevertheless, foreseeing the looming struggle against fascism he chose to accept this theoretical censorship. He rationalised this decision as a strategic withdrawal for the sake of being on the side of historical progress in what he viewed to be the forthcoming world struggle between capitalism and socialism. He retreated from direct political writings and during the next two decades confined himself to literary theory, history of philosophy and aesthetics. It was during this time that he established his reputation as one of the greatest Marxist literary critics and aestheticians.

In another sense, Lukács' self-criticism was quite genuine. In the late 1920s, he moved to Moscow and helped to prepare Marx's early writings for publication by the Marxism–Leninism Institute. He then realised that his infamous reinterpretation of Marx had been seriously flawed. However, the pervading atmosphere of Stalinist terror made it quite impossible for him to revise his old ideas explicitly. This opportunity did not come until the middle 1950s and the post-Stalinist official repudiation of the so-called 'cult of the personality'. First of all, he completed the mammoth *Die Eigenart des Aesthetischen* (1963)[3] – a two volume systematic aesthetics – and, finally, he attempted to re-elaborate the philosophical foundations of Marxism. Completed in his old age, this final work, *The Ontology of Social Being*, was stillborn. It was so severely criticised by his young Budapest School colleagues that Lukács finally decided against publication.[4] He died in 1971 at the age of 86.

LUKÁCS' PHILOSOPHICAL ANTHROPOLOGY

Although *History and Class Consciousness* was seriously flawed, it did lay down the main lines of an influential alternative reading of Marx that would become the foundations of Western Marxism.[5] Against the emerging *diamat* view of Marxist philosophy as a science of the general laws of reality, Lukács viewed Marxism primarily as a philosophy of praxis. This needs to be understood in the following double sense. Firstly, humanity produces itself and its history, by and through its own activities. Human historical development is not deducible from so-called 'laws' of history. Lukács stresses that, rather than humanity being created by these abstract but supposedly necessary historical laws, historical transformation depends upon social conflict and revolutionary class struggle. Obviously, social conflict is generated by objective social conditions. However, on this view, these social conditions are always the product of human actions. Secondly, Marxism is not value-free science but an enlightened theoretical consciousness playing an active role in the proletariat's struggle to realise communism. It addresses itself to the empirical consciousness of the proletariat as a theoretical distillation of the objective conditions, opportunities and goals of present social struggles.[6] The theoretical and practical implications of this understanding of Marxism as a philosophy of praxis are fairly obvious. Understood in this way, Marxism could not be the preserve of a party elite who laid down to the masses in advance a course dictated by historical laws. History is now viewed as a process of human self-creation in which ideology, consciousness and struggle are pivotal subjective contributions to finely balanced historical situations. In this conception, individual action and political praxis play a decisive role.

With the assistance of Marx's manuscripts, Lukács had easily identified the major error of his own interpretation. He now saw his famous identification of the proletariat as the identical subject/object of history as a Hegelian-inspired idealist deviation. In *History and Class Consciousness*, he allowed 'class' in the shape of the proletariat to replace Marx's category of 'species being'. The framework of Marx's early manuscripts was a humanist anthropology. For the young Marx, history was a process of human species self-creation through alienated labour. The historical task standing before humanity was ultimately to realise all potential human species capacities. However, in all previous epochs this process has been undertaken in alienated social conditions. The prospect of a revolutionary overcoming of capitalism signifies the conscious transcendence of the epoch of alienation and the end of all historically created contradictions. Lukács incorporated this anthropological framework and commitment to a rich individuality into his subsequent literary criticism.[7] The subsequent prominence of the categories of 'human species' and 'individuality' in his later literary and aesthetic writings stems directly from this pointed self-criticism. His late systematic aesthetics was clearly founded on an explicit philosophy of history. The essence of art is realised in the individuality of the great works themselves. They may be creations of specific historical times and circumstances but they also attain a timeless validity: they are the memories of man. This is Lukács' gloss on the famous passage in which Marx attributed a paradigmatic cultural role to the Greeks as the 'normal childhood' of humanity. The history of art gives expression to the unity of individuality and the species in so far as each great work – as a self-contained individuality – also signifies a historical moment of species achievement. The great works cannot be ordered hierarchically, as they are all eternal: each signifies a stage in the evolutionary unfolding of human species capacities.

The philosophy of history underlying Lukács' aesthetics was conceived in the spirit of hope. In the 'dark times' of the 1930s – with the disappearance of concrete revolutionary scenarios, the victory of fascism, the all-consuming Stalinist terror and the threat of world conflict – he clung to philosophical anthropology. The cathartic experience of great art that unifies individual and species is a defetishising consciousness. It demands that the recipient change her life and presupposes the possibility of overcoming the fetishism of everyday life. Yet such an anthropological 'guarantee' remains merely an 'ought': it is without immediate political pay-off or historical prospect. History was now reinforcing the lesson of *History and Class Consciousness.* Any attempt to posit direct identities between concrete individualities like the proletariat and the total historical process involved irresolvable theoretical impasses.[8]

The short period of de-Stalinisation after 1953 allowed Lukács to think of returning to his old philosophical interests. The changed political conditions momentarily also loosened theoretical possibilities. However, these plans were soon shattered by the Russian overthrow of the reformist Nagy regime. His late symbolic entry into the Nagy government as a minister for education earned him several years of exile to Romania and delayed his return to 'great philosophy'. When he did finally return, he explicitly took up the rejuvenating philosophy of the young Marx. For Lukács, this foundation became an almost unquestionable absolute. On this view, Marx had produced a revolution in philosophy by resolving the basic contradictions of bourgeois ontology: the antinomies of subject and object, causality and teleology and freedom and necessity. Marx's anthropology would serve as the foundation of a new understanding of man and his relations with the surrounding environment. At the same time, an authentic philosophy of praxis would aid in the overcoming of the 'distortions' induced by the period under the 'cult of the personality'. The broad outlines of the first aspect of this 'Marx Renaissance' were worked out in Lukács' *Ontology of Social Being.* Yet, this left many remaining lacunae and openings in this programme. There was scope to both extend and enrich Marx's insights, to break new ground in domains Marx had scarcely had time to consider, and to apply his basic principles to newly emergent problems, both in theory and practice.

To consider Heller's early Marxist works in biographical sequence would take up too much space. I shall confine my treatment of these early Hungarian works to an account of her main interests and the way they fitted into the Lukácsian programme for the 'Renaissance of Marx'. Although she never mentions Marx in the titles of her books until *The Theory of Need in Marx* (1976), all her works contributed in various ways to the broad aims of this programme. Even her treatment of apparently solely theoretical issues, such as values and instincts, is just as charged with critical intent and practical relevance as her consideration of the more concrete and politically explosive topics of ethics, revolution and everyday life. In the whole of this Marxist phase, Heller moves towards the construction of her own philosophical identity in a climate dominated by the tensions between the promise and the reality of 'really existing socialism'. She is gradually drawn from a defence of the 'authentic' Marx to eventually recognising the tensions and shortcomings in Marx himself.

TO VIEW THE WORLD RATIONALLY

Heller's contribution to a *Festschrift* for Lukács' eightieth birthday is entitled '*The Moral Mission of the Philosopher*'. This is a good place to start an exposition of Heller's Marxist phase, because it elaborates her initial understanding of philosophy in the broadest possible terms. This short essay both serves as a homage to Lukács and asserts the essential link between philosophy and a presupposed Marxian *telos* of history. Heller aims to define the philosophical attitude. This requires more than the sort of abstraction that would produce a sociological type. To go beyond the plurality of empirical types of philosopher, it is necessary to introduce the concept of representation.[9] This is a category not of ideals but of essence expressing the substance of human progress. The demands of the day call into being a fundamental and basic passion which orientates the totality of an individual's behaviour. In the case of the philosopher, this basic organising passion is the unity of thinking and personal conduct.[10] The possibility of such a passion has existed since classical Greece, when processes of social differentiation separated theory and practice. These processes also saw the simultaneous emergence of the autonomous personality. In this new constellation, philosophy holds out the promise of a possible eventual reconciliation in everyday life. In Socratic mode, Heller views the philosopher as the guardian of substance; he (sic)[11] represents that which was in danger of being lost but can never be completely lost. However, Heller gives this substance a Lukácsian historicist twist; it persists despite dynamism and contradictory development. In an image strikingly opposed to Nietzsche's view of philosophers as lonely giants living on summits and calling to each other across the ages and wastelands of ordinary folk, she transforms these same summits into a continuous ideal line in human development. The philosopher represents that substance which in the present may only be captured by the exceptional personality, yet is inherently general, at least in its potentiality.[12] She argues that philosophers are no aristocratic caste but only one aspect of an infinitely rich human substance. Reinforcing this point, she maintains that however great the discrepancy between philosophy and everyday life, the link between the two is unbreakable. The measure of the really great philosopher is in fact his striving to reduce this discrepancy and to restore unity.[13] However much Heller will later come to revise her views on social differentiation, this belief in the unbreakable link between philosophy and the everyday will be a cornerstone of all her later thinking.

What is meant by this unity of personal conduct and *Weltanschauung*? It means that the philosopher's conduct follows from his thinking, principles and values. There is no hint of transcendence in this thinking. For Heller, the key to the riddle of humanity is humanity itself; she insists that philosophical thinking must be immanent and earthly. Just as substance itself is subject to the vagaries of historical development, she maintains that the character of this unity will also change. While the figure of Socrates could represent the direct realisation of this unity in his everyday inquisitions of friends at the Agora, the textual objectification of philosophy made this no longer possible. As a result, the requirement of immediate unity is sacrificed. On the one hand, the theory must reflect reality. Clearly Heller has something other than 'correspondence' in mind here. The reality aspired to by the philosopher is more the 'actual' of Hegel's becoming rationality. On the other hand, she still insists that a moment of personal commitment is essential to philosophical truth. Already here we can see the germ of a view that will make her so sympathetic to the process of subjectivisation that she will later write it into the history of modern philosophy. The philosopher must take responsibility for his views.[14] The philosopher must be prepared to own his personal and theoretical past in a way that is never required of the artist or the scientist. In unpacking this unity as personal responsibility and truth content, she suggests that it has both external and internal aspects. The former requires the endeavour to realise ideas in the world. The philosopher must be a teacher. Internally, the philosopher must become a living embodiment of his ideology by ordering his personal existence in accord with its prescriptions.

We see here an indication of Heller's resistance to the processes of modern differentiation. The contraction of public life in the modern world has forced the philosopher back into the domain of private life as an almost universal fate.[15] Not only do the new bourgeois conditions render the philosopher merely another private person, they also transform ideology into a commodity just like any other, which must find buyers on the market. Yet Heller refuses to accept these implications of privatisation. She argues that this bifurcation only intensifies the emphatic need for a connection between conduct and *Weltanschauung*. This generates the possibility of a confrontation between ideology and conduct.[16] Of course, in historical conditions of direct unity between these two, the mere accusation of a discrepancy was a well established way of discrediting the philosopher. However, in more differentiated societies, a space now opens up for ideology to challenge conduct and vice versa. Heller's response to the new historical conditions is a moral and conservative one. Taking her cue from the ancient Epicureans and Stoics, she calls for the recovery of at least the spirit of the original unity. This now becomes her model of philosophy in 'dark times'.[17] Privatisation only reinforces the need to objectify conduct in work and retrieve the ideal of philosophical conduct. The genuine philosophical attitude not only insists upon the confrontation with the most vital questions of the whole of mankind; it also claims that the philosopher who is unable to live a truly human life through his philosophy is not deserving of the title.[18]

While standing her ground for a classical renewal against the tide of bourgeois differentiation, Heller also feels impelled to further specify her own notion of the unity of conduct and *Weltanschauung* against the weighty Marxist tradition of the revolutionary unity of theory and praxis. She maintains that the philosopher can be neither a theoretical mandarin nor the philosopher–king engaged in founding the city. On the contrary, what is required is a synthesis of contemplation and activity in which the ultimate priority is finally decided only by philosophical character and the objective limits of the age.[19] Even more decisive, however, is the need to infuse action into the very meaning of philosophical truth. Theoretical insight alone is meaningless unless under the sway of the practical question of what to do. If the world is to become a 'being for us', every philosophical truth must be related back to man. This means that the truth value of a doctrine is inextricably linked both to the practical choices made by the philosopher and to the perspectives opened up with them.[20] These choices are themselves an

expression of a passionate commitment to activity. Here again we see
in activist terms one of the most enduring themes in the entire Heller
oeuvre. This is the sense of full engagement that embeds philosophy in
what for her will eventually become the flow of completely contingent
historical experience and the demand that it be tied to the real historical
options and choices of individual actors.

This emphatic practical commitment does not stop Heller from
repudiating the role of the philosopher–king and its illusions, so
grotesquely exemplified in Stalinist distortions. This has nothing to do
with the relative scarcity of exceptional philosophical personalities.
At this time, she was still prepared to believe that Marx was gifted
with the all-round capacities of the prospective philosopher–king.
Rather, the key is a fundamental difference of representative attitudes.
In the case of the philosopher, personal responsibility is conveyed by
the *Weltanschauung*. This is strikingly different from the case of the
politician, where responsibility lies not in ideology but in immediate
objectives. The politician must take responsibility for the consequences
of actions adopted to attain these objectives.[21] Of course, only rarely
do these two attitudes assume such an extremely one-sided form. In
everyday life, they appear both in parallel and interlinked. But Heller
emphasises that they cannot be hierarchised: both are expressions of the
substantive development of humanity.[22] Here the Marxian philosophy
of history overcomes the differentiation and underwrites their ultimate
reconcilability. Accordingly, she confidently endorses the double illusion
that the thinking of the great politician ultimately contains in embryo
the thinking and conduct of the philosopher, while the great philosopher
instinctively knows the cause representing the interests of the people
and historical progress.[23] The secret radar of both these attitudes and
their 'necessary interconnection' is an intuitive comprehension of the
direction of historical development. This is an early sign of Heller's
willingness to accept the solution that would allow 'everything to click'.
Yet she still cautions against the active involvement of the philosopher
in great politics. The philosophical gift lies in recognising the great
political cause and theoretically formulating its tasks and threats but it
does not include the capacities to either recommend or execute practical
alternatives.[24] The essential limit to philosophical activity lies in the
structural division between theoretical and practical capacities.

The source of philosophical wisdom lies at least in part in the
philosopher's capacity to view each concrete moment as part of a
process. Philosophy is therefore predisposed to be historical, but the
corrosive potential of history is forestalled by the Marxian philosophy
of history. Historical process is the gathering of continuity to a focal

point that has the same meaning as eternity.[25] The concentration on essence inoculates the philosopher against despair. The young Heller's heavily normative definition of the philosophical attitude allows her to condemn Heidegger's abandonment of the moral mission of the philosopher. The feeling which best expresses the great philosopher's insight into the historical substance is *indignation*: this attitude retains an orientation to the possibility of universal development.[26]

Within the framework of this Marxian anthropology and its underwriting philosophy of history, Heller characterizes the philosophical attitude as the representation of a threefold 'normalcy'. Rejecting the popular affinity of philosophical genius with madness, she aligns it with psychic sanity and its indispensable faith in progress.[27] More fundamentally, philosophy charts the main line of historical development. In so doing it expresses the moral norms of each age. The life of the philosopher may be centred in his work, but his goal is not the work but the desire to solve the mysteries of reality. Philosophical thinking is diminished if it is seen as wisdom for its own sake. As Heller sees it, the essence of the moral mission of the philosopher was to grasp this reality and the cause of mankind in a way that vindicated its rationality.[28] Up to this point, she seems unconcerned by Marx's simple identification of the path of 'normal' human evolution with that of the culture of Western Europe. And as we shall see, even after she explicitly abandons this philosophy of history, she will still cling to the universal significance of this Western legacy, both as the bearer of the leading value ideas of modernity and as a timeless reservoir of meaning and excellence.

IS THERE A PLACE FOR ETHICS IN MARXISM?

In a retrospective on her own intellectual development, Heller tells us that 1956 was decisive. In the Petöfi circle, a club for political debate that continued to gather large audiences right up to the revolution that installed the Nagy government, Heller heard the victims of Stalinist terror and determined that Marxists should address the fundamental philosophical problems:[29] for her that meant doing ethics.[30] A glance at her bibliography shows that she has certainly made good this commitment. She lectured extensively on ethics before her dismissal in 1958, her early books were heavily dominated by ethics and this has remained a life-long interest, culminating in the publication of a three-volume trilogy on ethics.

Her early reflections on this apparent lacunae in Marxism are summarised in a paper, 'The Place of Ethics in Marxism' (1967).

There she departs from the question of why the problems of ethics have received no real clarification by the most significant representatives of Marxism. She acknowledges that the workers' movement has had a morality and acted in accord with a code of morals, but distinguishes this from ethics. The latter is associated with choice, conscious individuality, personal risk, contradictions and novelty. Moral codes, on the other hand, are fixed, making choices relatively unproblematic for the individuals who live by them.[31] Ethics only becomes a central preoccupation of a movement when certain conditions are met. Firstly, the movement must no longer view itself as absolute, but in relation to other movements, society and history; secondly, the movement must no longer be dominated by spontaneous consciousness. This occurs when history no longer proceeds smoothly, but by revolution or epochs of crisis and new contradictions. Thirdly, ethics becomes possible and necessary in a society in which the roles of individual decision and praxis increase. Finally, for ethics to play a role in a social movement, consciousness, self-knowledge and self-critique of the movement are necessary. The individual must be consciously confronted with the contradictions of the movement appearing to her in the form of moral contradictions. The link is clear between this analysis and Heller's own biography from 1956.

Her brief retrospective of the history of Marxian socialism shows that these conditions were rarely met. However, she believes that all this might now be changing with the historical constellation emerging in the 1960s. Banishing moral motives from politics and economics, expunging the reality of individual decision making and negating individual responsibility, led to the horrific and tragic results of the recent past. On the broader historical stage, the attainment of relatively acceptable and constantly increasing levels of material welfare in the West now demanded a reformulation of the agenda of 'What is to be done?' Emancipation from economic poverty meant that the presuppositions of a fully human life no longer had to be created. What was now required was the immediate creation of such a life: the awakening of a new kind of class consciousness in which ethics would play a central role. Reformulating the Marxian adage that in transforming the world humanity transforms itself, Heller suggested we are able to transform the world if we thereby also reshape ourselves. The forceful new emphasis on subjective morality is quite unmistakable.

In line with the Lukácsian programme for the 'Renaissance of Marxism', it is not surprising to find that the basic framework of this new ethics was already latent in Marx. He interpreted society as praxis. The history of humanity is the birth and unfolding of freedom. Heller adopts this consistent *immanence*. Human motivation, whether or not wholly conscious, is always immanent. Freedom grows with the power and consciousness of immanent capacities. This train of thought contains the general contours of a Marxist ethics. This human capacity to gradually 'push back the limits of nature' means increasing room to move. The latitude of human action can be wide or narrow depending upon the individual's historical epoch, social strata and specific qualities involved. Nevertheless, there are always alternatives and results unfold only out of effective choices between them. This relative autonomy of human action is the second key point of departure for a Marxist ethics. It means two things: firstly, both the possibility and the postulate that individuals and social groups actively shape their own fate. Secondly, to avoid empty dreaming and moralising, the 'facts' as they are have to be taken into account. For Marx, morality is the relationship of particular individuals to their concrete circumstances and possibilities. It involves a conscious choice from the perspective of the species. The Marxian heroes deliberately choose to take responsibility for states of affairs and actions that enhance total human values. In this respect, purely ethical acts signal the *objective relation of the individual to the species*.

Why has such an ethics not been elaborated? Heller's answer is that, like philosophy, ethics is more than just a question of correctly understanding Marxist texts: it is a question of experience and praxis. Marxist ethics can only be propagated in a movement where this ethical attitude has become pervasive. While movements may have 'successes' and increase their influence and power, they cannot hope to fully transform society without meeting the conditions that engender an authentic ethics. This is clearly a call heavily laden with practical meaning and political implications.

EVERYDAY LIFE AND REVOLUTION

The question of the radical transformation of society and its impact on everyday life was not merely a theoretical question for the citizens of 'really existing socialism' in the 1960s and 1970s. This was a question that touched the very meaning of a socialist revolution, its present physiognomy and its future direction. Heller bravely and conscientiously confronted this question in her 1970 article 'Marx's Theory of Revolution and the Revolution in Everyday Life'.[32] In a thinly veiled criticism of orthodox Marxism, she presented a critique of 'really existing socialism' and a vague practical programme for the restoration of the authentic Marxian meaning of revolution. Within a few years, this was to serve as the pretext for her cultural ostracism

by the Communist Party. This was really a summary and application
of ideas already formulated in an earlier book, *Everyday Life* (1968).[33]
There she laid down the theoretical framework that was to become
the basis of much of her later work. I shall begin with the politically
charged question of revolution and connect this to her more systematic
presentation of everyday life. This will later become the basis of her
theory of rationality.

The question of revolution is a classical topic in Marxism, but its
coupling with everyday life is quite novel. For Heller, the linkage of
the two proves that history is continually unearthing new problems.
Marxists were required to deal with these if Marxism was to remain
a critical tool relevant to contemporary social life. Hungary appeared
to be the realisation of the orthodox Marxist scenario: a revolutionary
seizure of power was followed by the abolition of bourgeois property
relations. Yet this regime did not appear to be about to realise Marx's
communist dream. Heller argues that even the more or less successful
dismantling of Stalinism was not itself sufficient to fully ensure the sort
of humanisation of society envisaged by Marx. The seizure of political
and economic control was for Marx only the precondition of the radical
restructuring of everyday life that would finally signify the abolition
of alienation. However, the real impetus behind the problemisation
of everyday life comes not just from the *incomplete* character of
revolutionary transformation in the so-called socialist world; it was
reinforced by the evolution of capitalism in the West. The post-Second
World War boom that brought high material living standards appeared
to have integrated the Western working class into bourgeois society. The
'relative and temporary' success of this manipulation of the workers
in the West added warrant to the experience of deformed revolution
in the socialist countries. It vindicated a shift of focus towards a more
comprehensive critique of everyday life. It is worthwhile noting in
passing that here Heller appears to accept the Frankfurt School thesis
of consumer manipulation, and even views the accommodation of the
working class as only a 'temporary success'.[34] As we shall see, her
attitude to the consumer society has softened noticeably over time,
although she has always maintained reservations that easily matched
an awakening interest in the green, ecology movement in the 1980s.

The vital point in Heller's argument is the need for Marxists to find
an alternative understanding of revolution, beyond the mere seizure of
political and economic power. She calls this alternative 'total revolution',
despite the unfortunate totalitarian connotations that cling to this term.
She envisages, not just the conquest of strategic centres of power, nor the
political takeover of all other aspects of life, but the transformation of

a way of life by the actors themselves. Total revolution signifies workers' democracy: mass participation constantly extended to larger sectors of the population. The model is the young Marx's idea of a humanising social revolution, as opposed to a merely political revolution that only perpetuates the alienation of bourgeois life. This alternative requires a shift of the focus of revolution away from the labour process and the institutional structures that control it towards politics and ethics. In many ways, Heller anticipates the sort of thinking to be found in Habermas's later article on 'The Crisis of the Welfare State and Exhaustion of Utopian Energies'.[35] She acknowledges that only social revolution has the life-transforming power to institutionalise change. However, if the existing so-called socialist societies proved anything, it was that the seizure of political power did not automatically result in the reorganisation of the whole way of life. In the achievement of this goal, ethics becomes a crucial element. Only at the level of individual attitude and action could real change take root.

This programme of revolution as a transformation of the total way of life works as a rationale for turning attention to the question of everyday life in both Eastern Europe and the West. In the Preface to the English edition of *Everyday Life* (1984), reflecting on her earlier motives, Heller makes it clear that the practical intent of the book was to theorise the possibility of, and contribute to, the transformation of everyday life in a humanist, democratic direction. However, additionally, she wanted to break with the dominant tradition of historical materialism and to construct a new philosophical framework built on a synthesis of Aristotle and phenomenology. Aristotle was the first to theoretically divulge the specificity of the practical life by revealing its immanent standards and focusing his attention on a justification of the good life. Here we see another theme that will be a constant in Heller's ethical thought. While the idea of total revolution will completely disappear from her later thought, the pursuit of the good life remains a central aspect of her more classical view of ethics. Her motives for appropriating the phenomenological approach are similar. It redirected modern philosophy away from the narrow confines of scientific abstraction and towards the totality of the everyday. The new framework offers the beginning of a philosophical anthropology of intersubjectivity. It reconciles the idea of finite humanity with the proposition that individual actors are the ultimate subjects of history.[36] Her synthesis goes under the name of the paradigm of objectivation. This new paradigm constructs social existence from the standpoint of the human being *as a whole*. This theoretical framework was to remain the unchanging basis of all her further work.[37] However, in this initial

version it presupposes the Marxian philosophy of history inherited
with Lukács' humanist anthropology. As we shall see, this is finally
discarded in the early 1980s when Heller turns to Arendt's notion of
the human condition.

Heller repudiates previous philosophical attempts to theorise the
everyday. Philosophy's perennial suspicion of mere 'opinion' had
ensured that the topic of everyday life and thinking had remained
outside traditional philosophical concerns. However, this topic comes
to prominence at the turn of the twentieth century with the increasing
awareness of 'rationalisation' and 'reification'. Suddenly the everyday
was rendered problematic by the incursions of quantitative bourgeois
relations and scientific rationality. One response to the reification of
the everyday was the philosophical tradition that turned away from
the formless, empty and repetitive character of everyday life and
attempted to critically analyse it. Heidegger associated everydayness
with inauthenticity: it represented a flight from the burdens of finite
existence. Only a life that breaks with the everyday in order to live at
the height of possibilities and faces moments of crisis and death was
really authentic.[38]

The other response was Husserlian phenomenology. Launched
under the slogan of a 'return to the things themselves', this attempted
to capture the essential structures of the life-world in their pristine
immediacy. However, it risked falling into mere reduplication of the
existing because the 'natural attitude' studiously avoided evaluation.
It elevated eminently historical structures of the life-world into
timeless constants. This phenomenology had greatly influenced the
other paradigm founded within sociology by Alfred Schütz. Similarly,
Heller is determined to supply an account of the essential structures
of everydayness and its concrete particularity. However, she advocates
taking up the sociological paradigm with a double perspective. Sociology
must not only explain the basis of the everyday life in macro-structures
but must also be able to provide a critical perspective on these structures.
It must be able to capture the pressures of modern dynamism. A desire
for the transformation of everyday life in a progressive historical
direction towards socialism infuses her account. She needs to show how
the everyday produces out of itself the possibility of its own historical
transcendence. Here Lukács' philosophy of history comes to the fore.
The accumulated cultural achievements of the species are the immanent
source of ongoing social dynamism. Rather than being prisoners of the
eternal everyday, socialised individuals are the driving forces, the active
agents who choose and add something to the structures of the inherited

world. Before exploring the mechanisms of this dynamism, we must reconstruct the basic elements of Heller's vision of the everyday.

Despite the fact that its structures, contents and activities will change throughout history and even within a society, the everyday is a human universal. All societies must reproduce themselves, and the aggregate of all those heterogeneous activities constitutes the everyday. Without these activities, society and social reproduction would not exist at all.[39] The everyday is 'heterogeneous' because it involves the co-ordination of diverse activities; it is neither a system nor an institution, but the arena where systems and institutions intersect in the habitual life-world. The only natural institution of the everyday is the family, which has always been the agent of primary socialisation. At the core of the everyday is what Heller designates the sphere of *objectivation in itself*. The basic constituents of this sphere, which is constant throughout history, are *language, tools and customs*. The social reproduction of the individuality is orchestrated within the broader processes of social reproduction. The individual must be equipped to fulfil required social functions and assume the responsibilities of adulthood. Basic competencies of communication, manipulation and understanding of the life-world must be acquired. This is the minimal level of acculturation allowing orientation in the life-world; it can be more or less protracted depending upon the degree of social dynamism. Language enables and guides thinking and the use of tools, while customs co-ordinate and guide individual attitudes and social practices. In the everyday we learn to perceive, think and feel in socially preformed, undifferentiated and indissoluble unity. However, rather than being a realm of necessity, the *sphere of objectivation in itself* is the door to freedom. Primary socialisation facilitates access to all higher attainments. In this domain, individuals are more than mere 'relays' for reproducing the social world as its exists. They add their own personal experiences and contributions to the world passed on to others.[40] In *The Power of Shame* (1985), Heller will speak of the 'accrual of surpluses'.[41] Everyday life is broader than the *sphere of objectivation in itself*: its diverse activities are not confined to primary socialisation. Yet the two are interlinked. The everyday is the domain in which the task of acculturation is accomplished and effective orientation in the everyday life itself requires its acquisition. For this reason, Heller maintains that *the sphere of objectivation in itself* is *historically primordial*: the foundation of all later institutionally separated and specialised practices and accomplishments.[42] Here she reveals both her implicit critique and continuing commitment to Marxist orthodoxy. Her emphasis on the heterogeneous sphere of the everyday as the original source of all historical evolution puts into doubt the primacy of the economy and opens up a broader and richer understanding of conditioning circumstances. At the same time, she still views this sphere as the 'basic' component of socialisation, to which others are merely subsidiary developments.

From one aspect, the everyday is the atmosphere without which the individual cannot breathe. Just as we are hardly conscious of breathing, we are so immersed in the everyday we take it for granted; its existence is one of pervasive repetition and continuity. Everyday thinking is conservative and its content invariant. This is a fetishistic thinking prone to largely accepting the institutions and forms of the world as ready-made. Unlike scientific thinking, it does not abstract from our immediate perceptions because here it seems unnecessary. Technology may be increasingly introduced into the everyday, but only naturalistically, to serve purely anthropological purposes.[43] Invariably we rely on a pragmatics of success that is anchored in repetition and analogy from previous experience.

From the subjective angle, however, everyday life must still be viewed as *objectification*. Socialisation is not just a process of passive appropriation but of the externalisation of the subject. The talents and capacities of the individual assume objective shape. Our products commence their own life and are exposed to their own fate. Every generation finds ready-made an enormous reservoir of these *objectivations*, which it must transform to its own requirements before passing them on to future generations. Heller views history as a wave-like process of such objectification. It is essential to see the bidirectional character of the process.[44] In the first sense, objectification is a continuous externalisation of the subject. In the second, it reshapes the subject. Objectification produces new needs, abilities, skills and aptitudes.

The prospect of enhancing subjectivity through objectification brings into view the further dimensions of this paradigm. The sphere of *objectivation in itself* is both the realm of necessity and the door to freedom. This implies that there is another sphere beyond it. Heller calls this the sphere of *objectivation for itself*. In *Everyday Life* she maintains that this sphere is ontologically secondary because it is not a necessary component of sociality; some societies have managed to function without some aspects of it.[45] This view will later be rescinded when she becomes more critical of Marx and finally abandons the primacy of production. The label *objectivation for itself* designates accumulated cultural achievements that supply meaningful worldviews and interpretations. Of course, the norms and rules of the sphere of *objectivation in itself* also provide humans with meaning. However, the unity of these heterogeneous activities is ultimately secured by particular meaningful worldviews typically appropriated together with the sphere of *objectivation in itself*. This means primarily religion, art and philosophy, with science being the latest historical addition. These all express in universal form various aspects of humanity's self-and-world interpretation. On the one hand, all objectivations grow out of, and are ultimately parasitical on, everyday life. On the other, the constituents of this sphere also acquire relative autonomy and have the capacity to follow their own inherent developmental logic once the society has attained a certain level of historical development and spherical differentiation. However, the *sphere of objectivation for itself* always remains anchored within everyday life, responding to the problems thrown up by it.[46] Cultural objectivations reconfigure the contradictions of the everyday through *intellectualisation*, *rearrangement* and *distantiation* from *the universal standpoint of the species*. This implies a conscious working-up of problems into coherent visions that in their questions and answers represent the species-essential forms of human self-consciousness.[47]

This constellation of spheres is completed by another sphere: that of *objectivation in and for itself*. Surprisingly for a Marxist, Heller has little to say about economic relations and political institutions. They are only mentioned insofar as their effects infiltrate everyday life. This third sphere contains objectivations that have aspects of both immediacy and consciousness. She speaks of integrations or social clusters, political and economic institutions and the law. The extent to which each of these tends towards either pole of the 'in and for itself', immediacy or consciousness, will largely depend upon historical conditions and the degree of alienation.[48] However, taken all together, the institutions of this sphere constitute the identity of a particular social structure against the universality of the other spheres.[49]

Heller's theorisation focuses primarily on the interaction of the 'in itself' and 'for itself' spheres. Yet these are ideal–typical abstractions. In practice, they coexist in constant interchange and overlapping. As intimated, she argues that it is theoretically still valid to view the everyday *as ontologically primary* and the point of access to the 'for itself' sphere. The former is the basis for the latter because the sphere of *objectivations for itself* is the product of a process of differentiation and homogenisation initiated within everyday life. Within the everyday there will be more or less homogeneous activities varying in extent, type and intensity. For example, concentration of a single task tends to homogenise activity as it suspends the particular viewpoint. All objectifying activities within the *in itself* have a generic aspect. All elevate particular endowments, wishes and impulses by imparting a common level of minimal societal qualification. Yet she especially mentions work

and morality, where the everyday and the non-everyday coexist. At the
other pole, activity finally undulates towards religion, politics, law and
the *objectivations for itself* proper – art, philosophy and science.

As noted, the leading characteristic of the everyday is its 'givenness':
it is dominated by customs and pragmatism. This is a taken-for-granted
world of opinion and spontaneity dominated by pragmatic success and
reluctant to submit itself to careful scrutiny. However, this does not
mean that everyday thought is necessarily alienated. Heller makes the
point that alienation is the product not merely of a taken-for-granted
world but of the attitude towards it. The fundamental question is
whether or not it is possible in principle for us to direct critical scrutiny
to any aspect of the everyday world. Running through Heller's work on
the everyday is a polemic against the philosophical tradition that had
viewed the everyday as a site of irredeemable alienation. Her critique is
based on an ethical and practical attitude primarily concerned with the
transformation of the everyday. This is exemplified in her distinction
between two ideal–typical life orientations that are empirically always
in flux.[50] The first is the particularist. This is not simply a consequence
of the fact that all affects are related to a specific viewpoint: after all,
we are not born with particularistic motivations. Inborn qualities and
propensities are always socially mediated. This is the burden of the
Marxist philosophical anthropology Heller will immediately go on to
develop. The social environment acts in conjunction with biological
potentials as a second mediating source of motivation. The self
appropriates a social environment through a process of identifications
that constitute various forms of 'we consciousness'.[51] The *particularist*
orientation is dominated by the requirements of self-maintenance
and need satisfaction rather than consciousness.[52] This life is lived
comfortably within the limits imposed by custom and spontaneously
identifies with them. The *individual*, on the other hand, makes her own
life the object of conscious reflection. She identifies not just with the
norms and values contingently structuring her everyday world but
evaluates according to standards abstracted from the higher sphere
of cultural objectivations, such as art and philosophy. Of course, the
extent to which this is possible is dependent upon the structure of the
given society and upon the contribution it makes to the development
of species essence.[53] While not even the sphere of high culture escapes
alienation, its existence provides opportunities for the transcendence
of *particularity* towards *individuality*. At the same time, the *individual*
cannot completely suppress her particularity and acts within the bounds
of natural endowments.

Here again we meet another major theme in Heller's ethics: her critique of revolutionary asceticism. *Individuals* choose to develop the most humanly valuable aspects of their capacities. This means that *individuality* is always *representative*, insofar as the individual is a measure of the value substance of a society, a synthesis whereby certain ambitions and attainments of the species have been appropriated and integrated into the *personality*.[54] The consciousness that conforms to the species is self-consciousness. Self-conscious individuality lives consciously and therefore distances itself from particularist motives and merely 'given' aspects of the world. As Heller puts it, a vital part of individuality is keeping a distance from one's own self.[55] This distance is the basis of the transcendence of the everyday. It supplies the perspective from which the individual can discern the factors hindering her development (towards the species). From this image of the world, the individual is able to formulate a *conduct of life* that breaks with mere conformity to reigning norms and values.[56] Such a worldview is an individual ideology that settles value conflicts and orientates towards either the restructuring or the conservation of reality. For Heller, *individuality* is not just an expression of dissatisfaction with self and world but the motivation to attempt to reform both.[57] Nor need this individuality be opposed to community. For Heller, the element of conscious choice involved in individuality makes community not the naturally given relation between individuals but a *creation* of individuals out of chosen human relations. In this small compass is contained the physiognomy of some of Heller's most central and constant ideas.

The main political message of these reflections was the view that Eastern Europe cannot wait for the creation of a community out of the abstract abolition of political and economic alienation. Like the young Marx, Heller conceives communism not primarily as an attained historical stage but as a permanent movement of revolutionary subjects. In its haste to form traditional political parties, Marxist politics lost sight of this. In practical terms, she looked favourably on the Western counter-culture and student movement and was influenced by both. The counter-culture offered an alternative paradigm that was concerned with transforming the world by transforming everyday life.[58] Anticipating future developments, it is interesting to find that Heller especially underscores the need to maintain a plurality of revolutionary ideals. Against some Western counter-cultural views that argued for a sort of return to nature, she holds firm to the view that the modern functional differentiation has forever destroyed immediate human relations and has imposed the historically novel task of creating new kinds of self-chosen human communities. In this latter respect, however, she offers nothing like a concrete programme. Yet she does underline the need for mass participation and democracy. At this time, an unresolved ambiguity permeates her thinking on practical reform. On one side there exists a vague messianic hope resting on the student movement and other cultural developments in the West. On the other, the main emphasis falls on the renewal of ethics in the shape of conscious individuality. This is the immediate product of the situation of the intellectual dissident in Eastern Europe bereft of any significant concrete social movement. In the light of the failure of the whole socialist experiment to transform everyday life, Heller was well aware of the importance of politics to bed down institutional change. Nevertheless, her own emphasis falls on individual virtue in the shape of the moral–cultural resistance of small groups, both to alienation and to the increased private egoism of the socialist life-world.[59] The very Stoic idea of *a conduct of life* evokes the dark historical times after the radical curtailment of public life, when political perspectives disappeared, leaving the individual to find her own meaning in personal conduct.

2
Towards a Philosophical Anthropology

The practical difficulties of the engaged intellectual struggling against official communist party censure in Eastern Europe should not be underestimated. Any attempt to promote the idea of Marxism as a theory of praxis in this context had to give serious attention to the role of individual choices, ethics and the cultural conditions of individual action. Heller could not view Marxism merely as a science of the laws of history that operated independently of the actions of individuals. And if she was concerned about social praxis itself guided by ethics she could not do without a theoretical framework that secured a richer understanding of the orientation to action. Lukács' *Specificity of the Aesthetic* (1963) had assumed that such a foundation was already implicit in Marx's work. Dismissing the idea that Marxian social theory was a form of value-free social science, Heller determined to further elaborate the philosophical foundations of this more comprehensive framework. Her early excavations of humanism in *Renaissance Man* (1967) had exposed the historical contribution of this formative epoch to the anthropological possibilities of cultural modernity.[1] There she located the emergence of an irreducible and conflictual plurality of values. This was not reducible to the antagonism of economic interests but represented the active response of individuals to the tensions of their time and estate, made possible by selective choices in relation to traditions that became binding precedents.[2] In her 1970 study, *Towards a Marxist Theory of Values*, the concern is narrower but more focused. She addresses explicitly the question of a Marxist value theory. However, in the course of this investigation into Marx's view of values and history she continually encounters the theoretical limits of orthodoxy and tests her precarious Marxist faith.

VALUES AND HISTORY

Heller argues that Marx chose abundance (*Reichtum*) as his primary value. She wants to show how this value can be concretised in terms of other values at all levels of human existence, including social struggles and everyday life, and be made the fundamental criterion of value choice in the contemporary situation.[3] It should be pointed out that even here Marx's choice of abundance is very closely associated in Heller's mind with the value of freedom. The many-sided unfolding of species potential is ultimately dependent upon the ability of individuals to *appropriate* that abundance and therefore on freedom to *access* these riches. This organic link between abundance and freedom will resonate through her later development. In the later move to post-Marxist radicalism, she will ultimately change her own highest-value choice from *abundance* to *freedom* and view the latter as the leading value idea of modernity. However, by raising the issue of values at this time, it was not her intention to transform Marxism into a mere voluntarism (the arbitrary subjective choice of values). For the moment still committed to the Marxist philosophy of history, she is intent on locating value development within the total social process of human self-creation and species objectivation. This project presupposes the universal validity of some historically created values in the shape of Lukács' anthropology of human species powers. Those struggling towards a future communist society could not be secure in their own value choices unless they were convinced that these values were universal and in accord with the objective development of history. It follows from this that Heller rejected historicism in favour of the Hegelian notion of Absolute spirit. This is the product of the sphere of *objectivation for itself* already elaborated in her theory of everyday life. Absolute spirit signifies the historically accumulated species-essential values possessing universal validity (art and philosophy).[4] Culture in this sense is the record of the highest, timeless human values: a register of the achievements of historical development and freedom.

Heller considers the question of whether there is such a thing as 'objective values'. Do some values have universal validity and, if so, is it plausible to speak of value development? The Marxist Heller is committed to providing answers to these questions. She wants to theoretically vindicate her own value choice, her commitment to the struggle for communism, and also to refute the view that Marxism is a value-free science. Conceiving it as a theory of praxis involves underlining its foundations in the dynamics of social movements, conscious value choice and individual decision making. Simultaneously she wants to secure the historical meaningfulness and validity of this praxis. For this to be so, the Marxist framework must conform to the objective direction of historical development. The values it affirms can be neither arbitrary nor relativist: they must be universal.

It follows from her theory of objectivation that history is nothing else than the combined social processes that actualise human-species potential. However, comparison with Lukács' position, outlined in Chapter 1, reveals Heller's increasing theoretical originality and intellectual doubts. Especially obvious is the radical open-endedness of her conception. First of all, she acknowledges that she offers not *the* Marxist theory of values but *one possible* theory. Not only was it quite unusual at that time to hear a Marxist discussing values; even more surprising is the concession that there could be more than one such valid theory. She sees a variety of possible ways of reconstructing Marx's theory. It is hard to ignore the explosive political message contained in this reading. This defiant celebration of pluralism also permeates her substantive historical vision. She repeats the emphatic statements of the young Marx: 'History has no goal'; its result is the consequence of the correlation of innumerable, uncoordinated individual and social goals. Individual activity plays itself out within a circumscribed domain of objective possibilities that condition a range of alternatives. These circumstances are both *limits* on the possible and the *source* material of human aims and aspirations. The individual never acts in a vacuum but chooses from amongst options raised by the existing ensemble of materials and possibilities.

Yet even while opening the door to value pluralism Heller upholds the idea of a value-free notion of development applicable to humanity as a whole. This value-free notion of development has three indices. (1) The productive forces – referring to the accumulated technique and abilities that are passed through generations and epochs as an axis of historical continuity. (2) Socialisation of the relations of production – the increasing extent to which social relations are conceived as man-made and changeable and thus as overcoming their previous merely natural interpretation. (3) Increasing universalisation of social integration – the individual increasingly identifying with more abstract groups; this culminates in the idea of humanity as the most universal grouping. The emergence of humanity from nature is due to the potency of sociality as it unfolds the immanent potentialities of human beings. However, Heller does not conceive this as a necessary process. The potential itself is not something that can be established in advance but only *post festum*. The first stone tool does possess the atomic bomb as its immanent potentiality but the realisation of this possibility is *neither necessary* nor could it *be predicted in advance* but only once development has attained a certain level.[5]

Aside from this value-free conception of development, Heller also distinguishes a value concept. The idea of development as progress entails a *direction* of development, in the sense of an evolution from *lower* to *higher*. Different philosophies conceive the value content of this development in different ways. However, Heller contends that with Marx the two concepts of development are fused. This is explained only partly by the dominance of the value of progress in the mid nineteenth century. It also follows from the priority Marx accords to the value 'abundance' (*Reichtum*). With abundance as the highest value, the unfolding of productive forces, sociality and the categories of integration are developments not only in the value-free sense but also in a value sense as well.[6] Marx sometimes spoke as if communism was a necessity, but this obscured the extent to which his concept of development was derived from his own choice of values. Heller is not interested in refuting all the charges of 'inevitiblism' against him. Instead she argues that even his sparse and highly qualified use of the concept of necessity contradicted his own ontology of praxis, which implied the irreducibly alternative character of all human action. With hindsight we know that capitalism found ways to further develop the productive forces. In this light, the idea of an ontology of praxis and of communism as an explicit value choice had displaced belief in historical necessity within Marxist theoretical discussion. Heller even reckons with the possibility that there may be an alternative to communism. If this were the case, she concludes that history could not be judged a development in terms of Marxian value content.[7]

Heller maintains that the Marxian value choice of abundance is shaped by the criterion of a humane society. Marx initially rejected capitalism on this basis. Only later did he *positively* choose the standpoint of the proletariat as the concrete historical representative of a humane society. Heller follows Marx. However, she simultaneously views this as an objective choice because it applies the same human standard to all historical periods. Yet this objectivity remains *conditional*: it presupposes the realisation of communism as the attainment of a human-species viewpoint.[8] At this point Heller has clarified the foundations of the Marxian vision of history and highlighted its dependence on value choice. However, the foundations of praxis are quite novel. The values determining this praxis have been located within a greater historical process and are dependent upon the vagaries of a dynamic social struggle and a political wager on a specific project. Historical necessity collapses before contingent social action, individual choice and responsibility. Of course, the other side of this novel foundation is a new contingency and an irreducible fragility. These notions will gain more prominence in her later thought. The idea of the indestructible value implied in the notion of abundance as ever increasing accumulation of essential species power is nothing more than a *faith*. Yet Heller never waivers. From this time, her commitment to Marxism was just as fragile as this faith. She concedes that were this faith to prove groundless, Marxism would forfeit its validity.[9] We shall see that ultimately this faith was to collapse completely.

THE PLASTICITY OF THE HUMAN

In the early 1930s, Lukács turned from the Hegelian-inspired idea of the proletariat as the identical subject/object of history to Marx's anthropological vision of 'species being' (*Gattungswesen*). This vision presupposed a plastic image of human nature: the full actualisation of all essential human species powers was a labour of the entire historical process. In this conception, the fully human society would result from removing all impediments to the development of essential human forces. Heller's own philosophical anthropology is an attempt to put some real flesh on the bones of this vision. Until her forced emigration, she tackled this task on a range of different fronts. The original conception included a theory of needs for which *The Theory of Need in Marx* (1976) was to have been a preliminary study.[10] Two volumes towards this project, written in Hungary, did not appear until the late 1970s: these were *A Theory of Feelings* (1978) and *On Instincts* (1979).[11] The overall conception was initially modified. It turned into a tetralogy that was to include the *Theory of History* (1982) and a *Theory of Personality*. However, the continuing evolution of Heller's philosophy in the freer intellectual atmosphere of the West finally undermined the original Lukácsian starting point. Ultimately Heller abandoned philosophical anthropology in favour of Hannah Arendt's idea of the 'human condition'. The rationale for this important shift will be explored when we consider Heller's eventual break with the Marxian philosophy of history. However, at this point it suffices to examine her original thoughts on instincts and feeling.

Heller's work on values, and particularly the priority accorded to the value of abundance, already presupposed an understanding of the human species unfolding its potentials in history and the conscious reappropriation of these capacities as a primary value concept. She now sets about augmenting her theory of value with a philosophical anthropology that actually spells out the more comprehensive underlying vision of man.[12] The basic premise of Heller's study of instincts is a determination to deny their existence for human beings.[13] The explanation of this apparent perversity is simple. To the contemporary reader, her decision to include the topic of instincts in her anthropology

seems almost unproblematic. Yet instincts have not always been the
obvious point of departure for philosophical anthropology. Popular
contemporary notions would have it that instincts represent the most
basic and unchanging level of animal and human compulsions. Yet
the ubiquity of this common view is the result of the inundation of
psychological and social-anthropological treatises in the twentieth
century. These all aspired to displace the flimsy creatures of philosophical
speculation with the sound scientific result of modern clinical and field
research. Amongst this welter of views from the behavioural and social
sciences, Heller had to clear a space for her own minority opinion – a
Marxian-inspired social anthropology of an *historically created human
essence*. She is well aware that speculation on human instincts is always
a product of abstraction and immured in the ideological contests of the
present.[14] On this basis she explicitly airs her own evaluative standpoint
and leading values. She then asserts that the theory constructed on this
basis must either best fit the contemporary empirical facts or be modified
in the light of them.[15] Her theory of instincts is a critical deconstruction
of the concept itself and especially of the significance attributed to it
in some domains of psychology and social psychology. She critically
appraises the spectrum of instinct theories from the biological theory
of drives to the social-psychological theories of personality.[16] Her aim
is to demolish the scientific claims of her fiercest ideological opponents
(the theories of basic instincts such as self-preservation, aggression
and sex) while, simultaneously, demonstrating that her theory is quite
compatible with the most promising results of others. She aims for a
theory of instincts that demolishes instincts as an explanatory tool in
building an image of the potentials and limits of historical humanity.

Heller departs from the proposition that humans do not have
instincts at all, but only instinct remnants.[17] She defines instincts in
the following way:

> compulsory behaviour mechanisms or movement co-ordinates
> which are species specific and, at the same time, action specific, are
> inherited through the genetic code, elicited by internal and external
> stimuli, which play a leading role in the preservation of the species
> within a certain stage of historical development and which surpass
> the intelligence of the given species from the point of view of this
> positive selective value.[18]

The virtue of this definition is that it excludes both the theory of
'basic' instincts and the theory of drives. In the case of alleged 'basic
instincts', such as aggression, self-preservation and sex, it is obvious

that so-called 'basic' behaviours are sequences of a great variety of different and separate movement co-ordinates that differ from one species to another.[19] Seen in this light, the behaviour allegedly stemming from 'basic instincts' evaporates into a multitude of movement co-ordinates, only some of which can possibly be ascribed to instinctual compulsion. The drive theory is ruled out for similar reasons. The above definition presupposes an inner stimulus that elicits the activity of the instincts. However, this inner stimulus is not an instinct but merely the condition of species-specific instinctive acts.[20] These initial movements are not stereotypical but rather individual. Only in some instances are movement co-ordinations species specific. The most rigid of these, such as chewing, swallowing, suckling and frictional movement, are instinct remnants.[21] However, the products of inner stimulus seem just too variegated to be described in terms of instincts.

Heller challenges both Hobbesian aggression theories and the crude Rousseauians who claim that all historical accretions are alienating and morally problematic. For her, humanity is neither a blank sheet of paper nor the repository of inalienable instincts.[22] As intimated, her alternative underlines the *historical basis* of human essence. Everything specifically human is the result of social evolution and conditioning.[23] This is why Heller favours the notion of *social* anthropology. Humanity is a social construct: biological stimulus functions always as social stimulus and human needs are always orientated to socially defined teleological action.[24] Man is not confronted by an environment of simple stimuli but rather by a 'world' of social expectations, objects, customs and norms. Future prospects turn on the transformation of this second nature. The history of human self-formation is one of demolition of instincts, or at least of instinctual guidance. The *differentia specifica* of the human species is the lack of both environmental specialisation and fixity of movement co-ordination and types of behaviour. The human social world mediates both stimulus and response. In other words, a large moment of *plasticity* is the distinctive feature of the human world. In humans, the instinctive 'security of action' was at some very early point handed over to a system of social customs and institutions. Emphasising the singularity of this fate, Heller corrects the Romans by designating human beings as social beings rather than social animals.[25]

Heller's alternative sits between the *closure* of human nature implied by the proponents of basic instincts and drives and the *radical openness* of the contemporary behaviourists who would abolish the concept of instincts altogether in favour of a conception of unlimited behavioural modification and relearning. While her position also implies the historical openness of humanity, what's crucial is not what unfolds from within according to genetically inherited patterns of behaviour but the infinite potentials of human plasticity.[26] The ideas of 'unfolding from within' and 'infinite building in' are not mutually exclusive; they are co-relative processes, despite the presence of historical forms of alienation that previously excluded their parallelism in the case of most individuals.[27]

A real tension appears here in Heller's conception, which is brim-full of consequences for her later development. Her idea of the infinite 'openness' of human nature is pervaded by a deep ambiguity. On the one hand, it expresses her conscious embrace of a certain utopianism. More than a mere theoretical proposition, the idea of infinite plasticity is a product of radical practical expectations. This is evident in her insistence that we are not obliged to extrapolate the man of the future from the man of the present.[28] Here socialism still represents the overcoming of alienation, the end of prehistory and the future expectation of a new communist humanity. On the other hand, this luminous vision is already deeply qualified by reservations. Heller is wary of the prospects for an infinite 'building in' of human nature. While Arendt is not mentioned, her strictures against the philosophy of 'everything is possible' seem already in evidence. They confirm Heller's own experience of the Holocaust and its aftermath. History teaches us that the 'good' is not all that can be built into human nature.[29] With this in mind, behaviourism is interpreted as a dystopian, scientific ideology of maximum manipulation. It reduces humanity to 'relearning' and the category of goal rationality displaces the pursuit of freedom and dignity as the aim of a humane society.[30] To avoid reductive and alienated dreams becoming real nightmares, awareness of the radical openness of humanity to historical enrichment must be tempered by recognition of limits over and above the restraints of genetic biology. Heller endorses the naturalist critique of behaviourism that claims that not everything can be built into human nature. The need for self-actualisation is an irreducible need of human beings. Repression on this scale in the long run only leads to dysfunctionality. However, she also rejects rosy, but dogmatic, naturalism. Her value commitment to the practical idea of the historical realisation of human species potential is the overriding element in this vision.

Heller argues that the Marxian concept of human essence has a particular affinity with the idea of the historical openness of humanity. She follows Márkus in elaborating the concept of human essence in terms of the constituents: sociality, consciousness, objectivation, universality and freedom.[31] These are the characteristics of a singular *human world* as well as human potentialities gradually actualised in history. On this reading, universality and freedom represent the direction of the historical process, whereas sociality, consciousness and objectivation signify its vectors. This will be the basis of a more even-handed, if unstable, reconciliation of the idea of the limits of human nature with that of radical historical plasticity.

Marx's acceptance of objectification as the fundamental constitutive human activity signified a break with Feuerbachian naturalism. We have already seen that the notion of objectivation is central to Heller's theory of everyday life. She has recourse to it again here to distinguish her position from the 'third way' in anthropology. The metabolic exchange with nature remains the fundamental ground of objectivation. While human objectivation never entirely abandons this ontological ground, all the same it is never completely reducible to it. This idea is captured in the observation that human intelligence has rendered instinct superfluous as a mechanism of adaptation to a given environment.[32] What is crucial here is not just the universality evident in enhanced human adaptive capacities but in what this flexibility consists. The Marxian understanding of objectivation turns on the fact that this plasticity does not simply unfold from within. The social division of labour brings into play potentials of the species development *without being built into individuals*. It follows that human essence *is not something inside human beings*, like instinct or genetics, but something outside them in the external constellation of institutions, social relations and activities. For human beings the activities of objectivation embedded in a world of social institutions, customs and values have displaced nature as the primary vehicle of human self-constitution.

This understanding of objectivation is paramount to the project to repudiate all notions of basic instincts. Heller rejects the notion of a sex instinct because human sexual behaviour exists only in the desire for objects. Human sexuality is not subordinated to instinctual regulation but to social institutions such as the incest taboo. Once again, objectivation overrides instinct.[33] She makes the same point in elaborating the deeper implications of human universality. Emancipation from the narrow constraints of an instinctual environment allows human beings to create and produce, even according to ideal laws and rules. Human universality is expressed in a complete absence of innate specialised capacities. In their stead, spheres of objectification evolved, structured and regulated by their own independent logics. Human universality is projected and sustained only by the existence of these institutional structures, which reproduce and constantly stimulate the enormous variety of human species powers.[34] This is illustrated by the fact that in human beings knowledge has become a need. Knowledge is perhaps the most profound example of those human needs that have become detached from biological stimuli and launched upon their own immanent dynamic, conditioned predominately by historical and cultural factors.

The priority given to this notion of objectivation in Heller's reading of the Marxian concept of essence underscores the primacy of *historical self-formation*. Yet only by abstraction from this real process can it be distinguished from its other aspects: consciousness and sociality. That Marx laid particular emphasis on objectivation is explicable by the denigration of work in traditional understandings of human uniqueness. While Heller underlines Marx's innovation, she is intent on not reducing the significance of sociality in the process of human self-formation. For her, humanity is just as much a *social construct* as a *historical one*: these are merely two sides of the same coin. Similarly, she devotes considerable space to elaborating the role of consciousness in the configuration of the distinctively human. This is especially important to her strategy to minimise the role played by instincts in understanding human behaviour. In regard to the trinity – instinct, conditioned action, intelligence – she explains that it is the latter which assumes the leading role in humanity. Language allows humanity to transcend mere perception, to formulate and transmit information. Social being is emphatically teleological: it is inexplicable without the setting of goals and choosing of adequate means towards the realisation of objectives.[35] This teleological activism indicates the extent to which instinct has been rendered superfluous as a mechanism of adaptation in human beings. Human homeostasis has extremely elastic limits that flow from this enormous capacity for transcendence.[36] Such flexibility and teleological energy is the product of the self-reflection that issues from linguistic thinking. Humans are conscious beings able to distance themselves from the world and view it as object. The mental distantiation that produces self-consciousness also has a social component: the ambiguity of self-alienation requires the capacity for the ego to be able to view itself from the standpoint of somebody else.

These reflections on the Marxian concept of human essence close with an elaboration of an apposite notion of freedom. Freedom means for Heller neither a public nor a private space, but openness to the future and to the possibility of consciously and intentionally realising radical novelty.[37] This freedom is intimately aligned with a philosophy of history that culminates in the realisation of an anthropologically ascribed many-sided human species richness. Freedom is a vital subordinate value that facilitates the process of self-creation. As long as Heller continued to view this philosophy of history as benign, the tensions between freedom and the primary value of human species wealth remained obscure.

Yet the ultimate ground of her later development is already evident in a concluding train of thought. Unlike the other constituents of the human essence, the distinctive thing about the value of freedom is that it cannot be realised in alienation. Universality, sociality and knowledge may all be attained at the cost of great masses of individuals. Freedom, however, she asserts, 'is not possible, never possible without the freedom of individuals'.[38] While the potential value conflict between individual freedom and species wealth is suspended by her faith in a non-alienated socialist society, the elements for a value choice that raises freedom to the highest value of modernity are already laid down in this recognition of the uncompromising singularity of freedom.

FEELINGS AND BOURGEOIS IMPOVERISHMENT

Righting the balance between nature and society on the question of instincts involves complementary tasks. Heller takes up another aspect of the allegedly extra-rational dimension of human beings in *A Theory of Feelings* (1978). Here she again ventures into theoretical terrain not previously covered by a Marxist thinker.[39] It is perhaps not surprising that a woman and mother would be the first Marxist to seriously engage this topic. However, her efforts are foreshadowed by Lukács' concern for the 'whole human' and express the New Left's similar counter-cultural worries about fragmentation under the sway of bourgeois culture.

The rationale of *A Theory of Feelings* is twofold. The first part of the book argues for the organic unity of man. Against the main tendency of the philosophical tradition to divide reason and feelings (passions), Heller provides a sustained defence of the unity of feeling, thinking and morality. In the Introduction, she maintains that this unity is an 'empirical fact'. A good example of this is her assertion that women are typically socialised for clairvoyance. She maintains that this is not an innate ability but an acquired cognitive capacity marked by the reintegration of emotion.[40] Of course we already know that this is one of the foundation stones of her conception of everyday life. Bourgeois society produces *particularist* feelings and splits the personality. This experience feeds the Marxian trope of alienation. Against this pervasive societal tendency, Heller counterposes the chosen value of personality. This is the individual who, in the sense previously outlined, *consciously shapes* her life according to a self-chosen hierarchy of values. She admits that the 'personality' in this sense exists today only as *an exception* and a *tendency*.[41] The latter part of the book is devoted to a sociological survey of the 'split personality' in bourgeois society and to a prognosis of its current prospects. In the following, we will briefly consider the contribution that the topic of feelings makes to Heller's philosophical anthropology. The focus then turns to the historical reconstruction and diagnosis of the contemporary situation as she viewed it in the 1970s.

Heller has already argued that human beings confront a basic antinomy. Species essence is genetically coded while the individual is an independent, idiosyncratic system. Everything that makes the individual human at birth is external to the individual organism.[42] This organism is like a genetically programmed machine that receives its tasks from the environment and its being-in-the-world. As we have seen, the primary tasks are the acquisition of language, the practice of customs and the use of tools. The antinomian double determination is reflected in the role played by the social in human homeostasis. Biological imbalance reflected in the so-called drives of thirst, hunger and pain is typically mediated by sociological factors. These are only very rarely a case of mere survival but normally of achieving this at a certain socially and culturally defined level. The two basic categories of human homeostasis are *preservation* and *expansion*. Both are always operative, but with differing emphasis in static and dynamic societies.[43]

Feelings play a crucial role in maintaining human homeostasis. They dictate the proportions between old and new, preservation and expansion, 'more' and 'enough', as well as the general reduction of psychological tension. Heller defines feeling as simply being involved in something.[44] The importance of this involvement is clear when it is recognised that human beings are intentional, essentially longing beings. They are also conscious and purposefully orientated towards the future. She underscores the point that feeling is philogenetically primary in as much as we feel even before we act or think.[45] Feelings play a vital role in ensuring the sustenance and continuity of the ego. The ego seeks and articulates problems from the standpoint of blank spots. But filling blank spots never completely resolves gaps: this filling merely brings about further gaps and thus modifies the overall structure.[46] However, in the process of socialisation, appropriation and filling the gaps produces the ego's own world. The aspects of this relation are internalisation, objectivation and self-expression. All three are simultaneously action, thinking, and feeling.[47] In forming its own world, the ego must selectively expand and preserve itself. Of course, there is no single relationship to the world; there are a variety of possible relationships to the world and various types of feeling.

Heller's insertion of feelings into her general anthropology allows her to elaborate a detailed classificatory typology that need not be reproduced here. However, her sociology of feelings is particularly interesting. It offers a contemporary diagnosis of society and her prognosis for a way beyond present antinomies.

She departs from the observation that differing emotional dynamics operate in different historical epochs. In her view, we are now fast receding from the bourgeois world epoch and its utilitarian housekeeping of feelings, which judged all things according to the value pair: useful/harmful. In contemporary society, adjustment is the chief consideration. The leading orientational categories are now correct/incorrect.[48] Historically, bourgeois society was the first society to allow the possibility of an individual housekeeping of feeling. In earlier societies, the value hierarchy of feeling was given and the task of the individual was to operate within the emotional economy of a fixed social position acquired naturally at birth. Only with the possibility of reversals of the socially given and the selection of values and tasks in accordance with particular disposition does an individual housekeeping of feelings become a real possibility. However, while this possibility was opened up by bourgeois society, it was rarely realised by the great mass of individuals constrained by the pseudo-natural laws of the bourgeois economy.[49]

Heller views the typical alienated bourgeois individual as a split personality deformed by the sharp division between civic and bourgeois consciousness familiar from Marx. Both sides of this split suffer from abstraction of the world of feelings. The citizen's acts are deduced from principles, while the bourgeois acts only according to the extension of individual interest or its generalisation as a group or class.[50] The bourgeois orientation is one of calculation. In this world of feeling, the passions play a decisive role, especially the desire for possession. This passion is theoretically boundless and this explains the *quantifiable* character of bourgeois needs. The ego entrapped within these quantitative passions is *abstract and homogenised*. Such an individual is increasingly absorbed into and transformed by like attitudes, values and aspirations. Heller maintains that bourgeois reality was increasingly resistant to qualitative value. This is registered in the world of art and the citizen. Unlike Shakespeare, who could allow principles to emanate from the life-situation of the concrete character (Brutus or Lear), Schiller settled for heroes who are merely the mouthpieces for ideas, because these ideas did not stem from concrete bourgeois life.[51] Such abstraction is just as evident in the life of the *citoyen*. Civic enthusiasm is equally a passion that homogenises the ego: it subordinates all emotions to a single dominant one. Such asceticism might flower in historical crises and emergency situations but is resisted by the bourgeois everyday.[52] We need to keep in mind here Heller's critique of asceticism.

It helps to shape her own vision of a way beyond the antinomies of bourgeois society.

The schizoid, abstract bourgeois world of feelings is in decline. The bourgeois social division of labour allowed a small elite the leisure to cultivate a world of feelings and rich emotional shadings. This culture of sensibility was achieved by turning its back on conventional culture and language. However, such an elite culture has a dialectic of its own that finally leads to emotional impoverishment. Having created a distinctive oppositional emotional world of culture and taste the adepts of emotional sensibility face the problem of communication. Rejecting the reigning socio-political norms, the bearers of sensibility were cut off from the society in which they lived. They failed to see the degree to which the culture of sensibility was built on privilege. It veiled another form of scarcity that revealed itself in their isolation from their peers.

Heller maintains that a new, more concrete world of feelings emerged in the post-Second World War environment linked to social adjustment. This is not just adjustment to society as a whole, but a *total adjustment* to every specific task, every place in the social division of labour.[53] Passions have not disappeared, but they now function within, and in relation to, adjustment. Compared to its predecessor this new structure of feelings is neither 'higher' nor 'lower': it contains contradictory potentials. The abstract quality of bourgeois passions and enthusiasm is on the wane.[54]

A close look at the new structure of feeling associated with total adjustment suggests increased neurosis. The new modern world of feelings is ordered around what Heller calls the quasi-orientational feelings: these are 'yes' or 'no' feelings in regard to any aspect of life, including action, thinking and judgement. These feelings play a role in all aspects of life and are thus universal. They lead to either living up to expectations or deviating from them. Typically these feelings have no value reference (they are correct/incorrect) and, consequentially, are not constitutive of the personality. Characteristic of this structure of feelings is the weakened ego that can *change* but not *grow*. It receives its selection readymade from the external environment and simply adjusts; its own world is not structured and cannot expand.[55] The individual at the mercy of her roles is characterised by a state of permanent anxiety. Heller maintains that neurosis is not typical of every sort of alienation. It stems from the situation in which one and the same individual is divided between alienated work and idleness. In the bourgeois era these activities were distributed amongst distinct social classes. However, in contemporary society this class allocation has been introjected into the typical individual's life. In only a few lives is the need for the elemental pleasure of reaching a goal that is tied to needs other than work and idleness evident as a constitutive principle.[56] For the majority, goal orientation in respect to needs is fixated on work and leisure.

Heller interpreted the late 1960s counter-culture as a reaction symptom to the crisis of a society of adjustment. Some abandoned their roles to create their own hierarchy of feelings. They placed the emotional dispositions of love and friendship at the apex. Their goal was peak experiences: the dichotomy between subject and object overcome in a climactic moment. She calls this strategy the 'radicalism of mood'. Its obvious limitation was that no lasting world or society could be built on direct relations.[57] As the Marxist Heller then saw it, this was the impasse reached by the early 1970s. On the one side was the society of adjustment, with its concretisation of feelings and loss of personality. On the other side was the exodus from the division of labour and the 'radicalism of mood'. The latter was not a real solution for the masses. A housekeeping of feelings beyond the social division of labour could not be generalised. It was also inadequate from the standpoint of the idea of a many-sided individual, rich in needs. The individual without a socially valued work goal loses one of her main ordering principles.[58]

Heller's own exploration beyond this antinomy involved a synthesis of the 'radicalism of mood' with enthusiasm. Yet this is not the abstract, ascetic enthusiasm of the *citoyen*, but what she called concrete enthusiasm. The feeling composed of ideas must be supplemented by a sensual capacity that would invest feelings in the realisation of specific tasks feasible for concrete man (sic).[59] Strangely, to conjure up the spirit of concrete enthusiasm Heller returned to the surviving letters of condemned anti-fascists. This notion of concrete enthusiasm repudiated heroism and martyrdom; its motive was duty to others, orientated by love of human beings and by the simple love of life rather than ideas. These individuals did not consider themselves exceptional and therefore thought their conduct generalisable.[60] For Heller, the ideal of concrete enthusiasm exists not just because there are such 'good people'. The psychic structure of the 'good person' is not aristocratic even if such people constitute an elite in the present. Regardless of their actual numbers, she endorses this form of elitism: it signifies the only promising, future-bearing elite. The synthesis of idea and needs is the condition of beginning the work to create a new world.[61] However, she admits it is debatable whether the 'good person' can be imitated.

On the face of it, Heller here confronts a problem similar to the one she identified with the 'radicalism of mood'. Amongst the failings of this strategy was a lack of generalisability. Heller's alternative model attempts to humanise the ideal by removing asceticism and

underlining a simple love of life. Oddly, however, her exemplars come
from the extreme experiences of anti-Nazi martyrs. Is this not just peak
experience, albeit in another form? Just as remote from the routines of
the everyday as the direct experience encountered in the counter-culture!
True, border experience is far removed from the neurosis of the society
of adjustment. However, this is also its limitation from the standpoint
of mediation. The 'goodness' of an anti-Nazi hero is simply equated
to that of the bourgeois everyday. What possible relation could it have
to the adjustment society, when its urgency seems to be a product of
such extraordinary conditions?

The tension between normative ideals and empirical conditions is not
the most theoretically troubling problem in Heller's efforts towards a
philosophical anthropology. Of more concern is her absolute confidence
in the inherited Lukácsian framework. She accepted completely Lukács'
self-critique of the abstraction of *History and Class Consciousness*
and its supercession by the Marxian notion of species being. Yet
ultimately this move suffers from the same theoretical abstraction that
contaminated the idea of the proletariat as the subject/object of history.
In its basic categories, the philosophy of man articulates a project of
human self-creation that ideologically universalises the process in the
West. The categories man, labour, history stand here as transcendentals
that underwrite the universal significance of the bourgeois narrative. Its
ideological status resides in its co-option of otherness and difference into
a story that homogenises identities and eliminates alterity. Today, the
cognitive credibility of this tale has been dented by modern scholarship,
which has displaced the idea of a collective historical subject with a
model of plural subjects and mutual identity formation.[62] However,
while Heller remained committed to a Marxian philosophy of history,
the idea of providing it with a foundation in philosophical anthropology
was a meaningful project. Her breach with philosophy of history will
bring the problem of closure in the concept of human nature to the
forefront of her thinking and finally cause her to abandon the project
of a philosophical anthropology altogether. Heller was still some
distance from achieving this level of clarity, but already her doubts
were becoming more manifest.

NEEDS AND CAPITALIST DYNAMICS

The book that brought Heller to international attention and raised her
philosophical anthropology into the avant-garde of leftist thought was
The Theory of Needs in Marx (1976). Of all her works, this remains
the best known and the one that most clearly identified her with the

last gasps of Western humanist Marxism. As mentioned, she initially conceived this as a 'finger exercise' towards her own theory of needs. While still generally located within a programme of 'Marx Renaissance', her interpretation already shows signs of an increasing critical distance. The fact that it could not be published in Kádár's Hungary and received widespread critical acclaim when finally translated in 1976 is some measure of its theoretical radicality.[63] The political implications obvious to its contemporary readers are easily missed today. Although strategically avoiding any discussion of the concrete problem of the 'transition to socialism', ostensibly on the grounds that Marx himself had not treated this problem,[64] her general theorisation of the problem of needs in Marx had moved beyond the limits of official acceptability.[65] As we have seen already from her thoughts on everyday life, the crucible of her theory of needs is a conception of *total revolution* that signifies not just the overturning of political regimes or relations of production but the transformation of everyday life. This is also more than a politically courageous attack on official Marxism. Heller begins to extend her critique to Marx himself. While still deferential, she sets about pointing out tensions in his theory and his own illusions; she views his greatness primarily in his 'brilliant incoherence'.[66] The crux of this 'incoherence' was the deep ambiguity in Marx's explanation of the revolutionary overcoming of capitalist society, his fluctuation between viewing revolution as the necessary outcome of quasi-natural laws of the economy and as the conscious act of an increasingly radicalised collective subjective power.

Above all, Heller presents the humanist Marx, whose entire theory draws its critical power from the philosophical critique of alienation. She asserts that the concept of need plays one of the main, if not the main, role in Marx's critique. Whereas classical political economy had excluded all extra-economic needs and conceived the worker's needs only as a limit to wealth, Marx clearly rejected this standpoint as the ideological mainstay of capitalism: it speaks from the standpoint of the capitalist alienation of human needs.[67] For Marx, socialism presupposes a transformation of the entire structure of needs. Increased productivity no longer means a quantitative expansion of commodities and exchange value, but increases in both the quantity and quality of use values.[68] The society of 'associated producers' signifies primarily a system of non-alienated needs.[69] Need is primarily a category of value. For Marx, the category of need functions as an *anthropological value category*, allowing him to *evaluate* the alienated needs of capitalist society.[70] As Heller's work on values already made clear, for Marx the most important category of value is *wealth* in the sense of rich needs;

it is the condition for the unfolding of 'human' needs and the basis for the free development of all aspects of individuality. In Marx's critique of capitalism, every judgement is articulated from a basis of positive values. This is critique that transcends the limits of capitalism, for its measure is humanity rich in human needs.[71] While it was the young Marx who elaborated this category of need, Heller makes clear that it was presupposed in all his later works.[72]

Humanity 'rich in needs' is not only Marx's fundamental value ideal but also the basis of his immanent explanation of historical change. As we've seen, the underlying source of this idea of wealth of human needs is the paradigm of objectivation. All attempts to demarcate between 'natural' and 'socially produced', 'material' and 'spiritual', 'necessary' and 'luxury' needs are blurred by the essential historicity of Marx's understanding of human needs. Human needs expand in a dynamic historical process fuelled by labour. Objectification stimulates *need enrichment*. For Marx, needs are not only passions but *also capacities*. Unlike biologically fixed animal needs, human needs increasingly engage activities that generate capacities and a spiral of ever new needs.[73] The human dimension of satisfaction imparts to human needs an inherently qualitative dimension. This historical dimension of need creation and augmentation underlines th*e social construction* of humanity: that human needs are formed and conditioned within a cultural environment. However, this forming results not from a passive imprinting but from an *active response* in the shape of capacity-generating activities. For Marx, historicity is not the domain of super-individual processes and forces but the practical activity of concrete individuals, circumscribed but never determined by the pervading historical conditions. This signifies a new paradigm of human *finitude* that facilitates an understanding of individual creativity and recognises the social constitution of human need within the limits imposed by historical and natural determinations.

Reconstruction of the theoretical motives behind the Marxian concept of need allows Heller to challenge two ideologically charged notions within the orthodox reading. At the core of Marx's understanding of the alienation of needs was his belief that capitalism reduced humans to the status of *means* in the process of wealth accumulation. Bourgeois society is primarily focused on exchange value and demands the homogenisation of needs to meet the requirements of commodification. Money is the quantitative measure of needs, which reduces them to possessions. Use values that cannot be translated into exchange values cease to be objects of production. While Marx comes to acknowledge the emancipatory dimension of capitalism, Heller insists that he always rejected the homogenisation implied by the notion of interests. The category of interest was unknown to ancient and medieval philosophy. It becomes more prevalent only with the triumph of bourgeois social relations. As a motive of individual action, interest is nothing else than the reduction of quality to quantity. The philosophical generalisation of the category of interests to classes is the product of a society in which the essentially qualitative and concrete dimension of needs has been suppressed by the processes of homogenisation.[74] Bourgeois society is the first 'pure' society where abstract, impersonal social relations have been superimposed on the compulsions of nature and have assumed a quasi-natural independence and necessity. Only when translated into the quantitative currency of alienation is the qualitative dimension of individual need recognised.

In the light of Heller's background, it is not surprising that she sees the equation of 'social needs' with the category of general interests as more dangerous than smuggling bourgeois categories into Marxian discourse. If social needs are equated with general interests, they become somehow 'suspended above' real individuals and viewed as 'higher' or 'more general'. They are perceived as more 'real' and authentic, while the needs of concrete individuals are devalued as partial and self-interested. In cases of conflict, this identification legitimates the subordination of individual needs to general interests. At this point, Heller has not yet questioned the pivotal Marxian distinction between class consciousness and empirical consciousness. However, she is already quite clear that in practice the theoretical distinction between individual and social needs legitimates an oppressive privileged perspective that always serves the needs of a dominant class or group.

Heller's relentless pursuit of Marx's genuine thoughts on revolution and interests exposes tensions in his understanding of the dynamics of capitalism. These surface with her signature concept of 'radical needs'. Her critique of the notion of interests leads to the conviction that the aspirations of the working class is not an interest in revolutionary transcendence, but rather in a struggle for wages and other incremental improvements. In other words, it only captures the working class in its alienated capitalist persona. Revolution presupposed a further development in the level of class struggle, moving beyond issues of economic distribution to those implicating a direct political challenge to the total bourgeois organisation of society as a whole. According to Heller, Marx sees the key to this transcending political self-consciousness in *radical needs*, generated by the life situation of the workers. The bourgeois system cannot function without workers: they are essential to capitalist society.[75] Marx's emphasis here falls on the social totality. The capitalist structure of needs is not some independent variable but an integral moment of an organic unity of production, distribution and exchange. In this totality, needs are not allocated by birth but by status ascribed according to political and economic institutions and functions. This link between need ascription and political and economic functionality introduces the moment of social dynamism and individual striving. This link is responsible for an accompanying shift in the character of bourgeois needs, from the dominance of quality to that of quantity. Radical needs are immanent within capitalist society; their radicality consists not in their mere expression (e.g. the desire for free time) but in their satisfaction, which could not be realised without the transcendence of capitalism.[76] The transcendent quality of these needs lies in their objects. Capitalism allows the individual to more actively shape their own need structure. Markets loosen social prescription and generate a broad proliferation of individualised packages of need satisfaction in the shape of various combinations of free time, artistic activity and personal development. At the same time, capitalism is simply unable to accommodate the satisfaction of these needs. This would breach the structural mechanisms of inequality and exploitation that are the foundation of the system. But Heller is not content merely to define radical needs negatively. Socialism involves an entirely new structure of needs, implying not just greater quantitative satisfaction but a fundamentally altered quality. Marx's value choice of wealth implies a need structure that promotes quality: free time, labour as intellectual work and artistic activity, personal development and freely chosen and enriched forms of community.[77]

The third defining aspect of radical needs is quality. Despite having attained a much higher level of material wealth, socialism entails that consumer goods play a limited role.[78] Social wealth would no longer be measured solely in terms of productivity and non-material values like free self-activity and personal development would transform the need structure towards even more heterogeneous, individualised packages. In such a society, material wealth is merely a condition of freedom but not freedom itself. In socialism, the only limit imposed on individual need would be that of other qualitatively different needs.[79] This notion of radical needs now becomes the key both to Heller's reconstruction of the ambiguities in Marx and to her forceful implicit critique of 'really existing socialism'. She argues that Marx the philosopher was faced with the problem of how his subjectively affirmed 'ought' was to be realised.[80] In the light of his own emphatic critique of the impotence of the whole philosophical tradition, it was essential for Marx that this infirmity be overcome, at least theoretically. He employs two ways of materialising his philosophical 'ought'. Although his two 'solutions' are ultimately contradictory and imply opposed practical strategies, in Marx's mind they became unconsciously fused together and he fluctuated between them for the rest of his life.[81]

Heller describes the first of these solutions as Fichtean because the emphasis falls upon *active subjectivity*. The subjective 'ought' permeating the philosophical figure of alienation is transformed into the material claim of a *collective social actor* in the shape of the proletariat. Alienation stimulates radical needs as the working masses strive collectively to realise their aspirations. The second solution is essentially Hegelian. Here the emphasis shifts from active subjectivity towards *objective dynamics* and the inherent laws of the economy. The antinomies of capitalist society represent only a particular instantiation of the general laws of historical development. In other words, the 'ought' now assumes the form of *causal necessity*. Heller acknowledges that consistent adherence to this understanding renders the idea of radical needs superfluous.[82] The notion that the economy operates according to quasi-natural laws is merely another appearance of fetishised commodity relations. By contrast, the intellectual force of the idea of radical needs is the stimulation of needs that shatter this fetishised appearance.

The revolutionary scenario involving radical needs relies not on historical laws but on a specific analysis of the dynamics of the capitalist commodity form. Bourgeois society produces not only *alienation* but also increasingly the *consciousness of alienation*: the formally free but concretely exploited wage labourer develops radical needs not just for improved material conditions but also as *enhanced species capacities*. The class that formerly had no particular goals within bourgeois society finally discovers its own universal subjective potentials. This gradually maturing universality is the source of both the emancipatory perspective of Marx's theory and of the concrete agent of total revolution. Despite the economic cast of his later works the underlying structure of this scenario remains. However, the emphasis shifts towards the proletariat's development of universal capacities in the form of collective activity, increased consciousness and the integral development of the worker as machinery replaces skilled labour.[83] In both scenarios, the philosophical critique of capitalism assumes an immanent historical form: an increasingly unified and politically cohesive class subject, constantly combating and contesting reified capitalist relations.

But not even all this impressive theoretical effort can ultimately conceal the illusory character of Marx's analysis and of the immanent power ascribed to the workers. The belief that revolution was guaranteed by radical needs cannot mask the truth that Marx *invented radical needs*.

They were a theoretical construct, the consciousness of alienation: perhaps more than his own subjective dreams but definitely not the empirical consciousness of the working class.[84] This consciousness was not actualised in Marx's own time. Even 100 years later, Heller could not convincingly determine whether or not capitalism produces such needs.[85] Yet, while distancing herself from Marx's illusions, she insisted that this posited collective 'ought' remained a 'practical necessity'. Still entranced by some of the dreams of the New Left, she continued to nurture a few illusions of her own. While Marx had been compelled to 'invent' radical needs, she asserted that we could now see them 'with our own eyes'.[86] Under the sway of New Left optimism, she viewed the Western student protest and counter-culture as another manifestation of emergent radical needs. Like Marcuse, she believed that the working class had been displaced from its position as the primary bearer of radical needs.[87]

Heller's book on Marx very successfully released the contemporary critical core of his own thought. In the course of doing so, she managed to formulate her own theory of radical needs. The illusory status of Marx's normative standpoint is exposed in the assertion that the radical needs attributed to the proletariat were in fact Marx's own invention. She also significantly loosened her commitment to the philosophy of history and categorically rejected the idea of historical inevitability. On the one hand, she maintains that history has not yet decided whether capitalism immanently produces radical needs. On the other, in an almost apparent contradiction, she argues that radical needs are now manifest both at the heart and at the margins of the orthodox working-class movement. Her book on Marx's theory of needs reveals clearly an internal theoretical struggle that will be carried over into the early works of her post-Marxist period. She soon made the decisive step in this latter direction when she finally abandoned the Marxian philosophy of history. However, the tensions and struggle she discovered in Marx between immanent analysis and revolutionary hope will persist in her own views even beyond her commitment to Marxism.

3
Critique of
'Really Existing Socialism'

In retrospect, it is easy to see in Heller's Marxist works the Lukácsian programme for the 'Renaissance of Marx' in the process of self-dissolution. Not only was the tradition of orthodox Marxism found wanting in relation to many of her own philosophical concerns, but she increasingly came to see tensions, ambiguities and lacunae in Marx himself. After a courageous public statement to the international media against the Soviet invasion of Czechoslovakia, the leading figures of the Budapest School faced escalating political pressure. With the death of Lukács in 1971, they lost the protection provided by his international reputation. Finally, the party moved against them. Some were sacked from their research positions in 1973 and others resigned in solidarity. For some years, Heller, Fehér and Márkus eked out a living from translation. Heller was refused permission to publish and also excluded from public life. Even so, the unofficial circulation of her writings produced more political retribution and harassment. Eventually, in 1977, both families decided on emigration to Australia. Heller and Fehér found themselves in a new environment in Melbourne suburbia. With plenty of time to write, Heller was able to continue the review of her erstwhile philosophical consciousness unimpeded.[1] The result was a decade of great productivity.

Heller immediately radicalised her critique of Marx and ventured the first tentative steps towards a post-Marxist philosophy. However, underpinning these philosophical efforts was the desire to finally come to a theoretical reckoning with 'really existing socialism'. Along with Fehér and Márkus, she took the opportunity to turn their collective disillusionment in an explicitly political direction with a critique of the Soviet style systems of Eastern Europe. This co-authored work, entitled *Dictatorship over Needs* (1983), deserves a full discussion.[2] It not only presents the most complete and fully elaborated version of the Budapest School's critique of these societies. It also fills out the experiential foundations of Heller's break with Marxism. Even more

61

important from the standpoint of Heller's future development, however, it initiates the radical rethinking of modern historical dynamics that will soon issue in a challenging new theory of modernity.

In an essential way, *Dictatorship over Needs* is still a Marxist work. While critical of various aspects of Marx, the authors employ a Marxian framework, categories and values to argue that 'really existing socialism' is a travesty of his vision. At the same time, they offer a 'thin' abstract analysis of the main structural components of the mature form of this society rather than a historical narrative. The authors are concerned more to capture what is the essential identity of these forms of society rather than the myriad of differences between them. As we shall see, this approach is both a strength and a weakness.[3] They maintain that this framework still offers a 'theoretically deeper and practically more radical/critical understanding than its liberal alternative'.[4] Exposing the essence of 'really existing socialism' becomes a test case for the efficacy of the future viability of the Marxist *instrumentarium*. The authors view themselves as exponents of a non-Leninist brand of socialist theory especially committed to the radicalisation of democracy. However, they relinquish former reformist illusions that somehow these regimes could be made to live up to their concept. On the contrary, the Soviet style societies represent a *new configuration of modernity* that finds no place in the Marxian philosophy of history. This society is not in transition to some higher social form, but is a ruthless dictatorship over subject populations. Whether taking the form of outright terror or subsiding into authoritarian conservatism, it continually reproduces itself and remains committed to the expansion of the resources and territory under its exclusive control. The book's title resonates both with the themes from Heller's earlier work on needs and also with the Marxist tradition that had tended to view capitalism as a system that distorted and manipulated human needs. The specificity of their claim is that the practical attempt to transcend this alienation with the project of a substantively rational society had produced an even greater disaster: a social system of total political control that exercised a dictatorship over the satisfaction of all needs.[5]

As political émigrés, the authors do not expect resonance in Eastern European societies. After all, there the book was prohibited and the subject populations already largely viewed Marxism as merely an ideological façade. Nevertheless, exploring the essence of real socialism remained meaningful and even urgent for Western leftists and the dissident oppositions still embracing democratic aspirations. At that time, Euro-communists found it politically more convenient to remain silent about these regimes than to accept a degree of co-responsibility for their crimes and accelerate their own processes of internal democratisation.[6] By contrast, the Budapest authors argue that confrontation with the reality of really existing socialism is vital: exploring the unforeseen conceptual ambiguities and inadequacies of Marxism in its classical form is a contribution to resolving the crisis, while the new allegedly democratic commitment must be substantiated.[7] The book is divided into three distinct parts, each written individually by one of the authors.

THE CLASSICAL OPTIONS

The precise economic and social character of really existing socialist societies is specified by Márkus. The classical Marxist tradition had already supplied the three basic explanatory alternatives. He insists that all of these are fundamentally inadequate, but that only their demolition provides space for an alternative model of 'dictatorship over needs'.[8]

The best-known explanatory model, associated with Trotsky, views the Soviet Union as a society *in transition*. It is located somewhere on the road from capitalism to socialism, but political distortions have arrested its development, producing a hybrid under the domination of bureaucracy and a privileged party elite. Trotsky stressed the progressive character of the already achieved socialist relations of production while explaining bureaucratic distortion as a result of historical backwardness or the residual influence of capitalism.[9] The critical thrust of the theory connects the lack of democracy with the existence of deep social and economic inequalities generated by uncontrolled political domination.[10] However, this strongest aspect also ultimately reveals the inadequacies and immanent apologetic potentials of the theory. On the one hand, it views party domination as the primary source of inequalities. At the same time, it continues to view central planning as the essential antidote to the same bureaucratic tendency. Márkus argues that this dichotomy relies on a disembodied notion of planning that associates it with democracy and rationality. Yet, in the case of Eastern Europe, planning has no independent logic and is subordinated to the power relations of complex bureaucratic hierarchies.[11] It is a crucial mistake simply to identify central planning as a socialist constituent and the market with capitalism. Without viewing the market as a universal panacea, he argues that only the imposition of limits upon the mechanisms of the command economy will check the power of the bureaucratic apparatus. Without limits, on the other hand, the mechanisms of the apparatus continue to expand and impotent citizens have no effective means of counteracting their utter irrationality.[12] If the workers in Eastern Europe are to overcome a permanent position of passive subordination and exercise some prerogatives, the false dichotomy between planning and the market must be demolished. The much vaunted 'dictatorship of the proletariat' obscures the need for this. This is merely another ideological fiction. In Eastern Europe, social rule does not mean collective control over the processes of social reproduction; rather it signifies the extension of the state's paternalist control over every aspect of life.[13]

This uncritical presumption of historical progress with the extension of state control is a major failing of the theory of transition. It presupposes that modernity faces an epochal choice between capitalism and socialism as the sole viable options. While this reading has the weight of the orthodox Marxist tradition behind it, Márkus insists that it is one-sided even from Marx's own standpoint. His theory implies a distinction between *nationalisation*, as a legal–political act transferring ownership of major resources to the public, and *socialisation*, as an effective transformation of economic relations that gives real power and actual disposition to the immediate producers. However, Marx never envisaged a socialist society retaining market mechanisms. The existence of problems to systematic reproduction and continuing instability in Eastern Europe, where the market exists but is subordinated to central planning, appeared to indicate a society in transition. Yet Márkus contends that these societies in fact show great continuity and oppressive stability. Even the obvious shift from mass terror to conservative authoritarianism concealed a remarkable underlying capacity for successful reproduction. This judgement turned out to be premature, as it preceded the birth of Solidarity in Poland. Nevertheless, this shortcoming must be offset by anticipation of coming crisis. The regime's proven capacity to survive crisis was no guarantee into the future. All the signs forewarned of the approach of a global systemic crisis.[14] Most striking in this analysis is that even belief in the total irrationality of the regime and prediction of global crisis never shook the shared conviction that these regimes represented a *hybrid* constellation of modernity impressively capable of surviving even grave instability. In these societies, even crisis was an immanent safety valve and not incompatible with the cycle of reproduction. The comprehensibility of this view follows from the analysis of the self-reproduction of these regimes.

The second conventional description of these regimes within the Marxist tradition views them as instances of *state capitalism*: the extreme centralisation and concentration of capital. On this view, bureaucratic domination is not a socialist deformation but a realisation of an inherent tendency of capitalism.[15] The bureaucracy becomes a collective capitalist and the society is prone to the class conflict familiar to Western society. The anti-capitalist credentials of these regimes are no obstacle to this interpretation. However, its main weakness is what it takes as proof of their 'capitalist' character. The existence of analogous features of economy and social structure between East and West cannot disguise the fact that the private appropriation of profit is non-existent in the command economies:[16] this is a difference of kind, not of degree. These societies simply ignore the principle of profit maximisation. The ruling apparatus is swayed primarily by broader social–political considerations. Invariably, it is motivated by the enhancement of its own power rather than by any thought of profitability. From the standpoint of theories of state capitalism, the governing logic of these societies always remains obscure or irrational. Yet the failure to pursue profitability is no defect or malfunction but the very key to their peculiar 'rationality'. Márkus argues that it is vital to discover the peculiar logic of this reproduction and understand why such excessive inefficiency can be perfectly reasonable from its own standpoint.[17]

In the command economy, the distinction between use value and exchange value is inapplicable. The former is directly produced and appropriated: it need not bear any relation to the real needs of consumers. The basic contradiction of these economies is between administrative use values and their social utility.[18] Proof of this is the endemic concrescence of shortages and waste that follows from the fact that administrative requirements and not real demand direct production. At the same time, consumers suffer the regular absence of goods. Furthermore, in these economies the division between subjective and objective factors of production is never complete. The apparatus has effective command not only over the means of production and appropriation of surpluses but also over portions of aggregate labour. Unlike the capitalist compelled to bargain over the wage contract, the state apparatus is in a position, within certain limits, to set the conditions of employment. While always constrained by a range of other factors, such as paternalistic intolerance of unemployment or explicit inequality, it maintains great overall control and inhibits the freedom of the worker. Against this power colossus, the worker's only defence is a guerilla resistance of non-compliance and sabotage. It is precisely the inflated power and reach of the apparatus that creates the distinctive economic and social matrix of these regimes. This difference does not amount to an alternative logic to instrumental rationality. However, while dependence on instrumental rationality bring these regimes into the vicinity of capitalism, the singular lack of innovative capacity only magnifies their monstrous otherness.

The final traditional Marxist alternative assimilates these regimes to the so-called 'Asiatic mode of production'. This alternative normally plays a supplementary explanatory role rather than an exclusive one.[19] It operates on the basis of vague analogies rather than as an explanation of the specific features of these regimes, and points to a variety of characteristics that these regimes share with some pre-capitalist societies.[20] Márkus argues that such loose analogies are hardly the basis for a critical understanding of the regimes' essential dynamics. In these regimes the activity of the state is not confined merely to redistribution, it is directly involved in the organisation of production. Clearly, a central message of *Dictatorship over Needs* is that this is an *integral social system* with the capacity to reproduce itself in a range of diverse local conditions and environments. Whatever the degree of dependence upon the capitalist world, the essential structure of these societies represents an *alternative contemporary* form of modernity. These regimes cannot be explained away in terms of the survival of some backward historical form, nor simply dismissed as a catastrophic 'social experiment'. They demonstrate that socialism is not the only historical alternative to barbarism, that certain non-democratic forms of modern socialism have the potential to assume new totalitarian shapes.

On this basis, Márkus begins the task of providing the economic and social elements of an *alternative new theory* better able to explain the structural features of this system and its unique functional rationality.

All the previous accounts identified the privileged role of the bureaucratic elite in these societies as their distinctive characteristic. Márkus unpacks this privilege by revealing how it works in a society where politics dominates over economics. The bureaucratic apparatus in these countries is a self-selecting elite. It replenishes itself through arbitrary co-option. By this means, it controls all techno-economic decisions concerning production.[21] Maintaining this disposition over the main factors of production makes the elite the *subject* of power while the actual workers have no effective control or leverage. Even the individual enterprise manager ultimately holds his position not on the basis of profit or efficiency but due to his influence within the political hierarchy. Enterprise autonomy is greatly restricted. The manager's hands are largely already tied by decisions of the higher party elite. It makes the final decisions and arbitrates between the lower bureaucratic hierarchies and levels of management that compete for favour. The role of the individual manager is to reach targets that are institutionally set by the party apparatus in a plan that is supposed to integrate the economy into the social totality. However, in practice these targets are always *unachievable*. The elite's power is never matched by knowledge. The unpredictability of external conditions, patterns of consumption and the supply of labour power are all disturbing factors that render some objectives of the plan contradictory or inadequate.[22] A permanent tension exists between the national interests as determined by the elite and subordinate local requirements.

The difficulty in determining in whose interests this system functions leads Márkus to suggest that *objective interests* is not as good an indicator of functionality in these societies as in the analysis of capitalism. The effective functioning of the system in no way corresponds directly to any perceived notion of individual interests. The party leadership has almost absolute power and is therefore able to perpetuate its identity. Yet this position is not reflected in the material advantages derived by its members. While inequalities and privileges of the leading apparatchiks abound, the individual member has no right to privately appropriate any part of surplus under the elite's control. Furthermore, the political will or interests of the ruling group is not the final determinant of the functional logic and direction of these economies. The economy has a relative autonomy of its own that limits and constrains the political will of the elite.[23]

To better explain the idiosyncratic functionality of these societies, Márkus revives Marx's concept of the goal function of the economy used in relation to the pre-capitalist world. This indicates that each distinct historical economy defines what constitutes its own costs and useful results, thereby positing a historically specific principle of maximalisation governing economic reproduction.[24] In the case of the command economies, this goal function turns out to be the maximalisation of the volume of material means under the global disposition of the apparatus of power.[25] This implies a notion of corporate property that is hard to assimilate to Marx's own schema of property forms. Strictly speaking, the apparatus is *only the trustee*. However, this in no way detracts from its power. The very meaning of the domination of politics over economics in these societies is that the fundamental economic relations are universally constituted, both in origin and principles of organisation, through and at the behest of the power apparatus. This system borrows its criteria of economic effectivity from imitating the market. However, the goal function is quite insensitive both to efficiency and to real social utility. This helps to explain a whole range of social and economic peculiarities. The most obvious are the degree of bureaucratic incursion into everyday life and the endemic but seemingly incurable economic irrationalities.

POLITICS AND CULTURE IN A LEGITIMISATION VACUUM

Heller focuses on the political physiognomy of 'really existing socialism'. Her immediate object is the *permanent legitimisation crisis* of regimes, at least in all the Eastern European countries. This amounts to something much greater than dissatisfaction, because the great majority of the populations also have a concrete image of an alternative political order in the shape of Western liberal democracy. This means legitimacy is in permanent question.[26] However, Heller distinguishes between this legitimisation crisis and the conditions of the collapse of the regime. While these two are clearly connected, she argues that legitimisation is not terminally impaired unless the confidence of the ruling elite also is undermined. Without this, the transition from crisis to collapse cannot be taken for granted.[27] In the light of the important role played by this factor in the rapid internal dissolution of the Soviet Union only a few years later, this distinction was prescient. At that time, however, she could see no significant alternative political vision operative in the internal politics of the Soviet Union.[28]

Heller locates the legitimisation deficit in Eastern Europe within its historical context. The Bolsheviks set up a Jacobin dictatorship: they viewed themselves primarily as the executors of World History. Eschewing all narrow claims to legitimacy proper, they did not even initially consider the new system of domination a permanent order.[29] All of this changed with the turn to 'socialism in one country'. Then the real need for legitimisation arose with real urgency. The construction of socialism required some form of consent and the reinterpretation of power as something other than domination. The final result was a shift to a charismatic version of legitimisation.[30] Stalin was a result of the party taking the terrorist road rather than a democratic one in its proposal to construct socialism in one country. Terrorist totalitarianism in the immediate post-revolutionary years turned subsequently into charismatic legitimisation. This strategy was supplemented by a claim to mythic substantive rationality in the form of the true science of society: historical materialism. However, because the discrepancy between theory and reality was so blatant, science could play only a supplementary role.[31] Charismatic legitimisation meant a potent mixture of omnipotent leadership and the creation of a climate of universal fear. The so-called 'cult of the personality' expressed the posited identity of the leader and the regime. Against Arendt, however, Heller insists that totalitarianism survived Stalin, even if without terror. She equates the former only with a political society that liquidates civil society, pluralism and human rights.[32] With Khrushchev, the quest for legitimacy shifted more towards substantive rationality in the shape of planning and economic competition with the West. When this failed, the ruling elite was left without a viable political alternative. Having established a stable regime and acquired superpower status, the elite chose to fall back on legitimisation by tradition.[33] Traditional legitimisation implies conservatism and the banning of all social and economic experiments. Tradition in this context was the fusion of Russian national and Soviet elements. Mass acquiescence and acceptance of the domination of the regime was the measure of its success.

Heller is overly pessimistic to believe that this success had exterminated all traditions of democratic thinking and eliminated the democratic imagination.[34] She maintains that behavioural patterns of autocratic government were deeply rooted in the Russian tradition. Things were quite otherwise in Eastern Europe. Nationalism would never work in its favour, there was no mass basis for legitimisation and not even all party members privately endorsed the system. Heller's analysis ends where she began: the permanent legitimisation crisis of the regimes in Eastern Europe. Yet this analysis seems almost to defy gravity. However, hindsight is always deceptively clear. Her caution is understandable in the light of the sad record of failed Marxist optimism. Furthermore, in the early 1980s the terminal crisis that was soon to engulf these regimes was far from evident.

In her substantive analysis, Heller explores the meaning of totalitarian political domination. A one-party political system 'solves' the problem of sovereign power by asserting the sovereignty of the party. Its leading role requires an institutional duality with tentacles that reach into all quarters and monitor conformity to its dictates. In formal terms, the sovereignty of the party signifies the sovereignty of the people, but in actuality, the majority of the people and even the majority of the party are excluded from all crucial decisions. The sovereignty of the party is a *form* that disguises the *real power* that lies with the leading bodies of the party. There exists a yawning abyss between the ideal and the reality of power.[35] Democratic centralism means the radical centralisation of decision making in which the first secretary who selects and controls party members is the real master of the state.

The logic of totalitarianism is relentless and irresistible. After the revolution, the destruction of all forms of traditional organisation necessitated transformation of the soviets into administrative machinery. This created the internal tension between the absolutely emanative logic of the state and the residual democratic spirit of the soviets. The totalitarian state required the homogenisation of belief systems, behaviour and institutions according to it own absolutist will.

The internal struggle was finally resolved in the 1930s in favour of the state and promulgated in the substantive claims of the much lauded Soviet constitution. The very meaning of the domination of the political meant in general the identity of public and private, that there was no life beyond the interests of the state. Unlike the identity of pre-capitalist times, totalitarian identity was not organic but arbitrarily superimposed to outlaw pluralism. The essentially arbitrary character of this interest substantiates Heller's cautious assessment of emancipatory prospects. In the period of terror, pluralism retreated into the recesses of private life. It was once again tolerated in the post-Stalin era, but subsequent revisions of the constitution still left the specific degree and content of various rights undefined. The elasticity of the totalitarian state was indeterminate and remained ultimately at the behest of the political elite. All concessions ultimately fall into the category of privileges that might be withdrawn at any time and remain contrary to the logic of the absolutist system.[36]

The strategic retreat from terror did not lessen the essential totalitarian character of these regimes. This truth is vindicated by a structure of power that emanated only from the center. Yet this still allowed for a variety of balances corresponding to specific historical periods and conditions.[37] The early period of Bolshevik control saw the rule of aristocracy.[38] The old Bolsheviks were the elite of the working class, hierarchised according to virtue and suffering. The first secretary was only *primus inter pares*. Only when the party lost its aura and its moral authority could autocracy triumph. The retreat from Stalinist terror to collective leadership signified retreat to oligarchy. Continuity then relied upon inbreeding and corporate selection in which status depended less upon heroic deeds than upon long obedient service; the asceticism of the revolutionary fathers was replaced by the privilege and obedience of the apparatchiks.[39]

The centralisation of totalitarian power excludes the independence of the functions of government. A singular unitary power lies with the executive and the legislative: the judiciary becomes a mere instrument of execution.[40] This power cast its shadow over the whole society, with its agencies at work in every crevice. In practice, however, this unitary power was delegated to the ministries and the political police. In both instances, the practical autonomy of peripheral agencies was constrained and held in check by the supervision of the party. The ministries constituted a vast subsystem of hierarchical control, constantly orchestrated and mediated by power. In the final analysis, everything depended upon decisions ultimately made at the center. Heller contests the view that these regimes exemplified the rule of bureaucracy.

Centralisation and totalisation clearly demand immense, interconnected and highly hierarchised, bureaucracies. Yet the bureaucracy was not an independent source of power nor were the apparatchiks, like civil servants, ultimately responsible to the people. In accord with the power dynamics of totalitarianism, the apparatus presented a closed phalanx towards citizen subjects and an atomised fawning gaze towards the summit of power.[41] Heller challenges Weber's praise of the efficiency of the bureaucracy. In the Soviet-style regime, bureaucracy was notoriously inefficient. This stemmed in part from the lack of civil rights and partly from closure to the pressure of public opinion. Chaos attended not only the application of bureaucratic rules: bureaucracy was also required to execute directives that cancelled or temporarily annulled all rules.[42] Heller views this inefficiency not as failure but as the secret realisation of the true aim of the regime: to frustrate and defer the satisfaction of the needs of its own citizens.[43]

Such perversity did not end with the bureaucracy; it resided within every mode and instrument of power. The police were typically charged with the responsibility of suppressing criminality as defined in the statutes of criminal law. Yet, under Stalin's rule, almost the whole population was cast into potential criminality; almost any human activity could be interpreted as criminal and the law functioned to intensify the general climate of guilt. The shift away from terror mitigated rather than suppressed this tendency. Soviet paternalism continued to view the population as one big family. The state as *paterfamilias* determined entitlements and punished wayward children with draconian measures such as 'enforced' psychiatric hospitalisation.[44]

The elite apparatus also maintained a stranglehold over ideas and culture. Soviet ideology was not ideology in the conventional Marxist sense. It was deployed nakedly to defend party interests and the changing strategic directives of the leadership without the slightest pretence of expressing broader class interests.[45] Without critical challenge and underwritten by the power of the state it no longer needed to convince or maintain coherence; reduced to dogma, its key was not intrinsic meaningfulness, or the normal conditions of falsification, but the requirements of the party.[46] What passed as 'free discussion' in these societies served only to alleviate the pressure of mounting internal contradictions. However, this 'freedom' signified neither open-mindedness nor real debate. It is easy to understand why Heller and Fehér treated the early days of Gorbachev and glasnost with great scepticism.[47] In this regime, the main function of 'true science' was to totalise and control society. Ideological pluralism was always perceived as a danger and its exponents regularly harassed.[48] However, functional success was paid for at a high price, in terms of both general culture and individual psychology. The victory of totalisation demanded the tutelage of the whole population and a general relapse into cultural de-enlightenment. The individual had to choose between assuming a total incognito without commitment or accepting everything. Moreover, dogma obliged not just passive acceptance but active service: analysis, public declamation and internalisation. Heller's account here bespeaks debilitating personal experience. Living a lie puts enormous stress on social relations, intimacy and on the individual personality. Those who succumbed also tried to destroy the survivors. Even the dissident was rendered ridiculous, telling 'obvious' truths to a non-existent audience.[49]

Consistent with a regime based on unitary emanating power and supported by pseudo-scientific dogma was a complementary *single system of valid moral norms*. But this hardly deserved the name of morality: the mandated system was only a thinly disguised articulation of the interests of the party. Heller traces the displacement of authentic morality back to the tensions that finally imploded Lenin's own ethics. His was a crude utilitarianism in which changing class interests duelled with the permanent social interests of mutual coexistence. This reduction of morality to interests opened the way to crimes against morality. Lenin identified the interests of the party with those of the proletariat even after the party had begun to pursue its own interests with a calculation that defied morality.[50] The result was a true slave morality.

Loyalty and obedience became the only virtues and they relieved the good communist of the burden of moral choice. There was no higher measure than the party, and conscience and autonomous reflection were suppressed; the commanded action was good by definition.[51] This produced the shame morality evident in the excessive zeal and feelings of guilt and relief manifested by those arrested for alleged 'crimes' against the Soviet order. The concrescence of loyalty and obedience destroys the elementary norms of social coexistence. This milieu was assisted by the official 'purge' that weeded out anyone not already completely cowed. The other side of this was the irresistible attraction of the power emanating from the centre. To be in its proximity was an index of honour, while to move away was a great calamity.[52] Heller asserts that no society was more atomised than the Soviet Union. Conventional morality was crushed by the power of the centre, leaving the individual naked. Of course, this was an exaggeration. All organic ties were not cut and elementary norms were still valid.[53] Subsequent events demonstrated their resilience and even that the capacity for new social movements had not completely atrophied. The regime's move beyond terror allowed the gradual restoration of these powers. Nevertheless, Heller was surely correct to emphasize the dynamics of atomisation. The lonely crowd flourished in a climate of fear in which the conditions of civic tolerance were conspicuously absent. Those who did not turn away from Soviet morality and ideology with total cynicism were left with little more than the furtive practice of traditional religion. A state religion and slave morality ensured that no god or higher ethical standard was likely to compete with the unquestionable authority of the party.

THE NEGATIVE POTENTIAL OF MODERNITY

So far the analysis has outlined the economic, social, political and ideological contours of the hybrid new regimes that emerged in Eastern European satellites. The new regime was neither capitalism nor socialism, nor a state in transition between them. It could be recognised as a response to the contradictions of capitalism, yet it had an affinity with backwardness, without being derivable from it. Fehér looks at its historical prospects. On the one hand, he is quite categorical in viewing this 'something else' as a historical dead end and a degradation of values. On the other, he is just as emphatic in maintaining that this is a modern system with universal aspirations.[54] However, these descriptions are only *seemingly* contradictory. This new social formation is no local deformation but a reproducible, transportable and expansionary system. It offers nothing of historical value, only great oppression, suffering and ossification. Yet by underscoring its reproducibility and expansionary appetite, he highlights its threatening potential to the complacent left in the Western liberal democracies. Simultaneously, he underplays the authors' collective very cogent and convincing diagnosis of the crisis of this regime and the mounting difficulties to its own reproduction. Rather than factor in crisis as a cumulative problem that not even naked power could indefinitely stall, the authors prefer to view it almost as part of the cycle of self-reproducibility in these regimes, followed by collapse and immediate restoration.

This new hybrid configuration of modernity is not socialism. For Marx, the latter was associated with freedom, equality and the individual's acquisition of the wealth of human species powers. However, Fehér is reluctant to absolve socialists of the co-responsibility for the fact that this regime only augments problems it was designed to solve.[55] At the same time, he sees no virtue in them simply wringing their hands. What's required is a painstaking review of socialist doctrine to isolate those elements that turned the Bolshevik Revolution away from its Enlightenment heritage towards oppression. He quickly dismisses the popular explanations, such as the usurpation of power by anti-socialist class forces that never in fact happened or neo-Burkean appeals to a constant human nature that can never be rationally reconstructed by conscious reform. The future can never be exhausted by even plausible pragmatic evidence of past revolutionary degeneration into dictatorship.[56]

For Fehér, the infection of socialism was traceable to the Jacobin legacy. A double anthropology that combined public declarations of human perfectibility with a suspicion of the masses encouraged a virtuous elite to resort to the means of terror in the noble quest for moral improvement.[57] Furthermore, against Marx's advice to abolish the state, the task of moral improvement was allocated to an unusually strong state.[58] While complaining of the alienation between citizen and bourgeois, Marx advocated a single revolutionary project that homogenised these two spheres and the specific tasks of political emancipation. Moral arguments against capitalism took a back seat to those referring to its inefficiency and to the need for a technically competent elite. This technicisation of the fundamental problem subordinated all other socialist values to the exclusive productivist push for growth of social material wealth.[59] Thus moral zealotry and technocratic elitism fused with the paternalist streak to be found in all socialist theories. The technicist reading of the task of socialism not only underplayed the other conditions posited to realise socialism; in the more underdeveloped countries, it also led to its equation with social modernisation. All delays fed the critique of a Western conspiracy that reverberated around the world, engendering a growing contempt for liberal democratic institutions and values.[60]

The importance of underdevelopment is no concession to the thesis of 'historical backwardness'. Jacobinism is an essentially Western invention and the reality of 'really existing socialism' looked a lot like the negative utopias of industrialisation. The centralisation of management in the hands of an increasingly powerful state and the total subjection of the workforce to the central powers of capitalism were already features of bourgeois industrialisation.[61] Under the dictatorship over needs, this logic was merely extended, with no competitive pressure, to the power of the state. The communal economy is another element of every form of industrialisation. The inherent limits and dilemmas of infinite growth soon compromised the promise of global planning, planetary harmony and unlimited growth. What was promoted as a higher principle of industrial organisation against the irrationalities of the market turned out to be itself one of the major hindrances to economic growth.[62]

Other characteristics of socialist ideology were especially suited to ushering in the alternative potentials of modernity. Unlike fascism, which only appealed to an exclusive constituency, socialism was proclaimed as a universal project.[63] Its secularist, this-worldly focus was also a tremendous advantage in facilitating industrial development. The radicalism of this doctrine had an obvious mass appeal in an epoch of great social crisis. The very idea of transforming the fundamental conditions of life purported to strike at the root of man by removing supposedly eternal limits. Finally, Fehér argues that in hastening a necessary change in elites in underdeveloped countries, socialism contributed to rapid modernisation and to the latter's worldwide success.[64] But socialist theory on its own could never have expected to transform the world. Only by advancing the operative tendencies of industrialisation, and meeting halfway the real social demands immanent in failed efforts towards modernisation all over the world, did socialist doctrine produce that non-socialist, non-capitalist hybrid regime that seemed at that time to have transformed forever the physiognomy and prospects of modernity.[65]

The inflated rationalist aspirations of the command economy have already been mentioned. Fehér returns to this theme in challenging the Western left's own erstwhile rationalism and to salvage its remnants for a contemporary socialist project. Márkus argued that the apparent irrationalities of the command economy were nothing of the sort. For Fehér, the idea of social rationality was a product of bourgeois society. One legacy of the Enlightenment was a set of criteria meant to weigh the elements of social rationality. Fehér considers these criteria to be applicable to all post-Enlightenment societies. They include the shift from an organic to a planned society, affirmation of the values of freedom, equality and fraternity (despite varying interpretations), repudiation of all discrimination, certain public forums for the exercise of critical scrutiny, and belief in social harmony.[66] After the First World War had demonstrated the folly of the bourgeois contraction of the rationality question to the individual, socialism was challenged to realise a superior type of rationality.[67] Yet Fehér argues that the project to redeem substantive rationality engendered the hyper-rationality of the command economies, with their permanent crisis and irresolvable contradictions.

There are vital lessons to be learnt from the deformations of hyper-rationality. The replacement of market mechanisms by a goal of production leads to the structural disequilibria noted by Márkus. The desire to plan a harmonious future and the aspiration to abolish markets are incompatible demands. Market relations are the only system of computing that make mathematical prediction, though not always reliable, at least possible.[68] Economic contradictions are only aggravated by the conditions of dictatorship: they suppress the substantive values required for overall social rationality. Lacking democratic channels, these regimes could only ascribe, but not actually know, the real needs of the people. To underscore the importance of the neglected democratic conditions to contemporary reformulation of the socialist project, Fehér stresses that the will to a democratically planned future is not itself rational.[69] It is a mistake to assimilate substantive rationality to techno-economic rationality. Not even the latter can be realised without social deliberation. The embodiment of this hyper-rationality is the 'guaranteed society'. The destruction of market mechanisms, legal guarantees and political feedback produced the exact opposite of the welfare state.[70] Such a guarantee is not the issue of fundamental human rights. Rather, as Tocqueville long ago predicted, it becomes the dispensation of a paternalistic state that rewards the humble requests and loyal supplications of its client subjects. The reality of the hyper-rational dream was ongoing subjection and intermittent consumer concessions. Behind the myth of the classless society lay continuing inequality imposed upon a homogenised and atomised population bereft of all institutional means of resistance. In this still hierarchical corporate society, there was only 'equality in inequality'. Everybody had liberties towards those further down the hierarchy, but the upper echelons were quarantined by power from the pressures being exerted from below. The official public discourse was all about unity, harmony and general interests. Yet the whole system of civil society that previously existed in some of these societies was uprooted, and the particular, heterogeneous interests that resisted such formulation were completely ignored and marginalised.[71] Hyper-rationalism also demanded the *politicisation* of the social order. The will to substantive rationality demanded an overwhelming suspicion of the individual and the dynamic of unruly needs. This hostility found immediate expression both in restrictions upon individual self-expressions of needs and in the monopoly the apparatus exercised over the social prioritisation of needs. Finally, it required terror.

The reason that the regime's ultimate commitment to planning was disingenuous is not hard to find. The Marxian model of humanity rich in needs and in the freedom to articulate them was simply unacceptable to it. All efforts of the regime to act in the name of the future man while, simultaneously, denying the conditions its realisation produced only a perverted radicalism. The ideology of community remained, but without the will to provide its real preconditions, the reality was to be nothing more than a coerced togetherness.[72] Despite its totalitarian omnipotence, the regime continually collided with its own untranscendable limits. The shift from terror to reform was a fundamental acknowledgement of a limit to the exploitation of human resources. However, even this concession stood in stark contrast to the ideology of the Soviet-style societies. The party still maintained the prerogative of total mobilisation of the whole personality. Nevertheless, the post-Stalin regimes made concessions to their captive populations and loosened their grip upon private life and activities. Even so, Fehér still anticipates further rationalisation. He envisages slowly increasing standards of living but also increasingly refined methods, principles and objectives of oppression. The internal limit of the regime remained its refusal to countenance the free articulation of individual needs and the real reforms that would require.[73]

In retrospect, it is clear this limit needed to be conceived in more dynamic terms than Heller and her colleagues were prepared to admit at the beginning of the 1980s. We have already noted their careful analysis of a fast approaching global system crisis; the accumulation of contradictions that could not be indefinitely ignored and must eventually be confronted. Even Fehér's mention of the prospect of slowly increasing standards of living seems undermined by the realisation that the required increased industrial production was non-existent in the Soviet Union. [74] This threatened not only the post-Stalinist compromise but also the capacity of the military machine to maintain its competitive position.[75] Clearly, the compounding character of these contradictions narrowed options even further and undermined the apparatus's capacity to hold the absolute rejection of political pluralism as its bottom line. This does not mean that the eventual outcome was some sort of historical necessity. However, it does suggest that emphatic belief in the fundamental political immobility of the regime was unwarranted.

The same rigidity mars the Fehér–Heller thesis that this social formation possessed a universalising claim similar to capitalism, thus making it an alternative version of modernity. They judged the regime essentially modern and prepared to impose its own system of industrial development on others. The command economy's production goal required the expansion of material wealth and power under its own discretion. This logic of industrialisation was initially also attractive to the Third World. An imperialist 'escape forward' could fuel a thrust to world domination and the defeat of the Western alternative.[76] This universalising aspiration also distinguished it from other totalitarian regimes like the National Socialists, whose constituency was always restricted by claims of racial superiority. Yet the dominance of the political in this regime meant that the universality claim was not driven by the extreme logic of ideology, but remained under the control of pragmatic considerations and strategic opportunities.

For Fehér, the political aspect of this imperialism is the ultimate limit to its universality claim. He is especially concerned with the political will to totalisation and the limits imposed on its exportation. He notes the ideological and political weakness of the centre.[77] The Soviet Union lacked cultural hegemony over its Warsaw Pact confederates. The regime was unable to inspire new ways of life, socially generalisable norms and values. Stalin ruthlessly annihilated the worldwide charismatic appeal of the Bolshevik elite. This ideological strength was now lost forever. In retrospect, precisely this dimension of political/ideological weakness was to have telling effects on the Soviet elite in the Gorbachev era. Confidence to confront and solve the other, primarily economic, dimensions of the crisis was undermined by the loss of hegemonic self-belief. The will to repeat the violent suppression of opposition and protest had evaporated.

The theory of 'dictatorship over needs' at the opening of the 1980s rested in large part on the conviction that these regimes were stable self-reproducing social formations. On this basis, it was argued that they represented a deficient but alternative option for modernity, which the West needed to take seriously as a real threat. While their parasitic character, their reliance on Western instrumental rationality and their cultural and technological barrenness were acknowledged, these authors still did not foresee historical collapse. While Fehér never ruled out the possibility of a conflagration beginning in the Soviet Union, he favoured the dependent states as the epicentre of the crisis. Even in that case, he predicted not total collapse, but a continued uneasy competition and collaboration with the West in a sort of mutually hostile functionality.[78] What is important is not so much this failure, which was shared by virtually all commentators, but the reasons for it. In part, this was a result of the very project to capture the essential identity and essence of this form of modernity. Almost inevitably, this required a high degree of generalisation and abstraction. Even when employed, as in this case, with a consciousness of its limitations, this structural account still remained insensitive to the variety of regimes and their changing empirical circumstance.[79] Despite its ultimate failure, the depth of the analysis and its exemplary account of many other aspects of the crisis remain striking.

The benefit of hindsight allows us to say that by underplaying their own analysis of systemic weaknesses, they gave more credence to the universality claim of this regime than it could objectively support. They also underestimated the impact that the dual politico-cultural weaknesses were likely to have within the elite apparatus itself. The capitulation of the Soviet apparatus under Gorbachev was perhaps the most surprising aspect of this complex constellation. Anticipating types of potential crisis, Fehér mentions those involving inadequate rationality; political and cultural dissent; demands for an autonomous legal system and civil society; and open rebellion, in which the whole population rises to demand its rights.[80] As it turned out, the final denouement had elements of all of these. However, probably most decisive was the response of the Soviet leadership. Not the 'will to totalisation' but its ultimate erosion spelt the beginning of the end for the 'dictatorship over needs'. The political aspect was the ultimate limit of the regime's universality claim, yet in a sense quite opposite to that supposed by Fehér. It signified the exhaustion of the cultural hegemony of the Soviet leadership. While Fehér registered this lack of hegemony as an element of crisis, neither he nor his colleagues realised fully the degree to which it was already eroding the political will of elements of the Soviet elite. Of course, this knowledge was largely inaccessible at that time.[81]

At the conclusion of the book, the discussion turns from the looming crisis of the 'dictatorship over needs' to a summation of the crisis of Marxist theory. Lukács' hopes for the 'Renaissance of Marxism' died in 1968. The political intransigence of the Soviet elite and the transformation of Marxism in the mind of the masses into a language of domination killed it.[82] The slightest window of historical opportunity for a Marxian revival was missed because the dissident Marxists, like themselves, while increasingly critical, had remained committed to the rescue of the Leninist Jacobin project. This ending both foreshadows great theoretical promise and also anticipates looming political horrors. The authors are well aware of the likely historical costs of this demise. The debris was a fertile ground for the new religious and nationalist fundamentalisms quickly gaining ground even then. On the theoretical front, the Budapest inner circle had momentarily re-formed to issue their political warning, ironically, in the idiom, albeit critically, of Marxism. But Heller had already moved beyond the Marxian paradigm.[83] It comes as no surprise to know that she had turned to the task of reconstructing her own version of radical philosophy in the light of this final break.

Part II

Towards a Post-Marxist Radicalism

4
The Quest for
Philosophical Radicalism

One of the most striking characteristics of the thought of Agnes Heller is her constant engagement with contemporary social experience. Her model of philosophical authorship is that of the thinking individual 'who makes sense of the historically and socially contingent flow of experiences'.[1] It was precisely this will towards social relevance that finally sealed her breach with Marxism and determined her course towards rethinking the contemporary meaning of radical philosophy. From very early in her development she had determined that Marxists should address the fundamental philosophical problems.[2] However, the autonomy required for this enterprise increasingly came into conflict with a political regime that would not tolerate internal critique. Ultimately, she will realise that Marxism itself was not a sufficiently sharp critical tool. However, this degree of clarity is evident only in the general direction of her first attempt to articulate a contemporary vision of radical philosophy. Much of the detail still remains immured in a Marxist inheritance. Even while it was clear to her that a contemporary radical philosophy must go beyond Marx, she seemed equally certain that the only way to get there was through him. Marx was the master of left-wing radicalism.[3] At the same time as she strains to assert the autonomy of philosophy against the rigidity of regime and ideological orthodoxy, the general contours of her vision of radical thought remain identifiably Marxist.

However, this initial post-Marxian attempt to fashion a radical philosophy was only a temporary staging post. It was too much dominated by the shadow of her own past. During the 1980s this shadow receded in a rush of productivity and an increasing confidence in her capacity to sustain an independent perspective beyond Marxism. Heller was then able to fully absorb the cultural experience informing the great postmodern cultural turn of this period without abandoning her own fundamental values. Her own idiosyncratic synthesis will be examined in Chapter Ten under the signature of 'reflective postmodernism'. As this signature suggests, while celebrating the potential pluralism that accompanies the collapse of the grand narratives, this standpoint attempts to go beyond deconstructive fashion, to connect postmodernity to the deepest experiences of modern contingency and draw out its radical consequences in terms of subjectivisation and individual responsibility. However, this is to jump too far ahead. In this chapter, the first phase of her post-Marxist philosophical odyssey will be explored.

TO GIVE THE WORLD A NORM

Implicit in the German title of her first post-Marxist work, *Die Philosophie des linken Radicalismus* (1978), is Heller's determination to preserve and rethink the meaning of leftist radicalism. A philosophy is radical insofar as it implies a total critique of society.[4] Such critique is warranted by the fact that modern society rests on relations of domination. However, critique remains nothing more than an impotent subjective cry unless it becomes the will of human beings. Only when philosophy articulates real needs will it be realised, only when it has become the philosophy of radical movements.[5]

Anchoring this idea of radical philosophy is Heller's Marxist-inspired theories of everyday life and radical needs, which we have already examined. Philosophy must be viewed primarily from the standpoint of social life. Its roots lie in the fact that we are evaluative beings. We feel, think and act through systems of value categories, which provide orientation in all our social activities.[6] Value category pairs such as good/bad, true/false are the constitutive elements of the system of rules and prescriptions without which society would be impossible. Value orientative categories function as final and unquestionable theoretical and practical ideas. In everyday life they are typically intermixed and appear only in the synthesis of cognition and action that is the crucible of our social activity.[7] Yet this everyday heterogeneity belies a gradually emerging purity that appears with the historical differentiation of the spheres of objectivation and the development of specific cultural institutions and practices uncoupled from the everyday. As a result, the application of a value category is then determined by its objectification-specific situation.[8] Heller views the process of purification of value categories associated with cultural differentiation as distinct from the use of these categories as 'free ideas'. She attributes this more general emancipation of value categories to the emergence of dynamic societies. In societies such as classical Athens, where the *polis* attained an economic and sociological tempo sufficient to breach tradition, value categories act as vehicles of critical questioning.[9] In rapidly changing historical conditions it becomes possible not only to question whether something is 'good' or 'true' but for such judgements to change over time. This form of critical questioning is, for Heller, the sociological precondition for the cultural enterprise of philosophy. However, fundamental philosophical ideas of the 'good', the 'true' and the 'beautiful' only emerge from the generalisation of value-orientative categories.[10] On this basis, it becomes possible to hypothesise these values as independent, essential goods.

These reflections on the historical emergence of philosophy amplify the degree to which Heller views it as an essentially practical, inextricably socially embedded, enterprise. It responds to social needs expressing our most essential human characteristics. Philosophy is *cultural expression* in the service of ultimate orientation within a social universe. It offers values and a form of life that allows addressees to live their thoughts and transform them into action.[11] That orientation here means more than mere cognition is reinforced by Heller's reading of philosophical wisdom as the unity of knowledge and good conduct.[12] While autonomous cognition is the single determining moment in all functions of philosophy, she nevertheless upholds the Kantian primacy of practical reason. Practical orientation within the world is the principal function of philosophy.

THE CONSTITUTIVE TENSION OF PHILOSOPHY

The desire for a 'worldly' philosophy is not a call for a philosophy subordinate to the 'facts' of the world or its dominant pragmatics. Heller views the triumph of positivism in the second half of the nineteenth century as a lapse of philosophy into a 'dogmatic dream' from which it extricated itself only recently. Philosophy can only adequately fulfil its principal orientative function and satisfy the need for value rationality within the social world by asserting its own autonomy. Her own marginalisation and political exclusion accentuated this emphasis on critical autonomy. However, Heller makes this experience pivotal to understanding the general social function of philosophy. 'Dangerous times' and marginality become the natural conditions of philosophy. But more than mere conditions, the constitutive heart of philosophy is the tension between social embeddedness and critical autonomy, social functionality and transcendence.

Heller sees this constitutive tension acting at vital moments in the history of philosophy. It permeates the Platonic enterprise. Philosophy is an independent and autonomous objectification, which seeks the unity of the 'true' and the 'good' in transcending opinion.[13] The plurality of philosophy consists in the various criteria and the different paths by which this unity is sought. Reinforcing her emphasis on the practical, Heller argues that the unity of theoretical and practical illustrates philosophy's inherent double-sidedness. From the beginning, it was more than just a coherent, systematic form of knowledge. It was primarily an attitude that took the shape of a form of life.[14] Socrates stresses not the definitive possession of knowledge but its lack: this was his invitation to thinking. Nor did philosophies originally aspire to be mere systems of knowledge. Moreover, the philosophical system as we know it is a 'recent' philosophical invention, only foisted on the philosophers of the past by later reconstruction.

As an attitude of critical questioning, philosophy finds its highest task in *demythologisation*. We have already noted that the breach with tradition is one of the sociological preconditions of the philosophical enterprise. To the ambiguity of poetic myth it opposes the clarity of rational argument.[15] Thus the subject of philosophy is reason and its agent is the 'rational being' who perpetuates a dialogical, critical thinking. However, the apparent openness and childish naivety of this questioning cannot disguise the fact that every philosophy constitutes its own 'true' and 'good' in advance.[16] Philosophical innocence disguises a secret anticipation of the likely destination. Philosophical questioning is a critique of what exists from the standpoint of what ought to be as the unity of the 'true' and the 'good'. Every philosophy creates its own world founded on the tension between 'is' and 'ought'. This tension is constitutive of philosophy because the 'is' is constructed from the perspective of 'ought' while the 'ought must be deduced from what "is"'.[17] Only when the 'ought' is accessible through the 'is' is it possible to undertake the *defetishising* journey. In this way is it possible for every rational person to commence the ascent from prejudice and ignorance towards the philosophical 'ought'. While the derivation of 'is' from 'ought' and 'ought' from 'is' appears a troubling paradox, it is, according to Heller, the essence of philosophy's utopian character. Every philosophy claims its 'ought' as the most real of existences. In this essential light, the 'is' is relegated to the merely inessential. However, what distinguishes philosophy from other utopian thought is that it imparts a rational form to its utopias. Others must be allowed to endorse this reasoning autonomously through a process of disciplined and systematic thinking.[18] This makes philosophy the bearer of rational utopia.

For Heller, the 'alleged' inconsistency at the heart of philosophy is traceable to the philosophical attitude itself. This is further proof of the inextricable unity of theory and practice.[19] The childish naivety of *thaumazein* (wonder) is a genuine astonishment leading to the passionate search for the 'true' and the 'good'. Yet even this prescribed philosophical preconditionlessness is limited by conditions philosophy chooses to ignore. Clearly every philosopher is a child of her time. Philosophy cannot abstract from knowledge of the past but must engage in a process of argumentative negation with it.[20] Heller conceives neither of these limits as shortcomings, but rather as constitutive of the game of philosophy and its own famed irony. Historical conditioning does not prevent the philosopher from making choices between values, thoughts and alternatives nor from thinking through to the end what is thinkable in his/her time.[21] Nevertheless, philosophy is fated to awkwardly straddle the abyss between a foundational astonishment and an augmentation of past philosophy in a way that reflects the general development of human knowledge.[22] The desire for secure foundations and a highest good is the necessary false consciousness of philosophy, which is only gradually corrected by its own internal plurality and polemics.[23] The task of *demythologisation* cannot be prosecuted too far, for this would mean the end of philosophy itself.[24] The philosophical song is one of innocence *and* experience. The attainment of philosophical 'naivety' requires a managed abstraction from prejudice, opinion and false consciousness. However, this abstraction is orchestrated by prejudice itself. The characteristic feature of this hybrid attitude is its Janus face: lack of preconceptions and childish questioning of prejudice reside awkwardly with the thirst for knowledge and understanding. This 'awkwardness' is largely the product of historical consciousness. In the past, philosophy was not required to reflect upon the historical conditioning of its own ideas. Since the rise of the hermeneutics of suspicion, this naivety has become questionable and philosophy has been compelled to reflect on its historical conditioning. At the same time, it must continue to assert and justify its claim to universality.[25] For Heller, the trick is to keep hold of both horns of the philosophical dilemma. Philosophy is required to reflect on its own *conditionedness* without pressing this process of *demythologisation* to the point of self-destruction. Simultaneously, it must cast aside all partiality in its instinctual drive for totality and for the universal. We have noted that these elements of tension and paradox are not 'inconsistencies' but are constitutive of the very essence of philosophy. This emphasis on philosophical paradoxicality is a constant with Heller. If anything, it becomes more central to her understanding of philosophy as she comes to view the experience of contingency as the heart of modern self-understanding. At the moment of her liberation from Marxism, it remains only an elusive opening philosophical gamut she is sorely tempted to resolve.

This awkward unity of partial and whole, historical and universal, conditioned and unconditioned, is open to the prospective solution of a postulated unity of individual and species. While Heller was committed to the task of forging an autonomous radical philosophy, she was equally attracted to the idea of philosophical 'reconciliation'. She later admitted that it was only too easy to assume a positive answer to the idea of this unity. Here was the guarantee of a common basis of all philosophical ideals, of the historical efficacy of philosophy and of its utopian democratic shape. It signifies the historical attainment of the philosophical ideal of transcending particularity:[26] that there would be an end to the contradiction between the historicity of philosophical ideals and the philosophical claim to universality. Here the young Marx's solution to the riddle of history – the unity of individual and species – floats before her philosophical imagination in the shape of a regulative Kantian idea.[27] Yet this postulate of the ultimate unity of the particular and the species is no longer a *transcendental* but a *historical* idea. It confirms that utopias no longer stand outside of history but are present, effective ideals of our time.

In view of the constitutive ambivalence at its heart, it is not surprising that philosophy has always found its natural constituency in the young. Youth, as the embodiment of openness, questioning, thirst for knowledge and without preconceptions hardened against rational persuasion, is its 'natural' addressee.[28] Philosophical argument rarely seduces other philosophers. In this celebration of openness, mental agility and expansive appetite, philosophy sports not only its eternal youthfulness but also its *democratic* credentials. It requires no prerequisites, no special knowledge, and is open to all. Yet its paradoxical heart is again evident in the premium placed on mental capacity. Athenian democracy was not wrong to be suspicious of the allegiances of philosophy. Yet Heller finds neither duplicity nor inconsistency here, but only *constitutive tension*. Philosophers are teachers who encourage a *democratic* relation to their pupils. The opposition of authority and innocence is subsumed in an overarching equality founded on the presupposition that all humans are equipped with reason.[29]

PROFESSIONALISATION AND
THE CRISIS OF PHILOSOPHY

These constitutive tensions cannot obscure the fact that the primary function of philosophy presupposes the historical achievement of a pervasive aspiration to equality. Attention has already been drawn to Heller's view that philosophy responds to a pervasive need for orientation in a social world no longer clearly signposted by unquestioned tradition. That philosophy addresses a *general reason* means that the instrument that would illuminate the way is already in the possession of all and is only in need of cultivation. This point is reinforced by Heller's determination that philosophy should not be reduced to an occupation. Complete professionalisation would spell the cultural death of philosophy. Philosophy is not primarily concerned with producing philosophers nor even with the institutionalisation of rational and methodical thinking; its core is illuminating, critical engagement with the world. As we have already seen, it is clear that its most fertile ground is not the professional but uncommitted youth. It is not by chance that the 'school' has served as the vital institutional home in the history of philosophy. The aim of the school is the inculcation of a mode of thinking and its greatest confirmation is the graduate equipped to enter the world, the pupil who now surpasses the erstwhile teacher.[30] Nor is this surpassing simply the acquisition of greater expertise and skill but the creation of new utopias and attitudes to life that emerge from novel articulations and configurations of the unity of the 'true' and 'good'.

Heller acknowledges that today philosophy is at risk of succumbing to the triumphal inroads of professionalisation. Increasingly, the limitations of philosophy as a job impair the original vital idea of it as a form of life. Today philosophy is firmly in the grip of the professional division of labour. The essential features of the philosophical attitude – astonishment, autonomous thinking and ironic detachment – clash with the professional need to pass on positive knowledge.[31] A corresponding picture to the difficulties of contemporary philosophical appropriation emerges on the side of reception. Whereas in the past the most significant layer of the philosophical audience was the connoisseur who appropriated philosophical systems from the standpoint of their contribution to the evolution of general culture, now philosophy has become increasingly the private affair of the specialists. Whereas formerly the line between philosophers and recipients was more fluid, today a growing divide clearly separates philosophical creators and consumers. While this division is not confined to philosophy, it clearly reflects a broader social reality in which cultural creation is no longer an organic part of modern everyday life.[32]

Rather than view the entrapment of philosophy within the modern division of labour as a fait accompli, Heller upholds the responsibility of the genuine philosopher to resist the reduction of philosophy to the status of a mere occupation. The difficulties of the present situation do not amount to its impossibility.[33] It must be remembered that Heller views philosophy as a child of difficult times. Given that its task always involves the critique of existing facts, it is understandable that defenders of the status quo always view it as dangerous. Amidst the imminent threats to the autonomy of philosophy, she conceived that its most immediate task in the middle of the 1970s was to return to itself. This 'return' meant several things. The division of labour underpinning the current division between creators and reception must be overcome. Yet this was only one moment of a perspective still bearing traces of the revolution of everyday life. As we shall see, she progressively comes to view the idea of symmetrical reciprocity as a regulative idea that upholds a modern dynamic sense of justice in a social arrangement based on specialised functionality. While her critique of the cultural division of labour is now unsustainable in this form, it is also clear that she continues to view a more fluid relation between philosophical creation and reception as vital to the continuing viability of philosophy. This partly explains her willingness ultimately to accept the 'coffee-house' image of philosophy. She would willingly risk the cultural reputation of philosophy to maintain its vital social functionality.

In some respects, Heller's attack on the professionalisation of philosophy may appear conservative. However, her intention is not to preserve philosophy as an arcane practice divorced from the dynamics of modern society. What is at stake is a critical social function, whose power is dependent on deep bonds with the everyday and with an educated public, autonomous thought and critical questioning. If such a function is to have any impact beyond the narrow province of experts, then it is crucial not only that the conditions of autonomy be sustained but also that philosophy should continue to have a sufficiently wide audience to exercise at least a mediated social influence.

This initial post-Marxist diagnosis of the condition and tasks of philosophy is permeated with paradox. Despite the formidable difficulties Heller sees facing its healthy maintenance against a rising tide of professionalisation and audience erosion, her account of the contemporary outlook of philosophy at this time was almost redemptive. This analysis is more an index of her personality than an accurate clarification of the contemporary prospects for philosophy at that time. As mentioned, she is an 'organic optimist', who was unable to feign neuroticism even when she believed it to be the personality more fitted to philosophy.[34] Her determination to face the demands of the day is manifest in the way she grasps the positive elements of the contemporary philosophical landscape. These constitute the basis of a new era of philosophical renewal. She quickly, however, came to regret what she called the 'New Left rhetoric' that infused this stage of her thinking. While still adhering to its core ideas about philosophy, she would soon distance herself from its forced pronouncement of Parousia.[35]

PHILOSOPHY AS RATIONAL UTOPIA

Regardless of her retrospective critique of *A Radical Philosophy,* it is fascinating to follow its reconstruction of the history of philosophy. Heller employs it to diagnose the contemporary philosophical terrain and to find the most appropriate model for her own future ventures. She views this new millennium as an awakening from dogmatic slumbers. The allusion to Kant is apt. It is clear that the torch in her philosophical pantheon was passed back from Marx to Kant. Marx may be the father of leftist radicalism, but he does not provide a model for contemporary philosophy. This must be one of autonomous and critical self-reflection; one that is both conscious of its own limits yet sufficiently bold to hold before our eyes the regulative, utopian ideas orientating our practical life. Kant is the embodiment of a heroic sentimental philosophy committed to providing a unified philosophical answer to the intermeshed questions of how we should think, act and live.[36] This concern for a comprehensive and unified answer will remain throughout Heller's radical philosophy phase. In a clear retreat from her Marxian history of philosophy, the high point now retreats back from the post-Hegelian revolution to the Enlightenment's emphasis on critical self-reflection. The desire to transform the world remains, but it is now to be cautioned by the recognition of limits and philosophical responsibility.

Novalis's view that philosophy should explain, not nature, but philosophy itself, signals the modern change of focus away from the naive preoccupation with being and towards critical self-reflection. For Heller, Kant's greatness consists in the fact that critical philosophy gave form to this new sentimental insistence on self-reflection without retreating from the practical task of satisfying the ineradicable metaphysical need for orientation and meaning.[37] Needless to say, upgrading the relative achievements of sentimental philosophy demands a correspondingly more critical look at former heroes. For Heller, the nineteenth century can be divided between the philosophical dead end of positivism, which seemed to signal the victory of a completely fetishised consciousness, and those who advocated a radical reform of philosophy away from speculative contemplation towards the transformation of the world. This latter tendency culminates in Lukács' diatribe against the *total reification* of bourgeois society. This impending fate could only be diverted by a consciousness capable of unmasking reified appearance and its revolutionary overcoming.[38] Heller rejects her teacher's dichotomous scenario of socialism or barbarism as a fiction. The idea of a self-regulating market is a negative utopia.[39] The demise of both positivism and revolutionary Marxism, premised as they both were, in opposite senses, on a belief in total reification, leaves open the possibility of a rebirth of authentic philosophy in the twentieth century.

A retrospective glance at Heller's account of the obstacles to philosophical renewal is interesting. Of these, positivism looms largest. Since the mid nineteenth century, philosophy had retreated before the triumphant march of science. Philosophical positivism was only the most virulent form of this loss of confidence. Philosophy was required to meet not its own standards of scientificity but those borrowed from the hard sciences.[40] This extreme and defensive reaction signalled a continuing inferiority complex. Faced with the premium that modernity placed on immediate action and utilisable knowledge, philosophy continued to struggle with a sense of its own loss of functionality and superfluousness. Characteristically, Heller contests this defensive posture. She accepts the rational core of this lack of confidence, while dismissing its neurotic symptoms. It cannot be denied that philosophy has lost some of its former functions and must change in order to remain relevant. She agrees with Habermas that it can no longer pretend to be queen of the sciences. However, there is a growing need for philosophy that should ensure it a vital future role. Science may have emancipated itself from philosophy and no longer requires its methodological confirmation. Nevertheless, many scientists now see the dangers of a merely pragmatic social use of science and want philosophical answers to a range of issues concerning the relations between science and society.[41]

Heller here seems to be anticipating Habermas' view of philosophy as 'translator' between the everyday and high culture.[42] However, she goes much further. Philosophical prospects are even brighter in the domain of the social sciences. Here philosophy has always had an important clarificatory role. These sciences are demarcated from philosophy by the fact that they are not concerned with ideals, but confine their attention to the empirical and its possibilities. The empirical 'facts', however, must be ordered: philosophy has an indispensable role to play in consciously elaborating the value hierarchy that is constitutive of the theoretical framework that orders empirical material.[43] More generally, the need for philosophy is rife in a world where the division of labour and specialised knowledge has dissolved the connection between the partial and the whole. This discipline and specialization are twin expressions of social fragmentation. The divorce of the part from the whole turns one function of the individual against the others, leading to the dissolution of the personality.[44] The split between part and whole is not the product of an irrevocable total reification, but one tendency of modern dynamism, of which the need for philosophy is a counter-tendency.[45]

The capacity of philosophy to meet this burgeoning need depends upon its reassumption of autonomy. It must retain its own structural truth and not be merely a dull imitation of the hard sciences. Even in the guise of philosophy, instrumental rationality cannot fulfil its primary function of satisfying the need for value rationality. From the partial perspective of purposive rationality, there is no privative road to totality. Unlike Habermas, who is content to view philosophy as a fallible synthesis of critical reflection and the specialised sciences, Heller wants at least a regulative, utopian access to the whole, and more existential purchase. On the other hand, as a rational utopia engendered through autonomous thought, philosophy is perfectly suited to mediate between the partial perspective and totality.[46] Philosophy is a product of the desire to understand the world as a whole. As the unity of the 'true' and the 'good', as the fusion of theory and praxis, it also allows us, even on the personal level, to give shape to our own lives: it offers values and the opportunity to live our thoughts while transforming them into social action.[47]

AMBITIOUS TASKS AND RESIDUAL TENSIONS

Not content just to pinpoint the growing contemporary need for philosophy or simply to reconstruct its traditional functions as an independent cultural objectivation, Heller outlines a truly daunting set of tasks for philosophy. Her agenda for radical philosophy includes not just the development of utopian ideals and a heightened self-reflexivity in tune with contemporary historical consciousness; it also demands the maintenance of the full practical programme of classical philosophy to answer the question of how to live. If this is not sufficiently ambitious, she adds a range of predictive social-scientific tasks associated with critical social theory. Not surprisingly, she doubts whether any single radical philosophy can fulfil all these duties.[48] This philosophy should (1) develop ideals that are the embodiment of a rational utopia; (2a) develop critical social theory; (2b) consider the concrete prospects of this radical utopia; (2c) raise anthropological issues, such as whether currently elite radical needs can be generalised; (2d) pursue historical self-reflection; (3) be a philosophy of life and answer the question of how one should live. Yet even this project is a limited one. Radical philosophy is confined to the pursuit of existential answers to questions concerning the realisation of positive human possibilities.[49] It deals only with questions for which rational answers can be given. The further range of metaphysical questions, such as the finitude of the universe, death and nothingness, lie beyond the province of rationality and just make us giddy. Like Wittgenstein, Heller recommends philosophical silence before the rationally inaccessible domains.

What are the ideals of the rational utopia posited by radical philosophy? Initially the guiding ideal of radical philosophy is humanity as a universal social group.[50] All values ascribed to in the rational utopia must be compatible with, and guarantee, a plurality of values and ways of living. Before long, Heller will maintain that freedom is the highest value idea of modernity and that other values must relate to it without contradiction.[51] Despite this apparent uncertainty regarding the leading value idea, which reflects her own shift from the Marxian priority of abundance to a postmodern priority of freedom, this contradiction is more apparent than real. As we have already seen, *Towards a Marxist Theory of Values* had already linked the Marxian value of 'abundance' inextricably with the value freedom. After all, human abundance is clearly conditional on appropriation and therefore on freedom. However, it is clear that freedom by its very nature cannot be subordinated to the status of a means, even if it is inextricably linked to a rich universal humanity.

Increasingly, Heller asserts the priority of the value of freedom. Yet, now detached from its housing in the conceptual framework of the Marxian philosophy of history, the derivation of the universality of the value of freedom is far from clear. Of course, posited in the most abstract form, beyond the arguments regarding its concrete contents, the universality of the value of freedom seems at least plausible in Western liberal democratic societies. Things become more problematic once we move outside the orbit of the Western culture and contemplate the historical limits of this project. This is an issue that will occupy her thinking as she further develops the social and political dimension of her vision.

Despite her optimistic narrative of a prospective contemporary renewal of autonomous philosophy, this first attempt at post-Marxist philosophical radicalism was both overblown and understandably tentative. The comprehensive and enthusiastic programme for a newly liberated autonomous philosophy reflects more her own sense of personal emancipation than a completely clear vision of a philosophy apposite for the reflective, ambivalent postmodern mood that was to emerge in the subsequent decade. Her measured retreat from Hegel to Kant, from totality to regulative rational utopias, sits uneasily with the insistence on the fulfilment of the full practical aspirations of classical philosophy and the retention of a heavy social theory burden. The figure of totality may have disappeared, but her account of the programme and tasks confronting contemporary philosophy reveals that the aspirations behind it have hardly been moderated.[52]

5
Beyond Philosophy of History and the Ascription of Needs

Heller initially envisaged that a work on history would form part of her philosophical anthropology. As we have seen, towards this project she completed volumes on instinct and feelings, as well as one on values and another, indirectly, on needs. Yet she ultimately abandoned this project before its completion. This became necessary when she accepted Hannah Arendt's critique of philosophical anthropology. Discussion of the detailed reasoning behind this shift must await consideration of the first volume of her ethical trilogy, *General Ethics*. Despite the evolution in the broad architectonic of her work occasioned by increased distance from her Lukácsian roots, the volume on history appeared, but now within a greatly transformed framework. The need for a volume on history had initially followed from the logic of a social anthropology that underscored the open-ended, self-created and plastic character of humanity. Historicity is the essence of such a human unfolding as both the *terrain* and the *process* wherein humanity is self-formed. *A Theory of History* (1982) was no longer primarily a contribution to philosophical anthropology. Rather, it registered Heller's final break with Marxism as a specific version of the grand narrative of a philosophy of history. Until this point, she had continued to theoretically posit a unified historical process despite her previously considered reservations. This allowed her to tie up all the theoretical loose ends into a system and make her philosophy 'click' in the traditional way.[1] Only on this basis had she been able to posit the ultimate reconciliation of 'is' and 'ought' in the idea of the overcoming of alienation, a society that would allow the individual to acquire all species capacities while expressing its ineffable individuality. *A Theory of History* signifies the early post-Marxist phase of her work. She attempts to conceptualise history after the philosophy of history. But just because this 'after' is still tentative and very much immured in what is immediately past, much of the book represents her critique of, and attempted demarcation from, the philosophy of history.

CONSCIOUSNESS OF REFLECTED GENERALITY

The book begins with a typology of the *forms* of historical consciousness. Because humans are social and historical beings, it follows that their consciousness of history will assume different shapes in accord with changing social conditions. We do not have the space to explore all of these forms, only to say that, ironically, they conform to the usual progress of classical philosophy of history, except that they are no longer hypothesised as the unified evolution of a single subject. The last form, however, deserves special attention because within it Heller ventures to describe the theoretical task confronting the post-Marxist present. The previous forms conform to well-established historical eras and their apposite forms of historical consciousness (myth, state history, world history). However, the final stage is a product of the crisis and confusions arising from the decomposition of the fifth stage – *world historical consciousness* – and its articulation in the nineteenth-century philosophies of history. The newly emerging form of historical consciousness is that of *reflected generality*. Unlike the consciousness that arose with the empirical unity of the world in the shape of the capitalist market in the nineteenth century, this latter consciousness holds out the possibility of a *reflective* relationship to that imposed unity. Here Heller raises the prospect of a cultural complement to contemporary globalisation long before it registered on the radar of most diagnosticians of culture. This form of consciousness would allow the full ethical consequences of the idea of sharing a single world to permeate everyday consciousness. But whether this consciousness will emerge remains to be seen. Heller views it as her task to make a contribution to such a new consciousness, which will be marked by what she calls a sense of *planetary responsibility*.

The decomposition of the era of grand narratives and full-blown philosophies of history, which viewed history in simple emancipatory terms, generates a new task. The great historical catastrophes of the twentieth century (two world wars, the Holocaust, Hiroshima and the Gulag) finally shook historical optimism. Of course, many earlier intellectuals held that the philosophies of history based on science or on the new mythologies of class and race were in practice destructive and partly responsible for these disasters.[2] Heller singles out R. G. Collingwood for special mention in this respect. Nevertheless, she argues that previous polemics were largely recriminations amongst competing intellectuals, intended to shift the blame from their own idols elsewhere. The vogue of philosophy of history was to find objective responsibility in terms of a historical process theoretically reconstructed from a specific angle rather than demanding *subjective moral responsibility*. We recognise here core arguments from Heller's earlier efforts to raise the profile of ethics within Marxist discourse. The triumph of political democracy in the post-Second World War period had achieved stability in Western Europe, but it has not encouraged fundamental questioning of what man is; this is what she calls *reflection upon generality*. Instead, the time had largely been an epoch of ideological rhetoric, pragmatic politics and disenchantment with radical anthropological speculation.[3] Notwithstanding this turn, the twentieth century did not see the complete disappearance of the philosophy of history. In the confusion that followed the collapse of all consistent philosophies of history, three alternative paradigms presented themselves. Heller finds sound reasons to reject them all.

1. *Research Institute Facticity*. She associates this programme with neo-positivism. This paradigm rejects radical anthropology and generalised reflection. Freedom is understood as adjustment and the elimination of dysfunction in existing institutions while reason no longer means reflection on generality, neither of origins or ends. It is reduced to an instrumental faculty for mere problem solving.
2. *Grand Hotel Abyss*. Taking over Lukács' famous critique of the Frankfurt School, she argues that their critique directs its contempt towards all forms of pragmatic politics. For it, contemporary society is conceived as a negative totality: it is without emancipatory tendencies or redemptive possibilities. This turns out to be an aesthetic vision in which the lack of real prospects relieves us of moral commitments and permits continued consumption and indulgence in disinterested contemplation. The bleakness of the view does not generate despair. It is still possible to grasp hold of the most modest social movement as a sign of transfiguration while rejecting historical necessity.[4] This is the ambiguity of the unhappy consciousness.
3. *Mental Hospital: the Radicalisation of Evil*. The third paradigm represents the radicalisation of the logic of a variety of extreme critiques of modernity coming from what Heller will come to call 'naive postmodernism', anti-psychiatry and political extremism. This paradigm assumes a 'the worse the better' philosophy and even views the marginalised 'other' or the alien as the key to redemption.[5]

   In the light of the inadequacy of these alternatives, Heller attempts to evoke the mood to which a contemporary chastened theory of history must respond. Recent work in historical archaeology has greatly expanded our sense of the past and relativised the project of world history within the history of *Homo sapiens*. As a consequence, the philosophy of history has been reintegrated into the philosophy of nature.[6] Historical relativisation has allowed us to view nature not only as the precondition and source of the historical drama, but also as its *limit*. Ecological concern manifests the fragility of even the project of world history. We are also aware that we are testing the limits of nature, with a current world population equal to the number of all the people who have ever lived.[7] The proximity of vast numbers reinforces the idea of world history as a shared fate in which the planet must be a home for all or for none. The newly emerging historical consciousness of reflected generality is distinguished by its repudiation of the abstractions in whose names so many previous crimes were committed. Humanity is no longer an *abstract universal*; it must now be viewed as plural concrete communities. Just as language does not exist as a universal but as a multifarious variety of natural languages, which all adequately fulfil their functions, so too the mosaic of human communities must be regarded as equally human.[8] Hitherto, humanity has existed only as an 'in itself' integration. To become 'for itself', all concrete peoples must assume planetary responsibility. Heller identifies this responsibility with a commitment to ethics and the primacy of practical reason.[9] This commitment must marry *a radical anthropological vision* (the idea that there is nothing in human nature that prevents increased human co-operation and the belief that certain motivations and inclinations exist in us in the shape of radical needs) with *socio-political realism*. This latter signifies not a conservative commitment to maintaining institutions just as they are, but allegiance to the idea of learning from history. It means assent to the idea that all steps towards change must involve the active consent of all, in the sense of democratic participation.[10] Heller endorses the general contours of Enlightenment anthropology. A free and rational humanity is not a *fact* but an immanent potential that *ought* to be realised. Yet unlike the consciousness of *reflected universality*, which underpinned classical philosophies of history with their inherent necessity, the new consciousness of *reflected generality* is orientated by its knowledge of the heavy human costs of the belief in historical necessity. It is a summons to action, not out of necessity but out of a sense of subjective responsibility dictated by the awareness of human suffering: the conviction that all historical actions count and that ever present are moments of fertile action.[11] What we have here is the makings of a new critical humanism that has exchanged Promethean aspirations for a consciousness of contingency and ethical responsibility.

Heller's theory of history is constructed in this new spirit and with the tasks imposed by it. First amongst these is the settling of accounts with classical philosophy of history. This repudiation of the philosophy of history is grounded upon a number of arguments.

1. It is impossible to know the future.
2. The philosophy of history is the product of a unique form of modern historical consciousness that cannot simply be imposed on the entire historical process. It is the fruit not of history as such but of the dynamic social conditions of modernity.
3. The philosophy of history has obscured the moment of ethical choice in political action. It views 'is' and 'ought' as immanent products of an essential historical logic rather than as outcomes and options for human action.

This is not simply a rejection of classical philosophy of history. Above all, Heller wants also to render this cultural project historically intelligible and explicable. Modern historical consciousness is located in what she calls its 'logics'. In Chapter 8, we shall exhaustively review the major elements of her theory of modernity, including her understanding of the 'logics'. For now, it is sufficient to understand that Heller understands 'logics' as immanent developmental dynamics. While classical philosophy of history had already thematised contradictions, this was only in a very circumscribed fashion. It abstracted out only a single logic and attributed to it an overwhelming primacy. History became the story of the unfolding of this single developmental dynamic, e.g. civil society or capitalism. Heller's main contention is that modernity is not a harmonious but a *contradictory* social formation. Against this simplified model, she now insists that modernity is a constellation of *competing* and *complementary structural alternatives* ultimately actualised only by historical actors.

In this first attempt to formulate her idea of modernity as a constellation of multiple logics, Heller argues that modern civil society is the bearer of two logics:

1. Universalisation of the market and private property.
2. Freedom, as expressed in democratisation, decentralisation and the equality of civil society.

The third logic is industrialisation. Interestingly, this logic is not associated with that of science or technical progress but with the limitation of the market by state control.

In the context of this model of separable, complementary and competing logics, socialism is conceived as a variety of social movements aimed at resolving the contradictions of modernity by favouring one of the logics. Marx was mistaken to ground his revolutionary strategy on the view that the basic contradiction of modernity was between capitalism and industrialism. On the contrary, socialism must be committed to the first logic of civil society: that of democracy. While to view Marx solely as an advocate of the logic of industrialism seems arbitrary, to Heller this makes particularly good sense. Marx's relative neglect of the institutional question of democracy within socialism is no simple oversight but symptomatic of a fundamental, deeper preference for the logic of industrialism, which was subsequently endorsed and actualised by the Soviet regime.

CRITIQUE OF THE CONCEPT OF PROGRESS

This view of modernity as an unstable societal form pressured by alternative, conflicting, logics is not meant to be understood solely in negative terms. Instability here is not *dysfunction* but the constant renovation of tradition. The unstable equilibrium that Heller will soon characterise as the 'pendulum of modernity' turns out to be an identity maintained through dynamic non-identity. Modernity is a social formation in which thought assumes the shape of constant transcendence. The great mistake of the philosophy of history was to historicise this transcendence as the unfolding of an immanent 'ought/is', in the shape of an essential logic. The present is neither the preserve of a single logic nor of a single culture. European history is just one amongst a plurality of projects. Alignment with this project is not obedience to historical necessity; it is a value choice.[12] The idea of history must also be conceived as a project of one culture amongst others. Heller affirms her commitment to this project from the standpoint of the logic of democracy. Her own theory of history repudiates dogmatism. It remains philosophical, an interpretation of contemporary social reality that is deliberately incomplete: it abandons the idea of a necessary outcome of the whole process. First and foremost, theory of history, unlike philosophy of history, must be historically self-conscious.[13]

The recognition that the philosophy of history is the product of a specific form of modern consciousness requires us to acknowledge also that the categories of progress and regress are equally so. It is the false consciousness of the philosophy of history to attempt to apply these notions in an indiscriminant way to all other societies. Heller claims that in societies without notions of progress and regress, there is neither.[14] Having rejected the ontologisation of these categories as immanent historical tendencies, the description of our age in these terms depends upon the *value standpoint* adopted. Progress can only be designated in terms of a value that specifies the aspect of progress being claimed. However, Heller also now dismisses any idea of a calculus of progress. Balancing historical gains over losses ignores the fact that human suffering is incommensurable. Calculating progress reduces human suffering to a mere means in the accomplishment of this end and value. To measure progress is to stand outside history and usurp the position of God. Heller accepts Collingwood's proposal that we only speak about real historical progress where there are *gains without corresponding loses*. To do otherwise is to admit the ethically shocking calculus of treating some human suffering as inessential or of secondary importance. However, Collingwood's proposal does not resolve the problem of progress, because historical development always involves both gains and corresponding losses. Therefore we cannot legitimately talk about actual progress and regress in modern society.[15] While a theory of history, unlike the philosophy of history, cannot acknowledge progress, it can interpret the acceptance of the *idea of progress* in our society as progress. This is progress in the sense that the will to create progress is something real, whose existence signifies gain without loss. The idea of progress functions as a norm for the creation of progress and is really a signature of a dynamic society committed to the spirit of self-critique. On this argument, it is possible to universalise the idea of progress, because its norm can be viewed as binding on the whole of mankind.[16] However, this seems rather contentious. The question of whether we can accept even the idea of progress in this normative sense as 'progress' really seems to depend on how we define this latter idea. Yet Heller's meaning is clear enough. The theory of history endorses the idea of progress, not as a 'fact' but as 'regulative idea' that in its universality expresses modernity's form of existence and its desire to create progress.

The idea of progress expresses the essential constitutive experience of dissatisfaction pervasive to modern society. While regional or specific dissatisfaction has always been a powerful motive in social struggle, modern dissatisfaction expresses a distinctive desire to transcend all limitations, a restlessness which contests all limits: social, political, sexual and generational. It views every victory as a momentary lull in an infinite quest. The philosophy of history proposed redemption from this dissatisfaction through the attainment of a historical plateau or a final realm of freedom; that would finally alleviate tension. While abandoning redemptive projects, a theory of history intends to activate dissatisfaction by struggling against conditions that would use other human beings as means; it aims to activate the quest for gains without losses and human suffering.[17] At the same time, this strategy also *renounces asceticism*. Having done everything to achieve this ethical outcome (which is her duty), the finite individual is entitled to seek the greatest possible amount of personal satisfaction.

A THEORY OF HISTORY

The explicit repudiation of a redemptive project makes it clear that Heller's theory of history is an *incomplete* philosophy of history. This theory preserves links with the old philosophy of history, but these are only the consequence of their mutual historicity. The normative edge, the 'ought' of the theory of history, is not completely formal. As a form of our modern consciousness, this theory does advocate certain substantial values (freedom, life) that become universal value ideas in our own dynamic and unstable society.[18] These values are carried mainly by the second logic of civil society associated with democracy. This is one substantive aspect. The other involves an ethics in keeping with these universal values, which will be elaborated in Chapter 9. More than mere 'oughts', these value ideas are co-constitutive of our being, insofar as they regulate both theory and praxis. Quite crucially, however, the theory of history maintains the distinction between upholding value ideas and speculating on their actualisation. Rather than claiming, as Marx does, that history never sets itself goals that cannot be realised, the theory of history asserts that humanity never produces values that cannot be observed and constantly upheld.[19] A commitment to the idea of progress understood as gains without losses involves an idea of the future. Yet because the theory of history denies itself true statements about the future, its idea of the future must take the form of a utopia. This returns us to the essentially utopian dimension of radical philosophy, discussed in the previous chapter.

This utopia is the image of the factual universalisation and realisation of the values associated with the second logic of civil society.[20] Implicit in this utopia of gains without losses is a commitment to pluralism. Only a regulative image that accommodates the differences of tastes, inclinations, talents and interests can live up to the norm of gains without losses. The utopia of progress must promote a plurality of life forms corresponding to different structures of need. Contradictions between the priorities of these plural forms of life can be resolved as long as parties are committed to the supreme value ideas of modernity (freedom and life) and processes of rational dialogue similar to those propounded in Habermas' notion of distortion-free communication.[21] In this configuration, the Marxian idea of revolution as transcendence to an entirely new form of society gives way to the spell of political realism as a commitment to the increasing preponderance of the second logic of civil society.

While it is clear that Heller viewed her main task as constructing a radical alternative to the discredited philosophies of history, it would be a mistake to believe that philosophical anthropology has completely disappeared from this project. The utopia that she constructs as an alternative to the realised future, which the theory of history denies, is itself the image of a way of life. Just as all philosophy of history is anthropology insofar as it posits a *telos*, her theory of history also retains a moment of this earlier project. However, now her radical anthropology is mediated by political realism and this requires the capacity to learn from history and avoid all emphatic assertions regarding the historical future.[22]

THE FALSE ONTOLOGY OF NEEDS

It was already noted that Heller's critique of classical philosophy of history rests upon ethical as well as epistemological grounds. Not only is it the case that we cannot know the future in advance, it is also true that to conceive this future as a necessary tendency of the dynamics of contemporary society served to undercut the decisive moment of ethical choice and responsibility intrinsic to historical action. When action is viewed as the product of immanent contradictions, not only does historical necessity swamp individual ethical choices, but the party that possesses knowledge of this necessity holds a claim for special authority and usurps the autonomy of real historical actors. A decisive move against this epistemological and political privilege required changes to other elements of Heller's theory. This was most obvious with respect to her theory of needs. By the end of *Marx's Theory of Need*, it was clear that her commitment to the philosophy of history was wavering. At the same time, she was still optimistic. She believed that radical needs were immanent in capitalist society and had begun to manifest themselves at the margins of traditional working-class politics. The decisive question was whether this theory of radical needs could survive the abandonment of its original ascriptive theoretical structure.

The essay 'Can "True" and "False" Needs Be Posited' (1980) takes a significant step towards answering this question.[23] Heller recapitulates familiar themes and positions, but these are now treated analytically in a way that divorces them from the former Marxian framework.

The focus on needs was the most original and characteristic aspect of Heller's reading of Marx. The explicit critique of the concepts of interest and social needs expressed her repudiation of really existing socialism with its command economy and authoritarian politics. The substance of this critique was a rejection of concepts that privileged specific standpoints in relation to needs and in practice allowed powerful elites and institutions to hierarchise the needs of subordinate individuals. Precisely this idea now serves as her point of departure in articulating her own theory of needs. She rejects all attempts to distinguish between needs on the basis of their alleged 'imaginary' or 'real' character. To assume that one can designate some needs as true and others as false at the ontological level is to usurp the position of God standing above the world.[24] For mere mortals, knowledge is always the product of fetishised social conditions. All attempts to divide needs into 'true' and 'false' on naturalistic grounds fail, because needs are always historically conditioned and socially codified; convincing trans-historical objective criteria according to which they could be divided are simply lacking. Yet these theoretical problems are nothing compared to the practical dangers that emerge when closed and elite political institutions and social strata arrogate to themselves the task of hierarchising needs: this leads directly to the dictatorship over needs.[25] Against all proposals to discount the reality of various clusters of needs, Heller maintains that the distinction between 'true' and 'false' needs must not be identified with that between 'real' and 'imaginary'. All needs felt by humans are real and all must be acknowledged, without attempting to allocate them into ontologically distinct groups.[26] Heller encourages the acknowledgement of all needs, although she does not argue that all should be satisfied. This acknowledgement amounts to equal recognition of all needs, but it ignores the fact that in present dynamic societies there are more needs than can be satisfied under reigning conditions. What is essential is a democratic institutional mechanism through which priorities between conflicting needs can be established. Here the norm of acknowledging all needs is fused with democratic principles in order to produce consensually determined priorities.[27]

Her determination to repudiate an ontologically founded distinction between needs, and to leave the question of actual satisfaction to the political institutions of democratic priority setting, does not mean that Heller refuses to distinguish between needs on grounds of value. On the contrary, she argues that the general acknowledgement of all needs neglects the *ethical aspect*.[28] While she accepts that all needs felt by humans are equally real, this does not mean they are equally good. We cannot do without the distinction between good and evil: without it, the satisfaction of all needs have equal value, irrespective of whether they require oppression and exploitation. In practice this would undermine acknowledgement of the needs of the oppressed and exploited. This is the reason that all concrete societies have refused to acknowledge 'sinful' needs. However, in a dynamic modern society that has eroded all fixed value hierarchies, any attempt to reintroduce a fixed moral roster appears doomed because it presupposes a privileged standpoint that disappeared with divine knowledge.[29]

Confronting this difficulty, Heller appeals immediately to Kant, who provides an ethical norm that is both *formal* and *substantial*. The famous second formulation of the norm of the categorical imperative 'not to use another as a mere means' does not dictate circumstances, but it is sufficiently concrete to allow us to grasp instances.[30] For Heller, Kant is a moralist poised at the historical precipice of the explosion of the bourgeois quantification of needs. He speaks of 'thirsts': these are not concrete needs but alienated needs for unlimited quantities that cannot be satisfied. The Kantian norm allows for the recognition of all needs without having to proscribe particulars, because it disqualifies alienated needs based on quantification. The key point is not to morally condemn concrete needs, but to designate options that refer to preferred systems of needs and the ways of life reflected in them.[31] The important function of options here is to influence and guide the development of systems of needs while critiquing alternatives.

NEEDS AND PLURALISM

Modern dynamic societies are competitive and pluralist. Various ways of life claim to correspond to the needs of people. However, such correspondence rarely exists. Often needs are merely imputed; real needs are disregarded as inauthentic, or it is claimed that whole classes of individuals have needs of which they are entirely unaware. Heller categorically rejects this imputation. She distinguishes between desires and needs precisely on the basis that only the latter are conscious. Nevertheless, in keeping with her allegiance to the idea of radical needs, she questions whether the awareness of needs is always homogeneous; does it not differ in level and form? She recalls Sartre's distinction between 'need as deficiency' and 'need as project' to illustrate the point that a felt lack does not necessarily signify the shape of a potential satisfaction. It may be that the social institutions and objectivations required for the satisfaction of a particular need are simply absent.[32]

In this case, the need exists as a sense of lack, as an accumulating frustration that may be expressed in irrational forms. She validates the Sartrean distinction, because the ultimate prospect of the notion of radical needs depends upon being able to walk the very fine line between outright imputation of needs and acquiescence in the existing structures of bourgeois need. She rightfully repudiates the former as the theoretical precursor of the brutal dictatorial denial of needs. Her narrow avenue of hope consists in the existence amongst broad social strata of a type of need that has not yet found its voice in the form of appropriate social institutions and objectivations. She is aware that even the distinction between need as 'lack' and as 'project' involves imputation. Such imputation is always a pseudo-form of the fulfilment of needs. However, she argues that in this case imputation is 'reasonable', because what is being imputed is not the existence of the need itself, which already exists as 'lack', but the transformation of this 'lack' into a 'project' were the appropriate institutions and objectivations available. The value guiding the preference of a system of needs 'points out existing needs in present society whose satisfaction *may* lead towards the preferred system of needs'.[33] As this implies a judgement concerning the future, of which we can never be certain, it remains imputation and not true knowledge. Thus even this 'reasonable' form of need imputation remains counterfactual and, for this reason, is a pseudo-form of need fulfilment. Heller reiterates the point that ideas and values are only temporarily, in 'great historical moments', able to fulfil the function of guiding systems of needs. The tragic history of modern revolution reveals that even when their content is democratic, unless embodied within the institutions and objectivations of social life, these ideal objectivations remain elitist and cannot fulfil the function of actually transforming the old structure of needs and producing a new one.[34]

Here is a new version of Marx's old complaint against the impotence of philosophy. As a mere counterfactual, theory lacks the power of generalisation that belongs to the power structure of every society. Inherent preferences already materialised within these power structures generate their own systems of objectivations that designate certain needs and the forms of their satisfactions. It is this power of the existing that characterises the form of manipulation pervasive to bourgeois society. This is not the overt compulsion of the dictatorship over needs but it is just as effective in limiting the exploration of alternative structures of needs. Practically, it achieves precisely the sort of division of needs into 'real' and 'unreal' that Heller rejects as a false 'ontologisation' of needs.

While recognising its counterfactual fragility, Heller endorses the Kantian reading of the categorical imperative, because it refuses to countenance the degradation of other humans to the status of mere means. This norm is the signature of radical needs, because it is only conceivable together with the idea of a society that has transcended social relations based on hierarchy and exploitative subordination, and it therefore presupposes a need structure like that posited in Marx's society of 'associated producers'. Whether the norm could be anything more than a theoretical construct or a pious dream depends upon the empirical prevalence of radical needs. Having detached her theory from the Marxian philosophy of history, the dynamics of bourgeois society are no longer sure to deliver 'radical needs'. At this juncture Heller offers her own wager. She affirms the reality of radical needs but admits that the progressive forces struggling on their behalf constitute only a social minority.[35] Undeterred, she maintains that the aims and aspirations of precisely this minority represent all humanity. It will be recalled that Marx justified the proletariat's claim to represent a universal interest on the grounds that its own emancipation could not be won without the abolition of class society and therefore without the emancipation of all classes. Heller's argument for the universality of the minority perspective of radical needs toys with dispensing with this degree of outright ascription. The essence of the Kantian norm of radical needs is the satisfaction of all needs.[36] She argues that there is in fact no Chinese wall between ordinary empirical needs and radical needs. Social movements, parties and interest groups devoted to non-radical aims can generate radical needs just as some radical aims can be satisfied in present societies, as long as they remain democratic.[37] The very proposition of satisfying all needs is itself radical in the social context of relations of exploitation and subordination. Clearly, she is determined to remain as firmly based as possible in the substance of real empirical needs. The recognition accorded to the satisfaction of *all existing* needs (excluding those requiring the reduction of others to mere means) reinforces this preference. Nevertheless, a serious problem remains. By bridging the gap between ordinary and 'radical needs' and referring to unsatisfied existing needs, Heller hopes to avoid the Marxian imputation of need.

Also, aware of the potential dangers in too easily bridging the distinction between ordinary empirical and 'radical needs', Heller immediately raises the obvious question of whether the ascription of universality to the minority perspective of radical needs is ideological or not.[38] Her answer is that ascribing 'radical needs' to humanity may be ideological but is not necessarily so.[39] The conditions for perpetuating a contemporary non-ideological politics of radical needs are, as she sees it, the following. The perspective of radical needs is in the business of influencing society towards the adoption of the systems of needs demanded by democratic orientating values. This commitment to engagement requires a politics of persuasion rather than of compulsion. This implies acceptance of a democratic legal state and the pluralism of competing systems of needs within it. Radical needs are themselves pluralist insofar as this perspective rejects the subordination of the other to the status of mere means.[40] The resurgence of qualitative satisfaction requires the proliferation of a variety of ways of life and the rejection of the dominance of any single form. The standpoint of radical needs must continue to assert its right to criticise existing priorities and advocate forms of life in conformity with its own values. It must also explicitly repudiate manipulation and the temptation to reintroduce the false ontological distinction between 'true' and 'false' needs as a tactic useful in delegitimising non-radical needs.[41] A commitment to pluralism means that the politics of radical needs is always devoted to the creation of alternatives and diversity. Heller's commitment to pluralism goes even further than affirmation of democratic forms. Heller perceives democratic institutions as tools rather than as ends in themselves. They cannot be the source of new systems of needs but only provide the indispensable framework for the *labour of democracy* as an ongoing process of public debate and participation, of decentralisation, of new objectivations with their resulting transformed structures of need.[42]

The main feature of this reconstructed version of Heller's theory of needs is the attempt to distance it from its initial Marxian framework and to relocate the notion of radical needs within a pluralistic democratic politics. At this immediate post-Marxist stage, the focus of Heller's concerns is the dangerous political implications of a dogmatic ontological division of needs into 'true' and 'false'. She wants to make sure that her affirmation of radical needs as a vehicle for critique and qualitative change within pluralistic democracy does not serve as just another form of ideological consciousness serving authoritarian political ends. However, to ascribe the interests of humanity to the needs of a minority is such a blatantly substitutionalist act of faith that it is clearly inconsistent with her radically pluralist and democratic aspirations. The underlying difficulty that generates this unintended relapse is the yawning gap that still exists between 'is' and 'ought'. It cannot be concealed that 'radical needs', as she defines them, are not the needs that currently preoccupy the great majority. 'Radical needs' have a qualitative dimension that cannot be satisfied within present social arrangements. This is the basis not only of their transcendent impetus but also of their merely utopian status. While hard political experience awakened Heller to the great political dangers of the Marxian version of ascribed consciousness, its residual aspects persist unresolved in her attempt to preserve a critical perspective in a post-Marxist radical philosophy.

6
Rationality through the Prism of Everyday Life

Heller's immediate post-Marxist works can be roughly divided into two: those that broke entirely new ground, and those that renovated her early writings in the light of her break with Marxism. The book on history falls into the former category, while the reframed theory of needs is located in the latter. A new English-speaking audience and the desire to provide a contemporary summation of her early, untranslated works accentuated the need for revision. Yet *The Power of Shame* (1985) sits uneasily between these two categories. It is primarily devoted to presentation of a general theory of rationality. The publication of Habermas' *Theorie des Kommunikativen Handelns* (1981) provided a new impetus to an ongoing discussion of rationality within the English-speaking world.[1] However, it also provided the opportunity to renovate the basic framework of *Everyday Life* in the context of the rationality debate, by dispensing with the Marxian primacy of production. While Heller endorsed Habermas' 'communicative' challenge to the hegemony of positivist notions of rationality, she also proposed a broader alternative conception. This involved a close of link of rationality to its every-day life context and the reintroduction of the Lukácsian motif of the whole person. She wanted to reconnect the rationality problematic to human emotions and personal character.

THE PROBLEMISATION OF EVERYDAY LIFE

In Chapter 1 we saw how the philosophical thematisation of everyday life occurred only when it lost its taken-for-granted status within consciousness. Despite a grand tradition of philosophical scepticism, European culture had long presupposed the self-evident symmetry of the everyday world. Only with the modern revolutionisation of everyday life, and its consequential resistance to form, were artists and philosophers compelled to counter-pose various types of 'truth' to it. Sociology could hardly afford the luxurious attitude of outright rejection. In its case, critique was tempered by the need to explain this formlessness in terms of the transformation of macro-structures.[2] Philosophy soon adopted a similar stance. Paradoxically, it was precisely the fact that everyday life had become problematic that eventually stimulated the insight that everyday thinking was the foundation of rationality. It followed that it was the logical starting point for a modern theory of rationality.[3]

Recognising the historicity of the problem does not detract from its general significance. Heller argues that the categories of rationality and everyday life should be applied to all societies. This is because the consciousness of rationality and the distinction between the everyday and the non-everyday are empirical universals. While she associates the historical emergence of the specifically Western concept of rationality with Socrates and the breakdown of traditional authority, she nevertheless asserts that a primordial capacity for discrimination between fundamental categories of value orientation like 'good' and 'evil', 'true' and 'false', exists in all cultures. These value-orientating pairs of categories are hierarchically ordered. On this view, acting 'according to reason' means to abide by at least one positively discriminated category. Her most general definition of the concept of rationality is 'acting according to reason', where reason is this most general capacity for discrimination.[4] This universal social capacity is both problematised and enhanced with the birth of morality. When custom no longer possesses the power to legislate, a deliberative moment is introduced into individual decision making whereby questions of both interpretation and application are raised. From this time on, discrimination of the good requires further determinations. Heller views morality as the consciously negotiated relation between the external and internal authorities required for good judgement. Practical reason signifies the ability to discriminate between value categories in accord with the hierarchisation of these authorities.[5] Along with Kant, she posits the priority of practical reason. Rationality is the pursuit of truth under the auspices of practical reason. In the last instance, rationality remains a moral category, because the conscious relation to custom exemplified by Socratic questioning still requires intersubjective values and evidence.[6] By locating rationality in the primordial anthropological capacity for discrimination, she short-circuits all the arguments of historical relativism. In specifying the historical origins of morality, she also clearly wants to preserve the broad classical agenda of rationality orientated to practical life rather than see it reduced to the calculus of science or pragmatics. As everyday life is simply taken for granted, it does not even require a preliminary definition. Yet precisely this taken-for-granted quality testifies to the fact that we have failed to fully acknowledge its place as both the foundation and the *telos* of a harmonious, substantive rationality.

To vindicate these claims, Heller revisits the paradigm of objectivation. This involves a revision of the priority she had previously, as a Marxist, conceded to the sphere of '*objectivation in itself*' and the connection of the historical emergence and cultural differentiation of rationality to this more encompassing systematic framework.

THE SPHERE OF OBJECTIVATION IN ITSELF

The backbone of everyday life is the sphere of *objectivation in itself*. It conditions the essential intersubjectivity of knowledge, communication and action: it is the social a priori of human experience. Its basic constituents – *language*, *customs* and *manmade objects* – are only analytically separable. However, appropriated in the everyday they fit the typical subject with the requisite abilities to operate adequately in her social world. Heller maintains that the three basic characteristics of this sphere are *inherence*, *heterogeneity* and *taken-for-grantedness*. The former refers to the fact that these elements are appropriated not separately but combined in integral activity.[7] Effective application of norms and rules requires language skills, just as the proper use of tools requires more than technical knowledge. Heterogeneity refers to the diverse character of the activities that occupy the everyday. The denizen of the everyday is no specialist, but a jack-of-all-trades. The fully socialised individual must perform adequately across a conventional range of activities. Recall Lukács' reference to the human as a whole and the fact that the subject of everyday life is required to develop, at least to some degree, the most heterogeneous range of human capacities.[8]

Everyday life is the foundation of rationality. The acquisition of the sphere of *objectivation in itself* is the presupposition of being human. It is the condition not only of individual and societal survival but also of meaning. Language is more than a means of communication and norms and rules are more than instructions for use. They legislate the positive side of value orientation and are ultimately legitimated by meaningful worldviews that designate a sacred or at least a proper order.[9] However, Heller especially underlines the fact that the sphere of *objectivation in itself* does not circumscribe the scope of knowledge or the patterns of action within the life-world. With their specific genetic a priori, the unique human is hardwired for the receipt of the sphere of *objecitivation in itself*. The accident of birth determines which particular one it will be. As appropriation is the task confronting every human being, *intersubjectivity* has priority over *subjectivity*. However, the subject is the dynamic force of socialisation, its product never uniform. Individual attributes and experience condition the quality and the pace of appropriation.[10] Especially in modernity, everyday life is awash with knowledge derived from elsewhere; even the content of the norms and rules of this sphere are historically variable depending upon the degree of regulation required by existing norms and rules. The intensity of this regulation, its tightness or looseness, is a product of changing historical conditions and the character and complexity of other coexisting spheres of objectivation. The existence of these other spheres also explains why the everyday is not explicable in terms of the sphere of *objectivation in itself* alone. Increasing social complexity and differentiation complicates this picture. The social division of labour reveals not just this single sphere but several others, each with their own norms and rules corresponding to specific social functions and rungs of social stratification. Changing historical conditions impact on direct access to other sources of knowledge and values not mediated by the sphere of *objectivation in itself*. Heller goes on to argue that modernity has expanded this access by allowing the everyday subject direct access to various cultural resources formerly restricted by sacred taboos and ritual exclusions.

CULTURAL SURPLUS AND THE ATTITUDES OF REASON

The problem of rationality emerges from the crisis of customary norms and rules. Only the appearance of another horizon allowed *nomos* to be understood as such. Of course, the same point can be made in regard to the everyday. To designate the everyday as 'everyday' only makes sense from some external standpoint. This becomes available with access to other cultural sources of knowledge. This difference of perspective is ascribed to two attitudes Heller designates as two different types of rationality. The *rationality of reason* involves observing norms and rules. In the everyday context, this is mainly related to action. By contrast, the *rationality of intellect* is a higher attitude that does not simply accept existing norms and rules as taken-for-granted but *tests* them according to at least one value. She acknowledges the family resemblance between these two forms of rationality. Thinking itself involves the following of norms and rules and is a process taken under the direction of reason. Reason has priority as the all-embracing form of rationality. Its appropriation makes the individual human and there can be no social life without it; it is a cultural constant and empirical universal. Furthermore, both forms require various combinations of inventive, repetitive and intuitive thinking. This link intimates a common rationality beneath the fundamental difference of orientation.[11]

The common root of both rational attitudes is the process of *appropriation* itself. While socialisation is always achieved, the degree of accomplishment varies. In each individual case, this is a matter of knitting together a *genetic* and a *social* a priori. This is the differential accomplishment of a common human task. Human beings have the capacity to appropriate the cultural world at a level considerably in advance of primary appropriation. This is the origin of what Heller calls cultural and cognitive surplus. The experience of every individual is unique and, even if the ineffably unique is 'unspeakable', it can still be expressed in the language of art or the sacred. In this intersubjective form, it is accumulated as *cultural surplus* and later reabsorbed into the sphere of *objectivation in itself*.[12] The corollary of the surplus of pure subjective experience is the surplus accumulated in the recesses of everyday life and institutions. This scattered reservoir of know-how and technical innovation is what Heller calls *cognitive surplus*. Under conditions in which the existing norms and rules are tight, it remains largely dormant. However, under modern conditions, with institutionalised science and more flexible norms and rules, the massive build-up of cognitive surplus finds an outlet.[13]

The introduction of cultural and cognitive surpluses into the model allows for a better understanding of the dynamic potential within everyday life. The most severe inadequacy of Heller's earlier Marxist theory of everyday life was the *ontological priority* accorded to the sphere of *objectivation in itself*. She had even argued that the cultural sphere of *objectivation for itself* was *historically derivative* and not an empirical universal. These earlier concessions to Marxist orthodoxy are now abandoned. The sphere of *cultural objectivation* is no less a precondition of social life than that of *objectivation itself*.[14] We have already noted that the norms and rules of the sphere of *objectivation in itself* are not merely instructions for use but are bearers of positive values legitimated by worldviews. The source of these worldviews is the sphere of cultural objectivations which supply human life with meaning. Specific norms and rules are imaginatively located within an overarching authoritative interpretation of the world that makes sense of heterogeneous episodes and thereby unifies experience. As social life is quite unimaginable without this social function, Heller now confidently attributes empirical universality to both spheres. Not only does the sphere of *objectivation for itself* perform the indispensable function of making life meaningful but it also absorbs the cultural surplus of subjective experience and thus acts as an incubator for the expressions of human potential.[15]

Heller joins a long tradition in Western Marxism that has drawn attention to the critical potential and ambivalence of culture. Cultural objectivations fulfil two distinct social functions of *legitimisation* but also *desubstantialisation*. The latter demands critique of substance from the standpoint of a higher order.[16] This need not be explicit criticism; it may simply be the challenge of an alternative vision or contesting hierarchy of values. This critical potential is enhanced by some of the intrinsic characteristics of this sphere. In contrast to the heterogeneity of the sphere of the *in itself*, all cultural objectivations are *homogenous*. The meaning of all actions within this sphere is determined only in relation to other actions within the same sphere. All cultural objectivations have their own intrinsic norms and rules that are not related or interchangeable with those of another sphere. Even momentary disconnection from the norms and rules of a specific cultural objectivation is sufficient for expulsion into other spheres.[17] As reservoirs of cultural surplus, the cultural objectivations possess a remarkable capacity to survive the specific historical conditions that engendered them. They express the mortal's desire for immortality. The homogeneity of the cultural forms also allows this to be actualised. Works can be interpreted and understood in their own right, relying only on intrinsic norms and rules of composition, without reference to historical conditions and social institutions. This is the *paradox of reception*. The feeling of transience evoked by immortal symbols provides the present with an invisible temporal depth. The present age is always broader than the historical present because collective cultural memory preserves much of the past. Clearly, this helps explain the critical potential of the sphere of *cultural objectivations for itself.*[18]

Entry into the sphere of cultural objectivations requires the suspension of everyday heterogeneous activities. It is largely a historical question of the degree of practical demarcation between the everyday and cultural activity as to whether this signifies a rupture or a smooth transition. However, the task of acquiring the capacities of appropriation occupies both everyday and institutional life.[19] The suspension of everyday attitudes must finally surrender to the homogeneous norms and values of the sphere of objectivation in question. Heller describes this surrender as a 'naturalism' contrived in conformity to the norms and rules of the specific cultural objectivation. All individual faculties are unified, and expressed in and through the homogeneous medium. The catharsis of reception is simultaneously objectivation and the creation of a new form of conscious subjectivity. Following Lukács, she describes this heightening and concentration of disparately developed faculties in a unified receptive experience as a shift from the human-as-a-whole to human wholeness.[20] Heller insists that the 'reborn' subject is not likely to be the same as the pre-existing one. This is the benefit of participation in the domain of human wholeness. Visitation to the *sphere of objectivation for itself* requires and produces a revolution amongst the compositional elements of thought. It insists upon a different relation between the repetitive, inventive and intuitive components within thought, with the balance shifting more to the intuitive and inventive elements. The precise character of this balance depends always upon the type of objectivation and a combination of historical and individual factors. However, the main point is that cultural reception invigorates the everyday with elements of expanded human wholeness. In this regard, she notes that modernity has facilitated the modern subject's direct access to the higher objectivations and constant oscillation between the cultural sphere and everyday life.

SPECIALISATION AND THE SPHERE OF INSTITUTIONS

The need to expand her account of the *sphere of objectivation for itself* and underline its equivalent status and empirical universality to the sphere of *objectivation in itself* was not the principal motive behind Heller's revision. Her main theme is rationality and her focus quickly turns to the modern source and dynamics of rationalisation. In stark contrast to *universal constants*, the sphere of *objectivation in and for itself* stands for the sphere of *particularity*. Beyond the institution of the family that continues to occupy its natural home within the terrain of the everyday, all other modern institutions (economic, political and cultural) constitute the *sphere of objectivation in and for itself*. In fact, this sphere consists wholly of institutions. These are subsystems of society that in their interdependence reproduce social identity. All institutions are characterised by relatively homogeneous norms and rules but, in their mutual support, they create a particular social identity.[21] However, this requires neither harmony nor consensus. The processes of rationalisation, like the social division of labour, entail a *differentiation* of the *sphere of objectivation in itself* into a hierarchised structure of domination. Heller makes the historical point that in early societies identity was secured by the unity of customary norms, rules and traditional worldviews, without overt domination. Today, however, the particular social identity imposed by *the sphere of objectivation in and for itself* is a structure of domination. It is worthwhile noting that she refuses to read this historical association as a logical or causal

link between *social differentiation* and *domination*. She still holds out
at least the possibility of a society with a sophisticated institutional
sphere in which norms and rules are not determined by the social
division of labour.[22]

Given the basic similarity between her model and the Habermasian
distinction between life-world and subsystems, it is interesting to find
that Heller is especially critical of his account of the institutional
sphere of modernity. His division of the subsystems of modernity into
economic and political seems to exclude the hybrid states of 'really
existing socialism' from the ranks of modernity and muddies the
difference between capitalism and industrialisation. This conceptual
fuzziness also impairs his account of politics, in which a subsystem
mediated only by power seems unable to distinguish different types of
political rule.[23] Heller also questions a number of other assumptions
implied by the autonomy of the subsystems. Like other critics, she
argues that the norms and rules of these subsystems are only relatively
autonomous, as they are not only embedded in a social structure but
are also interconnected with other institutions. Institutional behaviour
always has a thicker normative content than merely minding the rules
and not cheating within the system in question. This indicates that the
social structure itself is a conglomeration of mutually interconnecting
and supportive institutions. An exclusive emphasis on the autonomy
of intra-spheric norms and rules leads to the loss of the capacity to
articulate this vital interdependence and mutuality.[24]

The individual who inhabits modern institutions gripped by the
processes of rationalisation is the specialised human. It is therefore
vital that Heller explores the dynamics and interstices of institutional
specialisation. Like cultural activity, institutional life must also conform
to sphere-specific rules and norms and to even more specialised training.
Institutional activity is typically neither the activity of the *individual as
a whole* nor that of *human wholeness*.[25] It demands the development and
accentuation of certain human capacities. Furthermore, institutional
reproduction requires not so much exceptional talent as expert skills
inculcated by training and education. This sphere functions *without the
production of cultural surplus*. It has a capacity to store and implement
cognitive surplus, but does not produce it.[26] In fact, intensified processes
of functional differentiation have radically transformed the production
of cultural surplus. Shifting the centre of productive activity away from
the sphere of everyday life into institutions has diminished production
of subjective surplus. The increasing role of cultural reflection has
compounded this tendency. Cultural surplus is today less an immediate
precipitate of subjective experience and more dependent upon reflection

within the domain of cultural objectivations.[27] This is not to say that institutions can do without ideological legitimisation. Repeating the argument we have already seen her mount against the autonomy of subsystems, Heller maintains that even the increase in social complexity and institutional differentiation has not lessened the need for a unifying meaning. Smoothly operating institutions require the legitimacy drawn from meaningful worldviews.[28] A meaningful worldview legitimates the underpinning social order while allowing for the accumulation of knowledge and training that is necessary for reproduction.

The dominant worldview must permeate not only all institutions but also the sphere of *objectivation in itself*. The norms and rules of everyday life must be infused with the spirit of the dominant worldview. As we have noted, this legitimising function is even more necessary in complex societies with an extended division of labour. In such societies it is necessary not only to reinforce a specific structure of social differentiation but also to do so for both dominators and dominated.[29] Only this can secure a taken-for-granted meaningful world. On this score, it might seem that science had little hope of competing with religion. The latter excels especially at the provision of meaning. By contrast, the scientific worldview thrives on scepticism and expels all questions of meaning from its own province. Surprisingly, Heller finds the emancipatory potential of science to lie precisely in its reluctance to consider norms and rules as anything other than instructions for use.[30] This insensitivity to the normative dimension of norms and rules diminishes the pressure to internalise norms characteristically felt by the individual before a sanctified order. While this relaxation carries its own potential dangers, it also opens up the possibility of highly individualised ways of life.

Its limitations as a dispenser of taken-for-granted meaning has not prevented modern science's triumph over religion. In the shape of rationalisation, it has come to permeate everyday life and has largely displaced religion. Nevertheless, Heller is reluctant to interpret this success in Habermasian terms as 'colonisation', on two grounds. Firstly, she argues that colonisation is not a new experience for everyday life. Religion has only rarely lost its hegemony. Only for brief periods, after church and state began to separate at the dawn of modernity, was it possible for the idea of colonisation to be formulated. At stake here is not radical historical rupture but a *continuity of ideological domination* that has only changed its form. Before the historical moment of its liberation, everyday life was simply a colony pure and simple of religious worldviews.[31] Heller wants not just to infuse a moment of historical realism into the talk of colonisation, she also questions whether it has radically disrupted the primary functioning of everyday life. The increasing role of institutions shows no signs of usurping the function of primary socialisation. Were such a takeover ever to occur, it would extinguish the very source of cultural and cognitive surplus: that is, the human being as a whole. Without this subject of everyday life and subjective surplus, culture would wither from lack of nutrients and the social order that depends upon legitimating meaningful worldviews would face inevitable collapse.[32] Far from impairing the constant features of *the sphere of objectivation in itself*, modern rationalisation has reinforced the heterogeneous character of this sphere by its refusal to provide a unifying meaning for these activities.[33]

While this final argument puts Heller's reservations against the Habermasian colonisation thesis, it also offers it definite concessions. Amongst other things, the dominant scientific worldview signifies a decreasing proportion of normative elements in everyday life and the contents of the rules are fed directly or indirectly by science into everyday life. Science now systematically usurps the role of producing cognitive surplus from the sphere of *objectivation in itself*, in which it was merely the residue of heterogeneous activities. Finally, personal contacts lose their richness and functionality in social reproduction.[34] On the other side, the weakness of science in the area of meaning provision, and its incapacity to unify heterogeneous activities, impairs the subject's capacity for identity formation. The result is alienation and tension that give rise to large quantities of cultural surplus and undermine the stability of everyday reproduction. The resulting surplus either becomes the fuel of cultural critique or functions as a cultural deficit in the shape of individual and collective hysteria.[35] Heller recognises the profound and continuing impact of colonisation on everyday life, but refuses to concede that colonisation disrupts the basic socialising function of the sphere of *objectivation in itself*. Like Habermas, she is not about to ignore the potentially emancipatory aspects of science's renunciation of unified meaning. The provision of technical but not moral legitimisation of contemporary structures of domination leaves class, sexual and race discrimination without the legitimacy provided by previous dominant worldviews.[36]

TOWARDS A THEORY OF MODERNITY

Exploration of the colonisation theme links up with the incipient theory of modernity that begins to appear in several of Heller's writings from the early 1980s. Earlier we noted that her critique of progress in *Theory of History* takes her in the direction of a more complex understanding of modernity and its conflicting 'logics'. Approaching this same issue from the problematic of rationality and its instantiation within the institutional sphere, she now unfolds her theory from the perspective of science. Early science liberated the cognitive surpluses scattered around the heterogeneous activities of the everyday from the constraints imposed by the previously dominant religious worldviews. These surpluses were harnessed and systematised in a quest for a truly universal truth. In early modernity, the accumulation of cultural surplus, arising from the erosion of traditional concrete norms and rules, shifted all the cultural objectivations towards universality.[37] The values of both truth and beauty are universalised as the projects of autonomous art and science.

Making the link between capitalism and culture, Heller argues that modern science develops a universal language that presupposes the universal equivalence of money.[38] Like money, this universal language is conspicuously free of normative requirements. The positing of normative claims involves interpretation related to values. But science categorically rejects authoritative interpretation of universal values. This is why modernity is bereft of universal norms. The quest for truth does not require the observance of universal norms. Science demonstrates the self-restraint of its own domination by the imposition of a strict fact/value dichotomy. The value side of this dichotomy is left to the struggles between religion and the other cultural objectivations. With the breakdown of an authoritative interpretation and allocation of traditional virtues, individual interpretation of abstract norms undermined the authority of traditional virtues. The cultural impulse of this corrosive scepticism comes, according to Heller, not from science itself but from philosophy. With its methodical critical questioning, philosophy is the midwife not only of science but also of democracy. The same critical spirit that overthrew theological cosmology was also abroad in the political struggles that promoted democratic institutions.[39]

In fact, the idea of an unruly synergy between the logics of the market, science and democracy is one of the key insights of her new theory of modernity. The universal language of science was only made possible because the universal equivalence of commerce had already eroded the barriers of particularistic ways of life.[40] However, the complete victory of this market utopia of universal equivalence was contested by the counterbalancing institutionalisation of science and democracy. In the mutual conflicts of these three logics, science confirmed its position as the dominant worldview. Whereas the institutions of democracy delimit the *imperium* of the market, science has the capacity to actually *intrude* into the logic of the market itself. Heller argues that the early expansion of the market is not to be explained by mere egoistic motivations. Rather it was the spirit of science and the implementation of new technological developments that gave the market its early modern thrust.[41]

Science demonstrates the same intrusive capacity in relation to democracy. Weber amply demonstrated the indispensable role of efficient organisation in the politics of mass society. The proliferation of bureaucracy as an institutional support and structural principle of modern democratic parties reveals the internal tensions inherent in the modernity project. The institutionalisation of a politics of freedom in modernity has paradoxically also seen the rise of the expert, whose role has enlarged in an increasingly complex and dynamic society in which the most important decisions require speed and specialised knowledge. But the consequences of such developments threaten the very substance of democracy.[42] The potential and the achievement of science are clearly Janus faced. Heller insists that people employed in rational–bureaucratic institutions 'cannot learn to practice democratic procedures and cannot channel the practice of these procedures into other everyday activities already deeply permeated by science'.[43] The specialist may command expert knowledge, but her survival largely depends on the observance of the norms and rules of the institution. Even the oscillating switch from the norms and rules of the institution to those of everyday life and vice versa is normally pragmatic rather than practical, and typically does not require selective evaluation and conscious selection. With the increasing impact of institutions on everyday life and on the human as a whole comes the danger of increasing conformity and uncritical acceptance of authoritative rules and norms. This general claim about the anti-democratic ethos of institutional life will be treated more fully in Heller's ethics.

CULTURAL OBJECTIVATION AND THE RATIONALITY OF INTELLECT

The general accessibility of the sphere of cultural objectivations is one of the essential characteristics of modernity. This sphere contains utopian forms of life that have critical potential when opposed to real life. For Heller, the unleashing of this critical potential on a mass scale signifies the unstable equilibrium of the social structures of modernity. It is also the precondition for the shift between *rationality of reason* and *rationality of intellect*. However, the suspension of everyday attitudes that comes with elevation to the sphere of cultural objectivations is not identical to the exercise of rationality of intellect.[44] The suspension of the *rationality of reason* does liberate impulses and subjective potentials that remained inexpressible within existing norms and rules. As these impulses are both intellectual and emotional, their release brings both satisfaction and happiness, deriving from the fact that living to the utmost is always pleasurable. The routinisation of the activity of normal science cannot disguise the reality of the pleasure that reasserts itself in conditions of revolutionary science. According to Heller, this also accounts for the pluralism of the sphere of cultural objectivations.[45]

Elevation to the sphere of cultural objectivations may involve the pleasurable release from the norms and rules endorsed by the *rationality of reason*, but it does not mean the liberation from all norms and rules. We have already noted that each cultural objectivation is its own homogeneous medium with its own norms and rules. While the receptive subject moves in this medium, its norms and rules are simply taken for granted. Yet free movement within these homogeneous media requires more than repetitive thinking: it demands a higher proportion of imagination and fantasy. The subject's elevation to the sphere of culture allows the *rationality of intellect* to access critical norms and, in more dynamic societies, to question the norms and rules of one cultural objectivation from the standpoint of another.[46] While philosophy is, for Heller, the rationality of intellect incarnate, she also suggests that rationality of intellect is just as perennial as the curiosity of the child. It is just as universal as the reason that could only fulfil its societal function of primary socialisation by extinguishing the wonder that would not cease from questioning. For her, this is equivalent to the proposition that all cultures possess practical reason *in nuce.*[47]

Heller's consistent strategy in this reconstruction of the conception of rationality is a Marxian-inspired *de-reification* which contests the so-called 'vivisection' of rationality in order to relocate the category in everyday life. The first leg of the strategy involves reconnecting the origins of this notion to the life-world of the human-as-a-whole and the dialectics of the two universal spheres of objectivation. The second leg follows the specialist human in the institutional sphere and the transformations linked to the rise of modernity. Here the focus is historical rationalisation and the impact of this project on human wholeness and the life-world. The last leg turns finally to the question of human wholeness: the meaning and prospects of such a category and its implications for the notion of rationality.

We have already seen that Heller refuses to hypothesise even the highest expressions of reason. The *rationality of intellect* is no special mental ability but an empirical universal, like childish curiosity. It would be a mistake to forget its perpetual ties to the more mundane *rationality of reason*. Reason and intellect are abilities that facilitate practical discrimination: an everyday activity that involves the *human-as-a-whole* in relation to the world as a whole. In this task, all human mental abilities have a role to play.[18] Heller applauds Arendt's and Castoriadis's recent efforts to bring the faculties of judgement and imagination back into vogue.[49] However, her main inspiration in this endeavour is again Aristotle. His identification of rationality with a form of life allowed for the inclusion of pre-rational aspects of the personality into an overarching conception of the good life. However, in the light of the modern reduction of rationality to a formal category and its identification with the rationalised institutions and the specialised person, this vision appears obsolete. The rational character today is equated with calculation and the pursuit of success: all other pre-and post-rational feelings are excluded.[50] The rise of science to become the dominant worldview has marginalised charisma and aura. Heller's previous analysis of colonisation indicated that she views this process of disenchantment as a gain. The diminution of human credulity opens up the possibility of individuals shaping their own ways of life in accord with consciously chosen values. However, from the perspective of human wholeness, these gains have been dearly bought. The expanded role of institutions and specialists have almost eliminated the contribution of everyday actors to science and demanded the accentuation of one-sided individual capacities. As a result, *minima ratio* does not feed back into human character.[51] Yet, the classical ideal of the harmonious development of all the individual's abilities remains close to Heller's heart. She defends the unity of reason and emotion as the best chance of developing a rich rationality. This idea of human wholeness only appears disruptive and irrational in the modern world of specialisation. This world identifies charisma with irrationalism. She offers an alternative Socratic view of charisma that locates it within the bounds of the prevailing rationality of reason.

We know only too well that a naive *rationality of intellect* can also be the bearer of irrationalism. Heller suggests that its seductions are best resisted if everyone works out a rational character for herself.[52] However, the general line of argument here seems to beg the question that she herself raises when she admits that the major obstacle to the resuscitation of the Aristotelian model of the rational life is the modern discrepancy between the rationality of reason and that of intellect.[53] What is really needed here is a demonstration of how the call for an individually tailored rational character can maintain its link with, and foundation in, the rationality of reason. As Heller sees it, the only concession modernity makes to human wholeness lies in the celebration of love. This celebration permits full reign to our pre-rational emotions and the individual is recognised by the beloved in his/her wholeness. Yet even such praise is only half-hearted when love is viewed as irrational. Although the 'blindness' of love is a well-worn cliché, Heller interprets it as the perception of potentialities in the place of actualities. It is recognition of a utopian *invisible wholeness*. While the dream of total recognition rarely comes to fruition, it suffuses lives with meaning, unless overtaken by the gradual erosion of routine.[54] It would be a mistake, however, to interpret Heller's defence of the substantive rationality of love as an endorsement of the intimate as a substitute for the good life.[55] Her vision of utopia refuses to be contained within such narrow confines.

Ostensibly, the very idea of a rational character seems at odds with Heller's desire to *contextualise* rationality. Moreover, when the general definition of rationality is reduced to 'acting according to reasons', the attribution of rationality to any institution or character seems illusory. Yet, when viewed from the contextualist perspective, rationality is an evaluative term, not a category of possession but one of relation.[56] Heller insists that this latter view is not inconsistent with the idea of a rational character. The latter is also comprehensively relational insofar as it covers all the actions taken by the subject and is conceived independently of the content of the norms and rules engaged. Here rationality is a quality of human character that is not at all dependent upon following rules.[57]

RATIONALITY AND THE WHOLE PERSON

We have already come across Heller's ideal–typical distinction between the particular and the individual. The former typically pursues her self-interest without self-reflection. Although this may occasionally lead to the transgression of existing norms and rules, these are not generally put into question. The individual, on the other hand, has a *reflective* relation to these norms and rules. This combines the *rationality of reason* with the *rationality of intellect*. The personality is the great beneficiary of the processes of rationalisation. This has augmented the general rationality of the life-world while also allowing for the development of a higher type of rational character. What this actually means is that the rational personality constructs her own idiosyncratic hierarchy amongst the existing norms and rules from the standpoint of certain values. But this does not mean that the personality simply observes self-given norms and rules; she must also employ her own good sense in a programme of testing and modification. The result is a real synthesis of subjectivity and intersubjectivity that bears the mark of the individual personality. Commitment to this idiosyncratic hierarchy requires as much repudiation of self-interest as the capacity for self-reflection allows.[58] While this notion of personality remains a *regulative idea*, it is not merely counterfactual. The rational character is the embodiment of a praxis that continuously homogenises the heterogeneous activities of the life-world from the perspective of an individual synthesis.[59] The actions of this personality spring from a character that they both express and reinforce. Non-rational impulses are consciously acknowledged and allowed free reign, as long as they do not infringe the self-chosen hierarchy of norms and rules. The rational person is characterised, not by the strength of character, but by self-reflectivity and the capacity to keep in balance the complete hierarchy of values to which she adheres.

What are the subjective conditions to be met if the rational character is to surmount the obstacles placed before it by modernity? Without ethical consensus, the rational character can only be an incontestable value if it is also a moral personality. Heller rejects the Habermasian equation of morality with the mere readiness for rational discourse. For Heller, it is the moral person who guarantees rational discussion.[60] Meeting the conditions of rational discourse requires the suspension of passions and interests as well as openness to others. This means that rational discourse itself is dependent upon other elements of morality that only come with the broader totality of the rational character.[61] This only vindicates the centrality of practical reason and its capacity for discrimination. The challenge of modernity requires the generalisation of this practical capacity in a dynamic form that facilitates individual, selective and critical application.[62]

Yet, as the capacity for self-rationalisation in modernity remains almost limitless, the primacy of practical reason remains an *empty* promise.[63] Modernity has given birth to a number of universal value ideas but no *universal moral norm*. Universal value ideas, such as freedom, have normative power for those who observe them from the standpoint of the rationality of intellect. However, as long as this perspective is opposed to, and contemptuous of, the rationality of reason, real universalisation is inconceivable.[64] Such corrosive scepticism is ultimately destructive, because it denies even provisional foundations. Here Heller anticipates what will become her fundamental critique of naive postmodernism. By contrast, the rational character possesses broader moral qualities that promote mutual respect and dialogue in a way that allows the two rational standpoints to negotiate beyond the impasse of an empty practical reason. This again brings into play Heller's incipient theory of modernity. The failing power of practical reason is indicative of a modern way of life that resists normative claims. In a climate of general scepticism and dissatisfaction, the modern person has become both more individualistic and more conformist, in the sense of other-directed.[65] This is evidence that in our age the *rationality of reason* lacks the authority to stabilise character. On the other hand, the *rationality of intellect* is too sceptical to make good this lack. Only the rational character reconciles the two rationalities under the guidance of the intellect. The *rational personality* as a synthesis of the social and the individual is both attuned to the widespread rationalism of our time and able to combat tendencies to other-directedness, egoism and the retreat to pre-modern conventional norms and rules.[66]

Clearly, Heller's rational character is merely a *normative solution* to the modern fragmentation of reason. Its evocation has practical intent but lacks the immanent power to transform reality.[67] Not content with evoking her own normative vision of the rational character, she counsels the *conduct of life* we have encountered in her earlier work, both as a value in itself and as a viable option when the good life is not available to all. She argues that the relevance of her general theory of rationality and the ethical model of the rational character depends on offering accommodation to contemporary individuals searching for an alternative to models of rational self-interest.[68]

A common objection to all this is that the ethics of 'dark times' is an ethics of escapism and acceptance. This is an ethics that perpetuates the illusion that social problems can be surmounted by individual ethical improvement. A convincing reply to this accusation hinges on an appreciation of the unprecedented character of the historical conditions that make the *conduct of life* relevant to contemporary modernity. This option can be justified if external conditions are especially inhospitable. Without conceding the necessary escapist consequences of this ethics, Heller focuses on the positive reasons it is especially appropriate for contemporary life. What is most attractive is its commitment to personal autonomy, understood in terms that facilitate both the rational character and a democratic means of rational argument and persuasion. She also underscores the reliability and trustworthiness of the ethical subject whose deeds flow from their character. Finally, she aligns this personal freedom with the logic of democracy. While modernity has demolished the conditions that engendered social character types, it has been a fertile ground for the propagation of rationalism. The logics of both capitalism and democracy contributed to the substantive rationality that is the only social character type of the modern era. While capitalism produced rational egoism orientated to success, chance and external determination, it does not actualise the inner-directed person.[69] Only the democratic character is able to live up to this ideal. Not only do the goals, aims and actions of the democrat spring from her character; they are based on universal standards that this personality has adopted as her own. Conversely, a radical democracy based on the idea of the fulfilment of 'radical needs' will not be achieved without the inculcation of radically democratic personality patterns.[70] Heller concedes that in modern times this democratic character type is exceptional and that its wider propagation must necessarily be envisaged as a long process. However, she concludes that only this regulative idea will satisfy the demands of the homecoming of reason and the resuscitation of the promise of the whole person.

It is clear from this conclusion that Heller's abandonment of the Marxist philosophy of history had not dulled her appetite for utopian thinking and radical societal alternatives. The rational character envisaged above remains a utopian moment of a radical philosophy that still hopes in the early 1980s that the imminent contradictions of modernity might yet furnish enclaves for such types and thus prefigure alternatives to 'really existing socialism' and liberal democratic capitalism.

7
The Limits of Modern Justice

Heller opens her reflections on contemporary theories of justice with the proposition that in modernity the problem of justice is located precisely where political, social and moral philosophy meet.[1] In ancient times these three aspects of philosophy were unified in a single conception. In Plato's *Republic* the balance of the best society requires everybody to do only that task for which they are best fitted by nature; the resulting equilibrium was ideally mirrored in the individual personality, in which the other psychological powers accepted the governance of reason. Modernity, with its increasing societal differentiation, dissolves this unity, fragmenting the theoretical object into its components and generating an assortment of different paradigms and alternative solutions. Heller calls her study *Beyond Justice*. It amounts to a historical reflection on the tradition, while critically demarcating her own position from that of the dominant modern paradigms and emphasising the limits of modern understandings of justice. She stakes out her own position in relation to contemporary debates between communitarians and liberal rights theories, while also invoking the classical insight that the 'good life' is an integral moment of justice that challenges us to go beyond these limits.

The centrality of justice as a nexus between political, social and moral dimensions of philosophy is also registered in the position that this question holds in Heller's socio-political thought. Her own theoretical endeavours fall on both sides of contemporary debates over the question of justice. In order to connect her inchoate theory of modernity and her more explicit political essays with her abiding ideas in the domain of ethics and moral theory, she felt compelled to provide her own interpretation of the concept of justice. The main lines of this alternative project she calls an *incomplete* ethico-political theory of justice. She wants to underline the contingency of the modern condition, while providing a theory of justice that is universalist but non-foundationalist.[2]

THE HISTORICITY OF JUSTICE AND
ITS CONCEPTUAL FRAGMENTATION

In the first chapter of *Beyond Justice* Heller debates substantive issues
with some of the leading figures within the analytical tradition, without
explicitly questioning the limits of their framework. In the following
chapters she addresses these limits and explores the possibilities of
going 'beyond justice'. Her strategy is double fronted. Firstly, she
contextualises the formal question of justice by revealing the *historical
conditions* of its emergence. Secondly, she reintegrates the question
of justice into the wider canvas of the ethico-political *as a whole* and
attempts to redeem the claim that is central to her systematic ethical
writings. This is the belief that the contemporary reduction of ethics
to the question of justice is an impoverishment that leaves philosophy
with nothing to say about some of the most important dimensions of
human happiness.

Heller's strategy is to broaden the terms of the discussion. She
achieves this by introducing the distinction between *ethical* and *political*
concepts of justice. The foundation of the former is that the good
should be happy, while the latter finds it sufficient that obedience to a
political order of heterogeneous rules and norms does not require the
infringement of moral norms.[3] While it is possible that righteousness
be complemented by a political order, this is the absolute utopia:
an exception rather than the rule. The project of an ethico-political
order requires knowledge of the good. But because there are various
understandings of the good, a variety of ethico-political projects is
possible. This variety is a consequence of the historical dynamism that
undermined the classical ethico-political concept of justice.

Awareness of the absence of moral consensus in modernity has struck
philosophical observers from Hegel to MacIntyre. Early modern political
philosophy already presupposes this disintegration. To legislate for both
individual conscience and for the body politic, it becomes crucial to find
evidence in human nature for the particular good deduced as the end to
be realised. This supposed eternal human nature encompasses freedom
and reason; the aim was to derive goodness from one or the other or some
optimal combination of the two. But this solution entailed considerable
cost. Philosophy was now to be required to supply theoretically the
substantive goal that had previously existed as an actual life-world. As
this was clearly beyond its modest powers, philosophy was condemned
to reside in the misty realm of abstractions. Hegel made an iconoclastic
attempt to breech this confinement, but it was not really successful.[4]
For Heller, his synthesis represents the swansong of the ethico-political

concept of justice. Although he reconceptualises modern society as a trinity (family, civil society and state) whose dynamic trust came from civil society, the unity of the project falls to pieces, despite his designation of the state as a higher and more universal purpose. His tripartite concept of *Sittlichkeit* already acknowledged this process of fragmentation. Even resorting to a self-contained philosophy of history and resituating philosophy as the expression of an immanent rationality could not reverse this process; ultimately this only accentuated the difficulties accompanying the growing modern awareness of philosophy's own historicity. Hegel wants an ethico-political conception adequate to modernity yet anchored in historical reality. The former signified freedom and the latter *Sittlichkeit*.[5] Needless to say, the accusations of political conservatism and positivism that have dogged his philosophical reception bear witness to the opposite danger of conceding too much to reality and not enough to individual freedom.

Heller's interpretation of the Hegelian ethico-political concept of justice is nuanced but clear-sighted. Hegel's reconstruction is both 'for and against modernity'. His differentiated account demanded a reconfiguration of the main elements of the traditional concept of justice in a way that would reveal some of its clearest fault lines in the future. At the same time, he reinvoked the classical tradition as a warning against some of the worse excesses of modernity. Yet, for all these theoretical achievements, the historical essence that he sought to express was already in dissolution and rapidly moving beyond his horizon.[6] The differentiation and divisions Hegel builds into the *Idée* of modernity are already anticipated by early developments in English moral philosophy. Like Marx, Heller views developments in English modernity as the historical pacesetter. Here the two parts of the old ethico-political project of justice, morality and socio-political justice, become separated and therefore transformed. The latter loses interest in the moral world and focuses more exclusively on individual rights, to the neglect of goodness. Its concern is retribution/ distribution, and justice is rapidly reduced to the question of fairness.[7] Without the diversion of the just city, moral theory concentrates on the subject and loses sight of its inter-subjective foundation. Fortunately, this concentration has definite limits: without general validity, morality easily collapses into taste. In modernity the only generality is universality. But this abstraction is not a social cluster and the problem of the subject and humankind having to coincide can be solved only by extreme formalisation that renders morality not just formalised but also procedural.[8]

In the domain of moral theory Heller sees only two candidates sufficiently well equipped to deal with all the problems associated with the fragmentation of the ethico-political concept of justice: Kantianism and utilitarianism. Of these, we know that she has a clear preference for Kant. His virtue consists in his determination not to reduce practical reason to calculation and to keep righteousness related to the postulate of the best possible moral world, with the idea of the 'good' remaining quite distinct from that of benefit.[9] For Kant, the only way to see righteousness achieved and the supreme moral and natural good unified was to have the moral law posit the supreme good. The moral law in the shape of the 'categorical imperative' must be given to nature.[10] Heller acknowledges the justice of the historical criticisms of Kant. Formulation of the categorical imperative as non-contradiction is redundant and empty. His rigorous dismissal of empirical nature is also incompatible with the pluralism of modern moral personality.[11] For all that, Heller views his solution as 'flawless' in its philosophical elegance and still the best on offer to the problems it addresses. The second formulation of Kant's imperative, 'that man must be treated as an end in himself', is, for her, the fundamental and unsurpassed maxim of all moral reckoning.[12]

Heller argues that Kant does not dismiss the formal concept of justice, but confines it to his doctrine of laws. His moral theory, on the other hand, is 'beyond justice'. It is addressed to all intelligible beings and thus presupposes an anthropological revolution. However, he did not dwell on the realisation of this revolution. He was content to posit it as a postulate of the best possible world. Later neither Marx nor Nietzsche could resist the temptation to attempt to realise this revolution in the flesh. For Marx, the liberation from alienation would institute a free society in which everyone was moral, whereas Nietzsche looked to the coming of the superman. Needless to say, both of these reconstructions fail. Neither the elimination of human social suffering nor the liberation of humanity from ascetic morality is the dawn of justice. Not surprisingly, Heller judges Marx's failure as a final signal of the failure of the ethico-political concept of justice and a warning against all attempts to revive it.[13]

DYNAMIC JUSTICE AND THE INCOMPLETE ETHICO-POLITICAL PROJECT

Heller does not recount the history of the ethico-political concept of justice only to record its ultimate collapse and to counsel against all proposals for resuscitation. Nor is she a Hegelian wanting to register the immanent progress of the concept of justice as it receives an increasingly adequate formulation. She sifts back through the debris and marginalia of the narrative of justice to find the model for her own attempt at a theory of justice. This is discovered in the largely neglected dialogue of Diderot, *Nameau's Nephew*. In this almost forgotten work the spirit of a new alternative ethico-political concept of justice is present. Its most striking characteristic is its *incompleteness*.

The attraction of this most idiosyncratic work lies in its renovation of the task of philosophy. Rather than provide 'solutions' that fail to explore the real depth of the problems they address, Diderot suggests that it is time for philosophy to live as a human being and citizen, to be content with raising questions and accepting contradictions resistant to actions and decisions.[14] Philosophy is not capable of providing solutions if life itself refuses to supply them with a solid basis. This is no counsel of despair in the face of intractable philosophical problems. On the contrary, Diderot encourages courageous persistence in addressing all issues without the will to premature foreclosure. While his efforts are inconclusive, he scrupulously rejects easy answers. His preference for the dialogical form expresses the desire to present problems as open-ended issues. However, it is vital that the idea of a solution remains as a regulative idea. We cannot accept the separation of theoretical from practical attitudes, but must live with the tension between them. Theoretical ambiguity is no excuse for failure to act as moral agents; nor does it permit the repudiation of the striving for the reunification of these aspects of reason.[15] This is the formulation of the first *deliberately incomplete* philosophical programme.

The idea of a deliberately incomplete philosophy taps into the social dynamism that has become one of the features of modernity. Diderot's emphasis on striving to transgress limits and his awareness that life had its own tempo that philosophy could not accelerate merely at will signal the possibility of an incomplete ethico-political concept of justice. Its core is a *dynamic* understanding of justice. This presupposes the distinction between *static* and *dynamic* justice. Heller derives her initial formal, *static* definition of justice from observation of social practice and its implicit critique of attempts to ground justice ontologically. She recognises that practices of inequality presuppose certain social conditions. However, assuming the high level of abstraction required by a formal concept of justice in general, her formulation is as follows: *the consistent and continuous application of the same norms and rules to each and every member of a social cluster to which the norms and rules apply.* Of course, it is always possible to question existing norms and rules. However, this very questioning assumes a standpoint beyond the horizon of static justice. The very idea of questioning norms and rules implies the idea of an alternative system whose *telos* would be a different configuration of social clusters. It implies the capacity to measure present norms and rules against overarching values of religious or secular provenance, which they may or may not meet. Yet this conceptual limitation of the notion of static justice points to a historical conditionedness of all such questioning. Although the history of dynamic justice predates modernity, only in the latter has dynamic justice permeated everyday attitudes and thinking. In the past, alternative values were only available from the experience of other societies or the values of religion or other cultural objectivations. In modernity, this sort of reflexivity has been generalised, so that it is regarded almost as an unconscious possession.[16]

In the case of static justice, dispute rages around questions of misapplication of rules and norms to particular social clusters or as a result of inconsistent application. However, static justice *never* brings the norms and rules of justice themselves into question. What makes justice dynamic is the questioning that always threatens to de-validate the reigning norms and rules. Sometimes this questioning results in validation but its essence is negation, since norms and rules can never be verified in a way that renders them immune from challenge.[17]

The claims of dynamic justice can be orientated using a variety of criteria. However, Heller maintains that all are ultimately reducible to substantive values. In modernity the ultimate substantive values are universal ones that can be appealed to either as principles or as goals.[18] We already know that Heller designates freedom and life as the highest value ideas of modernity. The universality of these values is asserted rather than derived. Having renounced the philosophy of history, and favouring contextualisation, Heller will increasingly argue that they have become empirical universals (that is, values that everyone agrees with and with which they cannot disagree). However, as Jean Cohen has remarked, it is difficult to imagine what this could mean in a world of religious fundamentalisms and various shades of totalitarianism.[19] The explanation seems to be double. Firstly, the self-acknowledged Eurocentric focus of Heller's thinking. More significantly, it seems that the universality of the idea of freedom is projected on to history as a residue of her theory of history. The problem is that these universal values are therefore arbitrarily asserted and dogmatically maintained.[20] The theoretical difficulty will become even greater as Heller moves closer to the pluralist, postmodern spirit.

In any case, Heller ultimately deduces the value of justice from these two value ideas. It might seem that prominent value ideas of modernity, such as equality and reason, also deserve a place as ultimate value ideas. However, Heller argues that the claim for equality is always in terms of some other thing. While this 'something' stands for many things, these are always expressible in terms of equality in freedom or life chances.[21] She concludes that equality is not an *independent universal value idea* but a condition for the complete realisation of the values of freedom and life.[22] That equality is *a condition* for the realisation of these values does not mean that it cannot come into conflict with these highest values. Precisely such conflicts undermined the proposal to raise equality to the highest value. When raised to the highest value, the claim for equality is self-contradictory and interpreted as 'factual' equality. Understood as the equality of the capacity to appropriate the instruments of cultural competence, this idea is perfectly acceptable. However, when interpreted to mean that all humans possess the same cognitive endowments or that they will make equal use of them, it contradicts the possibility of equality in freedom.[23]

Heller sees a real parallel in the tension between the ultimate value ideas of freedom and life, and the other signs of paradox and incompleteness that she views as integral to any fully adequate understanding of modernity. While there is no logical contradiction between the two universal value ideas, they invariably come into conflict in concrete situations. She goes so far as to claim that all value discussions that remain unsettled in modernity are reducible to those in which the values of freedom and life, or some of their interpretations, stand in irreconcilable struggle.[24] Faced with such choices, the actor has no alternative but to give priority to one or the other. Guided by *phronesis*, this is not a once and for all preference but a dilemma of constantly contesting options unavoidable in a dynamic society.

Dynamism also modifies the meaning of our sense of justice. In the context of static justice, this is understood as a moral sense orientated to questions of justice in the sense of *right application of norms and rules*. Of course, what we called in Chapter 6 the 'rationality of intellect' brings into play the potential to reject existing norms and rules from the perspective of an alternative value. Historically this is the result of the second major moral revolution, which saw conscience emerge as an internal authority sometimes even more compelling than the existing norms and rules.[25] This capacity to actualise this dynamic sense of justice depends on judgement, but this is not the equal endowment of all. However, modernity has created social conditions that provided the platform for the universalisation of this capacity.[26] No longer the preserve of cultural elites, the process of de-validation of existing norms and rules in contemporary society is an everyday occurrence.

In modernity the political and the social worlds are the main terrains of injustice. The clash of political and social convictions generates conflicts that are relieved either by force, compromise or argument. Few of these conflicts arise directly from ideas of justice. Rather, existing structures of human need generate claims for satisfaction that appeal to existing or alternative ideas of justice. In modernity these claims ultimately invoke the two ultimate universal value ideas of freedom and life, with equality serving as a *conditional value* and rationality as the *supreme procedural value*.[27] Political struggles tend to be orientated to the value of freedom, while social struggles tend to prioritise the value of life or life chances. The prospect of such conflicts being resolved by rational means depends upon the existence of norms and rules that allow conflict to be negotiated in this way.[28]

Heller's accomplishment so far is to construct a narrative of the demise of the classical ethico-political concept of justice, outline the distinction between *static* and *dynamic* justice and offer some insights into her alternative paradigm: the incomplete ethico-political concept of justice. In large measure, this deliberate call for 'incompleteness' is a response to the role that dynamism plays in contemporary society and an acknowledgement that the classical paradigm of the ethico-political concept of justice did not sufficiently assimilate awareness of dynamism into its own understanding. The following takes up this analysis of the fragmented corpus of the contemporary concept of justice and considers it from the standpoint of Heller's alternative proposal.

THE SCIENTIFISATION OF JUSTICE

In Heller's narrative, the ethico-political concept of justice succumbs to the strains imposed by the differentiating processes of modernity. The socio-political aspect of the justice question became emancipated from a moral perspective and addressed by a purely scientific understanding of society. This gave rise to a regional socio-political concept of justice in the last two centuries, culminating in the work of Rawls, Nozick and Dworkins. Heller argues that, notwithstanding the genuine insights of these works, justice cannot be restricted to matters of distribution and/or retribution.[29] Clearly the persistence of the inequalities of capitalism and the development of the 'dictatorship over needs' under a nominally Marxist project provided lessons that both complicate the picture and diminish the prospects of any purely socio-political concept of justice. In Heller's view, recent moves by the thinkers mentioned above to widen the socio-political paradigm is evidence of a crying need for a resuscitation of the ethico-political concept of justice along the incomplete lines she suggests.[30] This need is compounded by the ironical fact that today the very dynamism of modernity is taken for granted and treated in a flagrantly ahistorical fashion.[31] Heller underscores the fact that all contemporary theorists depart from, and presuppose, the structure of needs associated with Western man and the welfare state. Of course, the problems associated with this situation have become everywhere more obvious. While the socio-political concept of justice rests on these presuppositions, the inevitable tendency was not to expose them to real scrutiny.[32]

We now turn to Heller's examination of the constitutive components of the socio-political concept of justice. As the structure of needs associated with liberal democracy is addressed primarily under the topic of distribution, we shall confine our analysis to that topic.

Hume is credited as the founding father of the modern deflation of the concept of justice. Against both tradition and great early modern predecessors, he identified justice with the question of property distribution alone. Even more provocatively, he claimed that any interference with property rights was a suspension of justice for the sake of social utility.[33] In doing so he made explicit the fundamental issue that still dominates all contemporary discussion of distributive justice: this is the clash between the value ideas of freedom and life chances.[34] Heller maintains that the dominant liberal paradigm articulates this conflict in various versions. However, its biggest drawback is that the assumptions of the basic model are never questioned and the model itself is largely abstracted from broader ethico-political forms of life that may render other options or variations more attractive.[35]

The basic assumptions of the liberal model are well known: justice means equality understood as the equal distribution of life chances. This allows liberals to reject the proposition that all have equal needs, while asserting the need for equality of opportunity. While Heller accepts this interpretation of equality, she rejects the idea that this can be cashed out as equality of income.[36] This latter assumption forms a crucial element of what she calls the 'triadic' structure of the liberal model. This refers to its three key assumptions: the atomised individual as *competitor* and *receiver*, the government as *regulator* and money in the form of *income* and *services* that is paternally dispensed by the state and received by the needy individual atoms.[37] Heller maintains that the complete hegemony of this model over discussions of distribution narrows our understanding of key concepts in the articulation of life options and homogenises practical responses. Her strategy is conditioned by the need to contextualise distribution within a wider ethico-political way of life. Rejecting the possibilities of presenting either a *complete* ethico-political alternative or just another abstract model of distribution, she opts to challenge aspects of the triadic model and its various articulations in a way that points towards the outline of an *incomplete* utopia.

Acceptance of the goal of equality of life chances does not decide how the equality aimed at here is to be interpreted. Whether it is viewed in terms of 'satisfaction' or 'resources', problems abound.[38] Things do not improve when Heller explores the tensions between the supreme values of freedom and life in the triadic liberal model. The ideology of 'equality of opportunity' in liberal society masks a range of very awkward questions. It is not clear why differential social contribution should require monetary reward. Why reward natural aptitude rather than merit? Even more importantly, she points to the obvious fact that talent is not the principal determinant of remuneration in contemporary liberal societies. The reality is that making money and manoeuvring within institutional networks and constraints is the key to conventional 'success'. In contemporary society, the realisation of talent is conditioned by the choices that give access to wealth, power and fame. The best chance of talent actually being realised would require alternative social conditions in which the individual was provided with the greatest variety of potential developmental possibilities. In this regard, she critiques Rawls 'new utilitarianism', which would financially reward those who improved the lot of the worst off. This proposal simply perpetuates the liberal triadic model and fails to improve overall life chances. If success and failure continue to be measured and rewarded in terms of money, then only those talents facilitated by or reducible to monetarisation would be encouraged.[39]

Heller also rejects what she calls the fetishisation of talent. Nietzsche made us aware that developing endowments into talents can have mixed results for morality. Where the balance falls depends upon a range of other factors, such as will power, sacrifice, diligence and circumstances. Introducing a theme that will be crucial in working through her own existential ethics, she reminds us that the choice of talent often involves the sacrifice of moral conscience.[40] She acknowledges that even morality has a natural component and that virtue is, at least in part, a product of the genetic lottery.[41] However, she insists upon the norm that everyone should develop her *moral talent*.

The argument then moves to a frontal assault on the central assumptions of the triadic model. Realisation of the universal value idea of equal life chances for all requires neither the satisfaction of all needs nor an equal distribution of available resources.[42] What is required is *the satisfaction of all needs required for the cultivation of endowments into talents, unless their satisfaction reduces others to mere means*.[43] The principal condition for this realisation is the existence of a variety of forms of life and the freedom to choose and change. Heller underscores the radical pluralism at the heart of her utopia. This does not mandate a single way of life, but presupposes conditions for the realisation of all utopias.[44] Even ways of life based on the triadic model find a place in this proposal.

One of the keys to Heller's alternative model is the recognition that an equal start does not ensure the realisation of all talents. Not all are equally endowed and some talents require unequal expenditure of social resources. It is imperative to acknowledge these different endowments from the start. However, these should not be rewarded by higher incomes, as all talents are equally precious.[45] That income looms so large in these discussions demonstrates the *taken-for-granted* character of the structure of needs implicit to the triadic model. Once we break out of this circle and consider other structures of needs it becomes obvious that these would favour a model that affirms from the start *unequal distribution.*[46] Clearly for this alternative model to be just and fair it must be based not on atomised individuals but on communities. These would form particular ways of life and be based on communal ownership. At this point Heller is still searching for a third way between the liberal democratic welfare state and the dictatorship over needs. The political marginality of the demand for communal living in contemporary society is for her no argument against this proposal. Despite the hegemony of the structure of needs associated with the triadic model, she reminds us that need structures are dynamic and always changing. Moreover the alternative model of *initial inequality* is the ideal image of the current democratic family.[47] She also anticipates the objection that her model is based on the coercive normative potential of communitarianism. In her utopia, freedom remains the highest value idea of modernity; her aim is to reconcile universal values with communitarianism. The choice of a particular way of life does not exhaust the individual's right to change her mind and choice.[48] Nor is her commitment to the *initial inequality* model a repudiation of a concern for resource equality. While sceptical of the old socialist belief in the abolition of inheritance, she maintains that the idea of inheritance is not inconsistent with that of the continual redistribution of wealth. Indeed the realisation of all utopias presupposes the principles of redistribution.[49]

It is clear from the foregoing that Heller's critique of the triadic model is based on the desire to enhance both freedom and life chances. Her emphatic commitment to these values is evidence of her real affirmation of pluralism. Her continuing support of redistribution is very much linked to the social need to ensure that unique ways of life do not die out. There can be no general pattern of just distribution in regard to a way of life. Only the members of each community can determine for themselves a form of justice that is adequate to their needs.[50] This realisation undermines the universal aspirations of the triadic model and leaves the decision itself where it belongs: in the hands of the community members directly concerned.

RESUSCITATING THE
ETHICO-POLITICAL CONCEPT OF JUSTICE

We have now seen that for Heller both historical reconstruction and analytical analysis bring us back to the limits of contemporary socio-political concepts of justice and point towards the need for a new *incomplete* ethico-political notion of justice. The foundation of this project requires the rejection of the idea of a single best possible way of life, of an ideal pattern or of a single ethics.[51] This is the basis for Heller's distance from the communitarians. Her incomplete project includes a moment of universality that provides a normative foundation *allowing different ways of life to live together*. To those who have wanted to emphasise these differences, Heller maintains that this synthesis is not as difficult as it seems. While differences are real and not to be minimised, there are just as many common traditions, social needs, life experiences and affinities that provide the basis for shared normative foundations.[52]

Unlike the utopias of the past, this deliberately incomplete model forgoes the presuppositions of abundance or the perfection of human nature: the good life does not rest upon the realisation of either of these past hopes. Instead Heller turns to the Christian 'golden rule' of 'do unto others' as a normative foundation. The universalisation of this rule means the elimination of domination.[53] However, even this regulative 'golden rule' does not mean that a perfectly just society is either possible or desirable. In the contemporary epoch, in which dynamic justice has permeated the very fibre of social existence, the idea of justice becomes a receding chameleon as new dimensions of its realisation are put on the agenda.[54] A completely just society is impossible and undesirable; a dynamic society without injustice is absurd. Complete justice is static in the sense that the same norms would apply in all societies or multiple systems be uncontested by processes of delegitimisation. In either case the existence of dynamic justice would be at stake. Forfeiting the possibility of delegitimisation means that the universal value ideas of freedom and life forfeit the mechanism of their realisation. But not even an anthropological revolution could eliminate the need for justice.

The very idea of morality presupposes the existence of norms and rules and the possibility of wrongdoing.[55]

Heller identifies the project for an incomplete ethico-political concept of justice with the 'golden rule' that affirms both plurality and reciprocity. Clearly these guiding norms are neither irrationally chosen nor merely arbitrary.[56] Yet, while they are historical and located in specific traditions, they are contingent and not guaranteed by any teleological process. In the age of contingency there can be no other starting point than the *Sittlichkeit* of contemporary society. The chosen normative foundations are not arbitrary, because the values underlying them are already held by at least some people in contemporary societies. Heller wagers on the normative content of these convictions and extrapolates them into the future.[57] This wager is framed in value rational terms: it is grounded in good reasons.[58] Nevertheless, Heller refuses to equate this with certainty. We cannot know whether these values will remain relevant in the future.[59] Those who espouse a pluralist and symmetrical world without double standards advocate them. This is projected as the normative standard for the anticipated social cluster of humankind.[60] Nevertheless, Heller's frank admission as to the contingency of this project brings to the fore the tensions already encountered in her affirmation of universalism beyond historical teleology. In full consciousness, her synthesis occupies the grey area between the modern and the postmodern that will become the arena of the last phase of her work.

The great virtue of the incomplete ethico-political concept of justice, as Heller sees it, is the unity of both *universalising* and *de-universalising* moments.[61] It is this joint programme that constitutes the core of her *incomplete* concept of ethico-political justice and distinguishes it from her main contemporary competitors. Heller presents a detailed critique of both Rawls and Habermas. In her view, Rawls's *Theory of Justice* (1972) represents a contemporary attempt to rescue the complete ethico-political concept of justice.[62] He offers an idealised triadic model. As we have seen, Heller maintains that the cost of this concreteness is a *fundamentalist* universalisation of the modus operandi of a *particular way of life*: the triadic model. Habermas, on the other hand, has abandoned the complete ethico-political concept of justice. He argues for a *socio-political* conception of justice that accepts universalisation founded via a quasi-transcendental deduction from the conditions of argumentation as its *sole moral principle*. Heller certainly favours Habermas's discourse model over Rawls's revision of social contract theory. However, she still asserts that he cannot provide a complete normative foundation.[63] In order to highlight the strengths of Heller's position against these two much better-known alternatives it is worthwhile to briefly rehearse her main criticisms.

RAWLS AND HABERMAS

Rawls's quite self-conscious attempt to reconstruct social contract theory in an acceptable modern form, Heller argues, has only been a partial success. While the replacement of the 'state of nature' by the 'original position' serves to avoid false historical claims and ensure absolute impartiality in the choice of principles of justice, she asserts that it also undermines the very possibility of choice. It is impossible to choose, legislate or reason under a veil of ignorance.[64] Abstraction from position, interests and affiliations is a feasible fiction as it still leaves a core of individuality in values, commitments and ideas of the good. However, without these, all that remains is a vacuum that can only be filled by the theorist's own values, commitments and ideas of the good. Rawls commits the substitutionalist fallacy, which distorts all traditional social contract theory. In place of the unworkable fiction of the 'original position', Heller offers a discussion of values on the discourse model according to the principles of dynamic justice.[65]

A number of fundamental differences immediately distinguish Heller's proposal. She does not impose her own concrete model; nor does she disguise the parochial source of her own abstract universal ideals. She invites others committed to universalising the 'golden rule' to present their own social ideals, thus anticipating the realisation of a pluralist cultural universe committed to symmetrical reciprocity.[66] Nor is dynamic justice threatened by the fact that the 'golden rule' itself is not open to choice or disagreement. Heller argues that no other basis for just procedure is imaginable that would ensure the continuation of the process of validation. Furthermore it is precisely this agreement regarding higher values that enables a conclusive discussion over other values.[67] While this proposal exposes false concreteness, it also does not allow us to step outside of history. It recognises that dynamic justice is a relative latecomer on the historical scene and its generalisation into everyday practice is an achievement of modernity. In this sense, the maxims of both dynamic justice and value discourse are the products of modern historical consciousness.[68]

A key feature of the incomplete concept of justice is that it does not even pretend to offer *the* model of a just society. This results partly from belated recognition that not even a dynamic model of justice is able to foretell the future. It also follows from the fact that there may be various just systems that all meet the normative standards but in *quite different ways.* Heller's discourse model builds in this insight at the most fundamental level. It allows dialogue participants to find their own solution(s) without the imposition of a single vision.[69] Moreover, commitment to this just procedure does not entail any concrete norms: only that the norms arrived at are valid. Dynamic justice is no threat to stability when it is anchored procedurally in communal *Sittlichkeit*.[70] Unlike the problem of 'tacit consent' that haunts social contract theory, the genuine value discussion assumed by the discourse model issues explicitly in the promise of real consent.[71]

Clearly Heller endorses Habermas's basic theoretical framework. She accepts the procedure of discourse ethics as the *normative* foundation of an incomplete ethico-political concept of justice. The task is to provide a procedural, universalistic concept of justice that is neither empty nor reducible to a particular concept of the good. The clear advantage of the discourse model is its elimination of substitutionalism in favour of allowing the participants themselves to determine their own principles of justice through rational discourse. However, this basic agreement still allows a dispute with Habermas regarding the adequacy of his formulation of the normative foundations of justice.[72]

In his version, the possibility of consensus on norms resides in a discourse guided by the principle of *universalisation*. While sharing allegiance to this principle allows participants in discourse, at least ideally, to come to a true consensus, it also compels Habermas to restrict factual universality to matters that can be settled in the interest of all. In other words, he reduces morality to the principle of justice.[73] Heller contends that the principle of justice is neither a pure moral principle nor the basis for a complete normative foundation. While justice incorporates a moral aspect, its concern with interests and consequences means it is not purely moral. Furthermore, she insists that morality cannot be grounded on a single moral principle. She maintains that Kant's attempt to achieve this with the principle of universalisation fails because the idea of non-contradiction does not actually provide us with maxims of action. Similar objections dog Habermas. To avoid imposing the norms of his own culture, his principle of universalisation remains completely formal. Yet without normative content, this principle is unable to provide any moral guidance.[74] As Heller views it, the principle of universalisation serves well as a test of social and political norms. As such, its aim is solely will formation: consensus and not moral rightness becomes the sole criterion of rightness. We are left with no criteria for gauging the moral quality of the consensus.[75]

This consequence would appear to undermine the cognitivist aspirations of Habermas's own moral theory. The will is directly subordinate to interests and needs. However, the discussion of needs can never be conclusive, because one need is justified by another need in what appears to be a vicious regress.[76] Moreover, Heller maintains that if the notion of 'equality of life chances is taken seriously, we are forced to acknowledge that all needs require equal recognition. Yet, human needs are not "natural entities" but conditioned by values and norms.'[77] While the discussion of needs appears to meet its limit in their mere facticity, the values informing them are open to rational dialogue. Whereas needs are embedded in concrete structures that are strictly individual, value discourse permits a cognitive process in which the truth or rightness of values is tested by rational argumentation.[78] At this point, Heller also finds the ingredients of a more adequate solution. The only outcome of a dialogue about needs and interests is rational compromise, not consensus. The latter is differentiated from the former by the fact that participants in a value discussion have freely endorsed a shared value as supreme and thus given it a self-evident normative power that is beyond reasoning. When they determine that contesting values are either true (or false) because they relate to the supreme value without contradiction or are interpretations of that value (or not), then consensus is attained.[79]

The espousal of the universalisation principle as sole moral principle seems convincing, because Habermas already presupposes the other modern universal value ideas. Yet if we completely abstract from these silent presuppositions, it quickly becomes apparent that the principle of universalisation *alone* allows any norm to be approved as right and just.[80] The risk of such distortion can only be eliminated by amending the principle of universalisation so that consensus is explicitly extended to the proposition that such a valid norm would at the same time actualise the universal values of freedom and/or life.[81] Furthermore, it is clear that even amended in this way the principle of universalisation serves only as a normative principle for the governance of socio-political legislation. Discourse ethics becomes the central moral institution of the ethics of citizenship. However, this ethics is not confined to socio-political discourse.

This brings us back to Heller's initial claim that Habermas's principle of universalisation provides a basic but not *complete* normative foundation for the incomplete ethico-political concept of justice. This claim concerns an ambiguity in the very notion of universalisation itself.[82] The problem is that 'universal' can connote either a moral maxim that claims validity for *every human being* or it can signify the assent of a community or *all those effected by the specific norm*.[83] The thrust of this ambiguity is that the first connotation does not require the assent of all, because even those who might choose to transgress it still affirm its validity as a moral maxim. The second connotation implies no such demand on every human, but confines itself to a community of interested parties. Heller claims that Habermas typically raises genuine moral issues only to brush them aside as obstacles to the attainment of universal consensus.[84]

The confusion that results from this ambiguity and Habermas's desire to confine the whole moral terrain to the domain of justice is avoided only by redefining the principle of universalisability so that it connotes not every human being but only every human being to whom this issue is of concern.[85] This latter principle of universalisability, primarily concerned with guiding and testing, Heller calls the universal maxim of dynamic justice. What this means is simply a *procedure* grounded in the equity of symmetrical reciprocity. Heller views this as the counterpart of the maxim of justice that *no human should be treated as a mere means*. This maxim of justice entails the injunction to maximise freedom and life chances. Thus the *maxim of dynamic justice* draws its *moral right* from the universal maxim of justice. Clearly any norm or its interpretation that repudiates these implicit values must be rejected.[86] For Heller, to live in accord with the maxim of dynamic justice and its procedure is to aspire to the best of all possible socio-political worlds. Habermas is content to make this *regulative principle* the limit of his philosophical quest. Heller, on the other hand, still wants to salvage remnants of the complete ethico-political concept of justice. She is determined to save morality as a genuine topic for a *comprehensive* modern understanding of incomplete ethico-political justice.

Such a rescue attempt requires Heller to fill out the ethical dimension of her proposal for an *incomplete* ethico-political concept of justice. What is most characteristic of modernity is the way in which dynamic justice comes to permeate everyday life. This institutionalisation of dynamic justice narrows the gap between morality and *Sittlichkeit*.[87] When dynamic justice takes root in a community in this way, fundamental changes are evident. The most striking of these concern the authority of moral customs and the exclusivity of just procedure in respect to socio-political matters and the law. The hold of internal moral authority and just procedure becomes so strong that their infringement amounts to a moral transgression.[88] Nevertheless, unlike some of her postmodern contemporaries, Heller finds here not repression but an ethics of optimal freedom based on the absence of domination.

How pervasive this ethics becomes depends upon the extent to which just procedure is absorbed into the communal *Sittlichkeit*.[89] Even the character of justice as a virtue will be conditioned by the degree of this absorption. For Heller, the instantiated ideal is vital. She calls this Time One: its guiding maxim is: *recognition of all needs except those requiring the use of others as means.* Justice here is a cold virtue. It does not take sides for any need nor does it require that needs be either reflected upon or argued for.[90] All values connected to these needs can legitimately make a truth claim. Heller implicitly rejects the proposition that this value discourse secretly favours cultural elites. No special skill, training or professional knowledge is required to make claims. Rather than a refined discipline of experts, philosophical questioning is the schematic practice of naive childish questions; it requires nothing more than ordinary human rationality.[91] Yet while the acquisition of moral 'good sense' is an aspect of conventional socialisation, Heller acknowledges that it is not possessed by all to the same degree. Just procedure requires that the twin rationalities of reason and intellect merge.[92] This makes the employment of reason a moral matter involving the possibility of transgression. Good judgement is a cognitive virtue demanding self-discipline. What is required is impartiality, commitment to values, argumentative and applicative capacity. This judgement must be operative both at the level of value discussion and as *phronesis*.[93] Heller views such good judgement as the virtue of citizens; it is a facilitator that generates both the conditions for value diversity and the radical tolerance that allows the rational exploration of differences.[94] Nevertheless, sometimes even in ideal conditions consensus is impossible and, in such instances, we arrive at the limits of the virtue of citizenship.

It is clear from Heller's ideal treatment of the virtue of justice that much more is required than good judgement and citizenship when ideal conditions are absent. In these times before and after Time One, the good citizen requires the additional virtues that allow her to act *as if* just procedure were actualised. Conditions characterised by domination put more demands on the cognitive aspect of virtue and require that impartiality be replaced by solidarity.[95] The good person must be prepared to speak on behalf of the dominated. However, Heller insists that solidarity does not mean that 'the good' substitute her own values for those on whose behalf she speaks. Solidarity is a 'warm virtue' because its commitment to radical tolerance requires making efforts to achieve at least the recognition of the needs of the oppressed.[96] The cognitive dimension of this demand finds expression in what Heller calls the 'Cartesian moment'. This is not just a moment in time nor does it signify a retreat into the inner self. Heller views this as productive dissent based on uncompromised autonomy.[97] In contexts of domination, the good citizen must be prepared to challenge false consensus. Such a checking process need only be solitary when conditions make it impossible to find others willing or able to join in the activity of de-validation. Socratic self-knowledge avoids the pitfalls of introspection by anchoring discovery in deeds and in the mirror of others.[98] The intersubjective and active dimension becomes much more explicit when Heller incorporates civic courage as the principal virtue of citizenship. Speaking and acting within the public domain against domination and false consensus actualises the autonomy of the virtuous citizen.[99] Good citizens may be few but they constitute the synthesis of rational insight and radical needs. However, the existence of the good citizen is no guarantee that a just socio-political world will be realised. Heller has simply rearranged all the traditional ethico-political conceptions of justice and their contemporary fragments. They have been projected as an ideal of just procedure, the only one that conforms to the idea of humanity as an overarching social cluster and of a society based on symmetrical reciprocity.[100]

BEYOND JUSTICE

Let's momentarily recall Heller's original intentions. She views justice as a point of juncture between ethics and socio-political philosophy. She also intended to bring the weight of the classical legacy to bear on contemporary discussions that have abandoned the idea of justice as an integral whole. Heller wants to go beyond the limits of this contemporary consensus. She believes it a civic duty to question such a consensus and to explore its basis. She suggests that philosophy can still 'talk in a positive vein about the self, morality, ethics, emotions, creativity and reason'.[101] Positing the universality of the value ideas of modernity and, as we shall immediately see, leaving their realisation to the existential choices of contingent modern individuals, still leaves open fertile terrain for moral philosophy.[102] Beyond the good citizen and just procedure, lie the *good person* and the *good life*. As the latter will be dealt with in great depth in subsequent chapters, here we need only show how it fits into Heller's idea of an incomplete ethico-political concept of justice and expresses her desire for a more comprehensive philosophical treatment of justice.

In Heller's view the 'good life' is the starting point of moral philosophy and the 'decent person' is the subject of that life.[103] Both these are facilitated by just socio-political conditions, but are not reducible to them. The 'good life' has three constituent components. These are *goodness, transforming endowments into talents* and *deep personal attachments*.[104]

Morality is not a distinct sphere of life but a component of all forms of social integration: it is the internalised bonds between humans. These bonds can intensify or weaken and this will determine the strength of morals.[105] While Heller endorses MacIntyre's view of the modern decline in morality, she attributes this not to the incoherence of the contemporary moral vocabulary but to the changing character of social integration. Complex modern social differentiation has done away with shared meanings encompassing all activities and a hierarchy of ways of life.[106] The existence of highly differentiated moral norms, values and virtues, operating at distinct levels, means that there is no common interplay between these three constituents of normativity. Pluralisation generates a variety of forms of the good life.[107] The role of contemporary moral philosophy is neither to comment on the concrete properties of the 'good life' nor to prescribe what the individual should do. To uphold the modern value idea of freedom, morality must remain sufficiently abstract to avoid preaching and to leave motivation undecided.[108]

Allowing for this abstraction, Heller proposes a formal definition of 'goodness': the good person *'prefers to suffer injustice rather than commit it.'*[109] Such a negative definition says nothing concrete about a person's way of life and is compatible with a full range of different societies. However, Heller has no doubt that such 'good persons' exist. This is the foundation of her moral philosophy. The philosophical task is to outline the preconditions for the existence of good persons. These preconditions are summed up in the already familiar idea that the good person has a *conscious and self-conscious* relationship to the norms and values of their community.

The task of being such a person in modern pluralist conditions is complicated. The processes of differentiation have raised the profile of institutional life. Modern individuals spend large periods of their educational and employment lives in this context. They are required to follow institutional norms and rules they have not actually endorsed; nor are they normally encouraged to judge them against moral standards.[110] Simultaneously, modernity has largely released the individual from the grip of clusteral, hierarchical and taken-for-granted norms. Yet Heller is reluctant simply to equate this freedom of choice with rationality. If the latter is understood as 'rendering meaning to ones actions' by acting consistently in relation to certain values, she views the results as at least ambiguous.[111] The mere fact of choice does not mean that the options available are morally good: choices can be determined by a range of other factors, such as tastes, desires and interests. Furthermore, institutional existence often compels the individual to pursue goals rather than values. The modern individual is often quarantined in a moral vacuum.[112] To avoid this potential drift to increased irrationality of action, Heller offers her notion of the *existential choice*. This notion becomes the signature concept of Heller's ethics. This choice has potentially conflicting options corresponding to the first two components of the good life. The first concerns the individual's relation to morality and the second to her uniqueness.

The person who is able actually to check goal and actions against a value standard is one who has already adopted the moral point of view. This requires a prior choice between good and evil. Heller views this choice as an historical option made increasingly more available in modern conditions, in which the individual is less constrained by social and status affiliations.[113] While Heller's idea of the existential choice remains abstract, it does provide a substantive direction. The good person is committed to a range of bonds and the norms connected to them. As a first priority concerned only with moral maxims, she will contribute to the realisation of the best possible moral and socio-political worlds, be an enemy of domination and contribute to citizenship and value discourse.[114] With this first dimension of the existential choice of goodness, we have one aspect of the good life, but not the good life itself. Moral capacity is in large measure a negative element that resists the transgression of moral norms.[115] Clearly, however, in any understanding of the 'good life', positive virtuosity and accomplishment play at least as significant a part. All humans have a variety of endowments and not all of these are moral. If the 'good life' connotes human flourishing, it is essential to explore the full range of potentialities.

This element is captured in Heller's view that the second aspect of the 'good life' is the development of *endowments into talents*. On the whole, modern differentiated and functionalist society has improved the prospects for this self-realisation. Modernity has destroyed the social predestination of caste and estate. This is not to say there are no longer serious obstacles. Self-realisation still requires a complex division of labour and compels the individual to manoeuvre in institutions and make money.[116] Nevertheless, Heller views this moment of essential choice as the choice of 'difference' or 'of transforming contingency into destiny'. It involves the transformation of specific endowment into talents. Only this pole of existential choice fully elevates the distinctive capacities of the individual from the domain of contingency and nature into the realm of a distinctive ipseity and reflective developmental project.

Heller is a staunch defender of modern subjectivity. She rejects the view that 'selfhood' is nothing more than an expression of domination, repression and power. While not discounting the idea of repression in the constitution of the subject, she believes it an essential bearer of human freedom. The idea of releasing the self from normative regimes is not a journey into pleasure but into unfreedom.[117] The 'unmade self' of post-structuralism shares with the rational, self-interested and the aesthetic self, the mistaken conviction that there is 'no bond binding all (humans) together in the name of which you should say "no"'.[118] Heller refers to this bond as the moral standpoint that defines the existential choice of the decent person. The great danger of exploring non-moral endowments is the potentiality to homogenise the self in a way that loses sight of this ultimate moral bond.

Heller argues that the only way beyond this apparent dilemma is to embrace both moments of the existential choice. The individual must not only be prepared to adopt the moral point of view in choosing herself as a good person. With this moral confidence, it is also possible to navigate in the various subsystems and spheres of culture, testing their norms while, at the same time, fully developing individual talents. With this yardstick, individuals can act without viewing these spheres as embodiments of domination and power. That discourse can assume the form of domination does not mean that all cultural forms are inherently dominating. Forms can be appropriated and distinctive endowments transformed into talents without inevitably succumbing to the grip of domination.[119]

One of the most important aspects of the transformation of endowments into talents involves the unfolding of non-rational potentialities.[120] Heller's emphasis on essential difference facilitates the full exploration of human richness. This is a point of profound continuity with her early Marxist anthropological investigations and its celebration of human richness. This includes not just cognitive but also emotional and creative dimensions of the humanity that until recently have received little attention.[121] The importance of these dimensions is illustrated by the fact that Heller designates the development *of deep emotional attachments* as the third component of the good life. The corollary of a rigorous Enlightenment preference for *rational faculties* was the misconceived aim of *absolute freedom*. The emphasis placed on *autonomy* tended to eliminate *heteronomy*. Heller now views this ambition as overblown and dangerous. The desire to fortify self-reflection and bolster the capacity for both cognitive acuity and moral autonomy cannot be bought at the cost of stepping beyond the human condition.[122] This implies an acknowledgement of the fundamental intersubjectivity that makes us essentially social beings, and points to the increasing depth in Heller's humanism.

The good citizen gives to all other citizens the respect due to them in accord with the ties of symmetrical reciprocity. The good person extends beyond the limits of the political community to embrace the macrocosm of all others in *universal solidarity*.[123] The microcosmic dimension is found in deep emotional attachments, such as love. Such attachments confirm the *relative heteronomy* of the human condition in a special way. Here heteronomy is a *personal* choice bearing an emotional intensity that escapes social determination. Clearly emotional commitment to the degree of self-abandonment carries real risks. The regulative idea of personal attachment as pure mutuality is rarely actually attained or often only of short duration. Moreover, personal attachments always involve a degree of psychological subordination that easily passes over into the destruction of the good life.[124] Yet, as a crucial aspect of the good life, these personal attachments are worth the risk. No amount of public recognition is a substitute for love and its deep personal affirmation. To be the subject of such love does not make us better or freer individuals but it does make us more human. Therefore such private happiness must be viewed as a necessary constituent of the good life.[125] This choice is self-affirming as long as the object of love is not also endowed with a resultant social power or the degree of self-abandonment contravene morality.[126]

One of the things distinguishing the *incomplete* concept of justice from the *complete* is that the latter attempted to fuse the good life and justice into a meaningful synthesis. For the moderns, however, actualisation of capacities or success in love are purely private matters. Failure in these quests is viewed as a personal responsibility. Paradoxically, deregulation at the level of social mores has not seen the disappearance of other social pressures that now press upon the individual with a new intensity. Although Heller views goodness as the 'overarching' moment of the good life, because it reinforces the fundamental togetherness of its elements, the other constituent moments are not determined by it.[127] This relative independence ensures a plurality of incomparable 'good lives' each with their own particular flavour. The best possible socio-political world optimises plurality by enhancing freedom and a diverse variety of good ways of life, while excluding domination.[128] In doing so, it bolsters the conditions in which the good life is open to each and every one. However, it is not possible to give a general answer to the question of the good life or its exact relation to justice. In modernity it is not possible to be good without sometimes going beyond justice.[129] In a dynamic society, this limit is a challenge to the good to actualise a beyond that is an end in itself. Heller denies any novelty in her reflections on the good life. This is simply the reconstruction of the possibility of the contemporary good person.[130] This 'good life' is not to be grasped in terms of 'infinite progress'. The only mark of the 'beyond' is the contemporary good character striving to realise the 'good life' in her own unique way.

Heller's reflections on an *incomplete* conception of justice are underpinned by a new understanding of the dynamic of modernity. She charts the fortunes of the classical aspirations of justice, and its eventual fragmentation, into the partial domains familiar to contemporary analytic philosophy. But the contemporary discontent manifest at the edges of these fragments generates the need for a paradigm shift to an incomplete conception. This allows her to propose an alternative model that joins universal values with the *Sittlichkeit* of concrete community and the existential choice of contingent individuals. However, a certain tension exists between the components of the synthesis. Without the support of the philosophy of history, her universalism is reduced to a utopian aspiration relying on questionable premises or dogmatic assertion. At the same time, her moral theory abandons the heights of philosophical interpretation for the reality of everyday goodness. This radical reconciliation of philosophy with contingency puts a strain on her universal aspirations that cannot be easily ignored.

8
A New Theory of Modernity

When Heller finally sealed her breach with Marxism, she began a conscientious and systematic review of her earlier standpoint. We have seen how this renovation stimulated the quest for a new post-Marxist understanding of radical philosophy. The theoretical breach made in *A Radical Philosophy* and (along with Fehér and Markus) in *Dictatorship Over Needs*[1] was supplemented by Heller's forceful critique of philosophy of history in *A Theory of History*. In this wide-ranging treatment on various aspects of historiography, Part IV takes aim at the underlying form of historical consciousness and the assumptions that had sustained the dogmatic historical confidence of Marxism. Here Heller outlines her own alternative to the classical philosophy of history. This takes the shape of what she calls a 'theory of history'. Here she also presents the first remarks towards what will turn out to be an entirely new and comprehensive theory of modernity. If the general reassessment can be thought of as a coming to terms with her 'erstwhile politico-philosophical consciousness', this latter signified a breakthrough to a new critical understanding of the complex dynamics of the structures and experience of modern society.

FROM HISTORICAL MATERIALISM
TO RETHINKING MODERNITY

Throughout Heller's work, radical theoretical innovation is matched by a remarkable continuity. This is very apparent in her first thoughts on a new theory of modernity. Even at the point where she is about to formulate a whole constellation of new ideas that would finally lead her to reflective postmodernism, the continuities and links with central themes in her earlier Marxist work are clearly evident. This is most obvious if we take a look at the essays that first announced the rudiments of the new theory of modernity. Besides her brief comments on the multiple logics of modernity towards the end of *A Theory of History*, the key essays are 'Class, Modernity, Democracy' (1983), republished in *Eastern Left, Western Left: Totalitarianism, Freedom and Democracy*

(1986), and 'Dissatisfied Society', from *The Power of Shame: A Rational Perspective* (1985).[2] It is clear from the former that the idea of modernity as a dynamic symbiosis of multiple logics emerges directly out of a critique of conventional historical materialism and of the belief that the economic was determinant 'in the last instance'. We know from Heller's early work that one of the founding ideas of the Budapest School's 'Marx Renaissance' had been an emphatic resistance to the orthodox desire to allocate causal primacy to economic factors and to demote culture, ideology and consciousness to the status of epiphenomena. Yet this bold commitment to the humanist Marx that Lukács had rediscovered in *History and Class Consciousness* did not initially weaken Heller's allegiance to Marx's central diagnosis that the fate of modernity was largely to be decided by the struggle between capital and labour. However, this classical thesis could not survive the political experience of the members of the Budapest School. The tragic history of Soviet intervention, party purges and political domination, from the Budapest uprising to the invasion of Czechoslovakia, finally convinced Heller. The trajectory of modernity required a more complex model that did not reduce it to the unfolding of the productive forces conceived narrowly in terms of the logics of capitalism and industrialisation.

The Heller–Fehér reflections in 'Class, Modernity, Democracy' revolve around the proposition that no single logic of modernity, whether of capitalism, industrialisation or democracy, could determine the other two.[3] This constellation of logics is a 'conflict-ridden coexistence' of all three.[4] What's more, the authors also view the relation between capitalism and democracy as one of mutual interdependence, with each assisting in the creation of the other.[5] If this is true, then the monocausal conceptions of historical materialism simply fail to appreciate the real historical complexity of modernity. Of course, to fully elucidate this new set of propositions a great deal more needs to be said. For example, it is not yet quite clear what Heller means when she refers to 'logics' of modernity. Before going on to address this question, we explore more fully the reasoning that underlines the whole conception.

It is evident that despite their clear desire to break with monocausal, economistic accounts of modernity, Heller and Fehér were at this early stage keen to preserve key conceptual links with their Marxist heritage. While they view the privileging of economic causation as merely an empty generalisation of capitalist conditions to the whole of history, they are not about to adopt the 'trendy' renunciation of the concept of class.[6] Instead they opt for E. P. Thompson's understanding of class as 'class in the making'. What is decisive for them in this view is that it underscores the emancipatory meaning of the concept. To speak of class is to evoke not economic determinism but the existence of freedom. Unlike the slave, who faces a world of unalterable dependence, unable to distinguish him/herself from nature, workers have typically demonstrated wilful opposition to reification[7]. This notion of class primarily draws attention to the conflictual character of history. Its value lies neither in its being some all-embracing feature of all societies nor a universal basis for the interpretation of all social phenomena.[8] The conflictual understanding of class presupposes an appreciation of the oppositional and resistive character of social dynamics and a commitment to radical action that initially survives Heller and Fehér's break with Marxism.[9] Furthermore, and more importantly, at this point they hold that it is precisely this dichotomous, conflictual character of socio-economic class which unifies all three elements of modernity and thereby guarantees the self-reproduction of modernity as an ensemble.[10] Even in a liberal democratic society, a specific form of economic domination characterised by classes still exists and this carries with it other political and non-political relations of social hierarchy and asymmetry. However, Heller and Fehér insist that class affiliation is not 'destiny' but a matter of more or fewer opportunities and chances. In modernity, the dichotomous ensemble of social classes emanates 'lifestyles' into the outer space of society. What is most decisive is the bus on which the particular individual alights. As they put it 'the abstract chance to get on a better bus is in principle constantly present, and, equally in principle, for everyone'.[11]

Just as orthodox Marxists have often tended to view the class character of modern bourgeois society as a constraining straitjacket that determines individual options, a similar tendency reduced politics to an epiphenomenon of economic power and interest. A crucial motivation behind the multiple logics model of modernity is clearly the will to resurrect the autonomy of politics and provide the project of democracy with a new status previously denied to it in the Marxist tradition. This is the corollary of the critique of monocausality. Rather than view the victory of powerful capitalist interests in political decisions as the necessary outcome of allegedly economic interests in the last instance, Heller and Fehér prefer to find the explanation of this influence in the general functions of the modern state that must ensure continued economic growth.[12] The idea that liberal democratic politics is a sham that serves only to advance the interests of a capitalist conspiracy ignores the fact that it is difficult or impossible to introduce policies that serve the interests of the bourgeoisie alone. To avoid social dysfunction, various forms of compromise must be built into policy decisions.[13] The genuine relative autonomy of the state and of politics in liberal democratic society exposes another failing of Marxism. Not only is the belief that one sociological perspective could provide a universal interest illusory; the exaggeration of the role of the proletariat in social transformation also blinded Marxist theory to the contribution of the overwhelming majority.[14]

What follows from this renewed interest in the dynamics of democratic politics is the need to raise its profile within a more comprehensive understanding of modernity. We have already mentioned the fact that Fehér and Heller draw particular attention to the reciprocal interdependence of democracy and capitalism at the historical origins of modernity. However, clearly a more pressing reason to evaluate the status of democracy came from reflection on the character of post-capitalist modernity. As already noted, the 'dictatorship over needs' is an idiosyncratic form of modernity: the logic of industrialisation had been fully emancipated without the discipline of capitalist markets and the potential for critique immanent in democracy. The resulting deformations, both economic and political, provided strong evidence that the full harvest of the richness of modernity required the symbiotic input of all three logics and excluded the absolute hegemony of any single one.

THE 'LOGICS' OF MODERNITY

Heller and Fehér's first thoughts on a theory of modernity makes it clear that the basic outlines of their model emerged out of a critique of the theory and politics of Marxism. The idea of a conflictual ensemble of multiple logics captures modernity as a dynamic and decentered totality characterised by pluralism and social contest around alternative options and future possibilities. To get a better idea of the specifics of this general model we need to return to the question of these logics and take a closer look at their initial interpretation.

The first articulation of the Heller's idea of 'logics of modernity' comes early in Part IV of *A Theory of History* (1982). There she designates three basic components of the modern age: civil society, capitalism and manufacturing industry. The genesis of 'History' involves the further development of these three components in their compounded and complex interaction. Each of these components is a basic form of existence that has an internal logic of its own. This means that each 'possess (its) own *dynamis* which is tendentially self-unfolding'.[15] This '*dynamis*' is not especially modern but is that of the forms of existence of every society.[16] Thus denizens of modernity have a consciousness of their own forms of social existence that, insofar as it is co-constitutive of this same existence, reinforces its dynamic power. Here we are not talking about any sort of necessity, in the sense of laws. Unsurprisingly, the students of Lukács view historical process not as natural law but as the product of action and conscious struggle. Social forms have an inherent weak *telos* that once in motion develops as a process of ongoing socio-ontological concretisation. In the course of this identity formation, new constituents of these social forms make their appearance and others are relegated or disappear. But those not deleted are preserved in the network of institutions, structures and action types.[17] For Heller, what is distinctively modern about this form of *dynamis* is that it is no longer simply *homogeneous*, but contradictory. No single logic dominates completely. This means that modernity bears *alternatives* that are carried by the social actors who embody the alternative logics of the same social system.[18] Thus the fate of the present to a large extent depends upon the actors who resolve these contradictions by temporarily favouring one of the logics, only to see tensions repeatedly re-emerge at different sites and in different subsystems.

The conflictual and complex interdependence of the modern symbiosis of multiple logics underscores the decentered character of modernity. Without a clearly distinguishable centre, modernity appears especially opaque and it is difficult for social actors to locate the source of problems and allocate responsibilities. The emphasis on alternatives, uncertainty and choice allows us to recognise both new threats and political options while discarding the one-dimensional myths, such as that of the 'fully administered society', which had deformed previous attempts to capture the essence of modernity.

If modernity is a symbiosis, does it make any sense to speak of these 'logics' as separable and distinct? It should already be clear that 'logics' as 'forms of existence' have both institutional and conscious moments. Each logic also has its origins in the historical legacy of European civilisation. Wealth, technology and statecraft are the historical elements of the logics of capitalism, industrialisation and democracy. In Heller's initial account, 'civil society' is viewed as the historical source of both democracy and the universalised market. These early formulations are marred by a certain conceptual indeterminacy that is confusing. As civil society is the historical site of the origin of both capitalist relations and the discourse of public happiness, it is easy to view it as the source of both these logics. This also seems less problematic than deriving democracy from statecraft. Clearly the translation of statecraft into democracy is rather one-sided. After all, European statecraft it not without political ambiguities; it engendered modern totalitarianism as well as contemporary liberal democracy. In this respect the link between civil society and democracy, if not automatic, is less problematic. Ultimately these two derivations are probably quite compatible. If one understands 'statecraft' as something more than the technical skill of holding on to power, and 'governing' as having a democratic dimension, then clearly civil society is the early modern home of democratic innovation and practice. However, this is not the end of conceptual ambiguity. At another point Heller defines the logic of industrialisation in the following terms: 'the limitation of the market through the centralisation of the allocation of resources by the state'.[19] This definition reflects the Budapest School view of the Soviet 'dictatorship over needs' as a unique form of modernity under the exclusive domination of the logic of industrialisation. Somewhat later, Heller will attempt to understand this same 'logic' of industrialisation purely in terms of the developmental tendencies of technology. This seems like another discrepancy. It may be true that state domination allows for a more uninhibited unfolding of technological logic, unimpeded by the constraints of the market or democratic resistance. Yet it could just as easily be said that the state could inhibit a purely technological unfolding if this was directly against the perceived political interests of the state.

One finds similar conceptual ambiguities in the Heller–Fehér reading of the 'logic' of capitalism. In early formulations, this logic is defined in terms of the universalisation of the market, whereas later it will be accounted for in terms of the increasingly pervasive functional division of labour.[20] While commodification and functionalisation are closely related historically, these two definitions are not the same; such conceptual slippage betrays the difficulty of completely separating these 'logics' and distinguishing what each entails and excludes. Notwithstanding the difficulties in formulation, it is easy to see why such importance was placed on the question of separability. From the Budapest perspective, the separability thesis supported the interpretation of the Soviet Union as a distinctive form of modernity dominated by the logic of industrialisation. Heller and Fehér's insistence on the historical interdependence and complementarity of these 'logics', as well as on their antagonistic relations, did not obscure the fact that in this model each 'logic' represented a distinctive 'rationality', with its own inherent socio-political *telos*. It was this proposition that at that time sustained the Heller–Fehér position that the Soviet Union was both 'deformed' yet also a stable modern constellation that showed no signs of not being able to sustain itself for the foreseeable future. Yet there was a certain amount of contemporary empirical evidence that put this proposition in doubt. Virtually all societies into which capitalist markets and Western technology had been introduced as foreign imports, without the complementary development of democratic institutions, remained highly unstable. This suggests that these modernising logics are not as distinct and independent as the original thesis proposed. Of course, the *coup de grâce* for this thesis arrived with the collapse of 'really existing socialism' at the end of the 1980s. The original belief in a distinctive and relatively separable course of development for the 'dictatorship over needs' was based on a theoretical abstraction of the 'logic' of industrialisation from the context of European history, in which the three 'logics' had always been an interactive constellation.

An even more pressing question regarding the 'logics' of modernity arose in regard to the status of the 'logic' of democracy. The immediate issue was whether or not capitalism, industrialisation and democracy each manifested an independent 'logic' and whether this was so in the same sense? We have already seen that the idea of a 'logic' in Heller's sense involves the inherent reproductive dynamism of a 'form of life'. What this means in the case of the 'logic' of capitalism comes readily to mind. The market has its own immanent, quasi-automatic tendency to expand as an increasingly self-enclosed and self-unfolding system based on the accumulation of capital, class domination and inequality. Market institutions are both supported by, and generate, appropriate social imaginary forms. Together these drive the developmental dynamic of the logic of the market towards universality: the incorporation of previously alien social domains under these forms.[21] The 'logic' of industrialisation operates in an analogous way. Technological progress is similarly future-orientated and energised by the revolutionary problem-solving practice of science. In both cases, the imaginary forms of these 'logics' convey cumulative fantasy with a universalising tendency. Heller points to the expansionary dynamics of the market and monetarisation during the European Renaissance and how they disrupted the smooth functioning of *particularistic* life-worlds. They announced the passing of the isolated and parochial standards of the community and the modern reign of universal equivalence. The tendency towards universalisation in the economy is supplemented by complementary cultural shifts. Around this same time, cultural objectivations move in a similar direction towards universality. Both art and science are the products of universalisation.[22] The quest for beauty will now transcend the confines of estate and place. Science institutes a common medium of communication between all scientists irrespective of religious belief, race or ethnicity. All scientists must accept the pursuit of true knowledge as a universal value. The 'logics' of capitalism and science are morally indifferent. Each follows its own independence value – profit and truth – emancipated from alien standards. The dynamism of these logics is also aggressive: new territory is constantly appropriated and subordinated to the new authority of value or rationality. Yet the question arises as to the real independence of technology from other social processes.[23] This is especially so in regard to those societies Heller regards as dominated by the 'logic' of industrialisation. Clearly the role that political domination plays in the determination of overall social goals in these societies renders the notion of an independent 'logic' of technology problematic. But this problem is not confined merely to the 'dictatorship over needs'. Sociological evidence also suggests that even in capitalist societies, considerations of technological efficiency or cost are sometimes trumped by those of control in determining managerial decisions.

Heller argues that the same universalising tendency was also present in the logic of democracy. A common ancestry exists between science and democracy. It was philosophy, with its incessant attack on tradition and convention, that not only raised truth to the status of a universal value idea but also elevated the status of other values, such as freedom, humanity and personality.[24] Fuelled by this critical spirit of philosophy, early modern socio-political struggles breached hierarchical social arrangements by challenging the authority of existing privileges and their organic linkages to the 'natural' virtues of specific estates. As values such as freedom become more universalised, their emancipatory appeal and application is liberated from the confines of social hierarchy.[25] Clearly on this reading, the logic of democracy is also linked to a process of universalisation. It resides in the unfolding of the universal value ideas of freedom and equality, the political instantiation of human rights and resistance to monopolies of power.

It is this tendency towards universalisation that brings into play that other feature of the logics: their potential and real antagonism. Not only are the logics complementary, assisting each other to cultivate especially appropriate conditions for their own systemic expansion, but they are also conflicting and mutually checking. Each universalising dynamic ultimately collides and competes with the others. The capitalist market advances the values of freedom and equality behind the backs of actors, while universalising its own mechanisms, forms and relations. Yet the fullest expression of this tendency – the utopia of the self-regulating market – meets the resistance of the countervailing logics of democracy and industrialisation. The democratic struggles of the nineteenth century resisted the logic of the market, as did the logic of industrialisation, with its devotion to rationalisation, central planning and regulation. This phenomenon of mutual antagonism sometimes appears perverse. The increasing role of bureaucracy and expertise within everyday democratic politics is a commonplace. Equally, we find that today the *imperium* of scientific rationality has never been more under question from democratic forces.

Whatever the similarities between these allegedly universalising 'logics', democracy seems to lack the irresistibility of the market or of technological advance. It has clearly not had the same impact on everyday life as science.[26] Taking over the mantle of religion, science became the dominant worldview of modernity. Initially Heller identifies completely with the logic of democracy and its resistance to the imperialism of capitalism and industrialisation. She wants to redress the contemporary scene, in which democracy seems everywhere on the retreat against the combined cannibalising advances of these competing dynamics. However, her advocacy is tempered by the realisation that the other 'logics' make a crucial contribution to the vitality and equilibrium of modernity. The 'logic' of democracy is not even the sole bearer of emancipatory potential. With its corrosive impact on the traditional, rigidly hierarchical community and systematic propagation of the values of freedom and formal equality, the market struck an early historical blow for social emancipation. Similarly, the rise of the modern scientific worldview, with its explicit avoidance of normative restraints, released the pressure to internalise conventional norms and allowed the psychological space for modern subjects to assume real autonomy.[27]

While Heller argues convincingly for the historical contribution of democratic consciousness to the birth of the constellation of modernity, the physiognomy of the 'logic' of democracy was far from clear. The other 'logics' of modernity have a colonising potential that resides in systemic and quasi-automatic developmental tendencies. The democratic social imaginary possesses great power at particular historical junctures but it does not permeate everyday institutions and social relations with the same inexorability. The contemporary failure to export democracy to the Third World, along with capitalism and industrialisation, is proof enough of this. The problem seems to lie in the fact that the emancipatory values of the democratic tradition are congealed in the constitutional tradition and the institutional framework that instantiates them. In modernity, law and politics have become professionalised and no longer require a motivating ethos. The reality of existing democratic societies requires only certain behaviours, such as voting; but this is a poor school for firing the democratic imagination.[28] Democracy lacks the internal systematicity and dynamism of the market or technical progress. In trying to capture its specificity, Heller emphasises political experiment and learning. This only reinforces the fact that the prosperity and survival of democracy depend less on structural dynamics and more on invention and conscious propagation.

Obviously, experiments are just as likely to fail as to succeed. The mixed record of European history when it comes to democracy has already been mentioned. Heller readily acknowledges that totalitarianism is equally an offshoot of the Western cultural tradition. However, she remains reluctant to concede it equal standing in the modernity project. While such societies are essentially modern, they are 'failed experiments'. She resists the temptation to locate barbarism at the very heart of modernity. This underscores the 'reflective' aspect of her standpoint: at all costs she wants to avoid the naivety of a totalising critique of modern rationality.

While this refusal to take the option of total critique can be interpreted as a will to complex analysis, it has also been argued that the Heller–Fehér insistence on a tripartite logic model itself represents surrender to simplicity and arbitrariness. The initial burden of this criticism related to this theory's purported comprehensiveness. How does this model respond to the more complex phenomena of modernity, such as totalitarianism? Is it adequate to view this unprecedented system as merely a 'distortion' emerging from the triumphantly unified logics of capitalism and industrialisation?[29] Such questions provoke the suspicion that the tripartite model involves an arbitrary choice of the key elements of modernity. Amongst others, J. P. Arnason raised this charge. He questioned the adequacy of these factors as an explanatory *instrumentarium* and was especially keen to demonstrate the significance of nationalism and state formation in the understanding of modernity:

> While this view [the Heller–Fehér multiple 'logics'] is in principle less restrictive, it has so far not proved more receptive to the problematics of nationalism. The main reason is obvious: if the plurality of basic trends is reduced to three logics, the dynamics of state-formation and inter-state competition are thereby relegated at an even more derivative role. ... The implicit refusal to regard them as a fourth (and not necessarily the last) dimension also blocks the analysis of nationalism; although the relationship of the latter to the modern state is neither simple nor stable, it is ... a key element in a more complex structure.[30]

Arnason is surely correct to stress that nationalism has been, and continues to be, a weighty factor in the history of modernity. This is true despite the fact that in more recent times 'globalisation', and with it the crisis of the nation state, has come into prominence as one of the major trends of contemporary modernity.[31] Nationalism and ethnicity continue to play a prominent role in recent European history. The most obvious response to this objection is to underscore the contemporary perspectivism of Heller's model. She was not attempting to capture the elusive essence of modernity. She will later characterise this essence as 'inexhaustible'. As a Hungarian dissident writing in the early 1980s, she focused on the struggle for a free civil society and multi-party democracy. She was well aware of the significance of national struggles in the Soviet Union and Eastern Europe and criticised the old 'histomat' for its reductive treatment of nationalism.[32] Nevertheless, writing before the fragmentation of the Soviet system, nationalism did not appear to her as a first order issue for understanding contemporary modernity. This is the real reason why democracy and not nationalism attains the status of a 'logic' of modernity.

DISSATISFIED SOCIETY

The theoretical framework of multiple logics is not the only link between Heller's Marxist past and the theory of modernity that she begins to develop in the 1980s. Already her earlier work on 'radical needs' had argued that the capitalist logic of endlessly increasing quantitative needs engendered not only systemic dysfunction but also the tensions of qualitative demands and a potentially revolutionary dissatisfaction with the existing capitalist structure. One of the key insights driving the shift to the multiple-logics model was the recognition that modern Faustian man, with his insatiable needs, was not merely the product of capitalist logic. Radical needs were equally the outcome of the other logics of modernity: 'only the formally free individuals ... are capable of self-consciously positing their system of needs as infinite and insatiable'.[33] Here we see the organic link between Heller's earlier theory of radical needs and the leitmotif of 'dissatisfaction' that she comes to interpret as the defining existential experience of the denizens of modernity.

The theme of 'dissatisfaction' has a long history in classical social thought. Marx attributed it to commodity production; Weber located its sources in the Hydra's head of rationalisation. According to Heller, both these views were only partly correct. Their one-sidedness flowed from the failure to fully comprehend the multidimensionality of modernity.[34] In her understanding, this 'dissatisfaction' is not equivalent to the Marxian notion of alienation. She concedes that a structure of needs oriented mainly to quantitative satisfaction of 'wants' will manifest all the hallmarks of alienation.[35] She, nonetheless, argues that modern 'dissatisfaction' is not the sign of some systemic dysfunction that we might ultimately hope to remove or fix, but the motor of the very dynamic of the social arrangement that calls itself modernity. Modernity's dynamism is constituted by the fact that it generates more needs that it can possibly satisfy.[36] This 'dissatisfaction' is not eradicable; it is essential to the delicate balance of modernity. Just as Heller is determined to sacrifice the perspective of transcendence along with the Marxian philosophy of history, she must also forego the utopian Marxian desire for the end of contradiction and alienation. In Heller's vocabulary, 'dissatisfaction' signals not just the pain of unsatisfied needs but a positive social dynamic in which negation is the lifeblood of change.[37]

The democratic propagation of the modern universal value ideas of freedom and equality is also pivotal in feeding an increasingly unbridled discontent. Consequently, modernity expands the structure of human needs *as a whole*. Along with the thirst for consumption and the rationalism of science, the struggle for justice and self-determination fuels this restless dynamism. Heller makes the point that the structure of human needs is always symbolically articulated; that is, shaped by the reigning system of values. In modernity, the leading value ideas are universalised. This means that their content is no longer specified, concrete and limited. On the contrary, these value ideas remain abstract and open-ended. Lack of concrete specification here means without limitation. Every advance in the chosen direction becomes, in turn, merely another constraint to be overcome. Against the measure of the universal value, no partial realisation is adequate and the only result is the yawning abyss of denied fulfilment.[38] As Heller will put it later, the needs of moderns are insatiable because the reigning universal value ideas define them as such.[39] The essential point is that the 'denied' fulfilment is impersonal; it is inscribed in the very notion of accelerating movement towards the higher, better and more. The classic ideological expression of this insatiability is the modern idea of progress. This is a modern fantasy of incremental, ceaseless advance with momentary pause but no end.

Despite her personal nostalgia for the small community of friends and her willingness to find a place for it as a subordinate moment in modern conditions, Heller never bemoans the restless dynamism of modernity. The undeniable distortions and failures of this dynamism never diminish the fact that the universalisation of the value ideas of freedom and life are the *only* ethical progress achieved in the entire history of humanity.[40] This is the other side of 'reflective' rejection of totalising critique. She refuses to turn her back on what she judges to be the real emancipatory achievements of modernity. This commitment underwrites both the unique regulative humanitarianism of modernity and the modern individual's bold desire to assert her own unique individuality and be judged not by narrow provincial standards but only according to the universal values of humanity. Heller concedes that the demolition of the concrete and the limited meanings attached to particular ways of life impose heavy costs. At the same time, the new affirmation of the unique personality can degenerate into the mere quest for uniqueness as such. In this vein, Heller muses sardonically that no kind of power, wealth or fame is below the dignity of modern man.[41] In other words, the open-ended quest is never constrained by other normative limits or sense of discrimination; tycoons, criminals and sportsman share their moment of fame with thinkers, statesman and saints. The drive for success and celebrity is one of the outstanding characteristics of dissatisfied society. The undefined quest for achievement propels the modern individual into an unlimited future. Yet, by one of the many paradoxes that permeate the modern condition, ceaseless advance only leads to more generalised dissatisfaction. In any contest, not all competitors are winners and even those few cannot rest on their laurels. Neither repose nor contentment is a satisfying option when the spirit of modernity decrees innovation and striving as its essential meaning.

In Heller's earlier Marxist phase there are traces of the Frankfurt School thesis of the co-option of the Western working class by consumerism. Her growing reconciliation to modern 'dissatisfaction' does not mean that she now ignores the frequent vulgarity and emptiness of this ceaseless chase after success and celebrity. However, primarily, she wants to know how modern individuals can integrate the dynamism of modernity into an existentially satisfying life. One of the deepest impulses in Heller's philosophical personality is that she not only wants *to know* but she also wants to be able to *assist* the modern individual *practically* towards finding her own solution to this problem. The dissolution of tradition and the collapse of estatist ways of life place modern individuals before a historically unprecedented task. They face not only the age-old contingencies of genetics, time and place, but now also the radical open-ended possibilities of a social existence in which vocations and options are constrained but not decreed: to grasp the emancipatory possibilities of this moment and become a real personality without succumbing to insecurities and emptiness.[42] To see how this can be done, we shall have to await Heller's proposals in the second volume of her ethics.

Yet in the meantime it can be said that even the successful embrace of this challenge does not entirely eliminate the prevailing modern milieu of dissatisfaction; it serves only to inoculate the modern individual against the maelstrom of personal dissatisfaction. It is the antidote to the frequent discrepancy between modern expectations and experience, but it does not reconcile the individual to shortcomings in the general condition of the modern world. This latter point only reinforces Heller's insight into the depth and pervasiveness of modern dissatisfaction. Even rising standards of living and juster institutions cannot bridge the gap between expectations and experience. Between generations, expectations rise. Nothing can quell a dissatisfaction that is immanent in the very core of modern dynamism and openness.

REASSESSING CONSUMERISM

Reservations cling to Heller's analysis of the ideology of progress. However, these doubts are not so much the product of the, at that time, growing 'green' sensibility of environmentalists and conservationists, but point to the fact that this project of unlimited expansion represents one of the deepest problems of modernity.[43] This, for Heller, is the prospect of modernity dominated by the logics of capitalism and industrialisation. However, she again resists the temptation to indulge in a totalising critique of mass society. Rampant consumerism is a major problem with a variety of economic, moral and ecological implications. But it signifies neither the triumph of instrumental reason nor the contrived sedation of the entire population through a programme of 'false' manipulated and homogenised needs. Against such totalising and one-dimensional accounts, she argues that in fact mass society has resulted in an enormous pluralisation of needs, practices and tastes. The modern mass media must now appeal to an increasingly segmented market, in which the multitude of consumer options is embedded in a variety of lifestyles and subcultures that maximise the possibilities for individual choice and self-determination. While in no doubt that the depth and variety of these options could be increased by further democratisation of society beyond mere consumerism, Heller also repudiates the substitutionalist strategy, which assumes its own possession of a more enlightened perspective in order to dismiss consumerism as mass deception.

For the post-Marxist Heller, consumerism is the most democratic of the modern lusts. Unlike the thirst for wealth or power, which leads to the instrumental use of others as mere means, Heller argues that consumerism has no direct victims.[44] While acknowledging that it is in part sustained by the illusion of nefarious participation in exclusive circles and the heights of outstanding achievement, Heller now maintains that this is a harmless outlet through which all obtain some fulfilment of needs and identify with success. This softer attitude to consumerism is largely prompted by the key recognition that generalised 'dissatisfaction' operates as a compelling motivational force in modernity. Heller abandons the idea of the completely satisfied society.[45] Moderns never expect to be completely satisfied; the quest for personal happiness and achievement is not inconsistent with incomprehensibility of the idea that striving and seeking would cease. However, this affirmation of the intrinsic dynamism of modernity does not mean Heller provides an unqualified endorsement of the logics behind rampant consumerism. She recognises the moral implications of the consuming passion of modernity; it may be the least dangerous of the modern lusts, but it can, nonetheless, be infantile and irresponsible. Unconstrained consumption in the First World in the face of immiserating poverty and hunger in the Third reveals moral indifference and complacency.[46]

The residual ambiguity in Heller's attitude towards consumerism points to the antinomy lying at the very heart of the modern concept of progress. This idea incorporates an ensemble of contradictory values; not just the universal value ideas of freedom, equality and self-determination but also growth-orientated values like productivity, technological advance, increasing power and material wealth. Needless to say, this uneasy constellation bears an internal contradiction that expresses the competing logics of a conflictual and multidimensional modernity. Simultaneously, this complex dynamic produces *both* the indices of material progress and the modern moral sensitivity to the irrationality and inhumanity of ever-increasing growth for its own sake.[47]

Clearly the resulting paradoxes born from the idea of progress cannot be easily unravelled. We have already seen that Heller's theory of radical needs dispensed with the politically suspect strategy of imputing 'true' and 'false' needs to other historical actors. She introduced the distinction between 'wants' and 'needs' in order to preserve a non-ontological basis for discrimination. The needs that express the will to self-determination have *value priority* over mere 'wants' that are fulfilled by all the other satisfiers of growth. 'Needs' are orientated to the universal value ideas of modernity, such as freedom and life (understood as equal life chances), while 'wants', which are not always compatible with these leading universal value ideas, conform more to the category of lusts.[48] In our societies, 'wants' predominate over 'needs'; the great majority of modern individuals derive most of their satisfaction indirectly through the fulfilment of 'wants'. As we have seen in her treatment of consumerism, Heller has no desire to diminish the importance of 'wants'. However, 'needs' still have priority as an expression of self-determination. In the immediate post-Marxist phase, when Heller still entertained hopes for a self-managed democratic alternative to capitalism and 'the dictatorship over needs', she continued to assert the existence of needs for self-determination within the broad strata of the modern masses. However, these needs were typically latent and could not just be imputed to subordinate classes and groups by privileged ideologues or bureaucrats. On the contrary, such 'radical needs' would only emerge from the unrestrained democratic dialogue modelled on the normative ideal of Habermas's undistorted communication. While all the logics of modernity make a contribution to the production of satisfiers of self-determination, only the logic of democracy exclusively upholds and extends those needs directed at self-determination.[49] This logic transforms a given social context into one that is really an expression of the agents' freedom and desire for self-determination. Heller hoped the triumph of democratic values would gradually reorient consumption towards needs. Only this would dampen the ceaseless growth associated with the predominance of new technology and capitalist wants.

Clearly this optimistic scenario was rather too neat. The initial theory of radical needs had presupposed a Marxian reading of the immanent dynamics of bourgeois society. The abandonment of the philosophy of history rendered this dialectics problematic. When this is replaced by a posited 'logic' of democracy, this in turn required a rearticulation of the theory of radical needs. The distinction between consumerist 'wants' and the 'needs' for self-determination corresponds to the multiple-logics model, with the former aligned to the logics of capitalism and industrialisation and the latter to the logic of democracy. Yet the doubts that have already been raised in regard to the logic of democracy manifest themselves in similar suspicions as to the empirical prevalence and intensity of radical needs. Heller's initial commitment to the logic of democracy demands a similarly sympathetic reading of the prospects of radical needs.

Heller moves in this direction when she stresses the *global* character of the modern dynamism of needs. The process of the universalisation of values destroys all particularistic value systems. The quantitative orientation to the 'more', 'better' and 'success' is substituted for the qualitative one formerly associated with concrete communities and their orientation towards the good. However, aware that this transformation has eroded the virtues, Heller favours the scenario of a democratised future in which a variety of self-managed communities would create the required mediating norms.[50] By this means, the explosive tension between the industrial logic of growth and the democratic logic of autonomy can be moderated and contained. The potentially 'unlimited' character of the modern structure of needs orientated to universal values is thereby harmonised with diverse communities committed to a plurality of limited ways of life. As we have seen in Heller's attempted reconciliation of universalism and communitarianism in *Beyond Justice*, she favours the individual's right to choose the community most adequate to her personality and, if necessary, leave it. At the same time the variety of forms of life acts as an antidote to the cancerous growth of any single structure of needs.[51] Sensing the utopian symmetry of this solution, Heller calls this her 'pleasant dream'. She cannot predict its chances of realisation nor does she want to impose it on others who may have their own alternatives to the antinomies of progress. In this sense, her solution remains merely a theoretical utopia. But is it really a 'solution' at all?

A moment's reflection reveals that this dream 'solution' is more apparent than real. A well-known dilemma of modern anthropologists is that while they may participate in their subject's way of life, they can never completely share this 'closed' world. The moment of transcendence that consists in their own observer status cannot be expunged and necessarily impinges in the shape of their distance from the normative environment. A similar transcendence operates in Heller's dream communities. The universal perspective always has the upper hand and she would not want it any other way. However, it is hard not to believe that this awareness of the contingency and the ultimately voluntary character of the limited horizons impacts on their meaningfulness and stability. It is not surprising to find that this dream solution to the antinomies of progress faded almost as soon as it was articulated. This probably had less to do with these theoretical issues than with the dimming of the political prospects for any real socialist 'third way' after the demise of the 'dictatorship over needs'. Heller quickly moves on to her more sceptical postmodern phase, in which problems replace 'solutions'. From now on, the problem will be less focused on securing the victory of the logic of democracy than on keeping the 'pendulum' of modernity and its conflictual logics moving in a balanced way.

THE FUTURE OF DEMOCRACY

The key to understanding the shift in Heller's thinking lies in the need to bring her political vision into synchrony with the gist of the new decentered and 'dissatisfied' model of modernity. It follows from her theory of history that the future of modernity is uncertain and open-

ended. In the early phase of the modernity theory, Heller and Fehér
theorised this contradictory ensemble from the standpoint of its fragile,
but nevertheless real, emancipatory possibilities. Their initial hopes
rested with the logic of democracy, though they acknowledged that
the forces arraigned against it were considerable. Moreover, at this
time, Heller thought it highly unlikely that this unstable and explosive
ensemble would sustain its uneasy balance indefinitely. In the face of
this inherent instability, the real likelihood was that a single logic would
eventually overturn the equilibrium to establish its own domination.

> I have interpreted modern western society as a unique combination
> of three distinct logics: capitalism, industrialisation and democracy. I
> have also asserted that because these logics have become increasingly
> contradictory, one of the dynamics – and all three of them do exist
> – will limit the dynamics of the other two, and eventually establish
> itself as dominant. I do not pretend to know which of the three
> logics will in fact break through. It cannot be denied either that our
> history may end in the self-destruction of human culture and even
> of the human race.[52]

In a somewhat earlier companion analysis, they speculated about the
outlooks for the competing logics. In their view, capitalism possessed
the smallest long-term chance of global dominance. Marx's prediction
that capitalism would transform the entire world has been shown to be
exaggeration; only a minority of nations under the influence of previous
colonisation adopted it. However, more important from the standpoint
of prognosis was the belief that the more democratic capitalism becomes,
the less would it be able to meet the massive quantitative increase in
demands that it would generate. The existence of public forums, formal
individual rights and constitutionally recognised pluralism provides
political instruments that would overwhelm an economic system unable
to deliver satisfaction to this rising tide of needs.[53] Of course, at that
time there was plenty of evidence to support this thesis in the historical
evolution of capitalism. The contemporary liberal-democratic welfare
state represented a historic class compromise, with capitalism being
compelled to soften its edges under the electoral pressure of working-
class politics. It seemed that this sort of system adaptation was required
to ensure its continued survival. But it would be wrong to read this
historical evolution as involving some form of necessity. The partial
dismantling of the welfare state all over the Western world in the last
20 years demonstrates that there is no inevitability in the victory of the
forces of democracy and self-determination. The increased tensions of

a genuinely globalised economy create conditions of almost permanent crisis that further endanger this model. However, for Heller and Fehér, these reverses foreshadowed the demand for a new institutional basis incompatible with the capitalist nation state.[54]

The most extensive treatment of the question of democracy in this early phase of the theory of modernity is Heller's 'Past, Present and Future of Democracy'.[55] Not surprisingly for a socialist dissident, her point of departure is the civil liberties of modern liberal democracy. They are at the heart of the formal character of modern democracy: this entails a relative (never complete) separation of state and society, constitutional civil liberties, pluralism and contractual political representation. This arrangement is formal because the framework does not determine outcomes, is silent on economic structures and is therefore able to coexist with capitalism. Pluralism ensures the possibility of struggle for power without determining its contours, while civil liberties ensure the freedom of speech, association, belief and property without guaranteeing the effectivity of their use.[56] Rather than deplore the indeterminacy of this formal framework in relation to real outcomes, Heller celebrates it as the indispensable presupposition of democracy. Those like Marx, who favours substantial democracy in the shape of a totalising political reunification of society and the state, in fact surrendered democracy. Having fully absorbed the hard lessons of the 'dictatorship over needs', Heller prefers the in principle correctable 'errors' of the masses to the certainties of the 'only true science' reinforced by the prerogatives of absolute power.[57] In the context of formal democracy, the masses' false steps take place in a learning process in which the only true social objective is the one endorsed by the majority. For her, leftist radicalism can conceive transcendence of the present only in association with the power of the people and the formal democracy that guarantees their consultation and commitment. However, it is precisely the openness and indeterminacy of democracy that points to its fragility and the question of its survival.

Formal democracy is everywhere on the defensive, threatened both by the encirclement of anti-democratic regimes and by internal enemies. Heller sees these challenges to survival coming from multinational corporations, military establishments and internal security organisations.[58] While the former two do not in principle contradict the institutions of formal democracy, they both have agendas and even logics of their own that can come into conflict with democratic sentiment. In the light of more recent international events and the new preoccupation with internal security, we would do well to underline the hostility she reserves for the secret police. The very existence of these security organs is for reasons of principle in contradiction with formal democracy and therefore anti-democratic. This is why their advocates always have recourse not to democratic principles but to the 'emergency situation'. Heller allows that some emergency situations, such as war, may legitimate temporary infringements of the entitlements of formal democracy. However, she views the temptation to extend the emergency into a permanent condition as a pretext that abolishes the democracy in defence of which the security organs were created in the first place.[59] Unlike the police and the army, who defend the status quo within a legal framework, security organisations have goals and a modus operandi that must remain largely secret and hardly acknowledged by a democratic society.[60]

As if these menaces to formal democracy were not sufficient, Heller finds a paradox at the heart of formal democracy itself. This lies in the fact that formal democracy's silence on the question of economic relations allows the exercise of a capitalist right to private property that in practice excludes de facto the majority of the population from the full exercise of political power. As the latter always tends to be controlled or influenced by economic power, the majority find their political equality effectively reduced to inequality and subordination.[61] Heller has no illusions as to the obstacles confronting the contemporary democrat, but she does at this time at least see a theoretical way forward. The task is to resolve the paradox of formal democracy in a positive way that does not abolish the right to property and does not completely unify the society and state under an absolute political will. Her solution was a form of worker's self-management that generalised ownership without centralising it in the state. This proposal celebrates the right of everyone to property, without conceding the bourgeois right to private property that excludes the majority from the exercise of positive freedom. All members of a productive unit would thereby participate equally in determining the way of functioning, the objectives and the means of the institution concerned.[62] For Heller, this is a positive resolution of the paradox of formal democracy, because it signifies the abolition of the centralised economic power whether in the hands of a class or of the state. However, the impossibility in modern conditions of envisaging a serious social programme without the state means that the vital thing is to ensure the avoidance of political domination, by ensuring a system of representative contracts that guarantees the consultation of the democratic will of all. The state must be responsive to this will and leave space for the rights of citizens to autonomously exercise the possibilities of their private and public spheres.[63] This is not some random embellishment to a fully democratic society, but the vital complement to the workers' participation in all aspects of their enterprises.

A solution to the paradox of formal democracy is crucial in the light of the formidable threats confronting democracy both internally and externally. The fate of democracy largely depends upon its capacity to expand. A positive solution engenders confidence in those external observers who are unacquainted with democracy.

Of course, the idea that capitalism would be overwhelmed by its inability to meet its self-created needs and demands seems a little like wish-fulfilment. It is decidedly too like the Western version of orthodox Marxist crisis theory to be convincing. Moreover, as Heller now defines modernity in terms of its inherent dynamism and spirit of dissatisfaction, a rising tide of dissatisfaction does not necessarily have to be viewed as a radical destabilising force. In addition, the most striking aspect of the contemporary landscape of modernity, despite all the justified complaints against it, is the absence of a viable economic alternative to capitalism. Be that as it may, on the basis of this initial prognostication, the future of modernity is seen to lie in the domination of either the 'logic' of industrialisation or that of democracy. This former possibility signified the truly dark side of modernity. It could assume a range of totalitarian or authoritarian anti-democratic forms. That this was more than just a theoretical possibility, Heller knew well, both from her own experience and from the belief that 'the dictatorship over needs' was imperialistic and well able to reproduce itself indefinitely. On the other hand, the hopes invested in democracy appear endangered by the very fragility of its own 'logic'. By the middle of the 1980s Heller's vision of future self-managing democratic communities has the status only of a 'pleasant dream', without any thought of a concrete strategy for its realisation. Resigning from the business of predicting the future, she becomes increasingly reluctant to reduce the horizon of modernity to simple alternatives. After all, the modernity she now contemplates is dynamic, fluid, complex and open-ended. This means it can be the terrain neither of simple choices nor of assumed outcomes.

This uncertainty in respect to the future was finally compounded by the collapse of the 'dictatorship over needs'. From this time, the multiple logics of modernity take a subordinate position in Heller's thinking and attention shifts to the 'spirit' of modernity, its cultural antinomies and a critical analysis of the meaning of 'really existing' democracy:

> Even if modernity survives and symmetrical reciprocity takes democratic forms by opening up access to political decision making, action and rule by everyone concerned, the world could still end up

becoming spiritless, lacking in culture, void of subject and deprived of meaning.[64]

Somewhat anticipating Fukuyama in his widely read book *The End of History and the Last Man*, Heller quickly turns her attention to the apparent exhaustion of radical energies in liberal democratic society and its cultural diagnosis. She formulates the tension between the project of individual self-determination and even the prospect of egalitarian democracy as the 'disappearance of difference'. On the one hand, modernity cultivates and celebrates difference as no other age before it. Yet the very popularity of this lifestyle and its increasing universalisation lead, as Tocqueville foresaw, to mass uniformity and the disappearance of significant differences.[65] Nor is this uniformity simply a product of the combined transformative logics of capitalism and industrialisation. The beginning of the new critical horizon in the Heller–Fehér theory of modernity comes with a shift of focus to the logic of democracy and its contemporary instantiation. The language of modernity also engenders uniformity. Having given birth to its adequate political forms, the spirit of freedom can easily lose its enthusiasm. Without concretisation into forms of life and mediating community virtues, the democratic language of rights threatens to homogenise difference and to eliminate community and creative imagination.[66] Here the bluntness of the law and its stultifying effects on 'natural', communicative bonds that Habermas noted under the signature of 'juridification' begins to come into Heller's sights as the dangers of a social world entirely covered in prohibitions.[67]

Clearly this critique is no retreat from previous commitments to democracy and self-determination. But the lack of a plausible scenario for the radicalisation of the democratic component of liberal democratic society leaves a growing abyss between Heller's aspirations and existing society. The result is a heightened critical focus on the physiognomy of real democracy. Heller does not resile from questioning even the very logic of contemporary democracy. Like Habermas, she highlights the exhaustion of innovative cultural energies. But, for her, this is not the result of the historical obsolescence of productivist utopias. Now resituated in New York, amidst its racial, ethnic and cultural tensions, she sees the problem as an orgy of cultural pluralisation and relativism. Such radical innovation saps confidence in existing institutional forms. Political learning involves a careful balance between stability and innovation. Certain institutions and arrangements must have an untouchable legitimacy in order to secure the foundations for the flowering of future-orientated fantasy. However, a tension typically exists between these two requirements.[68] The danger is that radical pluralism and cultural relativism can sap cultural confidence and tip the balance against rational policy making.[69]

Such speculation on present 'discontents' has to be weighed against the fact that Heller still views liberal democracy as the only institutional arrangement invented by modernity capable of integrating cumulative reform and radical social imagination.[70] The twin threats of cultural fragmentation and social homogenisation cannot discount the deeply embedded nature of the logic of democracy in everyday life:

> Universal or quasi-universal imaginary institutions can serve as the frame of reference for all kinds of contestation. Men and women can thus politicise all issues that effect the conditions of the use of their political freedoms in non-political institutions as well as in daily life. Put briefly, the concretization of the universal values and other main effective political values proceed in modern societies at several levels, directly or indirectly, provided that there exists a public sphere to ensure and secure the contestation itself.[71]

It simply may be that the socio-cultural dynamics of modernity have supplied the logic of democracy with a new physiognomy. Under the aegis of democracy, politics no longer assumes the shape of the revolutionary eruptions. History is primarily social and cultural; revolutions on this plane are not cataclysmic but constantly happening. Contemporary feminism is the most decisive and paradigmatic example of modern social revolution.[72]

The main point here is that the fragility of the logic of modernity is in some very real sense offset by its pervasiveness. The process of democratisation proceeds in contestation and critique, amorphous struggles at all levels. From this perspective, the earlier view that democracy had 'very limited prospects' relates only to the utopian dream of a variety of self-managing democratic communities. But this dream now recedes, along with the idea of a 'satisfied society' that was already historically obsolete and no longer in tune with the essential dissatisfaction of modernity. In going on to fully elaborate her theory of modernity, Heller will now locate the prospects of modernity in the dispersed, informal and formal cross-currents of contemporary socio-political dynamism. This shift is expressed in the optimism that suffuses her philosophically inflected accounts of the modern everyday, in which dissatisfaction, dynamic justice and critique permeate quotidian life and come to exemplify critical philosophy in practice:

What hitherto has happened only in philosophy can and does now happen in political practice and life. Men and women constantly juxtapose Ought, that is, universal values, to Is, to their political and social institutions, which fail to match or live up to Ought. Men and women interpret and reinterpret those values in their daily practice and they go about using them as vehicles of critique and refutation, of realising philosophy, or philosophy's ultimate end.[73]

There can be no question that Heller's philosophically enhanced vision of the modern everyday will strike a chord of recognition in some. Yet it is important to consider whether this view can be sociologically substantiated, whether it really reflects the existential experience of most individuals in the contemporary modernity.

How are we to read Heller's reconsideration of the logic of democracy? Firstly, it can be viewed as a further move away from Marxism and her own earlier theory of 'total revolution'. She moves beyond revolutionary utopianism and makes her last stand in the decentred heart of the modern everyday. This is a call for pluralism and self-determination that still holds out emancipatory hopes. It still wants to stretch our boundaries beyond the narrow limits of reformist liberal democracy. Modern dynamism may generate homogeneity and a citizenry of client consumers, but it also has an emancipatory potential. However, the second reading, which is not inconsistent with this, interprets Heller's shift more sceptically. Heller was one of a generation of critical theorists who came to the conclusion that even a theory with practical intent cannot transform life.[74] She ultimately rejected the idea of immanent revolutionary dynamics. However, her exceedingly upbeat account of the modern everyday can appear as an unadorned ersatz for the old story of an ontological–historical guarantee. In the face of the real fragility of the logic of democracy and the apparent reluctance of real historical actors to take the historical task of self-determination, this interpretation of the modern everyday as philosophy in practice serves as a sort of mythic warrant of empirically feeble claims. This gentle optimism with respect to the democratic credentials of modernity is seductive, but hardly in keeping with a reflective postmodern stance that prides itself on measured scepticism.

9

The Ethical Imperative

From the beginning of her philosophical journey, ethics has been Heller's central preoccupation. We know that this concern is deeply anchored in her experience of the Holocaust. Her dissertation on the ethical views of Chernyshevsky was followed by a course of lectures on general ethics at the University of Budapest in 1958. These lectures finally appeared much later in somewhat modified version as *From Intention to Consequence* (1970). Her essay 'The Moral Mission of the Philosopher' from around this time still sees ethics as central to the understanding of philosophy. As Márkus has recognised, ethics stands at the heart of Heller's conception of the philosophical task and deeply informs her own philosophical persona.[1] While she does not prescribe virtues or actions,[2] a strong pedagogic voice inhabits all her writings. Her intent is to nurture sensitivity to the good in everyday life and sustain the classical philosophical unity of life and work. These preoccupations permeate her contributions to the Lukácsian programme for the 'Renaissance of Marx' and her reflections on the place of ethics in Marxism, discussed in Chapter 1. Her subsequent farewell to Marx was not a renunciation of the ethical perspective but its emancipation from the straitjacket of classical philosophy of history and the ethical compromises dictated by Marxist politics.

The ultimate result of all this ethical reflection was a multi-volume magnum opus written over the decade from the mid 1980s to the mid 1990s. However, this work should not be viewed as an entirely new venture. Certainly, Heller wants to give a final systematic shape to her ethical ideas. Yet the fundamental ideas of this project were taken over from the earlier Hungarian presentations.[3] This demonstrates the remarkable continuity of her ethical thinking across the first two phases of her work. Nevertheless, between volumes 2 and 3 she comes to feel that her systematic presentation was working against her efforts to capture the contingency that permeates modern ethical life. The final volume, *An Ethics of Personality* (1996), which we will discuss in Chapter 13, adopts the much more open-ended and fragmented form of lectures and dialogue. It is clearly situated on the postmodern terrain of a heightened sense of contingency and paradox. In this postmodern reflective mood, Heller takes up the challenge of reconciling ethics with the modern quest for freedom and authentic personality.

In the earlier volumes, Heller's point of departure is the existence of the good person. Acquaintance with 'goodness' is not an abstract philosophical problem but a familiar existential experience of everyday life. Heller presents the conceptual armoury for a contemporary ethics that accompanies the good person through the general moral dilemmas of individual conduct. As always, she is primarily concerned with everyday life, self-conscious ethical autonomy and responsibility. Every conceptual link in her account of modern morality, however, advances toward the central issue of contingency, the ambiguous potentialities of the modern condition and our increasing awareness of its ethical repercussions.

THE HISTORICITY OF MORALS
AND THE NEW CONTINGENCY

This comprehensive revision of the ethical terrain presupposes an acute awareness of its fundamental historicity. The times of mythical worldviews, legitimating a certain order of things and conveying an authoritative communal narrative, are past. The modern individual no longer believes in a hierarchy of norms and rules simply handed down authoritatively as the wisdom of the ages. The first great *structural revolution* in ethics delivered a distinctively subjective aspect of the individual's relationship to given norms and values in *conscience*. The modern beneficiaries of this evolution are now living through a *second revolution* that has shifted the balance between external and internal authority decisively towards the latter: this is manifest as tendencies towards pluralisation, universalisation and individualisation. Ethics has not reached the perilous condition supposed by MacIntyre. Elementary norms and rules are still passed on to the next generation through everyday socialisation.[4] No matter how chaotic the appearance of modern pluralist forms of life, the fundamental norms of civility are observed to a high degree. Without them the modern complex social world would hardly be able to function.

Heller concedes that historical evolution has dramatically impacted on both the physiognomy and the tasks of morals. Whereas Aristotle synthesised all of the elementary aspects of ethics into a comprehensive and balanced vision, modernity engenders differentiation of this whole into distinct questions defying harmonious synthesis.[5] The traditional domain of moral theory is divided into three. An interpretative question: What is morals? A normative question: What should we do? And finally, a pedagogic or therapeutic question: How can we live the good life? Since the early Enlightenment, the increasing interrogation of tradition has shifted the main focus to the interpretative aspect and a sceptical inquiry into the validity of norms. As a result, the questions of application and *paideia* have been eclipsed and, in some quarters, even excluded from moral theory altogether. While sharing many aspects of MacIntyre's diagnosis of contemporary moral theory, Heller takes issue with his view that the modern condition is one of disarray and decline. For her, the story of the second structural revolution in morals is charged with dialectic possibilities and still incomplete. Whether the result will be 'more sublime and less repressive' or will dismantle all previous moral achievements is still an open question.[6]

Without such a certain resolution, Heller attempts to provide a modern reflective answer to each of the differentiated questions of moral theory. She refuses either to inflate any single aspect or to unify them into a single theoretical proposal.[7] Most contemporary moral theory either complies with the wave of differentiation or pursues a Hegelian strategy of reunifying 'is' and 'ought'. For example, Habermas is located in the latter programme, but Heller maintains that his acknowledged concentration on the interpretative question leads to the detriment of the practical and pedagogic ones.[8] Her unique alternative strategy retains both the *comprehensiveness* and the *balance* of classical moral theory.

Achieving this without sacrificing differentiation requires that each moral question be given its due, while observing the complex interlinkages between them. This accounts for the trilogy format. Each book represents a full response to its respective question: What are morals? What should I do? How can the good life be led? She unites all three questions by viewing them as partial responses to the question: *Good people exist – how are they possible?* This is the fundamental question of moral theory. The existence of the 'good person' is both an *eternal truth* of everyday moral experience and the *presupposition of moral theory*. Without a few good persons, the ethical venture would make no sense.[9] Heller's proposal is to present theoretical, practical and existential–pedagogic answers to the reality of this existence.[10] However, the essential continuity and timelessness of this question should not obscure the *historicity of morals* and the need to pose this question anew in the specific conditions thrown up by modernity.

The unprecedented character of modernity brings us back to Heller's *second* structural revolution of morality. The trend towards pluralisation, universalisation and individualisation of morals represents a momentous change that has shifted the ethical balance decidedly in favour of internal authority. While the content of morals has always undergone historical change, an overarching continuity in values and virtues within traditions remained. Most striking in the modern moral condition is the erosion of the powers of tradition, community and moral consensus. The pre-modern philosopher invariably shared the moral universe of his addressees. But this bond can no longer be taken for granted. To be both comprehensive and concrete, moral philosophy must derive its authority from its addressees. The philosopher and the addressees share something. Yet in modernity the receptivity of an audience is ensured neither by cultural homogeneity or consensus of values. The tendencies towards pluralisation and individualisation represent a real challenge not only to *Sittlichkeit* but also to the reception of moral theory. We can no longer expect to find this elusive shared 'something' in membership of specific communities. Heller suggests that a substitute may be found in a specific aspect of the modern awareness of the human condition.

This is the historically unprecedented experience of feeling contingent not only in regard to circumstance of birth but also in respect of social station and vocation. Without a socially pre-patterned *telos*, the awareness of the utter accidentality of individual existence is revealed and accentuated. Beyond membership of any specific community, this *double contingency* provides the universal ground on the basis of which all modern individuals can understand each other: it is clearly a relation of symmetrical reciprocity.[11] Our shared predicament is equally a blessing and a curse: simultaneously a state of radical indeterminacy and of infinite possibility. Yet the awareness of the common condition is currently so abstract that contemporary philosophers must also be wary of its misuse. Without the crux of a philosophy of history that Heller consciously relinquished it cannot be known whether the whole world will become modern nor whether moral philosophy can in fact address itself to every human being.[12] With this important proviso, she wages on the existential–ontological conditions of modernity. Her aspiration is to address the question of goodness in a world conscious of its own contingency.

THE *INSTRUMENTARIUM* OF ETHICS

The first volume of Heller's trilogy, *General Ethics* (1988), is devoted to the interpretative question: What is ethics? All her historical and cultural scholarship is brought to bear in elucidating and defining the fundamental categories of ethics. Key concepts such as the human condition, *Sittlichkeit*, moral autonomy, responsibility, consequences and judgement are all re-examined and allotted their place within her categorical armoury. The analysis is both informed by the history of ethics and refracted through the prism of everyday modernity. This perspective comes into play immediately, with her discussion of the human condition. We saw earlier that the central focus of her Marxist work in the late 1960s was philosophical anthropology. The works on values, instincts, feelings, needs and history that we have outlined in Part I were contributions to this unfinished project. This is now finally abandoned. Under the auspices of Hannah Arendt, she opts for a new conceptual foundation to her ethics. The notion of the human condition is no mere synonym for human nature, but its explicit critique.

The concept of human nature is notoriously loose. Not only has it been interpreted in a variety of different, sometimes wholly contradictory, ways by alternative philosophical projects, but its metaphorical resonance also embraces entirely different readings. However, metaphorical confusion and vagueness is only part of the problem.[13] The notion of human nature elicits connotations of passivity associated with the idea of living in tune with a peaceful or conflictual nature. Investigation of 'nature of man' has diverted attention away from the *moral behaviour*. The notion of the 'human condition' is also not without it own metaphorical baggage, but Heller maintains that her own reading of it as an ontological background to investigation of the *possibility* of goodness makes it a more reliable metaphor.[14]

According to Heller, the newly born infant is neither 'nature' nor 'system' but an independent 'system' in its own right. As if to underscore her break with Marx, she stresses that humanisation has nothing to do with history.[15] As social beings, we are human from birth; from the beginning, social regulation takes priority and instincts are mere remnants. The infant is programmed for society and its condition of realisation is to be brought up in and by society. This achieves the dovetailing of genetic and social a priori that constitutes a unique personal history. Heller calls this 'dovetailing' of a prioris historicity: it signifies the constitution of a unique life narrative, the double contingency of conception and 'thrownness' transformed into a personal history. Historicity overcomes the potential hiatus confronted in the infinite variations of social possibility and the ineffable idiosyncrasy of the personal genetic a priori.[16]

The process of 'dovetailing' invariably involves conflict. Yet the absence of a harmonious fit is not tragic, but the very stuff of human life. When mobilised and played out in worldviews, this tension is the energy of cultural creation.[17] For Heller, the human condition is constituted by the following elements:

1. Social regulation displaces instincts.
2. Historicity is conceived as determination and self-determination.
3. Historicity also means living in tension.[18]

Unlike general theories of human nature in which the map of the self has a regulative status against which individuals may vary, this alternative model allows for personal variability in the quality, quantity and character of the tension. The latter varies across societies as does the mechanisms constructed to absorb it. Interestingly, the pendulum movement Heller identifies with modern dynamism would seem to be nothing more than the amplified reflex of this deeper existential tension.[19]

Human experience is the product of tensions expressed in the pendulum movement between the self and social regulation. This is not a matter of stark oppositions but the poles of co-constitution. The self is an irreducible ipseity born to self-awareness and privileged access that assures us we know ourselves better than anyone else does. However, the truth is that others know us better than we know ourselves; they see us in action and social relations. The necessary corrective to the self's sense of privilege is the knowledge that it is co-created by other selves in the form of recognition and shared evaluations. The techniques used to understand our own internal perceptions are socially constituted general tools.[20] This point is clarified by the distinction between *self-awareness* and *self-consciousness*. We are already familiar with Heller's early distinction between particularity and individuality. While self-awareness is a constant of the individual human life, *self-consciousness* is tied to a *double* quality form of self-reflection. This takes the self as an object of scrutiny and creates a depth that is a function of its guiding value perspective. Every society has a certain kind of 'alternation tolerance' that defines 'normalcy' in regard to the exploration of this internal depth. This is more liberal in complex modern societies but even this tolerance has limits and transgression leads to loss of recognition and meaning deficit.[21]

MEANING, NORMS AND RULES

As with her earlier defence of subjectivity, the centrality of social regulation to Heller's view of the human condition suggests the impossibility of a world without ethics. 'Having a world' presupposes rules and norms.[22] Our actions are meaningful because they express, and are governed by, a hierarchy of norms and rules. This hierarchy is embodied in worldviews that authorise and justify actions. Heller calls these worldviews 'historical consciousness': they make sense of, and legitimate, a particular order of things.[23]

This framework allows Heller to integrate moral change into the very heart of her theory of morals. In principle open to interpretation, in practice norms are embedded in a *Sittlichkeit* that constitutes the moral customs of the world in question.[24] The tension between the more abstract norms and their concretely instantiated rules is *implicit* in dynamic social practices. Under specific historical conditions, it can become *explicit*. Heller acknowledges that total critique would completely destroy a particular *Sittlichkeit*. Yet this cannot disguise the fact that moral customs are also instruments of domination. In all pre-modern societies, moral customs imply social stratification. The individual is judged only in terms of the norm clusters relevant to her social estate. By contrast, in modernity norms become abstract, and general norms like justice are formally applied to all members of a society. While trans-clusteral virtues often existed, only in modernity are the supreme moral norms and virtues disassociated from the highest social class. The tendency towards universal norms inevitably leeches out all substantive content and leads to extreme formalism. This process of differentiation of abstract from concrete *Sittlichkeit* is the precondition of our theoretical and critical relation to morality. It is also the only contradiction-free moral progress in the history of changing ethical substance.[25] It introduces a potentially critical perspective towards conventional general norms and opens the prospect of overcoming extreme ethnocentrism. Free reign is given to the universalisation of general norms while, simultaneously and in concert, discovering empirical universality amidst moral diversity.[26] The modern claim for the universality of some general norms presupposes the existence of at least some ethical constants.[27]

Much of the analysis in *General Ethics* centres around the issues raised by intensified processes of differentiation in modernity and their consequences for the traditional fabric and vocabulary of ethics. A striking instance is the modern emphasis on moral autonomy and individual responsibility. In traditional society, the individual may even be required to answer for the actions of relatives. Ethical freedom only emerges when norms and rules are no longer taken for granted but are open to moral deliberation. Similarly, moral autonomy is another product of the alleviation of this opaque conventional world. Heller distinguishes between the problems of free choice and of moral autonomy. Each of these problems turns on the question of free choice or determination; however, the former concerns actions while the latter refers to character. The problem of autonomy emerges with the birth of a distinctive moral perspective. The morally autonomous individual exemplifies 'double quality' self-reflection.[28] Individual behaviour is self-monitored not merely from the standpoint of concrete norms but also from the transcendent perspective of abstract norms and ideas. The transcendent perspective overrides all merely external determination.[29]

The historical emergence of moral autonomy is not an argument for the existence of *absolute* moral autonomy. Heller argues for a notion of relative moral autonomy. She reconciles her Marxian-inspired recognition of historical conditioning with her own lifelong rehabilitation of the need for individual choice and responsibility. Starting from the everyday experience of moral life, in which we advise, judge and encourage alternative courses of action and individual character changes within certain limits, she asserts that determinist accounts of morality are theoretically false and morally wrong.[30] So are theories of free choice that ignore the limited character of practical options. Rational choice theory commits a double error. It treats all choices as *equal* if they all have an identical structure and weight and it *neutralises* the character of the individual doing the choosing.[31] For Heller, individual choice remains the cornerstone of morality. But choice is generated not by lack of restrictions in any given situation but by *our* attitude towards them.

This defense of *relative* moral autonomy acknowledges that the individual is subject to situational constraints that impact on morally relevant acts. Nevertheless, the very existence of morality presupposes a certain degree of autonomy. Its terrain is not rational discourse (Habermas) but the practical relationship of individuals to norms and rules, the continuous acting out of normative commitments. The idea of *relative* moral autonomy presupposes an environment of moral heteronomy, in which moral choices emerge from a field of social and pragmatic constraints. While these constraints do not amount to determination, they mould both character and action.[32] Yet it is precisely in this arena that we demand autonomous moral behaviour and authentic character. Heller insists that such goodness is possible. The existence of good people in everyday life is testimony to the practical nature of the challenge to resist the diversions of social constraint.

If choice is the cornerstone of morality, this also implies individual responsibility for the course of action chosen. Actions have irreversible consequences. For Heller, the assumption of responsibility is simply recognition of this fact. In a moral universe of *relative* moral responsibility, the *degree of responsibility* will vary according to a range of factors, including relational position to the action, knowledge, etc.

Such responsibility is typically *retrospective* in regard to actions but can also be *prospective* when an actor has taken up the obligations of a certain position.[33] The modern individual is commonly involved in complicated networks of obligation and responsibility. In traditional societies, a number of foundational virtues were ascribed to every member of a particular social cluster. While consensus is still common to ethical reflection, modernity has seen its erosion concerning fundamental virtues and vices. The increased differentiation of the spheres of modernity has dissolved most general virtues into sphere-specific sub-virtues and confined the former to everyday life.[34]

DIFFERENTIATION, MORALITY AND RESPONSIBILITY

The modern divorce between abstract and concrete norms has brought to the forefront the question of the responsibility of the person who transgresses norms for moral reasons. In fact, it is precisely this distance between abstract value ideas and concrete norms that requires a diachronic perspective. As we have seen, the possibility of the change is for Heller the cornerstone of moral progress. She cites Weber's reflections on an 'ethics of responsibility' as the paradigmatic treatment of this dilemma.[35] For him, the decisive issue was the consequences of value choices. If the choice does not lead to 'higher', more universal maxims than conventional norms, it can only be regarded as morally problematic. If it does, the subsequent action marks the beginning of a moral revolution.[36] Acknowledging the possibility of such retrospective vindication, as a former Marxist she feels compelled to underscore the enormous responsibility involved. It demands great certainty regarding an individual's chosen values. While this emphasis on individual certainty is no guarantee against crimes, such a wager is unavoidable if convention is ever to be challenged. Her greatest sympathy lies with marginalised individuals who take up 'world-historical responsibility' by upholding the good that has been trampled underfoot by various revolutionary regimes.[37]

While the latitude allowed to individual interpretation of moral action underscores individual responsibility and compels a heightened regard for consequences, it does not resolve all problems. The risk opened up by the modern possibility of contesting concrete norms is just as prevalent when attention is turned to consequences. The pluralism and complexity of modernity compounds the difficulty of judging consequences. In classical society, Aristotle could solve the problem of consequences. Within a given community there was an assumed consensus concerning the highest goods. The modern lack of consensus regarding highest values flows on to the assessment of consequences: judgement becomes subjective and problematic. This was the problem that motivated Kant's attempt to purify morals by universalising maxims and avoiding the context of moral choices.[38] Yet his attempt ultimately ran aground on what Heller calls the 'dilemma of morals'. The complexity of moral choices implies that action is always concretely situated. Some choices allow the universality of the maxim of action, but not for the action itself; context can render one maxim most appropriate for one situation but not another. This means that concrete deliberation is always essential and consequences must always be one of the factors considered.[39] In reality consequences continue to ripple with results not always foreseen. The complexity of this rippling has been accentuated by modernity. The intermeshing of quasi-autonomous subsystems and developmental logics generate a vastly increased risk of the unforeseen and unforeseeable.[40] The very dynamism of modernity has increased the indeterminacy of all social action and often renders concrete norms inadequate.

Recognising the necessity of contesting social norms, Heller is no longer a naive admirer of the Hegelian world-historical individual. Not even the certainty of individual conviction is a sufficiently secure basis on which to rest moral hopes. Practical judgement requires the assistance of principles. Only democratic principles are able to bear this weight. When consequences must be borne by millions of people in their concrete lives, Heller forsakes the wings of speculative fancy.[41]

THE CRISIS OF MORAL AUTHORITY

Heller's need to bolster practical judgement is not merely a response to the alleged sins of the philosophy of history and its overblown aspirations. The philosophy of history was itself a product of the modern crisis of moral authority. The increasing shift in favour of internal over external authority produced an increasing *pluralisation, universalisaton* and *subjectivisation* of morality.[42] Contra MacIntyre, she refuses to view this long historical trend as a decline; she credits it with the potential of even greater moral progress. However, this is not a unidirectional process and moral progress is not assured.[43] Moral authority is undermined by an internal conscience that seeks not alternative concrete norms but higher-level more abstract ones. These abstract norms can be grounded neither in reason nor in historical dynamism. Hegel's attempt to theoretically reintegrate *Sittlichkeit* into morality failed because it ultimately exposed the moral standpoint to historical contingency.

As Heller sees it, contemporary morality is fixed in a subjectivist mode but convulsed by tensions. This is no dialectic of contradictory values or between abstract and concrete norms, but a contest between two possible developmental logics inherent within the subjectivist moral structure.[44] Heller distinguishes between the *subject* as the *sole* and *practical reason* as the *ultimate* arbiter. Only the latter represents the emancipatory line of moral progress. Here the subject employs '*double quality*' reflection orientated to the standpoint of posited universal values. The interpretation of these values requires considerable effort even when they have been instantiated into a democratic–legal institutional structure. Whether monologically or dialogically chosen, they must be rationally supported by arguments accessible to scrutiny and debate.[45] The subject as sole arbiter represents the complete disappearance of the transcendental perspective and allows individualism to run amok. Without external moral authority, there are no binding moral norms and everything is permitted. The careful balance cultivated between deconstructivist and constructivist aspects of early modern conscience give way to nihilistic self-assertion. Here in embryo we see her later distinction between reflective and naive postmodernism. Like Hegel, Heller knows that sole arbitration can assume various different forms.[46] While she allows the possibility of moral progress, the persistence of these threatening forms of subjectivity makes her reluctant to simply identify the subjective arbiter with further evolutionary stages of moral development *à la* Kohlberg and Habermas. This is decided only by the commitment of modern actors.[47]

Whether this commitment exists and can be harnessed is a question that haunts an increasingly sceptical modernity. The traditional basis of moral philosophy was that virtue could be taught. The capacity to discriminate according to primary categories of value orientation is assumed to be present as an inherent outcome of the processes of socialisation.[48] The 'rightness' of moral judgements in the past was vindicated by an appeal to narratives of genesis that explained the legitimacy of the normative order. In this configuration, reason and faith are not antagonists but mutual supporters. Tradition and reason are the two anchors of legitimate belief. All this changes with the erosion of tradition and the increasing reliance on reason. When moral norms are justified by reason alone, the attitude of reason must also dramatically change. What is decisive is no longer the observance of existing rules and norms but the formulation of new laws. We are already familiar with Heller's distinction between the *rationality of reason*, concerned with the identification and application of unquestioned existing rules and norms, and the *rationality of intellect*, which brings into play a critical practical reason and its principal orientation to the good.[49] This latter higher form of reason empowers thought to both validate and de-validate rules and norms. Clearly, it is the *rationality of intellect* that must increasingly come to the forefront in modernity as the emphasis shifts from observation of, to the generation of new, moral norms. Having lost confidence in the moral viability of tradition, early modern philosophers were divided as to whether to locate the source of moral generation in reason or feeling or some combination of the two.[50] Heller rejects all proposed solutions along these lines. To draw a distinction between thinking and feeling is as arbitrary as to ignore the connection between reason and faith.

Picking up a theme already evident in her early writings on feelings, she argues that without the support of critical argument, both private sentiments and public passions must be viewed as morally ambivalent. The quest to enhance the quality of moral sentiment can easily be transformed into a celebration of sentiment for its own sake. The idea that certain sentiments are endowed with the power to generate moral norms is a psychologism that reduces morality to a mere epiphenomenon.[51] To make morality the province of psychology is to negate the moral autonomy of the individual and treat transgression as an illness to be handled by scientific discourse. The advance of modern pluralism and its real variety of 'good ways of living' should not obscure the fact that there must be moral norms shared by all. The increasing theoretical recognition of the proximity of reason and feeling has not translated into the general culture. As things stand, views are polarised between the domination of scientific discourse, in which the subject is treated as epiphenomenon, and the domination of sensibility, with the dismissal of all intersubjective norms. At stake is the future possibility of uniting the idea of self-development in the fullest sense with the idea of the rational constitution of norms in dialogue and argument.[52]

This polarisation of views is compounded by other centrifugal forces in modernity, such as the more complex division of labour and extended cultural differentiation. The modern dissolution of social stratification sees a shift from a virtue-oriented to an imperative-oriented moral culture and the birth of *practical reason*. However, the propagation of transfunctional value ideas such as justice, freedom and democracy does not prevent modernity generating its own differentiated moral terrain. Weber provided the paradigmatic version of this development with his account of the 'warring gods'. His account allows for both the relative autonomy of the spheres themselves in relation to each other and the autonomy of actors who adopt differing attitudes in accord with the norms of different spheres.[53]

Today opinions are divided over the meaning of the process of cultural differentiation. A strong thesis holds that all modern spheres, except religion, have been emptied of moral content. A weaker thesis puts the emphasis on the increasing autonomy of the spheres and the development of specific ethical environments within them. Heller explores the way in which this process of spherical differentiation impacts on the individual's relation to morality. Cultural differentiation is a bearer of possible emancipation. However, her model quarantines everyday life and views morality as a trans-spherical phenomenon. She argues that science has become the dominant worldview but this has not issued in any common ethos.[54] Cultural modernity is characterised by a 'weak' ethos sustained by the universal value idea of freedom. The democratic traditions of modernity encourage transfunctional action and an ethos that does not impede spherical relative autonomy.[55] She is therefore reluctant to identify modernity completely with differentiated spherical ethics.

Heller's acceptance of the Weberian account of cultural differentiation is not extended to faith in his prognosis. In the meaningless world constructed by modern science, he opted for the individual making a radical vocational choice that would determine both the central meaning of her life and the norms according to which she would expect to behave. Heller asserts the Weber's strategy rests upon a number of confusions. The idea of existential choice that Weber took over from Kierkegaard was not a choice of value spheres but of meaning-constituting attitudes within everyday life. The choice of such a form of life was no bar against activities in a range of spheres.[56] Nor did this require a choice between everyday life and the pursuit of higher cultural excellence. Weber mistakenly connected these two to a choice between different cultural value spheres. His error lay in ignoring everyday life and in viewing general morality itself as a value sphere. Heller maintains that *the primary* existential choice is that of becoming moral beings. This is no mere choice of spheres but one that encompasses all spheres and monitors all personal activity within them. This does not eliminate spherical differences but allows the individual to test inner spherical rules and norms against the standpoint of morality.[57] While acknowledging that cultural value spheres do have their own norms and rules, she contests the proposition that the modern individual is condemned to monotheism. The rounded personality should not be required to reify itself. Furthermore, she forcefully rejects the idea that a vocational choice is more fundamentally existential than choosing an ethical way in everyday life. Weber glamourised the idea of choice where the real moral issue is living up to the commitments it entails.[58]

These two levels of morality remain compatible as long as the general imperatives are pitched at a sufficiently high level of abstraction. The greater danger is the impact of sphere-immanent norms on everyday life in a way that drains it of moral content. The only antidote for this is the maintenance of pluralism and rethinking the possibility of re-centering positive lifestyles around particular ways of life.[59]

Heller concludes her reflections on the general conditions of ethics and the conceptual armoury of moral theory where she started: with the 'good'. This is not in order to review her argument, but to get some purchase on the concept of evil. While she has never allowed her own experience of the Holocaust to dominate her thinking, it is hardly surprising that she would consider any theory of ethics that excluded it to be inadequate. Nevertheless, her approach to the question of evil is as matter-of-fact as is her attitude to the 'good'. Just as the good exists empirically in the shape of good people, so does evil. As with the 'good', she can neither explain the existence of evil nor does she want to explain it away. It is usually associated with practices that in one way or another attack the social fabric. However, she contends that only those actions and programmes aimed at the destruction of morality really deserve the name of absolute evil.[60] With the rise of science as the dominant worldview, evil is no longer viewed as part of the order of things. This is especially compatible with the view that evil would be reduced to the minimum by the existence of optimal human institutions.[61] This insight into the institutional conditioning of evil brings into focus the modern association of great evil with power: particularly the rationalist conviction that everything is possible on the basis of rapidly accumulating knowledge. This extremity of evil she holds to be rare. More common are the 'good' and the 'bad' who assume opposing views of the Socratic maxim that 'it is better to suffer wrong than to do it'. She distinguishes between the *genius* of morality who embraces goodness beyond the need for formal maxims and *everyday goodness* which does not require extreme altruism. It only enjoins us to live according to the maxim of 'suffering rather than committing wrong'.[62] Yet even this is a high standard for everyday goodness. It requires not only the conscious renunciation of immoral action but demands also a capacity for forbearance under duress.

Heller's 'good person' can neither prove this choice 'rational' nor does she require such proof. Heller argues that philosophical advocacy of the 'good' from Plato to Kant ultimately fails. This reduces adherence to moral dictums to a confession of faith.[63] She views the moral attitude of taking responsibility for actions as the key to authenticity. In so doing, the individual unites her normative and empirical selves. For the purposes of the act, she steps outside of history and assumes the momentary mantle of immortality.[64] But such momentary transcendence is no denial of the historicity of morals. Nevertheless, the existence of 'good' people remains, for her, a trans-historical empirical universal that both assures us of the practical necessity of morality and promises us the possibility of a better world.[65]

THE NORMATIVE QUESTION
AND THE EXISTENTIAL CHOICE

At the centre of Heller's moral theory is her desire to reverse the twentieth-century truncation of ethics to the single issue of *interpreting* the good. She still favours the classical vision that also offers *normative* and *pedagogical* dimensions. Her strategy is to accompany a 'good' person in the course of her everyday life. The normative role of Heller's ethics is neither to create moral norms nor somehow to miraculously convert the rascal from a life of transgression. Moral theory is a *reflective enterprise* whose resources and scope are severely limited. Norms are the product of social interaction and cannot be summoned according to the wishes of philosophers. Moreover, moral theory is only accessible to those who already value the aspiration to 'goodness'. The moral message is not exclusive, but some individuals are simply deaf to its counsel. However, the demise of ethical prescription and the changed role of moral theory has not eliminated its *practical function*. The modern aspirant to goodness is even more in need of ethical clarification and moral advice. The contemporary everyday constantly engenders ethical dilemmas and questioning. The modern individual faces a complex social environment without a secure framework and the assurance of always knowing what should be done. The decline of fixed virtues and the rise of abstract universal values generate an ever-widening abyss and perplexity over questions of application. In this context, Heller believes that moral reflection provides the 'crutches' that keeps the modern aspirant to goodness on the right track.

Unlike the pre-modern individual whose character and behaviour options were largely predetermined by birth and conventional social ideals, the modern individual must find her character through a choice of destiny. As we have seen in Chapter 7, this choice is portrayed as the *existential* choice. This is so because it actually *constitutes* a self with an irreversible and irrevocable self-chosen destiny. The choice is irrevocable by definition because revocation would mean loss of self and lapse into contingency.[66] The existential choice is a metaphorical moment of life-changing revelation that is not always manifest in a single gesture. It is the result of a series of intentional acts that lead to increasing moral rationality.[67] However, the idea of existential choice does not mean artistic self-creation as an act of moulding raw material into a pre-designed shape. The individual actor is already determined in infinite ways for which she is not responsible. Nor can such a choice be assimilated to the model of rational choice, in which steps are chosen rationally in accord with a predetermined goal or life strategy.[68] While this choice can be rendered plausible in terms of psychology, personal history and moral reasoning, the actual choice itself cannot be reduced to rational explanation.[69] Heller prefers the classical paradigm of 'knowing thyself' as the template of self-choice. The character chosen as a personal destiny is not a product of mere introspection but the result of action; this is a 'proving' or a 'becoming' whereby the self reaches out to find the kind of actions appropriate to the self-chosen character and destiny. This is the meaning of the idea of choosing 'to become the person you already are'. This framework allows the individual to continue making consecutive choices bound by the *telos* of the initial existential one. In this sense, *existence* precedes *essence*.[70] The individual is already the bearer of an envelope of genetic and social a prioris. Yet it is only with the choice of all these determinations that the individual assumes full autonomy and pursues a personal destiny that is beyond contingency and external determination. This account reveals the crux of Heller's defence of the idea of modern subjectivity against its postmodern critique. Against a vision of a palimpsest's identity in which the emphasis is on forgetting, experimenting and disassembling shapes, she opts for a model in which learning that is either gradual or life-altering constitutes a real personal continuity.[71] Against Bauman's rhetorical objection that only a few people would change nothing in their life given the chance, she would surely reply that her affirmation of contingency as destiny means not the embrace of every detail but the realisation of the best possibilities.[72] This choice is a *leap* into authenticity neither determined nor directed by any external rule or norm. Authenticity signifies bringing the self's empirical existence into accord with these chosen best possibilities.[73] While accidentality remains an inescapable element of this context, for the actor this choice possesses an irresistible attraction that alienates all that went before.[74]

Heller's idea of existential choice entails a self-chosen destiny that has to be realised in a series of challenges and subsequent choices put to the character of the individual. But, as we have seen in Chapter 7, this self-choice is multifaceted. In one dimension, it concerns developing personal endowments into talents. This is the existential choice according to *difference*. In this choice, the chooser distinguishes herself from, rather than uniting with, others. In this gamble on difference, the individual is especially exposed to the external powers of good and bad fortune. Without the defensive armor of moral limits, the choice of difference is easily poisoned.[75] The personally chosen destiny may be pursued with absolute single-mindedness past the point of moral transgression. The single-mindedness of existential consistency may seem irrational or unethical to the external observer.

While the existential choice of difference underlines the moment of reflection and personal responsibility, its openness to moral transgression is a serious weakness. It is primarily this moral concern that motivated Heller to adumbrate the other dimension of existential choice orientated to the category of the *universal*; this is the choice of *goodness*. While the existential choice of difference implies that not everybody will make the same choice or possess the same level of endowments, the existential choice under the category of the universal is open to *all* individuals.[76] This is a choice of morality. Here the moral temptations linked to choosing uniqueness are extinguished at their source. The good person consciously chooses goodness over evil and adopts the maxims of personal behaviour equally valid for all. While the fate of the individual existentially choosing difference is subject to the vagaries of luck, the good person can never be led to regret her choice by fluctuations of fortune. Habituation to the good is the perfect inoculation against the poison of fate.

Heller's strategy is to de-radicalise the notion of existential choice by making it compatible with everyday experience and a variety of philosophical perspectives. She insists that this is a choice of the good person that *already exists*. While such a choice is undoubtedly transformational, the fact that it is a choice of all determinations reinforces the idiosyncrasy of the personal history at the same time as allowing no trace of external determination to impugn the freedom and personal responsibility of the good person.[77] The existential choice is not a metaphysical condition but historically situated in modernity. It presupposes the modern condition of *contingency* and the absence of pre-given ways of life. Moreover, it depends upon the specific historical attainments of subjective moral reflexivity and the increasing autonomy of the cultural value spheres that have allowed moderns to distinguish between excellence and goodness.[78] These cultural achievements allow the modern individual to combine the two choices despite their ultimate irreconcilability. Heller's concern for morality is not moral absolutism. In a cultural universe of struggling deities, no single choice can bring closure. However, the hierarchisation of choices at least allows for the autonomy and talents of the individual. She insists that the two

modes of existential choice can be combined as long as the distinction
is maintained between the *absolute* and the *fundamental* choice. This
distinction allows that, in instances of existential clash, the *fundamental*
will be subordinated to the *absolute*.[79] While the ethical remains
absolute, the individual is able to relinquish the objects of choice
when authenticity is threatened. However, giving absolute priority to
difference releases individual development from ethical precautions
and may risk the dissolution of the personality.[80]

The existential choice of goodness remains an exercise in radical
autonomy. Insofar as this choice requires moral categories, it draws on
the good that already exists in the person as a potentiality. Yet, as the
advice of conscience can always be rejected, this is not determination.
Here autonomy and morality lie in a precarious balance that befits
the paradoxical character of modernity. The condition of 'double
contingency' leaves the modern individual without a banister in
deciding what to do. Morality is indispensable to authentic character yet
ultimately this choice lies in the hands of the individual. This explains
Heller's preference for Kierkegaard over Kant. For the latter, the moral
law remains a definitive crutch in the world of dangerous and fraudulent
alternatives. But this constraint is at odds with the modern freedom and
subjectivisation. The superiority of the existentialist ethics lies in its
theoretical openness on this question of the ethical crutch. The ethics of
the personality does not single out any ethical crutch as definitive, but
allows the good person to be so in her own way.[81] Modernity has seen
the demise of all former *arche*. The only remaining ethical certainty is
the goodness of the decent person.[82] A product of the Romantic critique
of rationalist abstraction, the existentialist ethic asserts the unity of
the individual and the universal, with all their determinations, in the
concrete person. Yet this emphatic endorsement of moral autonomy is
quite compatible with the tradition of *Sittlichkeit*. The modern ethical
actor remains dependent upon the quality of her moral crutch. This
means that the existentialist ethic is also inherently dialogical, inviting
real moral discussion.[83]

THE NEW *SITTLICHKEIT*

The provision of meaningful moral advice presupposes reproduction of
the conditions of real moral discussion. In modernity, neither the old
republican model of a shared *Sittlichkeit* nor the utopian conditions
of discourse ethics are tenable.[84] The contemporary good person faces
the challenge of sustaining goodness overwhelmed by awareness of
contingency, increasingly inhabiting institutional subsystems and facing

escalating incidents of ethical collision.[85] In a world of conflicting values and virtues, differing normative engagements and increased opacity of interconnections and consequences, the possibility of dialogue and action depends upon being able to discover a common value or norm. The sheer variety of contemporary integrations and the resulting fragmentation of loyalties and commitments erode the prospects of consensus. In the absence of an established hierarchy of loyalties, Heller recommends the categorical imperative as a universalistic moral crutch whenever everyday rules and norms are in question. She admits that the good person is typically good without consulting universal formulas. Deeply conditioned by Judeo-Christian traditions, she does the good for its own sake.[86] Nevertheless, moral theory must anticipate the decent person's need for advice. No longer able to provide custom-made advice for every individual, theory must at least be in a position to provide general moral advice in all situations.[87]

Against the modern tendency to reduce morality to the question of justice, Heller views modernity as the bearer of a new form of *Sittlichkeit*. The increased atomisation of modern human relations loosens the former organic ties between norms, values and virtues, but intensifies the constant human need for others.[88] For Heller, care for others is a *universal orientative principle* of modern morals. However, such principles are not commandments and must be sensitively interpreted in the context of the particular carer. The ancient art of *phronesis* now comes into its own in a dynamic process of mutual caring that requires constant adjustments.[89] All of this has a deceptively traditional ring. Yet Heller insists that orientative principles remain abstract and avoid reference to concrete norms, rules or even virtue norms.[90] Abstraction functions to both *broaden* and *narrow* the territory of what is permitted. It allows guidance without the acceptance of any concrete norm and, simultaneously, proscribes any practice that infringes the principle itself. For precisely this reason, many traditional practices are today impermissible.[91]

Reciprocity is one of the most elementary ethical norms. Without symmetrical reciprocity, social existence is impossible. Only modern societies have emancipated this norm from the restrictions of social hierarchy.[92] Heller argues that the emergence of dynamic justice and freely chosen social interactions enhances the role of symmetrical reciprocity. If anything, this refutes the proposition that justice is all that remains of morality in modernity. After all, most contemporary acts of reciprocity have little to do with justice and much more to do with civility, generosity and kindness.[93] This is true despite the expanded role of institutions in modern life. Typically, modern institutions are founded on asymmetrical relations. Heller asserts that the good person should observe a natural equality in all relations external to institutions and refrain from relationships of service and patronage unless moral maxims dictate otherwise. However, the diverse range of modern patterns of reciprocity dictates that the precise details of reciprocity are left to the judgement of the individual.[94] Only wisdom and the consultation of everyday custom assists negotiating these delicate matters.

While it is true that moderns can no longer abide the idea of a pre-given form of life, Heller argues that virtue talk can still be meaningfully employed in a modified way.[95] Virtue no longer connotes some aspect of the form of the good life, but *character traits* that predispose individuals to the actualisation of certain values. The social *telos* has disappeared, but the virtues can be *reassigned* to accommodate the more dynamic and flexible modern social order. While moral theory is still concerned with forming, human beings can no longer be conceived as *raw material* nor forms as *ready-made* patterns.[96] Individuals do not create the forms of life, but are responsible for their own conduct. The notion of 'conduct' also better reflects the dynamism of modern life: its open-endedness and the role of reflection.[97] There is no direct link between virtues and the ways of life chosen by individuals, because this is precisely where ineffable individuality and contingency of the modern person assert themselves.

AUTHENTICITY, INSTITUTIONAL EXISTENCE AND CIVIL COURAGE

The notion of authenticity comes to the centre of discussion in the twentieth century with the demise of traditional virtue and increasing consciousness of contingency. Beyond moral virtue, authenticity is a personality term.[98] We have seen that the authentic person is characterised by the unity of existence and essence. How is this unity achieved if the existential choice involves choosing all previous determinations? Heller relies on the metaphors of 'dying' and 'resurrection'. The existential choice itself is a *timeless* moment of isolation after which everything is both the same and different. Paradoxically, the choice of all determinations is a release from the past insofar as from this point on the individual assumes full responsibility for all her actions. However, as already intimated, this does not mean that everything in her personality and past is taken as a value.[99] Much of the old person dies, because the existential choice affirms the cultivation of only her best traits and capacities. Everything is different, because she now evaluates and acts from the perspective of the chosen attributes and their affiliated values. Confronted by infinite possibilities, the authentic person raises herself by 'her own hair'. By contrast, the inauthentic person avoids the choice, remaining 'fake' and not 'real'. Heller wants to avoid the aristocratic connotations associated with the notion of authenticity. Her commitment to the modern universal value idea of freedom is tempered by the need for the existential choice of the universal as an absolute choice. Of course, this form of existential choice is open to all.[100]

This is the sociable choice of the public–political person who wishes to practise virtue. Authenticity here has to do neither with isolation nor with 'techniques of the self'. Authentic self-knowledge is a product of social relationships and disclosure to other human beings. Self-knowledge requires interaction with, and knowledge of, others. Others will sometimes know us better than we know ourselves. The virtues of being candid, truthful and trustworthy are reciprocal.[101] This mutual disclosure is a practical hermeneutics that does not require consensus. Heller is wary of the pressures of public opinion. Yet it is vital to pay attention to others and to possess the ability to tune in to the complex psychology and differences between persons.[102]

The modern individual not only experiences a heightened consciousness of contingency, she also inhabits an increasingly functionalised world of institutions and subsystems. These are a 'second habitat' that operates according to its own rules and residential obligations.[103] Moral dilemmas arise when functional rules and norms clash with the ethics of symmetrical reciprocity. Functional institutions are typically hierarchical and the decent person is not always able to quarantine her own interactions from the impact of asymmetrical imperatives. Heller acknowledges the modern priority of institutional rules and norms in instances of conflict, but with the important qualification that human beings are not reducible to functions.[104] Institutional constraints do not annul orientating moral principles nor prevent individuals observing and practising the virtues. But they do affect their interpretation and application as well as the intensity with which certain values are realised.[105] Contra Habermas, Heller does not simply identify the system with the demise of communicative rationality. Institutional life still requires a great deal of intersubjective negotiation. She terms the quiet observation of general orientating moral norms 'civility'.[106] However, the constraints of institutional orders mean that certain acts of reciprocity clash directly with institutional orders.

An elementary consequence of Heller's interpretation of the existential choice is that the individual's choice of all her determinations implies not just the conditions of her own life but, indirectly, that of others as well.[107] This becomes explicit in her commitment to pluralism and democracy. This throws up the immediate problem of interaction between the good person and those with fewer moral scruples. These interactions are inescapable and should not cause the good person to abandon observance of universal moral maxims.[108] In this context, the good person's attitude is one of concern. She must be ready both to understand and to assist in the alleviation of remediable misery. Of course, how and to what extent this concern can be operationalised remains a question for *phronesis*. However, social action often throws the good person into projects with those who are self-interested. To maintain her own integrity, the good person must be prepared to pass moral judgements in cases of moral relevance. Such judgements may be made public when they concern the public performance of those in question.[109]

Understandably, conscience reveals its full value in the context of 'dark times'. Yet Heller offers it only a partial defence. In modern totalitarian societies that have assaulted the very idea of individual autonomy, conscience is the only antidote and a bulwark against capitulation. However, this attitude has inherent limits and cannot be generalised. Consulting only conscience, without utilitarian considerations and 'reality checking', may also be a victory for ignorance and self-deception.[110] However, in totalitarian contexts, goodness can sometimes assume political relevance and be momentarily unified with 'concern'. While here conscience plays a vital role, it is not in itself sufficient. Fear can only be overcome by Heller's favourite civic virtue: courage. This is the all-encompassing virtue that underpins the capacity for all others.[111] In circumstances of universal suspicion in which trust is withheld, even the observance of elementary virtues like reciprocity require real fortitude. Only courage activates the bravery necessary to surmount fear and offer resistance. Such an investment has real costs in terms of time, energy, interests and money. Good citizenship can compete with other dimensions of a good life. Today there seems to be an increasing indifference to active citizenship. In this climate, civic courage again comes into its own as the vital virtue necessary to resist conventional power and uphold cherished values.

The distinction between the good person and the good citizen is not the result of dysfunction but of the deeply entrenched dynamics of modernity. One of the fruits of modern differentiation is an indulgence of an individual's choice not to participate in political life. In this society, justice is contested as an impersonal value abstracted from particular fates. Yet the perfect actualisation of this ideal would be unattractive and undesirable for the modern contingent person. This internal ambivalence of modernity is the inspiration of Heller's new alternative path in moral theory. In the past, moral theory drew its authority from membership of groups either local or universal.[112] The result was a moral theory devoted either to particular local customs or to purely formal abstractions. Heller's approach follows the contingent person who chooses herself according to a universal that can yield general principles, norms and virtues which are not purely formal and offer concrete guidance.[113] The existential choice of universality does not render the chooser universal. She keeps all the determinations of her concrete singularity. In this instance, general principles, norms and virtues are not purely formal and do offer moral guidance.[114] At the same time, the content of this moral direction remains general and requires further specification. This juxtaposition of the 'general' and the 'specified' is completely in accord with the existence of modern pluralism and its variety of good forms of life.[115] As each way of life carries its own yardstick of measurement, general principles and norms should be sufficiently general to allow mutual toleration and to permit decent persons to be 'good' in their own way.[116]

PHRONESIS AND THE EVERYDAY

A rehabilitated notion of *phronesis* is at the centre of Heller's ethical thinking. This concept is inherent to the existential choice of goodness: the good person always visualises actions in advance so as to avoid the violation of moral norms.[117] However, moral appraisal confronts particular difficulties in the modern context. The loss of tradition and the demise of a common ethos seem to inhibit the capacity of moral theory to deal with the actual problems of life. The dynamism of moral change and the heterogeneity and complexity of situations all amplify the time needed for moral reflection, while eroding the competence of former 'natural counsellors'. These dynamics further subjectivise morality and favour the internalisation of moral dialogue. On the other hand, moral risk has diminished through a combination of the reduced density of rules and norms and their increased formalisation.[118] All in all, modernity offers a picture of disjointed moral experience in which the individual gains wisdom only by negotiating a range of different environments and imposing moral continuity across an uneven terrain.[119]

Heller addresses the charge that her conception of moral appraisal is stilted and non-naturalistic because it is focused on key strategic moments and decisions.[120] In her view, it makes sense to focus on life-shaping crises and junctures in which possibilities are narrowed down, in which situations are not simply given but dynamic, offering real choices and new options. She acknowledges that choices are always made within constraints, but argues that these make no difference from the moral point of view.[121] The good person appraises not just ends but also means and their likely consequences. Goodness is no longer simply a question of character; it also includes values, commitments, obligations and promises that express personal priorities. Modern pluralism allows for the possibility of the individual becoming a good person in her own way. It follows that we have no right to morally criticise another who comes to a different evaluation of priorities: the goals and preferences of another are beyond criticism as long as they do not lead to moral infraction. However, tolerance cannot be extended to condoning moral transgression. While the capacity to forgive is part of the armoury of the good person, this does not allow absolution for acts against third parties. On the contrary, goodness requires action on behalf of others as long as it does not infringe their autonomy and their prospects of attaining their own goals.[122] While all this sounds straightforward, the fact remains that in real life interest and value-related actions co-exist in intricate networks. In these webs, moral consequences are difficult to fathom. Heller insists that *phronesis* cannot manage without the support of full knowledge and dialogue with concerned parties.[123]

To preserve individual autonomy in practical action is one of her primary concerns and an enduring legacy of Heller's own experience in 'really existing socialism'. The modern elevation of values into abstract value ideas means that the good person is often required to pursue particular goals allegedly for the sake of realising ultimate values. The dangers involved here necessitate a distinction between abstract and concrete enthusiasm. Emotional investment in ideas is permissible as long as it does not involve the abandonment of autonomy. With this proviso, commitment towards ideal causes can be called concrete enthusiasm.[124] However, a cause that requires the loss of moral autonomy or sacrifice of the freedom of others is altogether different. The abstract and concrete enthusiasts share goals and values but differ dramatically over means. Heller is also wary of excessively universal goals. The concrete enthusiast distinguishes between the quasi-universal as a regulative idea and concrete goals. She is content to make a contribution to the process of enlightenment.[125] The only substantive idea that qualifies as a real universal is democracy as an institution of self-determination. The good citizen will oppose even a majoritarian infringement of democratic principles.

In the twentieth century, moral philosophy developed a penchant for dwelling on the borderline case of the potentially tragic 'dilemma of morals'. Lukács' choice between socialism and barbarism is a paradigmatic case. Heller regrets this turn. Despite the illumination that she readily admits can be gained from the analysis of the moment of existential crisis, she favours the relocation of moral appraisal within the general settings of everyday life.[126] Life nearly always allows for things to be put aright. In any case, for Heller, the crisis moment is simply a metaphor for life in general. The quest of the individual to become who she is lasts a lifetime. This is also why such a quest is best articulated by a moral philosophy that maintains its focus on the ordinary.[127]

As we have seen, in Heller's view the rationale of philosophy lies in the aspirations of everyday life. Practical philosophy is a utopian order of regulative ideas juxtaposed to, but at the same time, drawing upon the dynamics of, everyday life. Like the rest of absolute spirit, this is a normative realm that confronts us with something higher and renders meaning by relativising our own particular concerns, interests and goals against this standard.[128] Yet this philosophical utopia is not merely normative, it is also virtual. It operates as an agent of its own translation. It demands the integration of ideal aspirations into the institutional fabric of the everyday. The existence of the 'good' person fits squarely into this vision as a utopian promise of the best possible moral world. The fact of exemplary goodness in the world gives flesh to the ideas expressed in philosophy. While the world is not just, the existential choice of goodness before us a passionate quest to unify virtue and happiness. While moments of peak political and social experience foreshadow such a realised utopia, they quickly recede into the routine of everyday life. However, the goodness of the moral life perpetuates utopia within everyday life.[129] The discrepancy that is produced in the peak experience between the empirical and normative selves is closed by an authenticity that allows routine conduct to coincide with character.

The difficulties of Heller's effort at synthesis have not gone unnoticed. The most obvious of these concern the aspiration to generate the utopian and the universal out of the everyday. Habermas puts this point most forcefully. The philosopher who retreats from the role of expert will very quickly be faced with the limitations of their own historical situation.[130] Unlike Habermas, Heller eschews foundationalism willingly, to reside in the contingent terrain of the postmodern everyday. The values underpinning philosophical vision and the goodness to which she appeals are explicitly drawn from the images and life forms of contemporary everyday life. Yet this has not prevented her from asserting the universality of these values. The fact that their empirical universality has been questioned is just such a suggestion of the limitation of her cultural context, which she has not fully acknowledged. Of course, the same can be said in regard to her reluctance to relinquish a role for philosophy in providing moral 'crutches' for the orientation of individual action. Heller's observations on the contemporary 'good person' are clearly the reflections of another 'good person'. Yet this moral advice often has the flavour of an 'agony aunt'. This accusation has nothing to do with the quality of the moral advice but comes from the perceived mixing of genres, with sound conventional 'common sense' being elevated to the status of philosophy.[131] Clearly the popularity of self-help and other 'guide to life' literature demonstrates the contemporary need for moral crutches and the vacuum of authority that exists. However, the fact that this is the case suggests that philosophy is not going to be able to fill it. The dilemmas of modern morality are in large measure a product of the crisis in traditional moral authority. Philosophy itself is not immune to this crisis, as we know from its retreat from its Enlightenment claim to be able to speak for everyman (sic) and from the process of its historical subjectivisation, which looms so large in Heller's own account. Yet she sits rather awkwardly across the horns of this crisis. Upholding the freedom of the modern, she has abandoned all foundationalism. At the same time, she clings tightly to universal aspirations. It remains to be seen how she envisages that these two can be reconciled in her moral theory. This crisis of authority was certainly also behind some initial misunderstanding of Heller's moral project and the incorrect belief that she was prescribing moral advice. As we shall see, this reception compelled her to adjust her approach and find a more appropriate form to address the classical moral agenda in a contemporary postmodern context.

Part III

'Reflective Postmodernism'

10
The Spirit of Our Congregation

It wasn't too long before Heller recognised the shortcomings of her first formulation of a post-Marxist philosophy. In retrospective self-critique, she has acknowledged that her reformulation of the radical project in terms of philosophical ideals represented a defence of a kind of absolute and a closure. Her recourse to the ancient paradigm of philosophy was a last belated 'collection of faith before the jump into postmodern resignation'. This was nostalgia for grand philosophy presented in a New Left rhetoric that announced a philosophical Parousia too loudly. Clearly, this was against the anti-utopian grain of postmodern times and left Heller with little but a traditional and empty philosophical utopia.[1] Yet whatever its residual illusions and rhetorical overstatements, the first formulation of post-Marxist radical philosophy nevertheless contained the leading ideas of her mature standpoint. The break with classical philosophy of history was registered in an awareness of the historical contingency of the Western odyssey. This awareness feeds the heightened self-reflectivity that is especially characteristic of modern historical consciousness. Awareness of contingency is supplemented by the recognition of plurality. Without a privileged master narrative all that remains is multiple social perspectives, producing a plurality of competing philosophical utopias that vied for the allegiance of contemporary social actors. These elements now had to coalesce into a new philosophical constellation.

In the course of the 1980s Heller rethought the fundamentals of this position. What was required was a philosophy that moved with the spirit of the times without succumbing to its most dangerous excesses. This process of rethinking is already evident in *Beyond Justice*. There her idea of the *incomplete ethico-political concept of justice* was linked to the spirit of Diderot and to a philosophical vision that rejected easy solutions and that raised questions and explored real problems, but was still content to live with contradictions. The unprecedented character of this modern experience informs *A Philosophy of History: In Fragments.*[2]

THE SUBJECTIVISATION OF PHILOSOPHY

The modern individual is 'born free' in so far as their life is posited as
an open book of opportunities from which they will choose a self-made
destiny. This understanding gives expression to a heightened awareness
of contingency. The older pre-modern sense of cosmic contingency
is augmented by the new modern sense of social contingency as
'thrownness'. A social fate is now something to be made. But despite our
dearly won 'formal' freedom, we are still confined to the prison house of
historicity and to the reflective cultural consciousness that accompanies
it. This consciousness of our own historicity has now become absolute.
For Heller, it is crucial to fully integrate this sense of contingency and
its limits into a contemporary understanding of philosophy.

The postmodern consciousness clearly distinguishes itself from the
Hegelian. Hegel had conceived philosophy as a unity that unfolded in,
and through, its many shapes. For him, difference is only a determination
of identity. However, his successors could not share this vision. The post-
Hegelian history of philosophy is a story of permanent revolution and
the constant repudiation of previous reigning forms. Each new original
philosopher introduces a whole new cast of categories and drastically
rearranges the parts and characters of those that remain. This was a
real revolution. One of the distinctive traditional characteristics of
philosophy as a cultural genre has been the supposed eternality of its
categories. Moreover, philosophers formerly always drew their categories
from a common conceptual pool. Yet the last century especially has
seen a growing personalisation of philosophy and the invention of many
new categories that only rarely outlive the philosopher who created
them. In the light of this radical subjectivisation of speculation, Heller
ponders whether philosophy could survive without its common pool
of characters.

Her answer is a forceful affirmation that resonates through her reflective
postmodernism. This is evident in her meditation on the categorical
mainstays of this common pool: reason, will and truth. Only a radical
rethinking of these categories will allow contemporary philosophy to
meet the challenge imposed by the new historical spirit.

As we saw earlier, philosophy was originally conceived as a bulwark
against deception. The philosopher was the one who could be
deceived. Deception is avoided by the right use of reason.[3] Reason
was an institution of the philosophical imagination on which the whole
philosophical project could unconditionally rely. It assumed many forms
but always stood for certainty. It was the courage to know, which led
beyond the abyss to certainty. This in turn depended on that common

ratio that allowed us to share a world with others. Living in both a private and a public world, human beings only become fully human, however, when these two worlds intermix through creative imagination. Only philosophical reason and its distinction between *doxa* and *episteme* elevated its addressees beyond joyful and deceptive subjective dreams. It guarded against the excesses of rampant subjectivity. Yet is this precious item exhausted by the requirements of identity logic? In the face of the modern attack on the other extreme – homogenising identity thinking – Heller poses the question: How common does 'the common thing' have to be?[4] The loudly trumpeted apocalyptic slogans such as 'the end of reason' ignore the fact that reason cannot be dismissed without a replacement. The meaning behind such slogans is the call to abandon the quest for unachievable certitude. In so doing, we make peace with human finitude. Whether we leave the place formerly occupied by reason empty or substitute something that is less stringent, the key is that the vacant position is a healing one. We want it to join us, but not be the same for all of us.[5]

The travails that attend a contemporary rethinking of the category of reason are as nothing compared to the shifting ground that has undermined the category of will. Forged by Augustine as a major philosophical category to justify punishment for wilful acts, it has maintained a continuous central presence in a Christian culture in which sin was the central imaginary institution of morals.[6] However, for the modern contingent person ethical infringement is no sin against God but an indecency against oneself. Yet the residues of sin live on within moral philosophy in discussions of freedom and determinism. Heller dismisses these as remnants of the old paradigm. Locating authorship is now the decisive issue in ethics. Certainly former debates still resonate in the acknowledged complexity of every individual person. Yet, while acknowledging conditioning factors, Heller argues that we can still speak meaningfully of authorship.

Even the increasing philosophical drift to subjectivism does not displace ethics at the core of Heller's philosophical personality. Individuals may construct their philosophical dramas in all sorts of ways. She insists, however, that a philosophy only appeals to her if it upholds the centrality of practical reason, morality and responsibility.[7] This is why she views the question of authorship as crucial to modern ethics. This question is not identical to degree of responsibility or identification with the deed. Some deeds have multiple authors with varying degrees of responsibility and individuals do undergo moral transformations. Yet Heller anchors the question of authorship beyond interpretation, in the attitude of authenticity. The authentic person ascribes moral weight to the link between her own actions and the act.[8] For her, this self-attribution is an exercise in moral autonomy. This is the light in which she understands her own concept of existential choice. The existential choice of oneself is the clearest manifestation of the leap into autonomy. This choice annuls all previous determinations; all erstwhile determinations are now chosen as the individual becomes the full author of her own deeds. The category of authenticity is the modern kernel that has survived after the husk of sin and will have become obsolete. The authenticity of the good person is a modern utopia – a celebration of the continuing viability of ethics and of the fact that life is worth living.[9]

The historical tendency to subjectivisation of philosophy is closely connected with the loss of a dominant concept of truth in postmodern times. This culture tolerates a plurality of discourses, each with its own criteria of truth. Truth still resides in absolute spirit, but the latter has been privatised. The authority of tradition is abandoned for personal interpretation. Yet even this does not signify the disappearance of a common spirit. Today we are even more conscious of our ensnarement within a particular historical milieu. What Heller calls the 'spirit of our congregation' is that of hermeneutics and historical consciousness. Accumulating research has supplied contemporaries with a truth that encompasses all of the past and the present. This may be a *large* circle but Heller insists it is still a circle. Here Truth is immanent and subjective. The assertion that the Truth is both whole and subjective is no contradiction because the whole and the subjective imply one another. Infinite possible interpretations are offered to subjects 'thrown' within the prison house of historicity. Denizens of modernity are deficient Hegelians. They are intensely conscious of their historical entrapment and therefore simply repudiate all claims to know necessity. Even the truth of the whole cannot be an absolutist claim. It is only a truth *for us*. We cannot legitimately ascribe it to other cultures. In pursuit of their own personal salvation, modern individuals scour the whole past, seeking novel meaning. Yet this mass search only thins out absolute spirit. Compounding this subjectivisation, philosophy joins the general 'ironic turn' in all cultural forms. This is another instance of the 'double bind' that Heller will come to see at the heart of modern experience. The modern individual must maintain allegiance to both historical and technological imagination and show due respect to both past and future. It is self-defeating to try to escape this spirit of the age. The philosopher can do no more than explore the sense in which historicity has become the new absolute, by banging their head against the prison-house of historicity.

The *aporia* at the heart of this double bind is a product of modern philosophical self-reflection. All truths appear in time and are therefore historical. However, only in modernity is this brought to full self-consciousness. Only modern philosophers have ventured beyond traditional scepticism to explore the *aporias* of truth. Kierkegaard rejected Hegel's equation of the historical and the eternal. He brings to light the *aporia* of the historical emergence of eternal truth. Philosophy is a dialectical enterprise trading on truths born through negation. Yet the Enlightenment ideal of absolute truth appeared to finally exclude negation.[10] In response to this *aporia*, postmodern philosophers have abandoned the quest for absolutes and universality; they search for a truth that does not compel. Heller argues that the early modern quest for absolute certitude was tied to a socio-political agenda: to sweep away the remnants of traditional asymmetrical feudal social arrangements. Yet, beyond this historically conditioned choice, the quest for certitude was quite unwarranted. Later adventures in modern philosophy of science have dismissed correspondence and suggested that there will be no final definitive criteria of truth. The dominating power of science as an ideology still holds sway in many quarters, but postmodern denizens do not believe in any absolute world picture. Heller now foreshadows a chastened humanism that is especially aware of limitation and of the fragility of the human condition.

While she does not deny the possibility of assertions about truth in general, these do not interest her.[11] A truth that compels, which is reduced to correct inference, outlaws other alternatives. Humans have the capacity to inhabit more than one reality at the same time. Each of these has its own distinct rules, norms and concepts of truth.[12] In these various realities, there will be different criteria of truth. Taking into account these different kinds of truth, she argues that true knowledge must be understood pragmatically as a kind of 'know-how' and 'know-what', which facilitates our orientation in the world. Concepts of truth can be inflected and shaded in various ways as well as being ethically informed. Criteria of reliability will vary from sphere to sphere.[13] Our capacity to participate simultaneously in multiple realities and language games allows us to criticise some norms and rules from the standpoint of others. This means that the content and criteria of truth are in constant flux. As we have already seen in respect to institutional life, we do not have to accept all the criteria of a specific sphere in order to navigate successfully in it;[14] nor does it mean that we have abandoned the question of truth. All that is required is a post-epistemological concept of truth which has put aside any aspiration to be absolute, certain or overarching.

Heller encapsulates this as a venture into an idea of truth that is the dialectical sublation of the concept of truth and its negation. This conception of truth provides knowledge, informs whether a kind of truth is truth for you and for others. She enjoins us to recognise each other's truths as the highest form of recognition of the other.[15] Saying that truth is subjective is, for Heller, no concession to solipsism. It only redirects attention to the subjective aspect of truth after an epoch mesmerised by objectivity. The subjectivity of truth entails the inevitability of wager. The individual wagers on a Truth that is truth for her. However, as Heller underlines, 'truth for me' is not identical to 'my truth'. No one possesses the truth. The personal wager does not define the source of any single truth or whether its content is contingent or eternal.[16] The subjectivity of truth is, for Heller, embedded in its edifying potential. This is the truly existential meaning of truth. An edifying truth is connected to the whole of an individual's existence. The modern subject exists in the flux of an ever changing hierarchy of truths. But the idea of truth is the regulative idea of a meaningful conduct of life. The truth of an individual's life as a whole results from a subjective synthesis into a meaningful life. Here truth corresponds to no 'fact', but is a truth event within an individualised narrative, a synthetic quest to shape a meaningful life. Unlike the ancient citizen, who was assured of the identity of the good and a meaningful life, the modern individual must wrestle with a full awareness of her own contingency. Heller views this as more than just an indication of the historicity of truth, of its cultural embeddedness. She hopes it signals the birth of a new postmodern culture reconciled to, but celebrating, contingency. This would be a culture without a dominating concept of truth.[17]

ON THE RAILWAY STATION

Heller is clearly determined to articulate her own personal perspective within the spectrum of postmodern pluralism. She is at pains to distinguish her distinctive reflective version of postmodernism from much that sails under this banner. She rejects postmodern relativism as a naive perpetuation of the grand narratives it rejects. This is a reactive shadow of cynicism and fundamentalism. Correctly understood, postmodernity is no new stage or epoch after the modern, but a further version of enlightenment, a self-reflective consciousness of modernity itself.[18] The consciousness of historicity has finally attained a degree of intensity that destroys all naive narratives of 'progress'; in its place we find a new awareness of the finitude, fragility and contingency of the human condition. Acknowledging a family resemblance between her own account of a series of shapes of historical consciousness culminating in reflective postmodernism and the now discredited grand narratives of nineteenth-century modernism, Heller denies direct historical evaluation and therefore naive progressivism.[19] Yet this does not mean reduction to the role of uninvolved spectator. Even when construed as entirely contingent, denizens of modernity cannot escape the present. This contingency must be chosen as a destiny and a practical responsibility. Contemporaries are in charge of this present world, and its very importance lies in its absoluteness for us as fate. Being in charge means there can be no avoidance of responsibility; indirect evaluation is part and parcel of practically dealing with this contingent context. The attempt to provide the present with some historical legitimacy, either in the deep past or a distant future, is bogus and mere avoidance of the practical responsibility of the 'absolute present'.

Referring back to the typology of forms of historical consciousness outlined in *A Theory of History*, Heller designates this sense of responsibility with the abstract label of 'consciousness of reflected generality'. The economic and technological tentacles of modernity have created a single world in which an awareness of a common fate is at least potentially exchangeable for historically uneven consciousness.[20] However, the collapse of naive progressivism along with historical lawfulness has undermined the attachment of this awareness of a common fate to a perspective of privilege. Instead, reflective postmodern consciousness underscores the contingency of this fate by turning its sceptical gaze on all civilisatory illusions. Not only are there no historical laws or goals, but even the earlier Enlightenment faith in rationality as a salve to the wound of cosmic contingency has been unmasked as ideology.[21] As we have seen, this does not signify the devaluation of reason, but a rethinking and refusal to employ it naively without scepticism and self-consciousness. The modernist illusion to be the first to really know what history was about has dissolved, along with its scientistic pretensions. The various illusory progressivist narratives of the nineteenth century led to the transgressions of the twentieth century – to the Holocaust and to the Gulags. These horrific lessons suggest a need for theoretical humility. The philosopher can no longer rest assured that they are aboard some fast train speeding towards an appointed destination. Heller now counsels residence on the railway station of the present. This means philosophy must deal with contingency, fragility, lack of privileged insight and uncertainty about destinations. Modernism survives, but as a transcended moment within postmodern self-reflection.[22] Yet this contemporary hegemony of postmodern consciousness is no final victory. The 'facts' supporting the progressivist narrative remain.

Resigned to the rigours of life lived permanently in transit, Heller is still far from relinquishing the possibility of utopia. If we cannot know the future, we cannot know that the redeemer will never appear. For Heller, this reversion to the language of religion is conscious and appropriate. The chair of the redeemer must remain. We cannot know, but may hope. Permanently empty, the chair remains as a utopian possibility.[23] This new statement of her position on the status of utopia represents a dilution of her earlier strong position for the centrality of utopia to a post-Marxist radical philosophy. While it is vital not to close the door to all utopian thinking, it is clear that the immanent scepticism of her new reflective postmodern standpoint requires a subordination of its status within the main philosophical task of guarding the equilibrium of modernity.

Heller's reconciliation with a modern life on the railway station should not be viewed simply as a response to the duress of disappointed revolutionary hopes. Certainly, real political experience has engendered prudence and theoretical humility. Yet, more profound is a deeper insight into the very paradox at the heart of what she takes to be the modernity project. As we have seen, she holds that freedom is the highest universal value of modernity. Freedom serves both as highest value and as foundation. Whereas previous societies could rest upon tradition and metaphysically self-evident truths, both of these succumbed in modernity to an unbridled negative reason. Freedom becomes the *arche* of this world: in the theoretical dimension as pure reason and in the practical as the autonomy of the will. Not content with recognising freedom's hegemony over modern theory and practice, she also locates here the source of both triumphant daring and profound difficulties. The denizen of modernity sits astride a paradox. Freedom is simply unable to perform the task of foundation. The very meaning of the critique of tradition and metaphysics is the denial of foundation. The modern world is grounded upon a principle that negates grounding.[24] This means that everything remains ungrounded and necessarily so. The real task is of constantly grounding anew. This is the radical emancipatory meaning of the modernity project. All the paradoxes of modernity arise from this paradox.

The main task of reflective postmodern consciousness is to think through this paradox.[25] While both *naive* and *self-reflective* postmodern consciousnesses are grounded in freedom, only the constant self-reflection of the latter *thinks through* the paradoxes of freedom. Nevertheless, it is hard to live without certainties.[26] Although Hegel was the first to temporise paradox, he eventually bowed to the absolute. Naive postmodern consciousness, whose scepticism does not amount to full self-consciousness, capitulates either to self-righteousness or to cynicism. To avoid this risk, a *self-reflective* postmodern consciousness must recognise the existential ground of the modern quest for certainties. This is not a desire for technical knowledge, but for meaning. The quest for meaning can neither be justified nor eradicated. The modern desire for truth is the existential desire of the finite being, born of involvement.[27] Because in modernity the subjective truth of involvement no longer has a common ground, each individual posits her own historical truth. This generates the dilemma first recognised by Kierkegaard. A merely subjective truth cannot solve the problem of truth. Without a sense of the absolute, existential involvement is bereft of meaning.[28] Each individual can speak with absolute conviction of her own truth without fear of falsification. The only way beyond this paradox is the 'leap' into truth, the existential choice whereby the individual takes responsibility for her truth. Ultimately, Heller affirms that this practical choice with its consequential assumption of responsibility is the only way to meet the demands of paradoxical modernity and its ungrounded grounding in freedom.

CONTINUITY AND REFLECTION

When this reflective postmodern articulation is compared to Heller's immediate post-Marxist philosophical paradigm, a fundamental continuity in her understanding of the philosophical project becomes obvious. For the reflective postmodern Heller, philosophy remains rational self-reflection concerned with demythologisation, critique and self-orientation. Yet other essential details have changed. This is not just an issue of nuance and terminology but an altered mood that adds a different inflection to her understanding of philosophical radicalism.

Heller's book on radical philosophy broke with the Marxist grand narrative and celebrated pluralism. The postmodern Heller has continued to explore the consequences of this pluralism and its impact on a viable contemporary philosophy. We have already noted her reconstruction of the history of modern philosophy as a tendency towards subjectivisation. The dominance of philosophical schools gives way to individual revolutions that often do not even survive the life of their initiator. Heller notes the impact of this change on the utopian moment of philosophy. In pre-modern times characterised by traditional virtues and by static need structures, an individual's utopia could be offered as a panacea.[29] This is no longer possible in the age of individualisation. As need structures and dreams of happiness become more individualised, the images of social and political conditions that might realise them become more idiosyncratic. The classical utopias offered a holistic vision of the unity of goodness and felicity. Yet increased individualisation rendered this so idiosyncratic that no contemporary thinker could promise such a perfect whole. The result is a *fragmentation* of contemporary utopian reality.[30]

Another of the most decisive consequences of Heller's conception of an increasingly individualised philosophy is the erosion of a rationalist bias in her understanding of the limits of philosophy. *A Radical Philosophy* demarcated philosophy from the domain of religion by restricting it from those questions of finitude, death and nothingness that simply make us 'dizzy'. While such a demarcation seemed to her critics quite arbitrary and narrowly prescriptive in its construction of the scope of philosophy,[31] it became quite untenable for Heller herself once she affiliated philosophy so clearly to the liberated individual imagination. To avoid potential ethico-political disaster attending an unmediated identity of philosophy with subjective imagination, she offers a strategy with two elements. This emphasises the limits of the human condition: historical conditionedness, human finitude, frailty and the dangers of the redemptive paradigm. She also asserts the necessity of a divorce between speculative and practical philosophy. The former is identified with a distinctive originality that is more personal and subjective. The philosopher gives shape to her own idiosyncratic set of philosophical characters less dependent on the traditional pool. This radical freedom extends even to those 'dizzy' topics that she formerly excluded from the consideration of rational philosophy. Yet, the same idiosyncrasy is proscribed from the domain of practical philosophy. In this province, the subjective imagination is constrained by the need to address the common thing we all share: the *res publica*. This constraint militates against the pure subjectivism permitted to speculative philosophy. Whether such a Chinese wall between speculative and practical philosophy is ultimately sustainable is open to question. While this is not a metaphysical dualism in the Kantian sense, it appears to constrain the dynamism and interplay between subjective imagination and social normativity in a wholly artificial and ultimately unsustainable way. For example, it is hard to see how radical needs can migrate from margins to the masses without the possibility of uninhibited transmission. Be this as it may, the motives underpinning Heller's strategy here become even clearer when we contemplate her reflective postmodern radicalism.

The Heller of *A Radical Philosophy* also associated radicalism with the total critique of society and with Marx's desire to get to the root of things.[32] While critique remains an indispensable and central element of Heller's understanding of philosophy, her reflective postmodern turn introduces greater nuance and complexity into her appreciation of radicalism. Like Marx, she refuses the title of 'radical' to any claim modelled on perfection and absolute transcendence. For her, radicalism implies immanence and the exploration not of some abstract beyond but of existing possibilities within dynamic modernity.[33] For Heller, such exploration is always utopian and she understands radical utopias as those that explore the possibilities within modernity, bearing the promise of symmetrical reciprocity. However, because there are almost as many such worlds as there are philosophers, the task of discriminating between them requires criteria. This is where Heller reasserts what she calls her 'thin rationalism'. Having liberated subjective imagination within the domain of speculative philosophy, criteria of rationality still remain in the domain of the practical. In order to avoid deception she has always maintained that the essential core of philosophy is the right use of reason. Even in its modern configuration, which has abandoned certainty and the logic of identity, rationality must be understood as the best remedy against deception and chaos. The radical has two choices that both take their cue from the Enlightenment. Here we return to the options of naive and reflective postmodernism. Reason in its deconstructive postmodern form is a destructive negating of all norms and taboos. In its naive version it lacks the ironic distance and self-reflection that would allow the termination of this destructive spiral short of the authoritarian self-assertion of particularity. Reflective postmodernism, on the other hand, has learnt fully the lessons of the failed nineteenth-century grand narratives. It takes the contingency, historicity and fallibility of the human condition seriously as an inherent limit to the aspirations of rationalism. Questioning must be sustained not only against all idols but also as self-questioning.[34]

It is precisely this constant questioning that allows the reflective postmodernist to appreciate the paradoxical character of the modern and the dual commitments that Heller calls the 'double bind'. While paradox assumes a variety of forms in modernity, she finds its principal manifestation in modernity's dual allegiance to both technological and historical consciousness. The former is associated with action and problem solving. For it, the world is nothing more than a standing reserve for potential instrumentalisation. The latter, on the other hand, is a spectatorial recollection that abstracts from utility in the quest for meaning as an end in itself. A radical philosophy is 'rational' when it contributes to the balance between the two. Somehow the pursuit of universality and regard for particularity must find a sustainable equilibrium. Only in this manner can the chaos of self-destructive negating critique be avoided, along with the one-dimensional worship of the existing. Heller no longer identifies radical philosophy with total critique. A philosophy can be radical as an agent of conservation and balance in a dynamic world pledged to the ideals of symmetrical reciprocity.[35] The immediate post-Marxist Heller articulated her concept of radicalism in continuity with the socio-political emphasis laid down by Marx. By contrast, the *reflective postmodern* Heller has absorbed fully all the implications of the practical failures of total critique. The ethical concerns that have always orientated her work are now registered in the heart of the concept of radicalism itself. It is radical to treat humans as ends rather than as mere means.[36] The incorporation of this ethical maxim into its pursuit of the utopian idea of symmetrical reciprocity makes a philosophy radical.[37]

In acknowledging the fragility of her practical rationalism, Heller goes further than Habermas in celebrating human contingency. She is determined to anchor her position not in the quasi-transcendental domain of language but in the more volatile terrain of history. Since modernity lacks the prospect of certainty, rational discussion cannot begin without the acceptance of at least one value as a first gesture. Heller wagers for freedom as the leading value ideal of modernity. This value is the manifestation of the norm inherent in the modern social arrangement of symmetrical reciprocity and the one supposedly accepted as the highest substantive value by a modern consensus.[38] Against the objection that the value of freedom is itself too abstract and in need of more supplementary definition in order to arrive at the sort of value agreement she implies, Heller's response is that such a move would 'spoil the whole argument' and 'tell an entirely different story'.[39] This can be taken to mean that contemporary social life is engaged in a value discussion around precisely this value. To specify it in any more precise way is to foreclose the debate and theoretically suppress the full expression of modern pluralism. Yet her reply begs the question of whether the possibility of such a value discussion is premised on the general consensus surrounding this value. In arguing that freedom has become an empirical universal, Heller assumes the consensus that is supposed to be the condition for the ongoing debate. Yet, as Cohen and others have mentioned, many individuals and groups contest modernity and reject the value of freedom. That Heller ignores this obvious fact suggests that there is even a normative edge to her understanding of empirical universality. Her universal appeal is to 'moderns' and not to the various shades of modern fundamentalism. However, to acknowledge counter-tendencies and opposition is completely in keeping with Heller's agnosticism. Unlike illustrious predecessors, she refuses to predict the future or even the survival of modernity.

PHILOSOPHY IN THE AGE OF CONTINGENCY

While, on one side, Heller struggles to defend the idea of empirical universal values, on the other, she must meet charges that she has conceded too much to postmodernism. György Márkus argues that her concessions to contingency threaten the very project of philosophy as an autonomous cultural objectivation. While he shares Heller's desire to dilute the traditional philosophical fixation on certainty and rethink philosophical rationality in accord with the modern cultural need for orientation, he holds firm to the need for a normative concept of truth.[40] For Márkus, the very unity of philosophy as a cultural enterprise relies upon the appeal to common criteria codified in the assertion of truth. Beyond the dissension of the philosophical past and the normative pluralism of the present, he argues that allegiance to a normative concept of truth sustains the fragile unity of philosophy and its very existence as a genre. Other cultural objectivations offer orientation and reflection, but only philosophy stakes its existence on the distinction between *episteme* and *doxa* and on a commitment to the argumentative methodology implied by it. Philosophy must not be reduced to 'coffee house' chatter.[41] Commitment to a minimal rationality condensed in the commitment to truth requires that claims be backed by argument and that this be orientated using vaguely common criteria.

We have already seen that Heller has not abandoned the concept of truth, but suggests a more multidimensional understanding and a more relaxed attitude to genre switching. She rises to the defence of the 'coffee house' model.[42] For her, the Márkus position represents a failure to fully digest all the consequences of modern contingency. She sees nothing wrong with some philosophers engaging publicly in edifying conversation, elucidating and problematising issues without pretending to know the answers to their questions. They may pursue their 'truth' as long as they do not deny to others the option of building more impressive structures. For Heller, this is completely in tune with the historical trend to subjectivisation, confronting the tyranny of false objectivism and part and parcel of recognising contingency and cultural pluralism. She is also determined not to exclude a whole range of practices and forms facilitating subjective orientation and meaning.

The gist of her claim is that the denial of normative truth does not necessarily mean a descent into irrationality. Even those 'literary'

philosophies that suspend their truth claim are not adverse to
philosophical argumentation and are quite willing to defend themselves
using conventional means. One may even challenge on historical grounds
the normative claim to which Márkus attributes the cultural unity
of philosophy. After all, he acknowledges disputation as the normal
condition of the philosophical schools. Of even more relevance, he notes
that on the rare occasions when alternative programmes within the
contemporary terrain do deign to address each other, this is more often
a case of defamation or of talking past one another.[43] Yet he insists
that the uniqueness of philosophy as a cultural enterprise depends
not on such empirical difficulties but upon the force of its normative
unity implied by the 'dogmatic' assertion of truth. Furthermore, it
could be added that it is a concession to his position to allow that the
postmodernists often resort to conventional argumentation. Surely,
this suggests their performative contradiction and the irreplaceability
of the notion of truth that is in debate.

Heller rejects any interpretation of her move as a concession to
relativism. She insists that for those playing the game of philosophy the
assertion of truth remains a serious business with high stakes. However,
there is also the question of the authenticity of its players. *Reflective
postmodernism* is indicative of a changed philosophical mood. For
Heller, it expresses the fact that some philosophers have lost interest
in cancelling the game and are happy to continue playing without the
illusion of consensus.[44] Contingency must be allowed to infect the
very normative status of philosophy itself. Whether or not the cultural
institution formerly recognised as philosophy will or should survive a
devaluation that ensues from falling cultural status and reduction to the
rank of 'coffee house' chatter is not for her the primary question. She
wagers on a persisting need for orientation in the increasing dynamic
conditions confronting the modern contingent individual. Even if genre
switching does blur the integrity of long established genre norms, this
seems to ensure the continuing vitality of a cultural enterprise similar to
philosophy. Never one to be confined by narrow disciplinary boundaries
or conventional genre forms, Heller believes the indispensability of
philosophy's cultural function will sustain it against all vagaries of
form. For Heller, this is the fate of a contingent cultural enterprise and
the cost that must be paid to fulfil the task of orientation in a language
that expresses the 'spirit of the times'. As we have seen, Heller views
the primary task of philosophy as making sense of the contingent flow
of social existence. Philosophy must engage with contemporaneity. Yet
philosophical radicalism requires that this 'sense' be both critical and
rational. Doesn't the very functionality of philosophy depend upon

normative requirements that compel discussants to meet on the same ground? How else could an activity such as philosophy distinguish itself from other cultural forms and ensure a fallible method of resolution? Heller may want to allow more voices to participate in the chatter, but it still seems that ultimately rules and criteria are required so that the chatter does not descend into chaos.

Heller's development between the post-Marxist radical and reflective postmodern phases has seen a change of emphasis in her understanding of rational critique. Reflection on the past and potential political and ethical costs of 'total critique' and 'naive' deconstruction have caused her to adopt a more nuanced understanding of philosophical radicalism. The fact that radicalism in this formulation is no longer associated with either political or cultural revolution is likely to engender accusations of accommodation from some political and philosophical avant-gardes. Yet these are mainly predictable and superficial reactions. The real sophistication of Heller's philosophical radicalism lies in its continued engagement with all the paradoxes of modernity without betraying ideals, critical edge or reflective capacity.

11
The Pendulum of Modernity

By the end of the initial examination of Heller's theory of modernity in Chapter 8, it was clear that some of her central ideas had begun to mutate. In 1986, Heller and Fehér both took positions in New York with the Graduate Faculty of the New School. This move to the symbolic centre of contemporary modernity, the subsequent dramatic collapse of the 'dictatorship over needs', the end of the cold war in 1989 and the need to refocus on the reality of liberal democratic societies hastened the rethinking of Heller's theoretical priorities and perspective. This re-evaluation sees a shift from the initial defence of the logic of democracy against the colonisation by the other logics to a more detached exploration of the spirit of the democratic ethos. The principal concern is now maintaining the equilibrium of the dynamic and inherently conflictual modern constellation. This shift first becomes obvious in the 1992 essay 'Modernity's Pendulum'[1] and comes to fruition with the publication of the comprehensive *A Theory of Modernity* (1999).[2] In this chapter we investigate these innovations and analyse their impact on the main outlines of the mature theory.

The ideas that Heller presented in 'Modernity's Pendulum' are not an entirely new departure.[3] Her post-Marxist reflections on the fate of modernity and its prospects of survival always hinged on the question of its multiple ingredients and dimensions and on the need to keep these precarious constellations in balance. However, in the earlier treatments of these constant themes the focus is on the ultimately incompatible and mutually destructive logics that threatened the very physical survival of the denizens of modernity. Against the background of a new arms race in the early 1980s, these worries hardly seemed idle fancy. But in the post-cold war historical conjuncture, the logics are reinterpreted and move into the background. Heller's attention turns to the internal structure of modern societies and to the question of their equilibrium.

This changed interest is most clearly registered in the figure of the 'pendulum'; this metaphor now usurps the position of priority formerly occupied by the idea of 'multiple logics'. In fact, in the paper

'Modernity's Pendulum' the 'logics' are not even mentioned. The previous talk of 'incompatible' and 'mutually conflicting' logics is supplanted by the image of the uniform and synchronised swing of the pendulum, maintaining its uniform motion within circumscribed limits. Only when constrained in this way does modernity avoid destructively overbalancing in a single direction under the pressure of one or more 'logics'. Heller is also now less concerned with the potential trajectories of modernity than with its essential structural components. These are now designated as the modern 'dynamic' and 'social arrangement'. The former is the spirit of modernity: the dialectics of dynamic justice that permeate the life-world as a spirit of permanent critique. Complementing this 'dynamic' is a 'social arrangement', whose essential modernity is attested by the fact that functional performance and the norms of symmetrical reciprocity displace social hierarchy as the fundamental norms of allocation and distribution. This focus on the 'constituents' of modernity reflects the critical insight that both components are crucial to the vitality and equilibrium of a dynamic but balanced modernity. For Heller, the lesson to be drawn from the 'distorted' character of the Soviet debacle is that critical dynamism is an integral moment of all permutations of modernity. Only its harmony with the norms of the modern social arrangement ensures the long-term viability and reproduction of the constellation of modernity.

A Theory of Modernity presents a synthesis in which these new insights and changed perspectives are brought into accord with what remained contemporary in her initial multiple logics model and its critical intentions. Heller commences with methodological reflections on her underpinning standpoint. The '*A*' in *A Theory of Modernity* is crucial because it underscores that this vision of the essence of modernity allows Heller to make sense of her own experience. In line with her reflective postmodern stance, she dispenses with the idea of a definitive account of modernity. Hers is merely *one* amongst *many possible* 'modernities'. While such an approach must be idiosyncratic, she also never loses sight of the fact of the shared character of social reality. Her vision will be 'true' to the extent that it captures not only her own but also common experiences. In doing so, it raises a theoretical claim to essence that fuses perspectives. However, this essentially practical *theoria* cannot rise above the level of opinion: this essence can neither be proven nor conclusively falsified. All that can be offered is the plausibility of a unique perspective that strikes a chord as one of the possibly true visions of an inexhaustible modernity.

THE CONSTITUENTS OF MODERNITY

The essence of modernity is a correlation between the modern 'dynamic' and the 'social arrangement' as the two constituents of modernity. This correlation promotes the relative stability of modernity despite its constant internal dynamism. Although the modern 'social arrange-ment', understood as a functional distribution of social positions, is essential to modernity, by itself it would be unstable without a comple-mentary 'dynamic'. This implies Heller's interpretation of the collapse of the 'dictatorship over needs'.[4] However, while this 'dynamic' is indis-pensable to the relative stability of modernity, it is not indigenous to the modern terrain. It emerges in Athenian life and assumes the literary form of Socratic questioning, reappears in several critical historical epochs and is implicated in all the narratives of the European Enlightenment, before assuming the voracious, destructive form of 'undialectical dialectics'.[5]

The 'undialectical' character of this questioning consists in the fact that it brooks no internal limit. In Hegelian terms, this is the logic of the 'bad infinite'. Rational deconstruction is corrosive when it finds nothing on which it can rest as taken for granted.[6] This sort of critique was vital to the delegitimation of tradition and to the delivery of the modern social arrangement. At that time, it served to legitimate the new language game of metaphysics. Yet, without the prospect of ushering in a new social world, this critique became destructive.[7] The affinity between this dialectics and modern social experience is obvious. Questioning, dissent, dissatisfaction and challenge are its essence. The modern 'dynamic' complements a world receptive to the claims of justice. It allows these claims to be contested in accordance with the rationality of intellect.[8] This dynamic goes even further, to challenge the concept of justice itself. Might not it be that justice itself rests upon metaphysical prejudice? This lack of critical inhibition prompts Heller to raise the question as to whether humans are able to live without something solid.[9]

Deconstruction reaches its limit when there is nothing left to deconstruct.[10] The modern dynamic is intoxicated with the process of universalisation. The world of distinctions was displaced by the newly created universal categories of man, art and culture. The modern subject was posited as endowed with a limitless subjective freedom, yet is, like all beings, limited: finite, conditioned and contingent. Here the Romantic voice of Enlightenment announces its presence. Life is not reducible to a technological problem. From the Romantic perspective, a view that makes efficiency the principle evaluative criterion is reductive and ugly. The Enlightenment itself manifests paradox when recommending both the destruction and the preservation of distinction. At stake here is more than a logical problem. Having defeated all distinction, the dynamic of modernity – in the shape of the process of universalisation – becomes nihilistic, turning against the previously acclaimed universality in the attempt to validate new 'differences'.[11] For Heller, contemporary fundamentalism is the natural offspring of this logic of nihilism. The danger of the 'undialectical dialectic' is a potential turn against critical discourse and the modern social arrangement. Naive commitment to either side of the paradox of universality and difference is an expression of undialectical consciousness and its incapacity to sustain the tension. For Heller, this is just as evident in the modern democratic pursuit of universal equality as it is in Nietzsche's celebration of particularity for its own sake. Only a reflective postmodern consciousness can face and think through the multiple paradoxes immanent in modernity.

The 'modern dynamic' appeared sporadically in pre-modern times but never bore permanent fruit. Yet, in ensemble with the 'modern social arrangement', it has conquered the world. Making a late appearance on the historical scene with its lift-off in Europe, this social arrangement expanded remorselessly, regardless of local affinity. However, without the modern dynamic, the modern social arrangement is unstable and quickly ossifies.[12] Spectacular growth was accompanied by the corresponding, potentially destructive, nihilism mentioned above. Heller insists that the essence of modernity cannot be dissected.[13] Nor is the unity of arrangement and dynamic a normative index of perfect development. Every society that has switched from the pre-modern to the modern social arrangement (functional allocation) is modern in its own way. Although unprecedented, modernity is no paradise. Neither paeans to progress nor nostalgia for the past are appropriate. The modern is the only social arrangement able to support present populations.[14]

Modernity signifies the end of a society organised on the basis of social stratification by birth. Society remains stratified, but the principle of this stratification is institutional functionality. Modernity promotes itself with the slogan of 'equal opportunity' under the assumption that 'all are born free'. The ideological character of this slogan matters less than the fact that in the modern social arrangement, assymetrical reciprocity is the *result* of functional performance. As function and being are no longer identical, the trampoline of 'equal opportunity' gives each individual her chance to change function.[15] This distinction is an index of the importance of institutions in establishing the hierarchy of the modern social arrangement. We have already seen that modernity has raised the profile of institutions. Everyday life shrinks to the family and adult life only begins with the assumption of a functional role within an institution outside the family. The network of institutions plays the primary role in establishing and perpetuating social hierarchy. This transformation emerges in conjunction with the dynamic of modernity and its gospel of equality and justice.

The ideology of 'equal opportunity' fuels the dynamic of modernity. The discrepancy between normative concept and empirical reality, between 'born freedom' and 'social slavery', opens up a wide terrain in which dissatisfaction engenders critique. Heller insists that the values of rationality and equality are not utopian ideas, but a virtual reality. The dynamic of modernity expands reality by constantly working to approximate these norms.[16] However, a chronic discrepancy means that dynamic justice is never short of causes and proposed compensations.

MULTIPLE 'LOGICS'

Previously we mentioned the young Heller's desire for a philosophy where 'everything clicked'. Her deliberate repudiation of this early philosophical ideal is one of the keys to understanding her mature theory of modernity. Whether all trace of this predisposition has been extinguished or not,[17] the portrait of modernity that has so far emerged is one of paradox, tensions and dynamism. The relationship between the modern dynamic and the modern social arrangement assumes a variety of shapes where 'nothing fits perfectly'. This is seen as an advantage, because it suggests that modernity is not a seamless totality without potentials and options, both good and bad.

This embrace of imperfection was part of the rationale of the idea of multiple logics. Heller now suggests that the 'logics' are *developmental tendencies or potentials* immanent within the modern network of institutions, social structures and action types: they are processes of socio-ontological concretisation. As long as an institution possesses the power to maintain its identity, it develops its possibilities.[18] 'Logic' implies developmental self-propulsion. Yet this *dynamis* does not determine the actualisation of possibilities. Institutional/action potentials remain open to the influence of competing logics. Historical immanence does not mean historical teleology. While it is theoretically possible to construct teleological sequences retrospectively, this should not be misconstrued as immanent unfolding.

The idea of multiple logics dispels a view of history as a single immanent story and a vision of society as a homogenised whole. In its place, we have real historical alternatives and a fragmented, decentred totality in which no single logic has primacy. This model suggests opacity, heterogeneity, indeterminacy, multiple social options and individual choices. Threats and dangers are difficult to identify because they have no single source. Likewise, at every stage of development there can be more than one outcome, because the logics are not entirely independent and direction is not internally determined.[19] Yet this marked heterogeneity, clash and confluence of potentialities, does not mean completely open or infinite possibilities. The menu of possibilities is constrained by limits. The nineteenth-century faith in unlimited progress and resources today seems incredibly naive. Our consciousness of limits is heightened by the increasing collision of the logics of modernity; technology, economics and politics. After a century of excesses in pursuing the illusions promoted and perpetuated by the domination of a single logic, awareness of limits is a safety valve and a warning of possible destruction. Moreover, it also reinforces an important element of Heller's anthropological vision: the fragility of the human condition.

Three logics are still identified as development potentials immanent within modernity. However, the contents of these logics have significantly changed. This is the crystallisation of a process of rethinking. The new contents are technology, functional allocation of social position and the logic of political power, understood as configurations of rule and domination.[20]

In earlier essays, Heller typically described the logics as industrialisation, capitalism and democracy. The new characterisation better reflects her distance from her Marxist heritage and her desire to maintain a critical, sceptical perspective. Whereas Marx thought that capitalism would conquer the world, Heller now maintains there is no capitalist society. From the start, she viewed capitalism as the bearer of both market mechanisms and civil society. This internal heterogeneity, and the influence of the other logics not determined by capitalism, rendered Marx's classical vision problematic. Heller also takes over Weber's insight that behind the Marxian culprit of commodification resides the more abstract and ambiguous figure of quantification. Rendering the second logic in functionalist terms allows her to leave behind the connotations of capitalism as a discrete societal form and to concentrate on the more pervasive market logic of quantification. This now becomes the functional allocation of social position.

The motives for replacing the logic of industrialisation with one of technology are both similar and different. The earlier emphasis on a logic of industrialisation already marked a departure from Marx. Heller's desire to theorise the 'dictatorship over needs' and warn of its potential as a new *sui generis* form of modernity prompted the initial elevation of industrialisation to the status of a logic equal to that of capitalism. Although she sometimes spoke about technology, the emphasis in her characterisation of the logic of industrialisation was more often levelled at centralisation and state control. The eclipse of the danger of the 'dictatorships over needs' facilitated a further abstraction from concrete historical scenarios and a concentration on a supposedly trans-historical developmental tendency. Heller clearly desires to penetrate behind the concrete expressions of institutional or action forms to an analysis of the allegedly deeper imagination in which they have their origin.

The change in the formulation of the third logic from democracy to that of political power reveals Heller's theoretical motives even more clearly. In the first tentative steps towards a theory of modernity, she threw herself behind the cause of democracy and gave this project the privileged status of a logic of modernity equal to capitalism and industrialisation – even while remaining uncertain of its ultimate victory. Just as time and theoretical evolution joined to distance her from the designation of logics in terms of concrete societal alternatives such as capitalism and industrialisation, the same has befallen democracy. Whereas the earlier Heller could view democracy as the only antidote to the threats to modernity, on closer acquaintance she realised that democracy itself was in need of constant critical scrutiny. This increasing scepticism towards 'really existing' democracy was also in keeping with the repudiation of historical forecasting signalled in her move beyond Marx. The shift from a logic of democracy to one of political power means that her analysis of the modern political is not even implicitly committed to a particular political form. The very idea of a 'logic of democracy' conjured up at least weak notions of historical teleology. Although Heller never practised the self-deception of value-free social critique, the explicit separation of her commitment to democratic values from the object of her analysis (political power) better sustains the perspective she previously called 'limited scepticism' and leaves completely open the political scenarios of modernity. This is especially apposite to her general understanding of these logics, in which the emphasis is very much on learning processes motored by historical actors.

THE 'LOGIC' OF TECHNOLOGY

A heterogeneous modernity with pluralised developmental possibilities does not mean a pluralist technology. What is distinctive about this logic is unilinear development without pluralisation. In contrast to the tensions and developmental options of political and social logics, the development of modern technology until the present shows no sign of splintering. It truly has become an empirical universal.[21] The singularity of technological development cannot be explained by the fact that in it cognition is reduced to mere problem solving. While this may be an adequate description of normal science, it fails to account for revolutionary science, in which innovative thinking cannot be reduced to questions of know-how. Heller agrees with Heidegger that at the most fundamental level the essence of technology resides in a particular mode of thinking that transforms humans into a standing reserve or instrumentalises them for use. This imagination compels humans to think in terms of subject/object, where the world becomes an arsenal for human use. However, Heller rejects both Heidegger's account of metaphysics as the cause of this imagination and his view that this mode of thinking exclusively dominates modernity. [22] She insists that there is more than one imaginary institution in modernity and the technological imagination always has competition. This reinforces her argument for the pluralisation and heterogeneity of modernity; it is enframed not by one but two non-aligned imaginary institutions: the technological and the historical.[23] The logics of politics and of functional division of social position are not entirely dominated by the technological imagination.

Both imaginations assisted at the birth of modernity and they have coexisted in constant interplay. [24] Heller associates the technological with action and the historical with recollection. The former gives priority to problem solving and the latter to interpretation and to the creativity of the spectator. Historical consciousness abstracts from utility and engenders a meaning that is an end in itself; it is a conversation with the past that renders it constantly present in its fragility, finitude and limit.[25] These marks of distinction should not, however, obscure the moments of fusion. The constant pursuit of novelty reveals the invasion of the logic of technology into hermeneutic practice, while the concentration on the particular discovery brings a moment of historical particularity into the continuum of technological consciousness.[26] The allegiance to two fundamentally conflicting imaginations is the dilemma Heller describes as the double bind of modernity.

The divided commitments of modernity do not stop Heller acknowledging that science has become the dominant world explanation. The former authority of tradition and religion has now passed over to science and allowed the technological imagination to become dominant. Founded on free inquiry, science pronounces its neutrality in questions of fundamental meaning. Its affinity with the modern spirit and its resulting authority has seen scientific explanation permeate all aspects of modern life. [27] Science is equated with truth, and a network of institutions, regimes of certification, journals and discourse legitimate this identity. Heller accepts Foucault's argument that the institutional authority of science also involves the exercise of power. When there are no external counterbalancing forces and it is allowed to impose the methods of the hard sciences on human subjects, it can become an oppressive force.[28] This de facto exercise of power reveals the possibility of interplay between the logic of technology and that of functionality. While the authority of science typically complements that of functionality, Heller makes clear that affinity can quickly turn into antagonism.[29] The authority of science retains trumping critical potential.

THE 'LOGIC' OF ALLOCATION

Heller views the second logic as the 'heart' of modernity.[30] This logic carries the main institutions of the modern social arrangement: the market, private property, private law and human rights. Clearly, this makes it the bearer of the essential difference between the pre-modern and modernity. It has shaped the distinctive modern social order, which has been able to fuse together formal equality and functional hierarchy. However the ideal of equality is elusive, because the mechanisms of social allocation must also reconcile initial equality with an unequal outcome; the synthesis remains imperfect. Functional justice is constantly accused of injustice before the bar of a higher dynamic justice. This quest for the ideal synthesis makes this logic the 'heart' of modernity. The concentration of claims for both justice and efficiency provides the heterogeneity Heller views as the core of modernity's vitality.[31] Corrective self-criticism is ensured by fact that the institutions of this logic push in different directions.

If the contestation of justice is one developmental tendency of the second logic, the other revolves around the market.[32] The market allocates individuals to a hierarchically structured division of functions. Even assuming the ideal market conditions of equality and freedom, the outcome is increasingly a social hierarchy based on differentiated function. In practice, this differentiation roughly corresponds to the level of access to control and management of the main institutions.[33] However, dynamic justice introduces heterogeneity into the pure logic of functional allocation. The struggle between the discourse of justice and functional allocation gives modern dynamism the appearance of a pendulum. It is only by the balancing of these two tendencies that social equilibrium is retained. This is why Heller maintains that a discrete capitalism no longer exists yet modernity continues to survive. She has not suddenly become blind to exploitation and social oppression. She is aware that a social underclass is no aberration but is essential to the functioning of modern states, yet still carries the greatest burden of injustice and exploitation.[34] Increasingly, only competition in the domain of education delivers access to a higher place in the social hierarchy. Exceptions become rarer as the exercise of power is increasingly enframed by the technological imagination.

The second logic manifests several unilinear developmental tendencies associated with the market. Heller mentions quantification, emergence of new needs and specialisation.[35]

In this second logic, the monetisation of the economy and the resulting deconstruction of the pre-modern social-arrangement-based natural differences gives free expression to quantification. Money reduces differences to quantities; it is the great equaliser that has shifted social distinction from birth to merit. Individuals are emancipated from personal dependence and this greater freedom activates adventure and risk taking.[36] But money has also had its Romantic critics, who highlighted the resulting social homogenisation and suppression of difference. Heller finds this critique exaggerated. Monetisation may tend to full quantification, but the pendulum of modernity in the shape of historical consciousness and cultural discourse resists this tendency, although the outcome is never certain.[37]

In modernity, the introduction of money as a homogeneous quantitative satisfier allows the individual increasingly to construct her own personal bundle of needs without being determined and limited by traditional social grouping. This tendency, driven by monetisation and technology, pushes the second logic towards infinite expansion.[38] However, this increasing autonomy of the individual consumer is not incompatible with the imposition of needs. The modern individual becomes prisoner of the technological imagination. Priority is accorded to novelty and increasingly technology is required to engineer specific 'ways of life'.[39] This is why Heller still finds value in the notion of alienated needs. Need structures are manufactured for, and imposed upon, individuals. As pure quantity, money does homogenise need structures. Again, this reflects the paradoxical character of modernity. The finite individual pursues the infinite in the form of an unending quantitative series.[40]

The third unilinear tendency of the second logic is specialisation. In this respect, the second logic complements forces already unleashed by the logic of technology. We previously noted how the modern social arrangement renders functional position decisive in the determination of social hierarchy. These positions are filled according to merit. As skills become increasingly concrete, a general education gives way to a specialised one.[11]Whether in the long term such specialisation is a benefit to humans has often been questioned. Heller sees the simultaneous historical emergence of culture as an antidote to a world where specialisation has marginalised the useless.[42]

At this point, Heller introduces a distinction inspired by Hannah Arendt: the modern gap between life and world. Life signifies production and reproduction focused on the pragmatics of survival. This activity, orientated solely to the useful, is distinguished from the good life. The latter rises above mere survival and pragmatics to the world of the imagination and ideas that have no immediate purpose.[43] This distinction introduces a normative dimension into Heller's theory of culture and modern subjectivity. The capacity for reflective subjectivity is an essential aspect of the second logic of modernity. This amount to the claim that historicity is essential to both the notion of the modern subject and the second logic of modernity. Historicity is both generalised and deeply ingrained in modernity. Yet Heller qualifies this interpretation by maintaining that life is possible without historicity. Historicity vitalises the reflection that is the core of the good life, but is not a necessary precondition of life.[44] Mere material reproduction requires skill, but not necessarily an identity-forming cultural narrative or 'world'.[45] The singularity of the modern subject is to ask questions and create distances. Yet clearly not all modern subjects achieve this. Only some attain the level of reflective historical consciousness. The level of reflection supposed as integral to personal identity and the critical dynamic of modern society is not as generalised or as deeply ingrained as some formulations suggest. In fact, the distinction between 'life' and 'world' corresponds to two qualitative levels of modern subjectivity. The notion of reflective historical consciousness is more than the narrative of mere ipseity. It is associated with cultural mediation of experience and critical distance. It opens up the possibility of an individual becoming a 'personality'. This notion is already familiar from Heller's earlier work: the exemplary figure who maintains a critical reflective relation to her particularity and the world. Once embedded in a Marxist framework linked to objective historical and species development, this notion is now measured by awareness of paradox. Both technological and historical consciousness vie for the imagination of the modern individual. Only those who become fully conscious of this determination experience what Heller calls the 'double bind' of modernity. The exemplary subject has a 'world'; he or she has risen above mere reproductive life to seek the 'good life' of imagination, 'useless' things and critical self-understanding.

'Having a world' does not mean this world is fully transparent. It entails a subject who is not the prisoner of one exclusive imaginary institution of modernity. This reflective subject accepts being conditioned by both technological and historical consciousness, and embraces the contest between these contradictory powers. Her identity is wrought from the force field of struggling powers induced by the 'double bind'.[46]

THE 'LOGIC' OF POLITICAL POWER AND DOMINATION

A constant theme in Heller's later work is raising the profile of the political. Marxism had always subsumed politics in an overarching historical movement that was ultimately determined by economic forces. Paradoxically, even the revolutionary goal of socialism did little to explicitly thematise politics. The multiple logics model of modernity amended this oversight in two ways. Firstly, it elevated democracy to the status of an independent logic with its own relatively autonomous causality and emphasised the practical need to struggle for it. Secondly, as we have seen, it drew attention to the threat of a form of modernity that had given absolute priority to the logic of industrialisation and suppressed the logic of democracy. Heller warned that the 'dictatorship over needs' was no mere historical aberration, but one of the possible configurations of modernity. If Heller has now found cause to abandon the terminology of a logic of democracy, due to its potential teleological reading, and to speak of the logic of political power, this means neither an implicit devaluation of the political nor a diminution of democratic sentiments and aspirations. Her discussion of the 'logic of the political' reflects the changed historical circumstances of the post-communist world. With the collapse of the Soviet system and its satellites, the threat of the 'dictatorship over needs' had receded. However, even in liberal democratic societies, the threat to the autonomy of the political persists in the aspiration of the technological imagination to reduce the problems of the political to exercises in problem solving.[47] Perhaps surprisingly, Heller's concern here is not so much the ideological drive for the minimal state. She views this as just another expression of the pendulum of modernity. This very motion can be viewed as a result of the ongoing tussle between the minimalist and the interventionist states.

On Heller's reading, the liberal democratic welfare compromise navigates between the minimalist Scylla of social unrest and the interventionist Charybdis of economic and social stagnation. The interplay of the second (social/economic) and the third (political) logic is indispensable to the dynamic equilibrium of modernity. Yet Heller sees this interplay endangered by a technicist interpretation that attempts to reduce all political problems to technical ones. This reduction would signify the annihilation of the double bind that generates the freedom and creative dynamism crucial to the survival of modernity.[48]

Heller maintains that historical consciousness is crucial to the political. The latter is not reducible to the technical pragmatics of life but also concerns the 'good life' and having a world for which historical consciousness is quite indispensable. Constitutions are never just products of technical drafting, but reveal the historical foundations of national traditions. They are not exportable in the same way as cars, televisions and other technology.[49] Adoption of aspects of constitutions is still possible, but this requires careful adaptations to bring the new into affinity with the local. Of course, the weight of historical imagination can vary greatly. The meagre political innovation of the moderns gives greater weight to the historical imagination: this recollection preserves worlds.[50] Labels such as 'false consciousness' and 'ideology' once denigrated the activity of 'worlding'. However, the post-Marxist Heller now defends ideology as the indispensable product of historical consciousness. Enlightenment once attacked ideology under the banner of universality. Everything particular was viewed with hostility and condescension as an obstacle to the acceptance of universality.[51] Yet in politics the only universal is an abstract 'humanity' bereft of stories. Collective stories are the products of historical consciousness centred on the ethical powers of family, civil society and the state. This does not mean Heller has renounced the critique of ideology. She recognises that, like ideology itself, it is indispensable to the modern world. Events in Kosovo and elsewhere have reminded us that historical imagination can sever all relation with 'reality' and 'rationality' and become immune to the impact of the other logics.[52] Nevertheless, Heller insists that there is no modern world without ideology. A meaningful concept of the political cannot be provided by scienticised critique. The values of rationality and universality cannot make up for the great mobilising power possessed by ideologies. This continued enticement is another manifestation of the 'double bind'. Modern individuals remain reliant on the workings of historical imagination even if they must simultaneously maintain a vigilant reality check and creatively struggle with the tension between particular and universal.[53]

Heller singles out totalitarianism, liberalism and democracy as the three major political inventions of modernity. Of course, these are especially pertinent to her biography. The new conceptual armoury provides real theoretical advantages in dealing with these. In Heller's earliest formulation of her modernity theory, the account of totalitarianism was unconvincing. As European statecraft has given rise not only to democracy but also to the twentieth-century catastrophe of totalitarianism, viewing the political as a logic of democracy seemed one-sided. Moreover, the attempt to account for totalitarianism in terms of the domination of the logics of capitalism and industrialisation and the suppression of the logic of democracy seemed reductive. After all, the most distinctive aspect of the two most notorious totalitarian regimes was their emphatic commitment to ideology.[54]

Heller's reclassification of the third logic of modernity as a logic of political power rather than democracy immediately overcomes the first difficulty. An added advantage accrues in viewing the logic of the political as operating through a struggle between technological and historical imagination. Ideology now plays a more central role. Totalitarianism is the most extreme form of modernity's double bind. The highest pitch of technological achievement and imagination is fused with the most exorbitant mythologisation of the historical imagination. The Nazis not only employed every technological means in the service of mass destruction but they even brought the technological imagination directly to bear on genocide as an issue of problem solving.[55] Yet clearly the task of extermination was not posed by the technological imagination but was translated from the ideologically construed world of historical consciousness. In the service of ideology without reality checks, historical consciousness becomes murderous. To make sense of this disturbing synthesis, Heller suggests that in the case of totalitarianism both poles of the 'double bind' pulled in the same direction. Acting in concert, the technological and historical imaginations overturned the pendulum movement of modernity and precipitated a catastrophe. The danger of totalitarianism looms when the 'double bind' is not genuinely double, when these two imaginations are not in contest in a way that binds modern individuals to competing evaluations, activities and historical perspectives.[56]

Liberal democracy is allegedly the bastion of this equilibrium. Heller concedes that there are good historical grounds for this view. Its mechanism of constitutional checks and division of powers has over centuries effectively sustained the productive tension between the multiple logics.[57] However, it remains to be seen whether these checks effectively avert all dangers. For Heller, the essence of democracy is the people's obedience to self-created laws that facilitate active political participation.[58] The combination of majority rule, representation and division of powers in modern democracy unites this positive liberty with the negative liberties of individual freedom. Rather than celebrate this remarkable historical convergence, Heller prefers to underscore the tension between the institutions of democracy and liberalism, their frequent divergence and collision.[59]

This concern surfaced soon after Heller's move to the United States of America in 1986. From this time, Tocquevillean themes become prominent in her thinking. In contemporary liberal democracy, democracy is simply identified with freedom, and civil liberties are typically taken for granted. Yet Heller insists that democracy aims at substantive equality and that this is not always advantageous to freedom. For Heller, the modern story of liberty reveals a gradual shift from formal to substantive equality. While endorsing the enhanced welfare rights associated with equality of opportunity, she rejects the view that all humans are of equal merit and worth. *Ressentiment* is not just a personal vice in democracy, but the spirit that pervades its institutions. This is the ugly face of democracy. Yet Heller concedes that all institutions have ugly faces and the aim of modern politics is not their elimination but a cyclical balance between them.[60] The *political corollary* of the oscillation between the pragmatics of life and the 'useless' things of the good life is the pendulum movement between liberalism and democracy. The optimal condition is a running equilibrium in which the formal and substantive features of liberalism and democracy counterbalance each other.[61]

Such a balance is the only hope of defending the fragile but vital combination of public sphere and formal institutional structures sustaining the highest modern value idea of freedom. For Heller, the 'political' means 'every act, discussion, decision concerning the determination of freedom in the public realm'.[62] In the spirit of Arendt, she reshapes her credo of republicanism around the politicisation of the issues of freedom. This republicanism is neither 'liberal' nor 'democratic' but *opportunistic*; it takes every opportunity provided by both these contesting orientations.[63] Abandoning all previous attempts to provide a new content in terms of political models,[64] Heller's new 'republicanism' is reduced to a *moment* and an *attitude*. The dreams of a *tertium datur* between communitarianism and liberalism has now given way to a degree of scepticism about conventional politics. Like Habermas' emphasis on 'crisis' as the ever present rejuvenating moment of democratic emancipation from the coils of functional subsystems and their power,[65] Heller's minimal republicanism is one of the moments of liberation preceding 'the constitution of liberties'. She is aware that this inchoate moment is rare and never long-lasting: it is quickly swallowed up by everyday politics, which is the business of the political class.[66] However, although reduced to a moment, this republican opportunity is *omnipresent*. It remains a permanent option accessible for all issues bearing on the determination of freedom. It cannot replace modern everyday politics, which has become trivial; but this triviality bears indeterminate moments of potential threat and the possibility of grandeur.[67] For Heller, republicanism means the perspicacity and readiness to recognise and seize precisely these historical moments.

THE QUALITY OF 'RADICAL NEEDS'

The staged retreat from a transcendent revolutionary perspective through a sort of communitarian/universalist *tertium datur* to a new 'republican scepticism' has required Heller to rethink her theory of radical needs. As the now obsolete revolutionary perspective itself grew out of Marx's critique of bourgeois society, the abandonment of the former presupposed revisions of the latter. Heller believes that the theory she and Fehér developed in the 1980s had new insights to offer into the contemporary dynamics of modernity. Obviously this theory also had a direct bearing on the previous meaning of the critique of needs. Whereas Marx was sufficiently confident of his target to direct his aim squarely at capitalism and the distortions of the need structure caused by commodification, Heller refocused her critical gaze on modernity and the more elusive and paradoxical figure of quantification. She argues that the Marxian critique of quantification turned out to be superficial and that a much more comprehensive understanding is required. A delicate balance must be maintained between outright Romantic hostility and a complacent liberal defence of quantifying processes. These processes permeate not just modern social institutions and experience but also our view of nature. Heller readily admits that we still do not completely understand it.[68] She accepts the substance of the Romantic critique even if its recommendations miss the main source of the modern predicament. In her view, a modern sense of community and solidarity can arise neither from communitarian restoration nor from the critique of freedom. On the other hand, liberal paeans to the efficiencies of self-regulation cannot conceal the gulf between market-effective signals and the actual need structures of real individuals. Yet, unlike Marx, Heller endorses the market and quantification essential to modernity. These quantifying mechanisms have enhanced social freedom and the autonomy of individuals. This amounts to an affirmation of the essential dynamism of modernity that finds its clearest expression in the 'dissatisfaction' that was first encountered in Chapter 8. On Heller's view, 'dissatisfaction' is merely the corollary of a denial of transcendence, a psychological mechanism of reconciling discontinuity with continuity within the limits prescribed by the delicate pendulum of modernity.

This new appreciation of the dynamics of modernity requires a more discriminating critique of quantification. The potential of markets to translate qualities and quantities has increasingly allowed individual need to be distinguished from political and social ascription of needs. As we have mentioned, Heller does not pretend to know what the ultimate consequences of the processes of quantification will be. She wagers on the longevity of the distinction between individual needs and the socio-political allocation of needs, while recognising that one of the profoundest problems facing modernity is the measurement of quality in a world which no longer recognises it in any other terms than individual choices. The problem is more than that of translating quantity back into quality at the point of individual life-worlds. This must happen anyway in order to sustain life. Rather it points to systems of needs and their relative qualities, from which all needs emanate and must be reinserted.[69] Obviously the reconciliation of quality and quantity in a modernity driven largely by quantitatively fired subsystems such as the economy and bureaucracy is one of the great challenges to be faced to keep the pendulum of modernity swinging evenly. In the coming era of limits, this question is likely to impose itself with even greater urgency. Chastened by the disastrous human consequences of rampant philosophy of history, Heller is understandably unwilling to predict the future. Nevertheless, she is still committed to a qualitative reform of modern structures of needs sufficient to meet this challenge by extending the achievement of free, pluralist and democratic societies without destabilising modernity's pendulum.

Even after she condemned the 'dictatorship over needs', she clung stubbornly to the idea of socialism as a this-worldly utopia of communitarian, democratic self-management. This perspective recedes from her 1993 revisit to the theory of needs. She continues to argue that radical needs exist, but now insists that they cannot be temporalised within a grand narrative.[70] Revolutionary projects in the twentieth century have been unmitigated disasters; they were premised on redemptive conceptions of politics and on presuppositions of unlimited growth, shared with liberalism, which must now be abandoned. As a result, there is a subtle shift of emphasis in Heller's characterisation of 'radical needs'. While Heller confirms her former definition of radical needs as structural unsatisfiability within the framework of existing bourgeois society, she employs a less specific and more normative formulation of the transcendence theme. Radical needs are now those 'not to be satisfied in a world based on subordination and super-ordination'. Yet, as Heller also now believes that 'a society free from social hierarchy, social conflicts....' cannot be achieved by 'the practical negation of the present phase of the modern social arrangement', the idea of radical needs appears in a changed light. It has a more traditional normative ring directed at the qualitative enhancement of the existing structure of needs. Rendering the transcendence theme less immanent and concrete is therefore coupled with this shift of emphasis to the qualitative aspect of radical needs. Radical needs are primarily those that cannot be quantitatively satisfied.

Heller's recognition of the spectre of limits becomes another good reason for overturning the Marxian philosophy of history. It dictates a special emphasis both on essentially qualitative needs and on the qualitative aspect of all other needs.[71] In fact, the perspective of limits prompts an array of questions that go to the very heart of modern dynamism. The problems of overuse and underuse of resources, both natural and human, are potential dimensions of instability. Even the possible depletion of the language game of science is seriously entertained as another possible threat on the horizon of modernity.[72] Concentration on the problem of limits reinforces the emphasis on the qualitative dimension of 'radical needs' otherwise already demanded by the disappearance of a revolutionary scenario. Heller now constructs her theory, not from the perspective of 'unalienated needs', but from the heart of liberal democracy and the embattled welfare state. The main feature of the modern social arrangement is the mixture of the market and other socio-political forces, such as movements and lobbies, in the reallocation of needs. Modern civil society is an open contest between various self-attributed clients, who appeal to the state for satisfiers and redistribution. Heller views this modern civil society as a great vehicle of justice, insofar as the inequalities of money and power can be counterbalanced by the sheer numbers of groups and individual claimants.[73] She believes it to be a model of universal significance. While only a minority of societies has adopted it and it may be surrounded by threats and burdened with internal problems, its emulation all over the world would signify progress on a great scale.[74] Having attained this plateau of historical development and assimilated the bitter lessons of history sufficiently to repudiate the perspective of radical transcendence, Heller believes that the focus of attention must now be on narrowing the gap between ascribed needs and the provision of satisfiers.[75]

Yet clearly this strategy appears to undermine the centrality of radical needs. In the context of a social democratic vision focused on the question of distributive justice and the narrowing of inequalities, the concept of radical needs seems reduced to a utopian imagination in a society whose relentless processes of quantification have dried up all sources of alternative cultural imagination. Heller refuses to consider this utopian imagination to be truly utopian. For her, the category of utopia is not consigned to some indefinite future; it exists as a virtual reality in the value preferences and forms of life of small communities. She understands such communities as groups of people who choose 'to live a common way of life inspired by shared spiritual and cultural values'.[76] Such communities are utopian because within them relations of subordination and super-ordination have been lifted and they have become the bearers of alternative qualitative need structures. For her, such communities constitute elites that are neither ascetic nor socio-economically privileged. She distinguishes such communities from the pressure groups of civil society. Instead, they are the anti-models of the model of infinite growth.[77]

This distinction raises questions regarding the sociological weight and empirical backing of this conception. Heller claims that her utopian imagination already exists in alternative communities. This is a substantial claim, offered without empirical support. Evidence of the vitality of such communities within, or on the margins of, existing welfare states in anything like sociologically significant numbers is less prominent than it was when Heller initially constructed her theory. Thirty years beyond the New Left and counter-culture movements this may be little more than wishful thinking. Almost by default this accentuates the drift of the idea of radical needs towards an exclusively normative role at the cost of the sociological emphasis still crucial to an immanent critical theory.

REAL NEEDS AND UTOPIAN RADICALISM

The tension in Heller's idea of radical needs expresses the uneasy resolution of the two strong motives in the development of her theory. We have seen how she derives this concept from Marx as the basis of a renewal of a contemporary humanist Marxism. It anticipated a revolutionary movement built not on the certainties of the objective laws of history but on the real qualitative needs of individuals. Nevertheless, it implied the immanent dialectics of bourgeois society. The modifications introduced into the theory have all been motivated by the desire to keep faith with a belief in modernity's immanent dynamics. The political and historical decomposition of 'real socialism' compelled her slowly and painfully to extract her notion of radical needs from Marxian ideology. We have noted the two stages of this recasting. It initially involved a critique of the substitutional political implications of the theory as initially conceived by Marx and moved on to the repudiation of the underlying philosophy of history. As a consequence, the idea of radical needs loses its guarantee as the immanent motor of revolutionary transcendence and is reduced to the status of one potential amongst a number of others connected to the conflictual logics of modernity. Without losing its immanent credentials, it assumes a more normatively accented role. The new emphasis falls upon the qualitative dimension of radical needs rather than upon their unsatisfiability within the framework of bourgeois society. On the one hand, she has tailored the cut of her theory of needs to fit the cloth of a less ideological and more complex understanding of modernity. On the other, despite her desire to keep pace with the dynamic of modernity and remain attuned to real needs, one cannot help feeling that the idea of radical needs stands as a last vestige of her original revolutionary inspiration of the theory. Only now, devoid of its revolutionary imprimatur, it is reduced to an emancipatory potential, a utopian image but with much weakened sociological weight. Even if we accept her reading of the needs of small alternative communities to whom she imputes radical needs, it is questionable to what extent they actually represent a significant social force.

Despite the drift towards pure normativity, Heller insists that radical needs still have objective social significance. Her version of utopia is not the appeal to some indistinct future but to virtual but minority consciousness within the present. She remains committed to the dialectics of deriving 'ought' from 'is' in spite of all the ideological dangers and teleological residues she herself has exposed in its Marxian formulation. Here it seems that her lifelong will towards social engagement and making sense of the immanent dynamics of modernity has tempted her one dialectical step too far. Ultimately, Heller's commitment to the idea of radical needs seems to represent the last residue of an abandoned philosophy of history that is somewhat out of tune with her more sceptical reflective postmodern mood.[78]

SURVIVING MODERNITY

While 'radical needs' stands as a signature for the emancipatory potentials of modernity, Heller's advocacy of 'republican politics' is indicative of her belief in the fragile condition of modernity. In the face of perpetual dynamism and uncertainty without secure foundations, it remains essential to maintain a sceptical watching brief on this fragile delicate balance. This is the only answer she provides to her own rhetorical question, which served as the title of her 1990 collection

Can Modernity Survive? Having repudiated historical teleology in all its forms, we have seen that she repudiates predicting the future. However this formal non-committal only accentuates the point that she believes the fate of modernity is in the hands of its own denizens. Only they can sustain the dynamism of modernity, maintaining the tenuous balance between systems functionality and politics, between technological and historical imaginations, between further emancipation and disaster.

To sustain this dynamic balance requires the appropriate correlation between the modern dynamic and its complementary social arrangement in which neither has primacy. On the contrary, the essence of modernity consists in this volatile union. The ongoing questioning and testing must not infringe the principle of symmetrical reciprocity even while it interrogates all of its concrete realisations. Yet the very core of this dynamic is a critical questioning that has no inherent limits and carries on the processes of delegitimisation ad infinitum.[79] Limitation comes from the collision of the multiple logics that not only *complement* but also *constrain* each other. The relationship between the dynamic and the social arrangement takes different shapes in each of the logics.[80] However, the modern dynamic must be present in all logics to avoid functional deficits. Although Heller does not elaborate this important remark, presumably it means that the dynamic's immanent negation operates differently in the logic of technology than in the other logics.[81] Just as the contest between small government and interventionism keeps the politics of modernity on an even keel by avoiding both social unrest and economic stagnation, the same dynamism is also immanent in the logic of technology. In this domain, however, the dynamic is not the negation of historical consciousness but that of problem solving. The processes of constant technical innovation resulting from cumulative problem solving have a different impact on the modern social arrangement (on unemployment say), than the operation of dynamic justice, which questions and negates all institutions failing to meet the demands of symmetrical reciprocity (legislative reform).

This difference in content of the logics of modernity means that each unfolds its own distinctive immanent potential. In the case of the logic of technology, this potential is a cumulative rationalisation based on problem solving. Heller underscores that this logic is unilinear; technology is an empirical universal and the historical imagination has far less impact on this logic than does the technological imagination on the other logics.[82] By contrast, the logic of functionality is the bearer of a contesting institution. Its dynamic therefore pulls in different directions. The content of this logic is the struggle between dynamic justice and the market. Insofar as this engenders pluralism, dissatisfaction and dynamism, this ambivalence makes it the heart of modernity. Heller maintains that the third logic, that of political domination, is not self-propelling, but is pushed by the historical actors within the institutions of the second logic.[83]

This admission gives focus to the problem that has plagued Heller's idea of 'multiple logics' of modernity from its initial formulation. We have already canvassed the questions initially raised about the autonomy of these 'logics' and also about the very idea of a 'logic' of democracy.[84] The domain of politics appears to lack an immanent principle of development, such as that of problem solving or profit. Heller insists that by 'logic' she means nothing more than a *dynamism* that develops the potentiality already present in a thing, does not specify content and thus allows for the specificity of the political. However, even this minimalist definition of logic implies the presence of an *internal developmental potential* that she seems to deny when she asserts that the logic of political domination is not self-propelling. The idea of a 'logic' of politics initially expressed her desire to raise the profile of the political. She wanted to underline its relative autonomy and enhance the capacity of democratic social forces to fashion their own 'republican' politics. Did these goals require the imputation of a 'logic' of any sort to politics? Heller notes the peculiarly of the political when she suggests that it expresses its universality differently.[85] Contrary to the logic of technology, which manifests its universality plainly as unilinear development and empirical universality, and the logic of functional allocation, which delivered consumerism to all the world, political universality can only be realised in translation to the particular. The logic of politics cannot survive without translation into its own local soil. While such institutions always have their own immanent potential, this particularity bears no relation to a general 'logic of political domination'. Undoubtedly, politics deserves the profile and importance Heller attributes to it for these, and other, reasons. However, this can be conceded without imputing to politics any sort of logic. Moreover, this would seem to be more in keeping with the idea of a modernity truly founded in contingency and freedom.

At the outset it was clear that Heller offers her theory as one amongst an infinite number of possible theories of modernity. Moving beyond the philosophy of history means that she stakes her theoretical claim only on the degree of resonance that her theory finds amongst contemporary denizens of modernity. At the same time, she presents a normative vision of modernity intended to harmonise with, and advance, universal value ideas. In early chapters, I raised objections to the alleged universal status of these supposedly empirical universals. Similar questions can be raised in regard to the normative status of Heller's general vision of modernity. We might encapsulate this problem by considering the issue of globalisation.[86]

Although Heller never explicitly employs this concept, the very idea of modernity as a spirit and social arrangement with potentially universal implications makes it implicit to her analysis. The idea of developmental logics in the domains of technology, functionality and politics only reinforces this potentiality. Heller even goes so far as to say, 'modernity can survive only if it survives on a global scale with or without heavy losses'.[87] As this statement remains unelaborated, its meaning can only be surmised. Marx clearly thought that capitalism conquered the world. While Heller maintains that capitalist society is a theoretical fiction, she, nevertheless, still asserts that modernity is a steamroller crushing all with its expansionary, universal, aspirations.[88] Heller's concerns about the 'steamroller' of modernity focus mainly on the logics of technology and functionality. While these promise great material benefits, she is more fearful for their homogenising and oppressive consequences. Her pendulum model suggests that the best prospect for the survival of modernity depends upon the propagation of a spirit of 'symmetrical reciprocity'. Only this allows for the real recognition of difference in accordance with universal value ideas of freedom, equality and life. Yet she acknowledges that cars and other consumer goods are far more readily exported than liberal democratic values. There seems little likelihood that liberal democracy is about to become the universal pattern of modernity.

Heller's aspiration to the universalisation of enhanced liberal democratic values in the form of symmetrical reciprocity reflects a Western bias that she would hardly deny. However, this emphatic normative element makes it difficult for her to encompass the real empirical diversity and variability that emerges with globalisation. Johann Arnason has pointed out that globalisation brings civilisatory complexes into contact, reveals contrasts and provokes divergent responses. While new integrative patterns are superimposed, they can never absorb all these divergences in their full variety. He concludes that globalisation compels us to seriously contemplate the possibility of different versions of modernity, such as those of the Soviet Union and Japan, both co-determined by their own traditions and historical backgrounds.[89] Although Heller asserts the global implications of her logics of modernity, this model seems a little too parochial to accommodate cultural traditions foreign to the West. While she certainly takes culture seriously and acknowledges that it permeates all spheres and logics, her normative model is so emphatically Western that it can hardly do justice to the historical diversity of multiple modernities. The initial model of the logics of modernity was intended to implicate the possibility of a variety of modernities. This aspect remains, but it has played a far less prominent role since the demise of the 'dictatorship over needs'.

A similar narrowness is evident in her discussion of the logic of political domination. The greatest part of her treatment of political power is concerned with the struggle over the role of state power and the dialectic between liberalism and interventionism. Heller interprets the present neo-liberal phase as just another swing of the pendulum. Yet this may also signify a more fundamental qualitative shift brought on by the demands of globalisation. What seems to be missing is some discussion of the prospects of the nation state in the era of globalisation. This is the issue that has increasingly come to exercise Habermas and others. Heller's almost exclusive focus on the internal dynamics of the modern liberal democratic state already seems a little dated by the emerging global dimension of economic, environmental and political problems.[90] With increasing evidence that global money markets, global communications and international political institutions will play a larger role in navigating its risks and ensuring its survival, a contemporary theory of modernity must be able to articulate theoretically the global dimensions of problems. Heller's model clearly has the capacity to accommodate this issue in terms of the multiple logics of development. However, her almost exclusive focus on political domination of the nation state forestalls such a consideration and neglects a whole range of new emerging issues that have now become even more pressing. In mitigation, it should be remembered that Heller does underscore the historicity of her own conceptualisation of modernity and expresses her reticence to repeat the mistakes of the philosophy of history by venturing to predict the future.

12
Paradoxical Cultural Modernity

The abiding value of high culture is one of the recurring themes of Agnes Heller's work. In *Renaissance Man,* she chartered the early evolution of cultural modernity. In *Everyday Life*, where she first laid out her own distinctive philosophical framework and began to catalogue the resources of resistance to the ' dictatorship over needs', the sphere of high culture was viewed as the first flowering of social differentiation and the first condition for individuality and a critical perspective. Yet theoretical allegiance to the Marxist paradigm of production compelled her to argue that this sphere was not a necessary component of socialisation in all cultures. Only after the break with classical philosophy of history did she rescind this view and argue in *The Power of Shame* for the *co*-originality of both the spheres of objectivation (primary socialisation) and high culture. If anything, the importance of culture increased as she came to embrace the postmodern challenge of contingency. This importance was accentuated by her concern that the processes of contemporary modernisation threatens to impair culture's traditional function of providing meaning and orientation. In the modern world, where even the highest value idea – freedom – does not provide illumination, culture serves as an indispensable reservoir of timeless human meaning. Heller's concerns go to the core of modernity and touch fundamental questions of value, authenticity, meaning, our sense of time and space, perfection and even happiness.

She views culture as the principal resistance to an increasingly technicised and homogenised modern world. In other words, culture is the primary antidote to the values of utility, quantification and instrumentalism that have rapidly marginalised the category of the 'useless'. For Heller, culture is not a distinct sphere or logic of modernity. It permeates all spheres and logics. As we have seen, at the heart of modernity lies a series of paradoxes and accompanying double binds that seem to bedevil all attempts at consistency and clarity. The claims of taste and democratic egalitarianism, universality and difference, critique and conservation, emancipation and enslavement, are just some of the recurring *aporias* that permeate modern experience. Heller counsels that this experience of paradoxicality is not to be whisked away. It is nothing but an expression of the fundamental 'double bind' that challenges the modern contingent person: the felt need to seek *foundations* in conditions most characterised by *groundlessness*. In this context, she offers her own tripartite articulation of the concept of culture. It purports to resolve the paradoxes resulting from the extreme polarisation of conventional concepts of culture.[1]

THREE CONCEPTS OF CULTURE

The conventional distinctions between ' high' and 'low', 'popular' and 'mass' culture are historical products. First came the concept of 'high culture'. The Greeks had no 'culture' in this modern sense because their creative activity simply belonged in an undifferentiated way to life. The idea of culture is a *post festum* theoretical construct born of comparison and judgement of superiority/inferiority that designates the canonical.[2] The cultural task is one of assimilation. To be 'uncultured' is a blemish that can be overcome by attainment. Access to the world of culture comes to signify elevation, ascension to the higher, truer, virtual, metaphysical reality above everyday life.[3] The condition of such an elevation is an alternative way of life that is relatively open to the possibility of assimilation. The distinction between 'high' and 'low' was once the property of estates and was not open to assimilation. However, supplied with a cultural inflection, the former designated refinement and an acquired capacity for judgement. These preconditions of relative openness, alternative 'others' and judgement makes clear that the dynamic of modernity was necessary for the existence of 'high culture'.

Ironically, this notion of taste unleashes a critical judgement that turns out to be mobile and changing. Eventually, in our time, this critical dialectic will turn on itself, questioning the relevance of such a distinction.[4] The slippery slope of this dialectic begins with the erosion of the *sensus communis* and ends with the suspicion that there is no objective standard of taste. Formerly, cultural elites avoided the awkward question of the grounding of their own judgements of taste. Finally, however, the pervasive impact of democratisation places the issue of cultural elitism on the agenda. As already noted, Heller views 'substantive equality' as the ultimate aim of the logic of democracy. Without objective standards of taste, the theoretical distinction between 'high' and 'low' culture collapses. The logic of this development would appear to be the disappearance of cultural elites. Heller notes that this is not the end of the story, but the beginning of another round of paradox. Taking the ground from under the feet of the cultural elite does not mean the practical dissolution of the cultural hierarchy, in favour of an egalitarianism in which all tastes count equally. The quantitative logic of the market has a big say in the contemporary world, but it has not yet eliminated cultural authority. Even if contemporary cultural elites have been partly responsible for the destruction of objective standards, their voices still carry a greater weight than that of the proverbial 'man in the street'.[5] The residual authority that lingers with this elite is indicative that the destruction of the notion of 'high culture', largely by factions of the cultural elite, is a mirage. Those loudly pronouncing the death of 'high culture' have already inherited this notion and function as its bearers.[6]

The paradox flowing from this first understanding of culture cannot be resolved. Heller does, however, offer an avoidance strategy. This requires the abandonment of two of the decisive innovations of the modern philosophy of art. The first requires that concept of taste as the distinction between 'good' and 'bad' taste be replaced by the idea of 'having' or 'not having' taste. This preserves a standard, but one that is no longer 'elitist'. The standard would be determined by *techné* or judgements of skill based on the assessment of perfection/imperfection within genres. Thus judgement would be guided by purely technical considerations and not by subjective interpretation of the spirit of the work.[7] While this does seem to restore the notion of an objective standard, it does not address the problem that interpretation has always been a vital part of constituting genres.

The second prong of this strategy involves circumventing the problem of the relativity of taste without resorting to unsustainable objective standards. The key here is both to mobilise the functionalist character of modernity and to inject historical imagination as the counterpoint to technical judgement. Assuming the form of hermeneutic consciousness, this would restore the other tie of the double bind. From the time of the Renaissance, intellectuals functioned to provide standards of taste. This function was an interpretative one of providing meaning. Great works are almost inexhaustible in their capacity to engender meaning. Their constant interpretation renders more meaning as it increases the aura of the works and evokes feelings of nostalgia and recognition.[8] Functional performance in rendering meaning can, Heller suggests, be the basis for discriminating between the great and the conventional work. The ranking of works would be determined not by beauty but by rendering meaning. What distinguishes the great work is the author's intention towards, and the created work's realisation of, meaning. In modernity, even great works find themselves on the market, but the market was not their inspiration. By contrast, the primary function of mass culture is entertainment. These products require the joint contribution of an author/creator, a producer and a distributor, but are designed from the standpoint of quick absorption and easy consumption. This does not mean that mass culture is without standards; on the contrary, it also has specific standards. However, these are not of meaning creation, but are linked to the specific functionality of consumption.[9] Heller maintains that it is essential to preserve the double bind of modernity. This marriage between functionality and interpretation restores the balance, with historical consciousness and the market each allocated its appropriate role.

For the moment, I will pass over Heller's second concept of culture, which is her theoretical key to resolving recurring paradoxes in the conventional dualist readings. Beginning with the third understanding of culture and its inherent tensions puts us in the best position to fully appreciate her attempts at mediation. If her first concept of culture is elevated, representing a 'higher' value and reality to which we might strive, her third concept is decidedly empirical, designating the fact that all human societies are cultures.[10]

The anthropological understanding of culture is exemplified by culture's empirical universality. To designate a variety of ways of life as 'cultures' has an emphatic political meaning. It implies a non-comparative norm of equal recognition. Each must be studied in its own right and no single culture judged better than another.[11] The desire to rank is the product of an external perspective which fails to acknowledge the immanent 'rationality' of the way of life but instead tries to impose its own alien standards. However, even this anthropological concept of culture bears within itself the tensions already noted in the normative notion of high culture. We know that there the paradox is concentrated in the notion of taste, which is allotted the role of arbiter between 'high' and 'low'. While it became increasingly problematic simply to identify this taste with a single cultural elite, it seems equally problematic to subside into cultural relativism and extinguish the very notion of taste. In the anthropological concept of culture, this paradox assumes another form in the shape of the bipolar distinction: universality/difference.[12] We have already noted that the universality claim of the anthropological concept implies a norm of equal recognition. What claims recognition here is the uniqueness of a whole way of life. Yet it does not follow from the recognition of every culture's being of worth as culture that they are all of *equal* worth.[13] The latter implies both quantitative measure and a value orientation based on standards of worth. While no standards of measure exist between incomparable ways of life, this does not mean that we shall not prefer one or the other on the basis of some partial aspect: its morality, for example, or the truth of its convictions. To think otherwise would be to abandon the possibility of arbitration between claims or critical judgements. Heller insists that we must distinguish between the claims of heterogeneous norms (where there are no standards of measure) and normativity and facticity (the claim of worth and the acceptance of that claim as true).[14]

The tension between these is apparent in every application of the anthropological concept of culture. With the anthropological concept, there is no outside or external perspective, and difference must be understood as undifferentiated pluralism. This concept of culture signifies a leap of the imagination beyond the tradition that denigrated the 'alien' and the 'other'. Furthermore, its extension to empirical universality represents an acknowledgement of the dignity of all societies. Yet it also narrows the concept of culture by limiting the application of the other concepts of culture. From its perspective, there can be no talk of 'high' and 'low' and no judgements of taste. All discussions of cultural worth are dogmatically disallowed.[15] Ironically, no pre-modern culture could have accepted the idea of the equal worthiness of all cultures: they were all ethnocentric, all grounded in the certainty of their own cultural convictions. Along with increasing self-reflexivity, modernity has lost its own self-certainty and relativised itself. This heightened self-reflexive doubt was temporarily veiled by Western self-legitimisation in terms of 'progress' and the empirical universalisation of its technology and markets. Yet this material self-justification has faltered in the post-colonial era with the radical questioning of 'progress'.

Heller sees a dual Western response to this challenge. The march of progress as the globalisation of modernity continues, but this has also provoked a resurgent romantic relativisation of Western culture.[16] While this strategy may ease the conscience of the former colonisers, it does nothing to resolve the paradoxes. Censuring overt claims to cultural superiority provides latitude for organic ethnocentrism to be reasserted. Each society asserts loudly that its culture is the best, at least, for it.[17] Obviously, such claims rely surreptitiously on the first concept of culture, which cannot be reconciled with the anthropological concept.[18] However, these theoretical paradoxes also have real practical bite. Authoritarian regimes rely on relativistic arguments to justify the suppression of political pluralism and to deny human rights in the name of cultural particularity. Heller insists that the norm of the anthropological concept clearly infringes the fundamental values of modernity (human rights, pluralism, publicity and political liberty) and must be restricted if it is not to constrain the universal value idea of freedom. She acknowledges that the normative heritage of the Enlightenment does not allow us to impose the cluster of Western norms on another culture. The denizens of other cultures are entitled to choose *unfreedom* should they really wish it. Nor is there any absolute basis for either rejecting or recognising fundamentalist cultures. However, in practice we are all required to make a decisive choice. For Heller, this is simply another instance of freedom as *the ungrounded ground of modernity* and the insight that we must take a leap. This leap cannot be theoretically, but only contextually, legitimated. Ultimately, this is an ethico-political choice for which each individual must take full responsibility.[19]

CULTURAL DISCOURSE AND NORMATIVE CULTURE

The most radical innovation in this reconstruction is Heller's introduction of another *concept of culture*. Like the normative and the empirical concepts of culture, this additional concept of culture is also a universal. According to her, this is an 'optative' concept, because it provides *equal opportunity* for participation.[20] This second concept, which she calls 'cultural discourse', is introduced as a means of resolving the paradoxes generated by pressing the extreme claims of the first and third concepts. Cultural discourse is a conversation which has no aim other then itself; it presupposes neither social nor professional qualifications; it is constrained neither by topics nor aims and presupposes only a delight in dialogue and enthusiastic individuals who value and cultivate conversation. Yet it does have historical preconditions. With the historical Enlightenment, critical discourse becomes deeply embedded in everyday life and assumes the function of critique. Because this conversation traverses the entire terrain from everyday life to high culture, a great deal flowed indirectly from it: it became the main bearer of the dynamic of modernity.[21]

While cultural discourse is an essentially unruly activity, it is nevertheless constrained by definite procedural rules. This *normative moment* is condensed in the single idea of 'disinterest'. The ethics of discourse requires the suspension of interests, making prejudices explicit, giving others a sympathetic hearing and accepting their sincerity. These conditions amount to a sort of moral code of discourse that instantiates the norm of equal opportunity. Unequal contributions by discussants do not infringe this norm. The realm of cultural conversation is a domain of suspended interests, a culturally constructed free space. No detrimental consequences flow from unequal real participation. To the extent that it avoids bipolarism, commercialisation and commodification, cultural discourse blunts the paradoxes arising from the other concepts of culture.[22] Take Heller's leading value idea of modernity, freedom: this is a paradoxical foundational value that does not provide cultural grounding, because certainty and self-evidence are missing. Free discussion unconstrained by power or interest produces a weak ethos that simply does not require foundation. Similarly with the dialectic of taste, which threatens to undermine the very concept of high culture. In an epoch in which truth has been eroded to the subjective and the historical and has lost its absolute imprimatur, a conversational judgement of taste can still claim universality despite being contested. The Kantian judgement of taste provides a generalisable model for all cultural discourse. The result is a utopian artifice of social sociability, where all interests – pragmatic, theoretical and practical – are suspended for the sake of the cultural dynamic alone. Such discussion is never value-free; but interests and prejudices, to the extent that they are known, should be openly declared. While this is socially constructed, quarantined free space, many things flow indirectly from it. Certainties are enthusiastically embraced and undermined, beliefs are queried and tested.[23] Yet such immunity has a down side: the same conversations can be frivolous and irresponsible. Recognising these possibilities, Heller is prepared to risk them for the sake of the overriding benefits.[24]

She is also reluctant to confine this utopia to the realm of the *virtual*. Cultural discourse is not an impotent ideal but a fiction shared around the dinner table and amongst friends. This reluctance deserves some comment. Heller's reflective postmodernism requires that she resist the sirens of the Hegelian dialectic of reality and actuality. This is most clearly expressed in her repudiation of classical philosophy of history. Yet, as we have seen with the theory of 'radical needs', this is more easily said than done. For her, expression of the immanent dynamics of society is crucial to the self-understanding of philosophy. When her thought turns to the sphere of cultural discourse, she again succumbs to this seductive melody. Discourse now becomes an actualised utopia, the coalescence of virtuality and actuality.[25] That she desires empirical confirmation of her utopian hopes is only to be expected. But when this hope struggles empirically to penetrate beyond the intimate sphere and finds its actuality only 'over the dinner table and amongst friends', then Heller's claim of the coalescence between the virtual and the actual seems to be stretching things. This could just as reasonably be described as a 'divorce'. The actualisation of the cultural template in private space is hardly confirmation of its impact on modern culture and its existing cultural institutions.

THE THREAT OF OMNIVOROUS CULTURE

Heller attributes universality to each of the concepts of culture, but only in a very circumscribed way. The empirical concept is universal in the most obvious sense that it *encompasses everything*; high culture is universal insofar as it *sets the standard*, and cultural discourse is also universal because it demands *equal opportunity*.[26] As we have seen, this third universality of cultural discourse is especially crucial to Heller's account. For her, culture is the source of spiritual sustenance. While it is possible to live without cultural discourse, it is not possible to live the 'good' modern life without it. A vital component of the latter is a 'high living' that results from the suspension of everyday routine and the surrender to self-transcendence in the form of sensuously dense and meaningful works. By selectively processing spiritual nourishment, the dominant cultural institutions create the reservoir of meaning that sustains modern individuals. However, Heller sees a threat to this cultural function with the emergence of *omnivorous culture* resulting from the multiple dynamics of modernity. Its cultural moment is the delegitimisation of the cultural authority of taste and the increasing dominance of the market. This leads to the homogenisation of cultural products and to the challenge to all qualitative distinctions. The result is a hermeneutic democracy of all texts. To the fundamental questions of who is selecting and which texts are selected, the only answer is a smorgasbord. As cultural elites disappear, the market fills the void. This cacophony of offerings and interpretations is ably assisted by the modern imaginations (historical and technical) which are only too willing to scour alien traditions and to raid the past and future in order to feed the ceaseless appetite for innovation and new spiritual food.

As Heller sees it, the omnivorous tendencies of modern culture engender the prospect of its crisis. Firstly, the hermeneutic feast leads to intimations of *cultural exhaustion*. This is already manifest in many features of modern culture. For example, the modest expectations placed on modern art. Modern works are no longer required to be creations of fantasy but merely indeterminate stimulants to the private imagination.[27] Falling expectations of creativity are matched by interpretative blurring of the distinction between original and fake. Originality gives way to the extraction of personal meaning. Yet this is far from all. Even more severe is the *fragmentation* of cultural discourse that is engendered by cultural rationalisation and professionalisation. In an environment of increasingly autonomous culture and professional specialisation, the circle of participants in cultural discourse is reduced to those who interpret to make a living. As a result, cultural discourse becomes fragmented into insular, contingent, and fluid mini-discourses. For Heller, the contemporary cultural milieu represents a new phase beyond avant-gardism. Not only is there no community of interpreters to legislate standards but there is also no shared *dense* cultural experience, which once provided a kind of common home, simultaneously familiar, evocative and novel.[28] The disappearance of cultural community leaves the individual interpreter as the sole mediator. In a cultural world reduced to individual mediation, the paradigms of language and hermeneutics are historically obsolete: there are no representative clashes of cultural horizons and the individual is constantly changing cultural languages.[29] The power of interpretation now lies in the hands of the individual interpreter. She is finally in the position to convey her own unique perspective in her own ineffable way. However, this is only the power of a *naked I*. Because this meaning is ever changing, shifting with every mood and mutation, it lacks authority and fails to convey a real message. Bereft of stability and authority, the naked subject is poorly equipped to assume the task of cultural selection. Whereas the modern quest for political freedom is always constrained by the common thing, the *res publica*, the modern thirst for meaning threatens to remain unquenched. The meandering of the indeterminate subject does not provide the required spiritual sustenance.[30]

It is not hard to see how the concept of cultural discourse fits into this picture. Where the notion of cultural community appears in terminal decline and cultural discourse has been fragmented into specialist mini-conferences, Heller's 'actual utopia' becomes a normative model of equal opportunity. Setting aside the constraints of modern functionality and the market, it both restores the original aspiration of modern high culture and acts as a barometer of its contemporary crisis. Moreover, as we have seen, Heller is reluctant to conceive her model of cultural discourse simply as subjective fancy or regulative idea. Clinging to a dialectic moment, she views this tantalising 'actual' utopia as being as close as our friendly conversations yet sufficiently ideal to still do normative service.

CULTURE AND TECHNICS

The paradoxicality and 'double binds' of modernity clearly transcend the domain of modern culture. The tensions both within and between the 'logics' of modernity permeate all aspects of the social totality, including everyday life. Heller explores these tensions in her discussion of 'civilisation' as the specifically modern form of everyday life. For her, 'civilisation' is a normative notion that signifies its bipolar opposite, 'uncivilised' or 'barbarian'.[31] Civilisation is both a norm that can be realised (behaviour) and a progressivist and optimistic orientation to the present that harnesses both technological and moral aspirations. The idea of 'civility' came late to European society. It emerges when the highest social rank no longer regards its own behaviour as naturally normative but as a bonus of disciplined habit. As the words 'civility' and 'urbanity' suggest, these habits were products of early modern towns, where proximity, rapidity and equality of social interaction required more elastic and more contextual regulation. This required a degree of impersonality consistent with a more complex social environment in which functionality plays a larger role.[32]

Precisely because individuals are not reducible to functions, informal rules develop that allows them to live closely together. The heterogeneous spaces where human beings dwell and interact must be habitable not just functionally, but in a way that allows the individual personality to shine through without creating the impression of superficiality or familiarity. The rules of civility apply technological and moral insight to the governance of even the smallest things of everyday life. 'Good manners' in context facilitate not just general socialisation but also the infusion of new social strata into society, by masking origins and even awkward individuality.[33]

In these civilisatory processes, the technological imagination is hard at work and even the body is reduced to the category of 'standing reserve'. Yet this imagination does not occupy the field exclusively. The historical imagination defends the modern idea of individuality against the demands of discipline.[34] The modern subject struggles to perform a difficult double role. On one side, she disciplines a body reduced to a mere object. Simultaneously, she struggles for liberation from such reifying treatment. This image of the internally divided modern individual captures the 'double bind' at the core of modernity's dynamic. The oscillation between social conformity and emancipatory chaos is just another expression of the pendulum of modernity, and is vital to its survival.[35]

The same tensions are evident in technological civilisation. This concept is founded on a dualistic description of the world as *nature/society*. The myth of technological civilisation sees an eternal struggle between these two, in which nature becomes a *standing-reserve* for the efforts of society to gain a final *technological* victory.[36] Yet this is a struggle in which resistance and reverses are only to be expected. The new thought, which Heller ascribes to contemporary ecological thinking, is the idea that the weapons of civilisation can become the weapons of nature against society.[37] This is the inversion of the older idea that science would conquer nature by usurping its own slumbering powers. Although civility and discipline are in part guided by the technological imagination, they are not objects and products. This underscores a second objective understanding of civilisation as technological objects and products. The objective characterisation views civilisation as a means indifferent to ends. The role of technology is the mediation of the relations between man and nature and between man and man, in a functional and impersonal way that goes beyond ethics.[38] Despite this emphasis upon technology as mere 'means', civilisation is also *efficient* and *rational*. These values of *Homo faber* and *Homo economicus* typify the 'work ethic' that supplied technological civilisation with its modern impetus. The civilised individual masters instincts and conduct in accordance with rationality, predictability and reliability. This legitimates technological civilisation beyond mere means/ends rationality.[39] Ironically, this same value constellation also threatens to render *Homo faber* superfluous. The bible of efficiency and economy is indifferent to humanist pleadings. As we have seen, Heller views technology as governed by an autonomous agenda that almost vindicates the claim that technology is simply about means, not ends. Yet what is really involved in technology is *fusion* of two forms of rationality: problem solving and the achievement of ends. In the former, the ends are *glued to means* whereas in the latter they are *distinct*. Typically, in modernity innovation becomes commonplace and is reduced to mere means. It would be a mistake, however, to conclude that technological civilisation lacks creativity or that rationality is without imagination. In modernity, civilisation has always been associated with science and a taken-for-granted 'progress'. Yet this simple identification is now becoming problematic. As Heller puts it, 'revolution and 'progress' are not straight lines leading in the same direction.[40] Heller here reverts to an earlier critique of crude rationalism and its divorce from human feelings. This also brings into the discussion a new complexity that was missing from her account of the logic of technology.

Almost inevitably, the exploration of this issue leads back to paradox. On evaluation, the hope that technological civilisation could be a neutral instrument of mediation in the human exchange with nature falters. Technology often involves opposites: easing/alienating, liberating/enslaving and enriching/impoverishing. Here value freedom and neutrality evaporate before the pressing questions of identity and direction that cannot be answered by appeals to the 'facts'. Both technological civilisation and its critics marshal evidence to support their particular standpoint. Clearly technological civilisation involves both gains and losses: it emancipates us from backbreaking labour while also rendering us prisoners of the constant pressure of time. Not only is there no simple way to compare these positions but even this polarised and one-sided advocacy is nothing but a moment of the dynamic of modernity.[41]

This conclusion assists Heller to live with all of the forgoing paradoxes. Qualms concerning the rationality of technological civilisation stems in large part from the increasing suspicion that the much-vaunted objective qualities of modern civilisation – reliability, predictability, efficiency and rationality – hold only for the micro-perspective and the short term. From the perspective of the long term, things are far less certain and the ecological doomsday scenario is not out of the question. Western claims of a superior rationality based on predictability and command seem even more problematic and questionable. Modern culture may be more *self-reflective* than other cultures, but does it follow from this that it is *more rational*? All cultures are rational insofar as they provide rules, norms and meanings that allow participants to function and to reproduce a way of life. As we have seen, Heller attributes the specific rationality of modernity to the *dialectics of cultural discourse*. Qualities of tolerance, good argument and openness accentuate the fragility of all truth except the moral truth.[42] Here her Kantian qualms come to the fore. While she endorses the Habermasian programme for a procedural rationality, stressing the provisional character of all foundations, she insists upon a 'warm reason' that, rather than being merely procedural, keeps in mind that it is always talking to some other.[43]

Accepting the rationality of all cultures does not commit us to the acceptance of all traditional rules and norms. The specificity of modern rationality consists in its constant testing and questioning. This is the basis of Heller's distinction between the 'rationality of reason' and the 'rationality of the intellect'. This expresses the idea of playing the game according to the given rules and questioning these very rules at the same time.[44] While the 'rationality of the intellect' is immanent within the dynamic of modernity, she does not ignore the importance of conservatism as a crucial element in a perspective truly cognisant of limits. The critical potential of a purely negative dialectic must be balanced by a reason committed to some rules and empirical certainties. These can also no longer be certain in the old sense of 'beyond discussion'. However, they supply a rigidity that preserves the homeostasis of everyday life. Clearly both forms of rationality are essential to the pendulum movement that sustains the equilibrium of modernity.[45]

The problems and paradoxes of cultural modernity reviewed in our understanding of foundational philosophical categories such as rationality have their corollary in everyday modern experience. The double bind that generates the paradoxes of high culture is just as manifest in more familiar but less examined aspects of everyday experience. One of the most profound changes that accompanied the birth of the modern world was a simultaneous shrinkage and expansion of the human world. This shrinkage resulted from the mechanistic revolution and the replacement of the Greco-Christian category of *place* by the scientific notion of *infinite space*. At the same time, the European exploration of new continents expanded the human world. This radical transformation is captured in Kant's distinction between 'knowing the world' and 'having a world'.[46] This signified the ever widening gap that has opened up between the world we have and the world we can know. There is an obvious difference in intensity between 'having' and 'knowing'. Rapid advances in transport and technology allowed us to conquer space, while assiduous historical consciousness brings glimpses of an even more remote past. Universal tourism can be viewed in this light as a valiant attempt to bridge this seemingly unbridgeable chasm. The nineteenth-century, representative locations such as Paris and London allowed a sort of reconciliation between knowing and having. The intensity of sensate experience was fused with the distance of the representative place. Today even these privileged places lose their representative status. Modernity is found everywhere and all places contain something of interest. Yet the 'virtual experience' of the universal tourist hardly qualifies as a 'having a world'.[47] This requires more than transitory visiting rights: it means the capacity to change this world for self and others. The universal tourist occupies a separate reality suspended in place and time. The specific bonds of tradition and historical imagination that constitute the privileges of 'home' are absent. 'Home' is a world of tacit pre-understandings, of shorthand communication that is an index of multidimensional closeness. Without these, Heller maintains, one forfeits the double bind that gives expression to the contradictory powers of both historical and technological imagination.[48]

Once again the paradoxical character of modernity raises its head. The increased social and spatial mobility of modernity problematises the possibility of familiarity and reconciliation. The experience of being sick of home yet immediately thereafter longing for return to it is commonplace. Greater mobility means that moderns are in eternal exile, deprived of the redemption that accompanies recognition of the familiar. 'Homesickness' is Heller's metaphor for this pervasive experience of *ambivalence* within modernity, the rhythmic embrace of contrary desires and wishes.[49] We are prisoners of the fact that we cannot have the world the way it was, while, simultaneously, suffering from its lack. Ultimately, this ambivalence resides in the already discussed intensity of the new experience of *modern contingency*. From the moment of birth, modern individuals are *aliens* condemned to the diaspora. Deprived of religious conviction and accustomed to mobility, they are more aware of finitude and transience. Because life is short, they desire new places to explore while they simultaneously covet a familiarity that is denied the traveller.[50] Standards of living and health have progressively increased, but modern life remains too brief for those who wish to be at home in the world.[51] Those who desire to realise all potentials and become truly familiar with the world they inhabit must inevitably fail. This deficit cannot be completely overcome and the authentic modern individual must simply learn to live with it as a final reconciliation with contingency.

DIAGNOSTIC DIFFICULTIES
AND THEORETICAL TENSIONS

While Heller's account of the paradoxical aspects of modern experience is compelling, both her diagnosis and the role that the concept of cultural discourse plays in her theoretical solution are open to question. While no one can doubt the corrosive impact of the market and the problems generated by the increasing autonomy of culture, her omnivorous culture thesis tends to totalise these trends. Other postmodernists applaud the so-called fragmentation of cultural dialogue into mini-discourses, not as restriction but as a *differentiation* that allows for the admission of many new, previously unheard voices, that both enrich and problematise the dominant culture. The expansion of tradition means a growth of artistic freedom and creative possibilities. The mere existence of a spectrum of mini-discourses does not in itself infringe the normative ideal of cultural discourse. This would be so only if the mini-discourses signified the cessation of cultural dialogue in Heller's sense of equal opportunity. Yet it could just as easily be argued that the phenomenon of mini-discourses merely exemplifies a more sophisticated system of *cultural filtration* required by a more complex society with its ensemble of semi-autonomous, instrumental subsystems. In this constellation, functional subsystems are essential, and it is vital that they incorporate flexible mechanisms able to select and hierarchise topics for relevant audiences.

Objections can also be raised regarding the coherence of Heller's diagnosis. Her view that contemporary culture signifies a qualitative leap where markets reign and cultural elites have disappeared seems to clash with her equally emphatic assertion that postmodern authors still trade on their own authority and that of the classics they interpret. She clearly believes the contradiction is in a naive postmodernism that would both employ and abuse the claims of cultural authority. Yet one could equally critique the concept of 'omnivorous culture' that perpetuates such a homogenous account of the dynamics of contemporary culture.

Heller's defense of an emphatic normative model of culture also seems to be in tension with other aspects of her theory of cultural evolution. We have already noted her view that 'omnivorous culture' is only the other side of modern contingency. These are, in her words, 'two sides of the same coin'. Clearly many features of modern culture have their ground in the modern awareness of contingency. The emancipation of the individual from a received tradition and social position has enhanced his/her sense of indeterminacy, freedom and autonomy. This has raised the profile of the individual in the process of cultural mediation. While we have noted the counter-tendencies in Heller's analysis, such as the increasing role of functionality and the professional expert in cultural life, the trend to subjectivisation remains one of the most pronounced and deeply entrenched tendencies of modern cultural evolution. Yet at this point Heller distances herself from most other theories sailing under the banner of postmodernism. Her 'reflective postmodernism' embraced contingency but cannot absolve the individual of responsibility and all the uncertainties that go with it. She cannot passively concede increased subjectivisation, when it appears to lead only to cultural exhaustion and issue in nothing more than the naked speaker stripped of authority and starving for spiritual food.

All this is also strangely at odds with Heller's favourite metaphor for the fragile equilibrium of modernity, which is that of the *pendulum*. The diagnosis of cultural exhaustion seems also somewhat in tension with her more comprehensive theory of modernity in which she maintains that functionality plays an increasing role. If the 'heart' of modernity is the *logic of allocation*, it follows that functional principles increasingly permeate all modern institutional systems, including those of culture. The problem is that it is hard to reconcile her normative idea of unconstrained, disinterested and open-ended dialogue with this empirical trend of increased functionality that is the direct bearer of interests. The disappearance of the connoisseur and modern trends towards institutionalisation and paid cultural elites signal, for Heller, obstacles to the possibility, and integrity, of real cultural discourse. While there can be little doubt that increasing cultural autonomy and commercial pressure impact on cultural discourse in various ways, it is unnecessary to extrapolate them all as unambiguous indices of crisis. Empirical surveys suggest that such pressures have not reduced the audience for high culture. Cultural institutions still uphold the demand for excellence (even if the criteria are hotly contested) and, on Heller's own reading, there are still those who claim the authority to judge it.

It is also interesting to consider Heller's diagnosis of culture in the context of the evolution of her general theory of modernity. Her theorisation of modernity's 'multiple logics' shows a decisive evolution away from a normative towards a more descriptive standpoint. Her preference for the idea of a 'logic of political power' over the earlier 'logic of democracy' is just one very important instance. Not wanting to identify with the worst excesses of 'substantive equality', and concerned to avoid all teleological connotations in her analysis of contemporary social dynamics, she has consciously distanced herself from the cause of democracy. Still a staunch democrat, she has, nevertheless, trained her sceptical gaze on the ugly features of contemporary liberal democracy. In this light, her unwavering commitment to an idealised nineteenth-century European culture as a normative model seems at odds with the increasingly sceptical and empirical trend of key aspects of the general theory.

13
Autonomy, Irony and Ethics

Heller is aware that the denizens of modernity are resistant to being told how to live their lives. Critical reaction to the second volume of her trilogy registered disquiet with the proposition that philosophy might want to provide moral advice even in the most general terms.[1] The significant lapse of six years between the publication of *A Philosophy of Morals* (1990) and *An Ethics of Personality* (1996) marks the pause that allowed her to review her approach. The Introduction makes clear that she began to feel the 'spirit of the age' was resistant not so much to advice but to the moral authority of philosophy. To deliver her essential message, Heller decided to abandon the strong pedagogic voice which, while it never legislated action nor prescribed virtues, assumed the authority to judge goodness and occasionally indulged in exhortations to goodness. The subjectivist and democratic 'spirit of the modern age' challenges the assumption of authority by the philosophical author. Pluralisation and individualisation are, for Heller, key tendencies of postmodern times. Consequentially, moral aesthetics must take account of the diverse shapes of the good life and of the growing demand that it be custom-made to the specific needs of modern individuals and their sense of autonomy.[2] To fully accommodate this spirit, Heller adopts a new form and a new authorial voice. Her ethics of the personality is delivered by an array of 'character-masks', employing lectures, dialogues and letters. These fragments offer a wealth of competing ethical opinions and options and they are presented with dogmatic naivety to wise, but less tutored, observers and correspondents. With this form, Heller injects a modicum of Socratic irony into her presentation, in keeping with the perspective of reflective postmodernism. This suggests the need for distance and an acknowledgement that these exchanges cannot decide the issue for others or close the debate. While knowing that she knows nothing, the philosopher is still allowed to wager on her knowledge in absolute good faith. In the final analysis, however, only the individual can fathom for herself how to be a good person. From Heller's perspective, this change of form does not vitiate the unity of the trilogy. As we shall see, this remains debatable. Certainly the earlier volumes serve as both a platform and a ladder to an ethics of personality. Yet in the final analysis the vital question is whether Heller's desire to provide the denizens of modernity with moral crutches is compatible with her equally strong respect for their moral autonomy.

Heller is not uncritical of the tradition of ethics of personality. The greatest part of the third volume involves her debate with this tradition. For her, this tradition is founded primarily on a belief in human contingency and on the gamble that the individual can be the sole and complete bearer of ethics.[3] From this common assumption the tradition fragments into a variety of contesting versions. The classicist version opts for the universal applicability of an ethics of personality. Free of external constraint, all individuals would be moral in their own unique way and able to participate in the many-sided development of their personalities. Opposed to this cultural optimism is an elitist stream that seeks concessions for exceptional individuals. A third more modern alternative rejects both elitism and the ethical tradition to rely solely on the individual fully facing the predicament of contingency and assuming self-responsibility.[4] Heller characterises this position as 'ethics without crutches'. An authentic ethics of personality must reside not in external claims but internally in the self-responsibility of the individual. While Heller shares these general sentiments, she is dismayed by the repudiation of ethical 'crutches'. As we have seen, she views these as indispensable assistance to the moral life of the typical modern individual who has lost the aid of authoritative tradition. All modern ethical decisions involve questions of priorities, self-responsibility and risk, which have no absolute answers. While knowledge plays a substantial role in our decisions, orienting moral principles and ethical reflection are of great assistance. Heller insists that it is crucial that moral theory occupy itself with the theoretical analysis of these crutches.[5]

The analysis of the ethics of personality has three parts: the lectures deal with *destiny*, the dialogues with *truth* and the letters with *wisdom*. The lectures treat Nietzsche's response to Wagner's Parsifal. As the ethics of personality resists abstract discursive analysis, she offers an illustrative paradigmatic case; Nietzsche's ethics of personality along with Heller's own doubts and queries.[6]

PERSONAL ETHICS AS DESTINY

The lectures present a fascinating account of Nietzsche's philosophical life. His relation to Wagner is represented as a growing obsession. The *Genealogy of Morals* is interpreted as Nietzsche's great anti-Parsifal. Nietzsche is viewed primarily as the man of existential destiny, the philosopher who lived his philosophy to the point of madness. At the time of his mental collapse, he had given complete shape to an ethics of personality intended to surpass the Wagnerian alternative and therefore annihilate the Christian worldview and values responsible for the sickness of contemporary European culture.

Heller argues that the break with Wagner was compelled by Nietzsche's need to follow his own philosophical star. Wagner's opera had fashioned an instinctive hero of an ethics of personality: the prototypical 'good man' of decadent culture. Yet Parsifal overcomes decadence through the redemptive act of saving the grail. This is an affirmative reading of Parsifal's virtue of compassion. Wagner gives new life and lustre to the ascetic ideals through the figure of Parsifal.[7] But this represented a direct challenge to Nietzsche's own ethics of personality. For him, the decisive issue was freedom and, ultimately, Parsifal was not a free man. His compassion is not chosen but felt; he does not make promises but only repeats the promises of transcendent voices; in committing himself to restoring the grail, he falls before God. Wagner proposes that Parsifal and his like will redeem the old values.[8] For Nietzsche, this is the antithesis of the strong and healthy hero whose commitments and promises are the product of his own instinctive will and self-responsibility.

In the light of this critique, the necessity to trans-value Wagner's values is obvious, but how to do it is not so clear. Nietzsche is faced the conumdrum of replacing the old Christian values such as compassion without announcing a new truth, a new set of ascetic ideals. This is why Heller concludes that the contra-Parsifal intention of the *Genealogy of Morals* could not be fully realised. While Nietzsche condemns the Wagnerian hero as a fictive restoration of the old values, he is in no position to celebrate new meaning. The only remaining option is a wager on the future and on the possibility of new values.[9] This assumes the form of Nietzsche's perspectivism, according to which there is no absolute perspective or truth: only the subjective truth, for which the individual must take full responsibility. While there can be no totality, there is at least complete engagement with a truth for which the individual lives wholly.[10] Yet this repudiation of metaphysical truth in favour of practical engagement and hope for the future brings with it familiar problems. Nietzsche's own commendable scepticism towards the ideological moment of philosophical abstractions such as 'humanity' and their linkage to ideas of 'progress' seems to utterly forsake him when his personal brainchildren are at stake. To tie history not to abstractions but to his own subjective dreams was just as much a case of the logic of madness.[11]

This lapse reveals deep dissonances in Nietzsche's ethics of personality. The tension between his radical anti-historicism and his equally radical historicism point towards cleavages between the form of his ethics of personality and its contents, his timeless ethics of the personality and its historical mission.[12] To explore these dissonances is to begin to see the cracks in the Nietzschean edifice.

The Nietzschean heroes are a 'lucky throw of the dice'. They represent themselves because they are a unique fusion of instinct and reason. Reason guided by affect constitutes a truly beautiful unity. The noble one does not follow others because this would be reactive. It goes without saying that such organic nobility occurs only infrequently and cannot be willed. That which is willed cannot be a 'lucky throw'. This means that the ethics of personality has nothing to do with history.[13] Yet, while the emergence of natural nobility is contingent and therefore essentially timeless, Nietzsche is still concerned to foster the conditions that facilitate it. The decadent values of Parsifal would hinder the promotion of an 'order of rank' and the prospects of such 'lucky throws'. However, when the focus turns to his own 'order of rank', the strains in Nietzsche's ethics of personality are immediately apparent. Heller poses an obvious question. Does Nietzsche discriminate between his 'lucky throws'? Are all such individuals noble embodiments of an ethics of personality, or only some? One of his standard strategies was to reverse signs and trans-value qualities like cynicism, cruelty, sensuality and egoism from vices into virtues. However, because he also despised some contemporary vices, he could not deal with them all in the same way. He tends to impose his own order of rank on the qualities of the self-created types. A purely formal ethics of personality was anathema to him. The idea of a diverse spectrum of noble natures manifesting variety similar to individual works of art was simply unacceptable. Nietzsche vacillated between a substantive ethics too narrow and overloaded with his own personal values and an ethical formalism of noble natures that was too broad and indiscriminate.[14] By identifying the 'lucky throw' with his strong, historically inscribed, values, he reduced the superman to a bridge, the individual being subsumed by a type standing for a general promise. Alternatively, he overdetermined his model aesthetically by adding additional formal criteria such as representation, gesture and uniqueness to the merely formal ethics of personality.[15] However, not even a synthesis of the two positions overcomes all the problems of a formal ethics of personality. An 'order of rank' constituted primarily by aesthetic criteria expresses not ethical but aesthetic taste.[16]

The fundamental question Heller asks is whether Nietzsche's ethical standards are reliable and have any ethical qualities.[17] She maintains that without the introduction of at least one purely ethical criterion he was trapped in mere formalism. While keen to enlist the resuscitation of moral aesthetics as a key part of her own ethical project, she recognised that it must take second place to moral concepts proper. Nietzsche's virtues fail to provide ethical content because they lack a moral centre, like the Kantian formulae of non-instrumentalisation.[18] Heroic personalities look down contemptuously on others, but not for reasons of moral censure. They have no morals. Programmed for their own perfection alone, they are self-contained consciences.[19] This is a licence that believes 'everything to be permitted'. For Heller, this is hubris: there can be no morality without something, whether divine or transcendental freedom, standing above all single human beings. This limitation clearly infringes Nietzsche's understanding of autonomy, but Heller questions whether such a 'full' autonomy is still human.[20] This is another instance of her stepping back from the excesses of illusory ambitions. For Nietzsche, Parsifal's resurrection of the ascetic ideals is a will to nothingness. Yet this is nothingness willed by others as well. Ascetic ideals continue to provide human suffering with meaning. Nietzsche's alternative wills a non-existent nothingness in the shape of a formal and empty alternative to ascetic ideals.[21] He fails to match Wagner's metaphysical totality because his alternative cannot raise a claim to truth. It is merely Nietzsche's own personal truth.

Heller concludes that Nietzsche was at least true to his philosophical destiny. Through his obsession with Parsifal he became what he was. He thought historical pessimism to its extreme, saying everything there was to say. In the process of doing so he posed riddles and problems that continue to preoccupy all contingent children of modernity.

THE TRUTH OF AN ETHICS OF PERSONALITY

While the first part of *An Ethics of Personality* treated the ethics of personality through the prism of the destiny of a personal philosophical life, the second examines the same question from the perspective of truth, in three dialogues. Each dialogue loosely addresses itself respectively to the questions of possibility, description and practice of this ethics. Heller's character-masks explore theoretical, practical and existential dimensions of the truth of an ethics of personality.[22] However, she cleverly mediates the naive ardour of her young interlocutors with ironic distance and playful exploration of sexual politics.

The first dialogue is a conversation between two philosophy students, Joachim and Lawrence, attending the Nietzsche lectures; later a female friend Vera joins them. She is the embodiment of non-professional womanly wisdom. Joachim presents the Kantian objections to the very idea of an ethics of personality while Lawrence counters these with a consistent Nietzschean defence. Vera mediates with a Kierkegaardian synthesis incorporating elements of universality and singularity.

The crux of the Kantian position is that ethics is not about the singular personality at all. By its very character as normative regulation, it imposes the same standard on all.[23] This is an equality that does not enchain.[24] To personalise ethics is to abandon it. It is imperative to maintain the separation between an ethical system and the life of its author. Philosophy should speak for itself and not succumb to the critique of universality: personal memoir should never acquire the status of philosophical ethics.[25] Ethics requires that the individual assimilate to the universal; indeed the individual's autonomy consists in this identification with the universal. Of course, morality is always embedded in historical context and conditions of discovery. Yet this does not mean that its eternal existence is undermined.[26] This eternity is not the figment of philosophical abstraction but an idealisation of the practice of decent people. In practical reason, the language of the everyday and eternity coalesce.[27] Kant maintained that human beings are crooked wood. They cannot be trusted and therefore it is essential to exclude the personal, phenomenal aspect of individuals from ethics.[28] Behaviour must be tested against maxims expressing the categorical imperative. This is our own internal crutch and warrant of individual autonomy ensuring that the moral centre of non-instrumentalisation is always approximated.[29]

Lawrence rehearses a litany of familiar objections against this stance in defence of an alternative ethics that breaks with the old ascetic ideals. He accepts the need for compulsion in the achievement of great things but insists that this compulsion must come from within.[30] The aspiration of traditional philosophy to universalism rested upon a metaphysical climate of absolute authority, but this philosophical pretension could not survive the death of God. The Kantian quest for universalism turns out to be nothing more than egoism. Respect for the diversity of otherness must be subordinated to the identity shared by the particular and the universal. The post-metaphysical world increasingly acknowledges that philosophy has always been dialogue with the facets of ourselves. In embracing Nietzschean perspectivism, the postmoderns have finally abandoned all naivety.[31] Lawrence rejects the charge that the accommodation of perspectivism inevitably leads to relativism and nihilism. This accusation is launched from the metaphysical heights of the absolute. In a post-metaphysical climate, however, this relativist charge is demolished at its source. Absolutes remain, but not the absolutes of knowledge. Lawrence claims to be a perspectivist committed to absolutes in the sense that he is absolutely committed to his own truth.[32]

After the initial interchange, the only thing the two friends seem to agree on is the existence of the 'lucky throw'. Both admit that conditions of historical dynamism have diminished the prospects of such individuals, owing to the competing demands of social differentiation. However, the sticking point for Joachim remains that even the existence of the naturally favoured individuals does not ensure their moral acceptability. This means that the very idea of an ethics of personality is in jeopardy.[33] The introduction of Vera pushes the dialogue forward by offering a philosophical account of the 'goodness' of decent people. Vera argues that her strategy allows an escape from the generalities of Kantian maxims to the synthesis of contingent singular experience and universality.[34] The existence of good people is evidence of the existential choice. This idea is already familiar from Heller's *A Philosophy of Morals*. Some individuals who make the existential choice for decency will require a crutch, but not for the leap itself, which is not an issue of rational knowledge. Yet, at crisis moments, when individuals seek solutions to difficult moral problems, crutches can be indispensable. This is where Vera integrates Kant into her Kierkegaardian ethics of personality.

Much of the second dialogue is devoted to illuminating the details and objections to the idea of the existential choice. Vera argues that there are both theoretical and practical advantages in the language of existential choice. The language of determination implies complete causal explanation; however, the individual is never completely self-transparent or predictable.[35] It is impossible for the individual to adopt a theoretical attitude to herself. Creative individuals fulfil themselves through action, but the actor cannot know in advance all her determinations at the point of decision. The existential choice is therefore not the issue of self-knowledge but a leap into a calling, into a destiny.[36]

We already know that one type of existential choice under the category of the universal is differentiated from another under the category of difference by the fact that its attraction is a moral imperative, not a specific activity.[37] In both cases, there is the pull of a strong affinity but, in the former, 'goodness' has priority across the spheres. The latter realm is the domain of the 'lucky throw', of those individuals who take the risk of gambling on authentic self-realisation. Primarily the choice of exceptionally creative individuals, there is a dimension of this question that goes beyond exceptional talent. The existential choice involves the whole person. Existing talent will in some cases push the individual in a certain direction. But this 'push' must be differentiated from the 'pull' that follows from the leap and is derived from the individual's total commitment to her chosen destiny. Vera explains that the existential leap is nothing like the choice of a profession. It is possible to practice a number of professions without ever having made an existential choice. The specificity of the existential choice of difference lies in the total identification of the individual with her talent. Life becomes galvanised around a singular purpose with an intensity that consumes all secondary attachments and relations. Heller's own existential leap into philosophy is a striking instance. Vera explains that such a choice does not exclude other activities, but these do not pull with such a compulsion of self-fulfilment.[38] Passionate commitment always involves great risks. These range from disappointment to the demonic: talent falling short of aspirations to moral transgression involving the sacrifice of others may be demanded. There can be many reasons for failure and not merely lack of natural endowments. Yet the despair of the exister is the same when robbed of the deepest pulse of her being. Vera insists that existential fulfilment should not be measured by the standards of external success. These are always captive to fortune, while existential fulfilment navigates by internal standards related to the activity itself.[39]

Authenticity is the leading virtue of the existential leap. To remain true to the self and one's best talents requires the blending of the virtues of truthfulness and fidelity. It may also involve great personal suffering and profound loneliness. The temptation to take an easier course, to abandon the central self for the allurements of money, power and fame, is ever present. What signifies truthfulness for the existential choice of difference remains a bone of contention. Vera connects its meaning to self-knowledge. However, all efforts towards self-knowledge must be approximate. Not fully self-transparent, the self lacks the power to fully illuminate all its motives.[40] The meaning of existential truthfulness also eludes a narrowly epistemological reading. In this context, truth signifies the pursuit of the difficult rather than the easy, the pursuit of the centre rather than an attractive diversion.[41] Against the suspicion that perhaps such unwavering commitment is an untimely notion in conditions of modernity, Lawrence retorts with the recognisably Hellerian view that this passionate engagement with personal fate is the condition of the very existence of culture.[42] Joachim reads this emphasis on personality as 'mystical' and against the democratic, egalitarian nature of ethics. He dismisses Lawrence's reliance on the mysterious 'facts' of personality as a retreat to class characteristics, which are never simply 'facts' but a product of historical becoming.[43] While Lawrence allows that class and cultural conditions may nourish personality, he nonetheless insists that they do not make it.

Despite the gradually consolidating consensus for the model of an ethics of personality as the only possible ethics in modernity, Joachim has moral qualms regarding the existential choice of difference.[44] What does the fusion of fidelity and truthfulness really mean when an individual is passionately committed to self-realisation? How much suffering is involved in the pursuit of a passion?[45] When it coincides with the individual pursuit of self-becoming, loyalty is drained of its conventional meaning. Yet Joachim sees the biggest difficulties associated with the passionate commitment to difference as stemming from the potential infringement of the moral law and the suffering imposed on others. If truthfulness requires the exister to keep faith with her internal promise, what is to be made of the promises and undertakings made to others? By the end of this dialogue, Joachim has conceded the existence of an ethics of personality. Nevertheless, his residual doubts and mounting fear that in agreeing to an ethics of personality he has betrayed his own personality form the bridge into the final dialogue.

This involves a move to the question of the subjective 'truth' and meaningfulness of this ethics. The focus begins to turn from primarily theoretical issues to the wisdom of how the subject actually lives the 'good life'. The gradual shift from theory to practice is signalled by Joachim's request to have the wise Vera as confidante. He feels that his Kantian interpretative framework best fitted his own feeling that he was two people in one: maxims served him as a 'crutch' to support his moral infirmity and awareness of internal division.[46] Vera argues that reliance on a moral 'crutch' is common amongst modern contingent persons who makes their moral way without the aid of tradition. Furthermore, she insists that reliance on an edifying personal crutch is no capitulation to relativism. She is primarily concerned to mediate the stark opposition Joachim experiences between universality and singularity. To this end, she recounts her theory of the 'human condition', as an attempt to alleviate Joachim's concerns and to illuminate the heightened modern consciousness of contingency.

The account of the modern human condition bears a striking resemblance to the one encountered in Heller's earlier volumes. Morality should not be conceived as some sort of repressive cap thrown over the tensions immanent within the life of the modern individual. Vera's account mediates the universal and the particular in a way that accounts for good, evil and a plurality of truths even if any singular throw always remains beyond explanation.[47] The representation of modern contingency with the idea of the 'throw' does not purport to be the truth about morality. Instead the narrative posits our openness to truth. The central truth of morality (that it is better to suffer wrong than to wrong others) is beyond proof. All that remains are gestures embracing this moral core in a personal way without being able to render it in a definitive form.[48]

The final dialogue goes on to make clear that even the individual's pursuit of her destiny is not necessarily a commitment to the lonely vigil of self-realisation. Lawrence argues that friendship without dependency is no mere habit to be cast off as a sacrifice to self-promise.[49] The demise of absolute truth underwrites the idea of a community of equals who think in their own way because there is no longer any secure metaphysical ground. Today, the focus of attention is innovative original minds. Lawrence dismisses the suggestion that this embrace of community is inconsistent. His equality is not the substantive equality poisoning the cultural heart of liberal democracy, but a self-chosen equality of the few. This is a negative equality not obsessed with equalisation but concerned only with the absence of domination. Lawrence's ideal is the Stoic–Epicurean enjoyment of the life of spiritual concerns with a few chosen friends.[50] Heller is not fazed by this recourse to an ancient model to exemplify the postmodern ideal of friendship.[51] Central here is not doctrine but attitude; this complements the existential choice insofar as it subordinates all other concerns to the one chosen as destiny. Only the retreat from heteronomy can preserve the good life and allow those who have chosen themselves existentially to pursue their destiny.[52] Joachim sees here only a thoughtless disregard of the other that is inconsistent with morality. Each of the interlocutors pursues their own interpretation of what such a destiny and happiness can mean from the Stoic–Epicurean perspective.[53] This only goes to reinforce the general message of the dialogues that an ethics of personality is possible and is compatible with a plurality of personal ethical 'crutches', all of which can assist their bearers to aspire to both goodness and self-realisation.

THE WISDOM OF MORAL AESTHETICS

From the outset we have seen that Heller set out to restore something like the full aspirations of classical moral theory. She chose to tackle not only the question: What is ethics? But, in addition, that of: What we should do? and, How should we live the good life? *An Ethics of Personality* addresses this final question. Only the third dialogue, 'Letters Concerning Moral Aesthetics: On the Beautiful and Sublime

Character, On Happiness and Love', moves on to the question of practising the good life. To reinforce the practical angle, Heller breathes more life into her character-masks, allowing them to assume lives of their own and confront the resulting existential choices. We now learn that the previous dialogue is the philosophical creation of Lawrence, the young Nietzschean-inspired student of philosophy. The letters are an exchange between Fifi, also a young humanities student, and her grandmother. The underlying topic is the moral-aesthetic education of Fifi and her developing romantic interest in Lawrence. Lawrence is the exemplification of a Nietzschean ethics of personality, Fifi is the beautiful person and the grandmother embodies the wisdom of age.

In the letters, Fifi requests existential advice from her grandmother over her romantic interest in Lawrence. The correspondence turns on questions of romance, wisdom, authentic self-realisation and, especially, the viability of a love between a beautiful and a sublime personality.[54]

Lawrence is an imposing figure: young, intelligent and passionately committed to self-realisation as a philosopher. Fifi realises that his commanding personality requires obedience and is incapable of reciprocating real love.[55] The grandmother agrees. While not narcissistic, Lawrence believes everybody loves him and acknowledges no vanity or envy because he believes all are like him. This amounts to closure and insensitivity. Lawrence is the sublime character whose promise is grandeur. However, living in prosaic times when inauthenticity reigns and there is no appreciation of 'greatness', the sublime character easily turns melancholic. The lack of appropriate tasks to release its internal tensions can lead to either disaster or to personal despair. Nevertheless, the grandmother favours real tragic greatness to mediocrity. This is the tragic potential of a time when real tragedy has disappeared. Such sublimity cannot be saved by love, and the lover faces the grave risk of losing herself in the quest.[56]

The wisdom of the grandmother allows Heller to clarify the notion of existential choice and to raise some objections not canvassed in her earlier purely theoretical presentation of this idea. For the grandmother, the notion of the existential choice is a beautiful metaphor. However, she is wary of it becoming a standard against which to measure all unique personal histories. The idea of a single, life-transforming commitment falsifies the experiential continuum between essential and conventional living. The grandmother is convinced that we do choose ourselves, but not entirely. The stark opposition between authentic choice and inauthentic indecision fails to recognise a gradient that includes indecision and partial choice.[57] The notion of existential choice really signifies an ideal that can only be approximated, not fully realised.

It is revealing that Lawrence has no vocabulary for the experience of approximation. The existential choice under the category of difference allows for sharp differentiation of success and failure, but such clarity is often missing in judgements of decency. The existence of the 'good person' cannot disguise the fact that most people live between good and evil. Nor would we want to think that anybody was beyond the possibility of rehabilitation.[58] The grandmother also brings her worldly wisdom to the idea of 'transforming contingency into destiny'. No human destiny can annul all contingencies. A rich life is one full of involvement with things and others. This implies that the possibility of our own loss of self is a mark of ineradicable contingency.[59]

These reservations in regard to the idea of the existential choice encourage the grandmother to offer an alternative conception. She rejects both the passionate homogeneity of the existential choice of difference and classical harmonious individuality. She recognises that the classical ideal is irreconcilable with the priority of the modern value ideal of freedom. It relies upon a hierarchy of command and obedience, as in the domination of Plato's reason over the heterogeneous elements of the soul.[60] Her alternative gives priority, not to an ideal or to planning, but to the coexistence of different kinds of openness. She likens it to the harmony of a modern orchestra, in which all instruments play the harmony together while each assume the lead in turn.[61] The harmony of the individual depends upon her following her own good sense. She surrenders to the 'pull' of a self-certainty, but this must remain open to strong and heterogeneous feelings. Heller interpolates some of her own heroes, Austen, Sand, Luxemburg and Arendt, as exemplars of this balance of freedoms in which personal nobility and self-direction were united with rich emotional density and the cultivation of friendships.[62] These examples show that even if beauty cannot be chosen, it can be cultivated.[63] None of these women was happy in the conventional sense. In various ways exiles, they nevertheless managed in difficult circumstances to cultivate emotional intensity, taste, friendship, and a joy for life that radiated from their personality and work.

Lawrence is not convinced by the grandmother's alternative to classical harmony. For him, the idea of harmony as a balance of freedoms smacks of the classicist tradition and tends to confuse beauty with freedom. The individual possessed by a single interpretation of freedom can still be free and lovable. Making her commitment to one direction only pushes all other freedoms into the background. The grandmother's residual classicism is a terrorist attack on individual uniqueness that misconstrues the very meaning of the existential choice. For modern individuals, the leap itself is the fundamental freedom and the basis of all others. The self-choice of all determinations means that only rarely is becoming a beautiful person an option without inauthenticity.[64] Decency and greatness infrequently dwell in the same soul and the issue of harmony must be secondary to that of freedom. The inharmonious person must be just as free as the harmonious one. From Lawrence's perspective, the grandmother wants to interpose herself between the individual doing the leaping and her freedom, by prescribing her choices.[65]

Heller's response to this critical defence of existential difference is interesting. The grandmother declines to meet this counter-attack head on. While she stands by the necessity to pass aesthetic and moral judgement on life projects, *phronesis* now dictates the momentary adoption of a purely observational perspective. Judgement and advice (or the assistance that may flow from it) have serious moral consequences that require the judging person to oscillate between the position of observer and actor.[66] She also acknowledges that Lawrence's version of the existential choice for self-perfection without a model can be a sort of work of art from which others derive great pleasure.[67] However, she defends her own archetype of the beautiful woman. In the final analysis, philosophy has an irreducible autobiographical moment. This concession is very much in keeping with Heller's postmodern turn and with her belief in the increasing subjectivisation of modern philosophy. She is fully aware of the historical obsolescence of her own classicist predilections. We already know that Heller largely endorses Lawrence's critique of American democracy and its drift towards substantive equality. These are the conditions of one-dimensionality, in which subjectivity is shrunken and individuals become other-directed, superficial and imitative without moral consideration.[68] This may mean the disappearance of beautiful people in her classicist sense. While the old woman takes solace in the richness of existing great works of philosophy and music, she wonders whether the disappearance of the beautiful person of taste and refinement might not also see the disappearance of high culture.[69] Without pretending to know the future, she still cannot contemplate the prospect with enthusiasm.

In the final letters, the grandmother outlines her theories of love and happiness. Yet when finally asked whether Fifi should declare her love for Lawrence she declines to give a definitive answer. Foreseeing the incompatibility between the sublime man and the beautiful woman, their opposed personalities and aspirations, the potential adviser has no way of foreseeing consequences and balks before her decision.[70] Existential decision always involves risk, for which only the leaping exister can take responsibility. Nevertheless, the grandmother is at least prepared to wager on the character of the beautiful person: no matter how she chooses, she will have no regrets.[71] Finally, Heller raises her voice in a final defence of her project of a comprehensive moral theory. The grandmother rejects the conclusion that theory can say nothing about morality. To theorise wisdom, beauty and love may be a 'love's labour lost'; however, not every philosopher can immediately embrace the 'crutchless' ethics of personality. Moral theory is just such a 'crutch' that remains available at any time for all those who feel the need to use it.

IS AN EXISTENTIALIST ETHICS OF PERSONALITY VIABLE?

At the beginning of this analysis of *An Ethics of Personality* we noted the tension between the postmodern spirit of the congregation and the role of moral authority that traditionally attached to the philosopher dispensing wisdom on the character of the good life and how to live it. Heller resolves this tension to her own satisfaction by a change of genre. She is convinced that the resistance of the material to the idea of the philosopher assuming the authority of moral adviser is a problem of form rather than of her philosophical ideas.[72] This change allows for dialogue and multiple perspectives, and promotes the idea of the actor choosing to be a good person in her own way. Rather than confronting Lawrence's critique headlong and usurping the role of moral judge, the grandmother momentarily assumes the observational role and allows the reader her own autonomous judgement. Similarly, the granddaughter's request for love advice is not answered directly, to avoid usurping a moral responsibility that today can belong only with Fifi. This strategy is intended to sustain the autonomy of the contemporary moral agent in choosing the good according to her own lights while, at the same time, preserving the moral 'crutch' for the increasing number of contemporaries who feel the need for it.

Mihaly Vajda reads Heller's shift of genre as symptomatic of a deeper problem with her ethical project.[73] His argument has two main components. Firstly, he suggests that the change in genre between *A Philosophy of Morals* and *An Ethics of Personality* is really a fundamental break in the programme of the trilogy. In a number of earlier formulations Heller suggested that the third volume would be a theory of proper conduct. In *General Ethics* she conceives the task of the third educational–therapeutic aspect of moral philosophy in the following way. It must answer the questions of 'how innate propensities of people can be moulded to enable them to live up to moral expectations' and, on the other hand, of 'how a way of life conforming to the standards of goodness can be secured against the threat of misery and unhappiness'.[74] To Vajda's mind, the realisation of this programme as a dialogue of different ethical views manifest in different personalities and behaviours bears no likeness to this initial programme formulated in terms of 'moral expectations' and 'standards of goodness' obliging conformity. In other words, Vajda maintains that in the third volume of her trilogy Heller actually abandoned her original philosophical ideas, which required a final theory of proper behaviour, in favour of something quite different: an ethics of personality. Secondly, he argues that the former and the latter never come into contact because they occupy entirely different ground.[75] For Vajda, the ethics of personality survives only in the domain of individual motivation and behaviour: it is ultimately resistant to explanation in theoretical terms. Because there can be no such thing as *the* ethics of personality, only its exemplification in the personal actions of the single individual who embodies it, ethics of personality falls completely outside and beyond the domain of moral philosophy.

Vajda's argument for a rupture in Heller's conception of the trilogy is convincing. Her difficulties in realising the initial conception point beyond the issue of genre to the substance of her conception. The idea of moral education to expectations that compel seems definitive in the original conception. The force of the Kantian argument presented by Joachim is deeply embedded in Heller's own moral conception. It took some time, under the pressure of the increasingly postmodern direction of her own thought, before she accepted the idea of an ethics of personality. That Joachim continues to have great misgivings over this concession is indicative of Heller's own residual doubts.

The arguments that Vajda's brings against the ethics of personality are already well-rehearsed in Joachim's trenchant defence of the Kantian position. Even so, Heller would reject the proposition that in opting for the ethics of personality she was delving into the non-theoretical terrain of 'individual motivations and behaviour'. From the outset, she excludes individual psychology from the domain of ethics. Remember that for her it is not possible to convince another of the Socratic maxim that it is 'better to endure than to cause suffering.' The individual choice of the universal is never fully transparent. It is an existential leap that defies rational reduction. Yet for her this is not the end of the story, but its beginning. Having abandoned the metaphysical absolute, existential ethics has to contend with an eternal that is nothing but the idealisation of the practices of 'good' people in everyday life. Having acknowledged that everyday life does present the 'lucky throw' of the individual who affirms goodness out of only an internal compulsion, Heller undertakes to theorise her possibility. Vera's version of this, and the accompanying alternative choice of difference, allow for a spectrum of possibilities that inhabit the postmodern ethical world.

Passionate engagement with a personal destiny is, for Heller, sublime. It unites the values of individual freedom and human richness that have been the orientating values of her life's work. This value is enhanced when we recognise that such engagement is the condition of the very existence of a high culture that today faces the pressures of the omnivorous market. Yet appreciating the rationale of Heller's reconciliation with the ethics of personality does not remove all doubts or completely meet Vajda's objections.

We have already seen that the programme for self-perfection can be a licence by which 'everything is permitted'. For Heller, this means that morality requires that there be something, whether divine or transcendental, standing above all single human beings.[76] Yet, in the dialogue that forms the second part, Joachim's misgivings, that the individual's passionate devotion to self-becoming leaves very open the possibility of moral transgression and the suffering of others, receive no direct or convincing answer. This corresponds to Vajda's claim that an ethics of personality falls completely outside and beyond the domain of moral theory. While Heller contests the claim that it falls outside moral theory, she would not deny that the existential choice of the category of difference involves definite moral risks. This is clear from her consideration of the existential despair that visits those who run aground in a passionate devotion to self-becoming. Yet, while such a choice can put the individual beyond the reach of moral claims, this is not the dissolution of morality itself. This moral standard remains as the idealisation of the everyday behaviour of 'good' people. At this point, Heller, like the grandmother, seems to have vacated momentarily the role of philosophical judge and assumed the position of conventional observer. But neither is this surprising. Heller's existential ethics places great emphasis on the notion of the 'wager'. This is part and parcel of a philosophy that claims to fully embrace the contingency of the modern human condition. In this epoch, there is no historical *telos*, no moral certainties and no avoiding the risks of life and moral transgression, only the prospect of making one's choices with the highest degree of self-reflection and sense of responsibility.

14

Conclusion

Evaluating the life work of a living philosopher is always awkward. Dilthey made the general hermeneutic point that it is not until the moment of death that the circle of interpretation is complete and the interpreter is in a position to broach the issue of meaning.[1] Heller has been a dynamic and productive thinker over a long period. She is always likely to spring a big surprise. Nevertheless, in her case there is at least some justification for attempting a preliminary assessment in her own oeuvre. Towards the end of *Der Affe auf dem Fahrrad* (1998) she asserts that in the domain of philosophy of history and ethics she has accomplished everything that was in her power.[2]

Interestingly, Heller reads her philosophical accomplishment as the fulfilment of a duty that stemmed from her sense of responsibility to the victims of the modern world who included her father and other friends amongst the countless innocents consumed in the Holocaust and the Gulags. Approaching old age, Heller viewed her philosophical life work as a sort of existential detour, albeit a satisfying one, imposed by the vortex of history and the obligations stemming from her survival. Until the age of fifteen, her exclusive interests had been books, poetry, beauty and the mysteries of the heavens. Yet from that time her fateful existential proximity to the great historical catastrophes of the twentieth century saw her childhood wonder displaced by the more pressing need to understand the events and forces that had turned her world upside down. Lukács provided her with the opportunity to commence this task and she grabbed it with both hands. From that time, she began to construct a theoretical world of her own that allowed her to understand these disasters and to share her knowledge with others.[3] This was a world centred round ethics and history and, as we have seen, Heller has returned to these topics continually throughout her life, deepening her insights and renovating her philosophical framework with each new phase of historical events and thought.

ETHICAL BURDENS AND LOST ILLUSIONS

The tenor of Heller's autobiographical reflections makes it clear that the completion of her systematic philosophy with *A Theory of Modernity* (1999) is both the fulfilment of a duty and a release. She is now liberated to return to her earliest interests in beauty, metaphysics and religion. Her subsequent works in the new century on Shakespeare, the historical Jesus and a theory of comedy make good this return to her initial preoccupations. At the same time, Heller feels genuine satisfaction in meeting her responsibility to history. The theoretical world through which she attempted to illuminate the 'dark times' of her century, for all its comprehensiveness and richness, may ultimately leave the fundamental questions unanswered. She admits as much in acknowledging that although we can understand the circumstances that made these tragic events possible, we are unable to understand them as a whole.[4] With this sober conclusion we return to the ultimate mysteries that orientated her initial philosophical questioning. However, this recognition of the limits of understanding is also one of the hardest lessons learnt by her in the course of her philosophical development.

At various times Heller has spoken of the illusions that underpinned the intellectual framework of her early work. These took two forms. Firstly, Heller, and her Budapest School colleagues believed that 'really existing socialism' was reformable and that she could make a cultural contribution to the reform process. The last vestige of that illusion disappeared with the Prague Spring in 1968. Secondly, there were the theoretical illusions connected to the Lukácsian programme of the 'renaissance of Marx'. These illusions are most evident in Heller's philosophical manifesto, 'The Moral Mission of the Philosopher', considered in Chapter 1. In this essay, the measure and the fate of the philosopher are tied to her understanding of the objective dynamics of the historical process. After the collapse of the hopes for reform, it did not take long for Heller also to release herself for the constraints of the Marxian philosophy of history. We saw in Chapter 3 how her commitment to this philosophy of history was already challenged by a humanist reading of Marx, with its emphasis on class struggle, consciousness, needs and ethical choices. By the conclusion of her Marxist theory of values, the realisation of socialism as the *telos* of history, far from being a matter of historical necessity, was reduced to a fragile article of philosophical faith. Even before 1977, when she left Hungary and the dissident life behind her, she had already dispensed with this faith and initiated the major task of reconstructing her philosophical worldview after Marx.

Yet to read Heller's escape from her theoretical illusions in this way is to capture only one side of her philosophical persona. She has an enormous capacity to absorb and master language games, to explore their limits and intricacies and to revel in the movement between them. At the same time, this purely philosophical acumen finds its best expression at the point of engagement with contemporary social experience. She has an unmatched capacity to move from everyday experience to philosophical theory and back again; to transform one into the other, all in the cause of making sense of the contingent flow of history. From this perspective, her retreat from the Marxian philosophy of history might seem a natural consequence of these strengths. It might even be questioned why these realisations came only when they did; why a philosopher so attuned to the breezes of contemporary culture, albeit one living in the narrow cultural confines of Kádár's Hungary, did not recognise the existential inevitability of her later course even sooner. To answer these questions we must look at the other side of Heller and delve deeper into her philosophical personality.

Looking back on her own philosophical life at the turn of the twenty-first century, Heller sees a striking continuity beyond the enormous diversity of output and the change of frameworks. She notes the centrality of ethics and history as the perpetual focus of her work. This sense of continuity is supplemented by a remarkable stability of fundamental orientating values. Besides the existential rupture that catapulted freedom to usurp the position of highest value previously occupied by abundance in her Marxian value hierarchy, Heller's main humanist values have remained remarkably constant and anchored her philosophical vision from the very outset to the present. Neither the existential fate that exiled her from Budapest and saw her make her home on two other continents, nor the changes she willingly embraced to ensure the contemporaneity of her philosophy, could disturb the core values of her worldview. They provided a constant point in navigating her way through the stormy seas of contemporary history, politics and culture. While she has become increasingly adventurous in searching for the vocabulary to construct her own theoretical world, a humanist moral mission has always informed the limits of the quest and the ultimate shape of its final contours.

This humanist worldview was initially forged with her allegiance to the Lukácsian-inspired Marxian philosophy of history. It signified a historical vision of a self-created humanity building a communal world that embodied the potential for the full exercise of individual theoretical judgement and ethical autonomy. The 'riddle of history' was solved in a neat fusion of Enlightenment values and the immanent dynamics of modernity. The perfect synthesis was also extremely attractive to the organic optimist in the young Heller, with her elective affinity for the system in which 'everything clicked'. While this native optimism left her susceptible to easy illusions shared by a whole generation of leftist intellectuals in the twentieth century, it also motivated a titanic theoretical labour that would build her own distinctive philosophy. However, the Janus face of her will towards a system was a dogged determination to revise failed illusions and ensure contemporaneity. This labour involved a multiple endeavour: to distance herself critically from her erstwhile philosophical consciousness, to fully absorb the lessons of the twentieth century by reconfiguring her fundamental orientating values and to make a meaningful contribution to the practical illumination of the present.

As we have seen, this theoretical odyssey passed through two main subsequent phases. The period immediately after the break with the Marxist philosophy of history produced the outline of a distinctive post-Marxist radicalism. Yet, in some crucial respects, this still bore the residues of her Marxist past and harboured further illusions in regard to the possibility of a non-totalitarian, democratic socialist third way. These dissolved with the rapidly moving historical events and diminishing options. They finally succumbed to the spirit of the reflective postmodernism that has remained Heller's perspective for more than a decade. Beyond these phases and the resulting theoretical modifications and shifts that we have considered in some detail, it is essential to consider the bigger picture that has emerged. If Heller's work is characterised by deep continuity of orientating values, how is this view to be reconciled with the changes in perspective and framework? What is the burden of the lessons she has learnt from the fateful intersection of her own personal history with that of the most defining events of the twentieth century?

CRITICAL HUMANISM

One of the repercussions of Heller's break with a Marxian philosophy of history was that she re-evaluated the project of a philosophical anthropology that had been at the very centre of her early work. The result of this critical reflection was the abandonment of the project and the adoption of the Arendtian concept of the human condition. While this move was undoubtedly influenced by the intensity of the emerging post-structuralist critique of humanism, there was never any question of her endorsing its wholesale repudiation of humanism. She also had very sound independent reasons to recognise the totalitarian fantasy implicit in a project that elevated humanity to the status of a self-creator. Arendt's emphasis on human conditionedness was the obvious philosophical antidote. Recognition of the fact that human affairs are bound in a web of social relations places inescapable limits on all illusions of human self-emancipation.[5] Heller wanted to refocus attention on moral action rather than being diverted by either passive conceptions of living in tune with nature or by activist dreams that connect humanisation to historical realisation in a way that might legitimate contemporary or past crimes. These principal concerns find their first programmatic expression in *Beyond Justice*, where they are articulated in the idea of an incomplete ethico-political concept of justice. They return with greater certainty and even more force in her account of the spirit of the postmodern congregation and the reflective perspective that she derives from it. The *Weltanschauung* derived from awareness of the human condition leaves the question of ultimate human essence unanswered as a matter of principle. While prepared to draw tentative inferences from experience and history, it draws inspiration from human freedom and remains open-ended and content to live with contradictions and unsolved problems. Delivered from divine hands, human fate is still to be made. But humanity is not the author of this story: individual humans are the actors, but they are not unequivocally responsible for the eventual outcome. The modern embrace of the value of freedom must always be qualified by our recognition of contingency; of the fact of human thrownness into times, places and contexts, that should always inhibit the aspiration to absolute mastery.

Looking for a terminology that captures the mood expressed in Heller's reflective postmodern philosophy it is hard to improve on the notion of critical humanism suggested by Tzvetan Todorov. Given the parallels in Heller's and Todorov's existential experiences, this is hardly surprising. Another political refugee from Eastern Europe who found a new life in the West, Todorov's reflections on morality in history are derived primarily from an interpretation of the centrality of totalitarianism to the history of the twentieth century.[6] He also wants to excavate a humanist tradition that cannot be accused of complicity in the genocides and the human right abuses that have become so common in our time. Whereas critics of humanism regularly equate humanism with the Enlightenment as a seamless ideology of instrumental domination, Todorov wants to clearly distinguish between scientism and humanism as two separable ideological components of the historical Enlightenment.[7] While the former is derived from the practice of science, its ultra-rationalism is not science but a worldview whose basic postulate – that the real is completely transparent – cannot be proved.[8] Humanism does not accept this postulate. It rejects the very idea that it is possible to know the universe without residue.

On Todorov's reading, human beings are the point of departure and of reference for all human actions. Unlike former worldviews that placed religion, tradition or nature in the central position, humanism is an anthropological doctrine with the focus of human affairs. Though part of the universe, the human world is a unique one because of human self-awareness and the capacity to act against expectations.[9] The anthropological core of humanism turns on three basic propositions: that all humans belong to the same species; that humans are inherently sociable (not just at the level of mutual interdependence but also at the level of consciousness); and that humans are essential indeterminate.[10] Humanism adds to this unvalorised and sparse anthropological core a morality and politics in accord with it. This provides the essential reconciliation between nature and liberty, between the given and the chosen. There is an affinity between the values of this humanist morality and the basic anthropological assumptions. The dignity of all humans must be recognised equally, the elevation of the other is the ultimate goal of my action and the free act is preferred over the constrained one. While it is important to see the anthropological core and the deliberative moment as compatible, the aim is neither to eliminate conflict between the two nor to reduce the claims of either.[11] Just as Heller highlights the complementary and conflicting 'logics' of modernity, Todorov designates the complementarity and tension between its constitutive values as the key strength of the humanist doctrine. The humanist grammar involves three persons: an *I*, a *you* and a *they*. Acclaim of the liberty of the *I* is constrained by the finality of the *you* and the universality of the *they*. Universality is not a constraint on the recognition of otherness, but the condition of it being fostered.[12] In this constellation, a deep appreciation of the value and irreducibility of human individuality and freedom is enhanced by sociality and shared values.

Todorov acknowledges that the link between humanism and politics is imprecise. At times this has led to an activist and ambitious politics. Belief in the inherent sociality of individuals can imply redefining the ends of society, and privileging the autonomy of the individual can amount to a relentless attack on social conformity. To counteract this tendency, Todorov cautions that the critical humanist does not believe in man (sic).[13] Neither does confidence in human capacities amount to the conviction that humans can do everything. Emancipation from many of the most arduous constraints of religion, tradition and nature is not the end of limits. Echoing Arendt, Todorov reminds us that because human desires rarely coincide, plurality is also a limit to the omnipotence of human aspirations. In addition, humans do not choose their physical being, history or culture. This list of conditioning factors and limits immediately recalls Heller's emphasis on the contingency of the postmodern human condition. Like Heller, Todorov is no believer in the inherent goodness of human nature. Human beings are capable of the very best and also the very worst. But this is nothing more than recognising their freedom and its imperfection.

We have explored Heller's fondness of the idea of the existential wager. The choice of the ethical life is a mystery for which not reasons but only the existential leap of will provide the most satisfactory account. Todorov carries this idea of the wager into the very heart of humanism. Current knowledge is neither absolute nor definitive: to believe otherwise is an act of faith that humanism cannot abide. This favours the principle of precaution, a distinction between theory and practice and a margin of error that takes account of human fallibility. This corresponds closely to Heller's own distinction between speculative fancy and the practical constrained by the common thing. Yet, because the most identifiable human attribute is the capacity for self-surpassing, the humanist enterprise remains open-ended. This is meant not as an act of faith but as a spur on human knowledge and will.

The above account of critical humanism encapsulates the lessons embedded in Heller's elaboration of reflective postmodernism. The youthful anthropological optimism that underpinned her early Marxist writings on instincts, needs and values and gained expression in the idea of 'total revolution of everyday life' as an implicit critique of distorted authoritarian revolution of the 'dictatorship over needs' has not disappeared. Her confidence in the possibility of humans exercising fully their reason and autonomy is now balanced by a clear appreciation of conditionedness, limits, contingency and the resulting need of humans to live with contradictions, to continually explore real problems and to reject all tempting ideas of closure. The tension within this balance is increasingly expressed in Heller's later work, but nowhere more keenly than in *An Ethics of Personality*. Her confidence that philosophy can still provide a moral crutch in the postmodern environment here struggles with the equally emphatic imperative that it be cut to the cloth of the individual personality, take into account contingency and repudiate the notion that it can decide on behalf of autonomous moral agents.

UTOPIAN AMBITIONS AND ORIENTATIVE PHILOSOPHY

The same tension is manifest in Heller's fascination with the idea of utopia and her enduring commitment to its centrality in the philosophical enterprise. We have seen that this commitment is deep in Heller's understanding of the very essence of philosophy as the exploration of the tension between what appears to be given and what is claimed to be essential.[14] It is reaffirmed after the break with the philosophy of history to ensure that philosophy still stands as guarantor for a transcendence, albeit one reduced to a regulative idea. Nevertheless, rational utopia is still posited as the expression of the immanent dynamics of modernity, whether it is the 'radical needs' of new marginalised social constituencies or a 'virtual' democratic culture of discourse actualised amongst family and friends. In all such instances, Heller is keen to hold on to the emancipatory potential of modernity against its equally formidable threats and subside neither into nihilism or despair.

This volatile combination of immanent critique and utopian imagination can sometimes leave Heller awkwardly straddled between normative ideals and real empirical dynamics, between assertions of value continuity and increasingly sceptical postmodern doubts. Her claims for the universality of modern value ideas such as freedom must confront the suspicion that this is a selective universality conditioned by a specific epoch and a Western cultural tradition. Having abandoned the security of traditional normativity, her 'rational utopias' are especially vulnerable to the charge that they lack convincing empirical confirmation. While Heller has sometimes even been prepared to admit the 'dream' status of her theoretical solutions, her stance as an immanent critic loses credibility if her claims for universality are merely dogmatic or her utopian imagination does not resonate with contemporary aspirations and find real support in sociological evidence. One of the suspicions engendered by an increasingly subjective culture is that the individual articulates merely her own view of the world and that the ground has slipped from under the feet of philosophy's utopian authority. Heller is entitled to continue affirming an immanent approach in search of the emancipatory possibilities thrown up by the dynamics of modernity. However, at times this dialectical commitment to utopian possibility flares out in a way that seems very much in tension with the sceptical cast of her reflective postmodernism.

Modern pluralism gains a higher profile in Heller's reflective postmodern phase. A relentless drift toward subjectivisation finds expression in the postmodern reality in which, like the windowless monads of Leibnizian metaphysics, all monads mirror the whole world, but each of them does it in its own way from its own unique perspective.[15] She is well aware that this dynamic undermines the cultural authority of philosophy, but her faith lies more in the social function of philosophy than in its institutional forms. She willingly embraces the coffee-house model of philosophy, noting its compatibility with the new appreciation of contingency and its will to problematise issues and to continue dialogue without the pretence of knowing all the answers. She is confident that a powerful subjective vision which gives wings to the thought of others will always find an audience and may even become its own paradigm. But there can be little doubt that today messianic power is in short supply. This may in part be connected, as Habermas believes, with the exhaustion that has overcome the transcendental notions of the nineteenth century,[16] but it seems also to express a general scepticism that has disqualified all former pretenders to the utopian mantle. Indicative of this demise, the profile of utopia is not as high as it formerly was in Heller's most recent formulations of her standpoint. Rather than assert the priority of rational utopia as the principal task of a reflective postmodernism, in *A Theory of Modernity* she is content to ensure that the place at the table remains set for the messiah, should he ever deem to make an appearance. The change in tone is unmistakable. Yet it still remains vital for Heller that the utopian space is not expunged, even if it is her intuition that for us moderns 'only emptiness is fullness' as there is no other 'hope beyond hope'.[17] The tenacity with which she holds on to utopia even in unpropitious times brings us back to the essential continuity of her thinking. Heller's achievement is to shape her reflections on ethics and history into a theoretical world that offers orientation and understanding of the present. In the contemporary philosophical world this seems an untimely and even obsolete project, though not without precedents and fellow travellers. Kolakowski and Bernstein, amongst others, have made eloquent cases for more utopian thinking on the grounds that it is culturally vital that common sense be subject to questioning and the inquisitive energy of the mind never go to sleep: as well as healers, we need diggers.[18] Nevertheless, this breaks various taboos venerated by the dominant philosophical paradigm.

In his survey of the contemporary philosophical landscape, György Márkus sees three main programmes.[19] The hegemonic one, which reflects the prestige of science in the contemporary society and culture, is associated with the scientifisation of philosophy and espouses programmes of scientific realism or naturalism. It takes science as its object and analyses the structure of its theories and their internal logic and method. Its focus is epistemology and metaphysics. Its professed aim, as far from being realised as ever, is to transform philosophy into a science.

Not surprisingly, given the increasing sense of disquiet and risk that have accompanied the very successes of modern science and its escalating technological impact upon the natural and human environment, an alternative programme has taken up the part of the excluded 'other' that is resistant to rational categorisation. The various strands of postmodernism are its most forceful representatives. It typically adopts the negative option of deconstructing the deep structures that have allegedly determined the whole direction of the Western intellectual tradition, and attempts the almost impossible task of giving voice to the excluded or that which is not at our disposal. The major difficulty with this position is that it effaces traditional genre boundaries, renders the criteria of legitimate critique uncertain and commits its advocates to an ironic relation to conventional philosophical means. The practical consequence of this principled externality is troubling. Viewing the present as the last phase of a modernity deeply contaminated by its metaphysical commitments, it counsels either restless expectation of a revolutionary 'turn' or unconditional acceptance of the contradictory present on the grounds that this tradition is what we are.[20]

Heller's philosophy finds its place in a third model, which Márkus has characterised as the orientative, narrative programme. The advocates of this programme, such as Charles Taylor, Jürgen Habermas and Alasdair MacIntyre, amongst others, try to determine the identity of philosophy with a more indirect but also more encompassing approach. The crisis of philosophical identity seems to be an element of a much more complicated modern socio-cultural complex. Today there is a prevailing uncertainty regarding our future destination and how to get there: our past and future do not seem to constitute an unbroken continuity. What is needed is orientation, and this programme attempts to provide a sense of where we have come from and where we might be going.[21]

The proponents of the dominant scientistic paradigm are defenders of the Western rationalist tradition, but they ignore serious questions about their own particular concept of reason. While they are quick to notice inconsistencies in the criteria of rationality, their narrow cultural and historical perspective means that they lack awareness of alternatives.[22] We have seen how Heller offers an alternative account of rationality and attempts to contextualise it in a much broader socio-historical framework. She is also very keen to shift it beyond its formalist and scientific frame and relocate it within the heart of everyday life. In this desire she is at one with some of the pragmatic liberals who also want to abandon the idea of philosophy's privileged access to reason and reaffirm the centrality of the everyday. In their view, modernity has forgotten that the project of living precedes the project of philosophy.[23] Their conviction is that we are naturally endowed with just enough epistemology and metaphysics, and that philosophy goes badly awry if it seeks to make these its core activities. Against the more reductive versions of naturalism that deny the specificity of the human world and require a standard of objectivity it cannot provide, they assert the need to focus on the normative core of human existence. This is also connected with a more nuanced relation to tradition. In contrast to the proselytising enthusiasm and naive optimism of Enlightenment scientism, they counsel no categorical rejection of tradition. Along with Heller, they recognise that without explicit reflection on historical origins and the richness of our traditions, we can easily forget the specificity of our own projects and allow many unacknowledged assumptions to creep in unnoticed.[24]

Heller's reflective postmodernism matches her critique of positivism and formalist rationality with a staunch defence of philosophical reason. Yet her dispute with Márkus demonstrates that this does not extend to a Platonic rejection of rhetoric. On this point she agrees with Rorty and his strong advocacy of an edifying component in philosophy. While not completely abandoning the concept of truth, she calls for a more differentiated notion that takes into account the human capacity to simultaneously inhabit multiple worlds and acknowledges that certainty has given way to falliblism and the desire to explore truth games that do not rely on compulsion. She accepts the inspiration of Kierkegaardian existentialism and the priority of maintaining the conversation over the discovery of truth. In her mind, the specificity of philosophy as a cultural objectivation counts for less than its social function in the dialectics of everyday life. This concern for the social effectivity of philosophy is warranted in an epoch of increasing differentiation and cultural specialisation. The coffee-house model of philosophy allows many new entrants to express a philosophical opinion. It also calls for a new pragmatism in relation to criteria that abandon the quest for certainty in favour of dynamism, flexibility and nuance. Yet can this social functionality really be sustained without some criteria that allow the discussants to mutually assess their claims?

Naturally Heller's social commitment is qualified by the loss of her former Marxist illusions. Like others within the orientative, narrative paradigm, she is sceptical of the grand narratives that aspired to totality and offered substantive images of the human predicament. She is, however, just as convinced that philosophy still has a unique orientative role to play in contemporary social life. I have outlined her belief in the escalating generalised need for ethical crutches in modern moral life and the role that striking images of modernity can still play as trampolines to individuals seeking orientation and self-reflection amidst the paradoxes of contemporary life. Her life's work has been to construct just such a worldview. Yet her general commitment to immanent critique is no longer matched by prediction of the future or a definite connection to concrete praxis in the form of even a vague political vision. Tormey sees in Heller's utopianism an invitation 'to reflect and debate, but not to act'.[25] This is both true and false, but it should not be grounds for criticism. It is true in the sense that her vision is no longer directly connected to praxis. This is why Beilharz is correct in speaking of her shift from 'a sociology of action' to a 'philosophy of experience'.[26] Yet, as I suggested earlier, her stance is not merely contemplative, nor does it preclude action. One of the lessons she has learnt from the tragedies of the twentieth century is that philosophically fuelled politics is dangerous. Heller's engagement with the dynamics of contemporary society suggests an ongoing concern for the human world and its fate. She encourages individual self-reflection. For her, this is the limit of philosophy, which it crosses at its peril. However, for philosophers and other citizens this can also be an indispensable prolegomenon to sound action.

Márkus draws attention to the diagnostic function of the orientative, narrative model of philosophy. Philosophy must analyse and reconstruct the tradition of the present. This involves illuminating the normative and factual preconditions of dominant contemporary practices and privileges. Gutting maintains that general visions are essential elements of human culture and that failure to provide them is a sure sign that a culture is in crisis.[27] The burden of the critique of the philosophy of history is that such diagnosis can no longer assume the form of closed *totality*. It has become vital to build scepticism even into the general vision of the human predicament. This is the burden of Heller's shift to the idea of the human condition. Yet it is still possible today to construct a *totalisation* within a given tradition from the standpoint of existing potentials and chosen values that permits a distantiation from certain practical and cognitive assumptions presently taken for granted.[28] Because philosophy purports to deal with the universal, it must relate the present to a general paradigm of the human relationship with the world conceivable on the basis of present possibilities. At the heart of the specificity of philosophy is this creative act of redescription that relates the present to this posited universal existential vision.

Philosophy also requires conceptual analysis and historical critique to sustain its vision; vision, conceptual analysis and historical knowledge must all work in concert to ensure the credibility, power and coherence of the world created. We have seen in Heller's own case that it is not easy to maintain this concert and that the resulting dissonance impairs philosophical credibility. Yet even successful synthesis does not render the created world definitive. In the postmodern world, the pervasive pluralism and trends towards the subjectivisation of culture, already noted by Heller, generate a variety of competing paradigms reflecting a diverse range of practical and value priorities. Philosophy, as we have seen, is no longer able to offer a single vision of the good life. Its cultural function consists in expressing the spectrum of socio-cultural options and criticising them with the other tools at its disposal in a way that makes possible a process of reflective evaluation and choice.[29]

There is hardly another living philosopher who has striven so determinedly to provide her own singular and comprehensive vision of that world. Recognising that the fate of a philosophy is ultimately decided on the plane of existential satisfaction, Heller has never been afraid to give the narrative and speculative moment of her philosophy its head. For her, the orientative moment of philosophy goes beyond the mere formulation of an evaluative attitude to the collisions and conflicts of the present.[30] The utopian moment remains a crucial component of philosophical vision even in times when the philosopher's credentials for this task seem no better than anyone else's. This speculative rhetoric has regularly got her into trouble. Recall the quite genuine self-critique of *A Radical Philosophy*! Yet, self-criticism has only moderated not extinguished Heller's utopian aspiration. Even in the heart of her sceptical postmodern reflections in *A Theory of Modernity*, she felt compelled to construct her utopian model of cultural conversation as a theoretical means of combating the antinomies of modern culture.[31] The downside of this propensity is that a speculative concrete image can easily lose contact with empirical knowledge. As we have seen, philosophical vision must be constrained by conceptual analysis and historical/empirical knowledge if creative redescription is to yield its most potent cultural impact. However, this balance is itself a philosophical utopia and most of the time even the best philosophy is an eternal struggle between the gods of its constitutive elements.

The overextension of Heller's utopian ambition must be set against its intrinsic strengths. Utopian aspirations are also the source of her panoramic vision. From her core interests in ethics and philosophy of history she has fashioned a rich and detailed analysis of the contemporary human world from the everyday to high culture, from the personal to the global, all informed by the history of philosophy from the classics to the postmodern. In exploring the essential continuity of values manifest in the shifting perspective of this achievement, I have highlighted the sense of duty that issued from the burdens of an existential experience of loss and survival and the will to render it meaningful. Yet such an interpretation runs the risk of viewing Heller's life work as some sort of existential detour. On Heller's account, she was drawn away from the things that were initially most important to her, only to be able to return to them in recent years when her duty was complete. On this point I would suggest that Heller has deceived herself. Although we might look to the burden of survival as the source of the sense of duty that sustained her systematic intent, it was wonder and the love of the starry heavens and beautiful things that populated Heller's theoretical world with its richness of insight and detail. A great part of the pleasure of reading her is that comprehensive vision is accompanied on almost every page with small gems of analysis, insight and wisdom that illuminate the unexamined and the already well known. Every one of Heller's works resonates with her devotion to absolute spirit and her fascination with all human things. The contingent historical fate that located her at the vortex of twentieth-century history provided the occasion, but her work and living spirit have always been a seamless unity. The curiosity, wonder and awe that inspired her first philosophical interests have not just made a belated return. They permeate all her writings and work in concert with an ethical imperative and felt need to allow the chaotic everyday to speak with a philosophical voice and provide her readers with orientation amidst the kaleidoscopic events of modernity.

Notes

INTRODUCTION

1. D. M. Brown, *Towards a Radical Democracy: The Political Economy of the Budapest School* (London: Unwyn Hyman, 1988); J. Burnheim (ed.), *The Social Philosophy of Agnes Heller* (Amsterdam: Rodopi, 1994).
2. S. Tormey, *Agnes Heller: Socialism, Autonomy and the Postmodern* (Manchester: Manchester University Press, 2001).
3. Peter Beilharz offers a similar explanation of Heller's relative marginalisation. For him, Heller's closeness to the Enlightenment and its spirit 'not only to think for yourself but to be, to act as yourself' is a strenuous demand not easily heard amidst the Babel of contemporary theories. P. Beilharz, 'Budapest Central: Agnes Heller's Theory of Modernity', *Thesis Eleven*, 75 (London: Sage, November 2003), p.112. While I agree that Heller's continuing proximity to the Enlightenment did not assist her reception in fashionable cultural circles in the 1980s, I think the problem lay less in the demands of her position than in the prejudice that these were already obsolete goods.
4. Beilharz, 'Budapest Central', p.110.
5. A. Heller, *The Time is Out of Joint* (Maryland: Rowman & Littlefield, 2002).
6. A. Heller, *Der Affe auf dem Fahrrad* (Berlin: Philo, 1999), pp.50–61.
7. Ibid., p.476.
8. Ibid., p.94.
9. Burnheim (ed.) *Social Philosophy of Agnes Heller*, p.285.
10. F. Fehér, *The Frozen Revolution: An Essay on Jacobinism* (Cambridge: Cambridge University Press, 1987); F. Fehér (ed.), *The French Revolution and the Birth of Modernity* (Berkeley: University of California Press, 1990); F. Fehér and A. Arato (eds), *Gorbachev: The Debate* (Cambridge: Polity, 1989) and *Crisis and Reform in Eastern Europe* (New Brunswick: Transaction Books, 1990); A. Heller and F. Fehér, *From Yalta to Glasnost: The Dismantling of Stalin's Empire* (Oxford: Blackwell, 1990).
11. *The Time is Out of Joint*; and *Die Auferstehung des jüdische Jesus* (Berlin, Philo, 2002).
12. A. Heller, '9/11, or Modernity and Terror', *Constellations*, 9/1 (Oxford: Blackwell, 2002), pp.53–65.
13. Ibid.
14. Heller, *Der Affe*, p.283.
15. M. Vajda, 'Agnes Heller: A Lover of Philosophy, A Lover of Europe', in J. Burnheim (ed.), *The Social Philosophy of Agnes Heller*, p.19.
16. Peter Murphy notes the poetical allusiveness that is at the core of all her accounts of the autonomous moral personality. P. Murphy, 'Agnes Heller's Great Society', *Thesis Eleven*, 75 (London: Sage, November 2003), p.101.

17. It is worth noting that in Heller's vast oeuvre there is the occasional paper on these questions. See her early essays 'Communism and the Family' (with Vajda) and 'The Future of Relations Between the Sexes', both in *The Humanisation of Socialism: Writings of the Budapest School* (London: Allison & Busby, 1976); and 'The Emotional Division of Labour Between the Sexes: Perspectives on Feminism and Socialism', *Thesis Eleven*, 5–6 (Clayton, Victoria: Department of Politics, Monash University, 1982).
18. Heller, *Der Affe*, pp.309–10.
19. Ibid., p.310.
20. G. Márkus, 'The Politics of Morals', in J. Burnheim (ed.), *The Social Philosophy of Agnes Heller*, pp.257–80.

CHAPTER 1

1. G. Márkus, 'Debates and Trends in Marxist Philosophy', in *Communism and Eastern Europe: A collection of Essays* (New York: Karz Publishers, 1979), p.109.
2. G. Lukács, *History and Class Consciousness* (London: Merlin, 1971).
3. G. Lukács, *Die Eigenart des Äesthetischen Werke Banden*, 11–12 (Luchterland, 1963).
4. Three sections of the manuscript were subsequently published in English: G. Lukács, *The Ontology of Social Being*, 1. Hegel; 2. Marx; 3. Labour (London: Merlin Press, 1980).
5. Márkus, 'Debates and Trends', p.107.
6. Ibid.
7. A. Heller, 'The Philosophy of the Late Lukács', *Philosophy and Social Criticism*, 6/1 (Boston: Boston College, 1980), pp.147–63.
8. Ibid.
9. A. Heller, 'The Moral Mission of the Philosopher', *New Hungarian Quarterly*, 13/47 (Budapest: Autumn 1972), p.156.
10. Ibid., p.157.
11. In this period, Heller typically uses the male pronoun form. In these cases, I will simply follow her usage without further emendation.
12. Ibid.
13. Ibid.
14. Ibid., p.158.
15. Ibid., p.160.
16. Ibid.
17. For an excellent discussion of Heller's appropriation of Epicurean and Stoic themes, see Marios Constantinou's 'Agnes Heller's Ecce Homo: A Neomodern Vision of Moral Anthropology', *Thesis Eleven*, 59 (London: Sage, 1999).
18. Heller, 'Moral Mission'.
19. Ibid., p.161.
20. Ibid.
21. Ibid., p.162.
22. Ibid., p.163.
23. Ibid.
24. Ibid., p.164.
25. Ibid., p.165.
26. Ibid.
27. Ibid., p.166.

28. Ibid., p.167.

29. For their own account of this time, see A. Heller and F. Fehér, *Hungary 1956 Revisited* (London: George Allen & Unwin, 1983).

30. A. Heller, 'A Reply To My Critics', in John Burnheim (ed.), *The Social Philosophy of Agnes Heller* (Amsterdam: Rodopi, 1994), p. 283.

31. A. Heller, 'Die Stellung der Ethik im Marxismus', *Praxis: Revue Philosophique Edition Internationale*, 2 (Zagreb: 1967), pp.244–252.

32. A. Heller, 'Marx's Theory of Revolution and the Revolution in Everyday Life', in *The Humanisation of Socialism: Writings of the Budapest School* (London: Allison & Busby, 1976).

33. Not published in Hungarian in 1970 and not until 1984 in English. A. Heller, *Everyday Life* (London: Routledge & Kegan Paul, 1984).

34. Ibid., p.43.

35. J. Habermas, 'The New Obscurity: The Crisis of the Welfare State and the Exhaustion of Utopian Energies', in *The New Conservatism: Cultural Criticism and the Historians' Debate* (Massachusetts: MIT Press, 1989).

36. G. Márkus, 'The Politics of Morals', in John Burnheim (ed.), *The Social Philosophy of Agnes Heller* (Amsterdam: Rodopi, 1994), p.272.

37. Heller, *Everyday Life*, p.ix.

38. R. Wolin, 'Heller's Theory of Everyday Life', in *The Social Philosophy of Agnes Heller*, pp.138–9.

39. Heller, *Everyday Life*, p.118.

40. Ibid., p.7.

41. A. Heller, *The Power of Shame* (London: Routledge & Kegan Paul, 1985). This is a reworking of the basic conceptual framework of *Everyday Life*. While virtually all adults achieve a basic level of competence, as subjective experience this achievement has an additional personal dimension that is only expressible in cultural creation. This cultural surplus represents a vital reservoir of potential innovation.

42. Márkus, 'Morals', p.275.

43. Heller, *Everyday Life*, p.51.

44. Ibid., p.47.

45. Ibid., p.118.

46. Tormey is mistaken when he attributes a Platonic interpretation of cultural objectivations to Heller. She does not ascribe to the view that this realm is 'separate from, if not held "above", that "visible" world'. While she does hold that access to culture provides knowledge and the prospects of greater self-reflectivity, she also views this domain as a product of historical processes and individual creation that is very much embedded in everyday life, and responsive to it. S. Tormey, *Agnes Heller: Socialism, Autonomy and the Postmodern* (Manchester: Manchester University Press, 2001), p.41.

47. Heller, *Everyday Life*.

48. Ibid., p.120.

49. Heller, *Shame*, p.104.

50. Heller, 'Marx's Theory of Revolution', p.50.

51. Heller, *Shame*, p.112.

52. In a post-Marxist refinement of her position she will introduce a distinction between 'needs' and 'wants', according to which only the latter is associated with external determination.

53. A. Heller, 'Individual and Community', *Social Praxis*, 1/1 (The Hague: 1973), p.20.

54. Ibid. Along with his objections to Heller's alleged Platonic theory of culture, Tormey is also worried by the elitist connotations of her distinction between particularity and individuality, Tormey, *Agnes Heller*, pp.41–3. This is part of a more general concern with her failure 'to analyse the interaction between individuals and mass movements', p.45. Yet on this point I think he fails to appreciate the specific context of Heller's situation. In Eastern Europe at this time, there were no mass movements for democracy or even the possibility of this sort of overt political activity. In this context, it is not surprising that that exemplary personality and cultural activity would possess the sort of political meaning that is not so customary in liberal democratic society.
55. Heller, 'Individual and Community', p.20.
56. Heller, *Everyday Life*, p.49.
57. Ibid., p.20.
58. Ibid., p.50.
59. Márkus, 'Morals', p.275.

CHAPTER 2

1. A. Heller, *Renaissance Man* (London: Routledge & Kegan Paul, 1978), pp.5–6.
2. G. Márkus, 'The Politics of Morals', in John Burnheim (ed.), *The Social Philosophy of Agnes Heller* (Amsterdam: Rodopi, 1994), pp.269–70.
3. A. Arato, Introduction, in A. Heller, 'Towards a Marxist Theory of Values', *Kinesis*, Graduate Journal in Philosophy, 5/1 (Carbondale Fall: Southern Illinois University, 1972), p.5.
4. Ibid., p.6.
5. Ibid., pp.63–4.
6. Ibid., p.66.
7. Ibid.
8. Ibid., p.70.
9. Ibid., p.76.
10. A. Heller, 'A Reply to My Critics', in John Burnheim (ed.), *The Social Philosophy of Agnes Heller* (Amsterdam: Rodopi, 1994), p.284.
11. Tormey locates these two later works outside the project of the 'Renaissance of Marx', when Heller moves towards her own personal thinking. S. Tormey, *Agnes Heller: Socialism, Autonomy and the Postmodern* (Manchester: Manchester University Press, 2001), p.15. While I agree that these works demonstrate a more autonomous treatment of many issues, they still very much form an integral part of Heller's project for a philosophical anthropology and therefore sit at the very centre of the 'Renaissance of Marx'. This is confirmed by Tormey's later comment that even Heller's post-1968 works show that 'her attachment to the spirit and ideals of the Renaissance of Marxism was if anything strengthened during the latter half of her Budapest School career' (p.51).
12. S. Benhabib, 'Review of *On Instincts* and *A Theory of Feelings*', *Telos*, 44 (St Louis: Telos Press, Summer 1980), p.213.
13. A. Heller, *On Instincts* (Assen: Van Gorcum, 1979).
14. Ibid., p.6.
15. Ibid., p.17.
16. Benhabib is correct in noting that Freud and the neo-Freudians receive only a perfunctory treatment.
17. Heller, *Instincts*, p.25.

18. Ibid., p.8.
19. Ibid., p.4.
20. Ibid., pp.14–15.
21. Ibid., p.15.
22. Ibid., p.96.
23. Ibid., p.1.
24. Ibid., p.11.
25. Ibid., p.16.
26. Ibid., p.17.
27. Ibid., p.2.
28. Ibid., p.1,
29. Ibid., p.95.
30. Ibid., p.69.
31. G. Márkus, *Marxism and Anthropology* (Assen: Van Gorcum, 1978).
32. Heller, *Instincts*, p.19.
33. Ibid., p.20.
34. Ibid., p.21.
35. Ibid., p.19.
36. Benhabib has drawn attention to the naturalism of the category of homeostasis. It postulates a natural evolution towards a state of preservation and expansion that sits uneasily with a being whose identity formation occurs through linguistically mediated social interaction. 'Review', p.216.
37. Heller, *Instincts*, p.19.
38. Ibid., p.22.
39. A. Heller, *A Theory of Feelings* (Assen: Van Gorcum, 1978).
40. A. Heller, 'The Emotional Division of Labour Between the Sexes: Perspectives on Feminism and Socialism', *Thesis Eleven*, 5/6 (Clayton, Victoria: 1982), p.65.
41. Heller, *Feelings*, p.4.
42. Ibid., p.18.
43. Ibid., p.35.
44. Ibid., p.7.
45. Ibid., p.110.
46. Ibid., p.41.
47. Ibid., p.110.
48. Ibid., p.150.
49. Ibid., pp.199–200.
50. Ibid., p.215.
51. Ibid., p.226.
52. Ibid., pp.221–3.
53. Ibid., p.228.
54. Ibid., p.227.
55. Ibid., p.233.
56. Ibid., p.206.
57. Ibid., p.236.
58. Ibid., p.237.
59. Ibid.
60. Ibid., pp.238–9.
61. Ibid., p.241.
62. Benhabib, 'Review', pp. 218–20.

63. A. Heller, *The Theory of Needs in Marx* (London: Allison & Busby, 1976). Written in the early 1970s, its publication was delayed by Heller's political excommunication. It was first published in Italian in 1974.
64. Ibid., p.100.
65. György Márkus recalls that it was the essay 'Theory and Practice From the Standpoint of Needs', a summary of the main theses of the book, which served as the official pretext for her removal from Hungarian cultural life in 1973. See his 'Politics of Morals', p.278.
66. Heller, *Needs in Marx*, p.88.
67. Ibid., p.26.
68. Ibid.
69. Ibid., p.27.
70. Ibid.
71. Ibid., p.39.
72. Ibid., p.38.
73. Ibid., p.41.
74. Ibid., p.57.
75. Ibid., p.76.
76. Ibid.
77. Tormey finds in Heller's theory of radical needs a reversion to the classical Marxist account of social transformation, from the mode in *Everyday Life* that had focused on the process of defetishisation. *Agnes Heller*, p.69. Yet the distinction he tries to draw between these two does not exist for Heller. For her, the very radicality of these needs has a qualitative aspect, which means that fetishised appearances are breached and cultural needs become more prominent.
78. Heller, *Needs in Marx*, p.102.
79. Ibid., p.105.
80. Ibid., p.74.
81. Ibid.
82. Ibid.
83. Ibid., pp.92–3.
84. Ibid., p.95.
85. Ibid.
86. Ibid., p.86. I do not agree with Tormey's reading that 'Heller almost revels in the impossibility of Marx's vision' for 'this does not invalidate it as an "ought" to inform action'. *Agnes Heller*, p.73. This renders Heller a conventional utopian thinker who is happy to affirm mere 'oughts'. On this point, she endorses Marx's critique of the impotence of philosophy. Her utopianism is historically immanent and implies a vision and values that are a virtual, becoming reality.
87. Heller, *Needs in Marx*, p.86.

CHAPTER 3

1. A. Heller, 'In einer fremden Welt', in *Der Affe auf dem Fahrrad*, pp.391–415.
2. Although the views of the authors were not identical and each wrote a particular section of the text, they had fully discussed the conception of the whole and in the foreword take authorial responsibility for a common position. F. Fehér et al., *Dictatorship Over Needs* (Oxford: Blackwell, 1983), p.xiii.

3. On this distinction between 'thin' and 'thick' descriptive accounts, see Tim Luke's contribution to I. Szelenyi et al., 'Review Symposium on Soviet-Type Societies', *Telos* 6 (New York: Telos Press, Summer 1984), pp.155–92.

4. Fehér et al., *Dictatorship Over Needs*, p.8.

5. Arato makes the point that each of the authors derive the notion of 'dictatorship over needs' in a slightly different way and that its significance is more symbolic than theoretical. A. Arato, *From Neo-Marxism to Democratic Theory: Essays in the Critical Theory of Soviet-Type Societies* (Armonk, New York: M.E. Sharpe. 1993), pp.123–4.

6. Fehér et al., *Dictatorship Over Needs*, p.2.

7. Ibid., p.8.

8. Ibid.

9. Ibid., p.9.

10. Ibid., p.10.

11. Ibid., p.12.

12. Ibid., p.13.

13. Ibid., p.16.

14. Ibid., p.21.

15. Ibid., p.22.

16. Ibid., p.24.

17. Ibid., p.30.

18. Ibid., p.32.

19. Ibid.

20. These include bureaucratic domination, a line of continuous development in the Russian case and the resuscitation of a deep conservatism, which followed the retreat from the period of mass terror under Stalin.

21. Fehér et al., *Dictatorship Over Needs*, p.45.

22. Ibid., p.53.

23. Ibid., p.59. This is evident in well-known negative structural phenomena such as the seller's market, in the consumption and production of goods, bottlenecks and overmanning, against the expressed and repeated resolutions of central committees.

24. Ibid., p.65.

25. Ibid.

26. Ibid., p.138. Of course, several authors have raised the question of the usefulness of the notion of legitimacy in regard to the Soviet-style societies. On this point, see Arato, *Neo-Marxism to Democratic Theory*, p.127.

27. Fehér et al., *Dictatorship Over Needs*.

28. Ibid.

29. Ibid., p.141.

30. Ibid., p.142.

31. Ibid., p.146. If we cast a look back at Hannah Arendt's analysis in 'Ideology and Terror', in *Origins of Totalitarianism*, second edition (London: George Allen & Unwin, 1958), the discrepancy between theory and reality is not such an important issue. She maintains that the essence of ideology is to mask this gap and even finally to replace it with a seamless ideological view of the world.

32. Fehér et al., *Dictatorship Over Needs*, p.147.

33. Ibid., p.151. Leaving aside the question of traditionalism as a mode of legitimisation in Eastern Europe, Arato also raised the problem of the tension between the recourse to traditional legitimisation and Heller's equally strong claim that these societies

were 'modern'. He asks the question as to how traditional legitimisation could work in a truly modern society. *Neo-Marxism to Democratic Theory*, p.129.

34. Fehér et al., *Dictatorship Over Needs*, p.153.
35. Ibid., p.158.
36. Ibid., p.163.
37. Ibid., p.167.
38. Ivan Szelenyi complains about Heller's continual recourse to antediluvian categories, suggesting that while it shows 'admirable imagination ... it is not clear to what extent these categories are used as metaphors or are sufficiently reconstructed to meet the realities of a complex industrial society'. Szelenyi et al., 'Review Symposium on Soviet-Type Societies', p.173.
39. Fehér et al., *Dictatorship Over Needs*, p.170.
40. Ibid., p.171.
41. Ibid., p.176.
42. Ibid., p.177.
43. Ibid., p.178.
44. Ibid., p.180.
45. Ibid., p.187.
46. Ibid., p.188.
47. F. Fehér and A. Heller, 'The Gorbachev Phenomenon', in F. Fehér and A. Arato (eds) *Gorbachev: The Debate* (Cambridge: Polity, 1989), pp.20–37.
48. Fehér et al., *Dictatorship Over Needs*, p.193.
49. Ibid., p.196.
50. Ibid., p.207.
51. Ibid., p.208.
52. Ibid., p.215.
53. Ibid.
54. Ibid., p.221.
55. Ibid., p.223.
56. Ibid., pp.224–5.
57. Ibid., p.225.
58. Ibid., p.226.
59. Ibid., p.227.
60. Ibid., p.229.
61. Ibid., p.230–1.
62. Ibid., p.232.
63. Ibid., p.233.
64. Ibid., p.235.
65. Ibid., p.236.
66. Ibid., pp.239–40.
67. Ibid., p.242.
68. Ibid., p.243.
69. Ibid., p.244.
70. Ibid., p.247.
71. Ibid., p.251.
72. Ibid., p.259.
73. Ibid., pp.262–3.
74. Ibid., p.262.
75. Ibid., p.277.
76. Ibid., pp.274–5.

77. Ibid., p.283.
78. Ibid., p.277.
79. For precisely this reason, Milhaly Vajda raised doubts about structuralist accounts of these regimes in his *The State and Socialism* (London: Allison & Busby, 1981).
80. Fehér et al., *Dictatorship Over Needs*, pp.285–6.
81. Interestingly, in his 1987 article on the Budapest School's analysis, Arato also claims that in the Soviet Union there was 'neither a broadly based democratic opposition nor any trace of reformism from above'. This only goes to highlight the great speed with which the dynamics of dissolution finely overcame the regime. *Neo-Marxism to Democratic Theory*, p.143.
82. Fehér et al., *Dictatorship over Needs,* p.291.
83. The authors subordinated their own personal theoretical differences in presenting a unified perspective. I owe this information to a conversation with György Márkus in 1999.

CHAPTER 4

1. A. Heller, 'A Reply to My Critics', in J. Burnheim (ed.), *The Social Philosophy of Agnes Heller*, p.282.
2. Ibid., p.283.
3. A. Heller, *A Radical Philosophy* (Oxford: Blackwell, 1984), p.137; first published as *Die Philosophie des linken Radicalismus* (Hamburg: VSA Verlag, 1978).
4. Heller, *Radical Philosophy*, p.134.
5. Ibid.
6. Ibid., p.53.
7. Ibid., p.55.
8. Ibid., p.57.
9. Ibid.
10. Ibid., p.58.
11. Ibid., p.5.
12. Ibid., p.8.
13. Ibid., p.7.
14. Ibid., p.10. For more detail see Pierre Hadot's *Philosophy as a Way of Life* (Oxford: Blackwell, 1995).
15. Heller, *Radical Philosophy*, p.9.
16. Ibid.
17. Ibid., p.13.
18. Ibid.
19. Ibid., p.14.
20. Ibid., p.16.
21. Ibid., pp.15–16.
22. Ibid., p.16.
23. Ibid., p.25.
24. Ibid., p.4.
25. Ibid., p.59.
26. Ibid., pp. 64–5.
27. Ibid., pp.64–6. Tormey argues that the major revision in *Radical Philosophy* is the breakdown of the identical subject/object that he attributes to the 'most idealist aspect of Marx'. S. Tormey, *Agnes Heller: Socialism, Autonomy and the Postmodern*, p.93. Yet this identical subject/object was the error not of Marx but of the young

Lukács in *History and Class Consciousness*, which he genuinely repudiated in self-criticisms from the early 1930s. Heller was quite aware of this and so her target is not so much Hegelian idealism as such, but its teleological implications. Thus the main philosophical movement is from Hegel to Kant.

28. Heller, *Radical Philosophy*, pp.17–18.
29. Ibid., p.19.
30. Ibid., p.20.
31. Ibid., p.21.
32. Ibid., p.35.
33. Ibid., p.21.
34. Heller, 'Reply', p.285.
35. Ibid., p.284.
36. Heller, *Radical Philosophy*, p.5.
37. Ibid., p.2.
38. It is not true that Lukács maintained a thesis of total reification in any other sense than that no reform programme could alleviate the 'absolute sinfulness' (Fichte) of bourgeois society. Of course, the very contradictory character of this society excluded the real possibility of total reification, since its dynamic produced the revolutionary proletariat as its own negation.
39. Heller, *Radical Philosophy*, p.4.
40. Ibid., p.2.
41. Ibid., pp.43–4.
42. See J. Habermas, 'Philosophy as Stand-In and Interpreter', in *Moral Consciousness and Communicative Action* (Massachusetts: MIT Press, 1990).
43. Ibid., p.44.
44. Ibid., pp.48–9.
45. Ibid., p.49.
46. Ibid., p.51.
47. Ibid.
48. Ibid., p.152.
49. Ibid.
50. Ibid., p.135.
51. Ibid., p.155.
52. Ibid., pp. 44–9.

CHAPTER 5

1. J. Burnheim (ed.) *The Social Philosophy of Agnes Heller*, p.284.
2. A. Heller, *A Theory of History* (London: Routledge & Kegan Paul, 1982), p.28.
3. Ibid., p.30.
4. Ibid., p.31.
5. Ibid., p.32.
6. Ibid., p.33.
7. Ibid.
8. Ibid.
9. Ibid., p.34.
10. Ibid., p.323.
11. Ibid., p.35. If anything, this motif will gain in weight as the consciousness of contingency moves to the centre of Heller's reflective postmodern standpoint.
12. Ibid., p.292.

13. Ibid.
14. Ibid., p.299.
15. Ibid., p.301.
16. Ibid., p.302.
17. Ibid., p.303.
18. Ibid., p.311.
19. Ibid.
20. Ibid., p.312.
21. Ibid., p.314. For Heller's early critique of Habermas' version of rational communication, see A. Heller, 'Habermas and Marxism', in *Habermas. Critical Debates* (Cambridge, Mass.: MIT Press, 1982).
22. Heller, *Theory of History*, p.333.
23. A. Heller, 'Can "True" and "False" Needs Be Posited?' in *The Power Of Shame: A Rational Perspective* (London: Routledge & Kegan Paul, 1985).
24. Ibid., p.285.
25. Ibid., p.287.
26. Ibid.
27. Ibid.
28. Ibid., p.288.
29. Ibid., p.289.
30. Ibid.
31. Ibid., p.291.
32. Ibid., p.293.
33. Ibid.
34. Ibid., p.294.
35. Ibid., p.296.
36. Ibid.
37. Ibid.
38. Ibid.
39. Ibid.
40. Ibid., p.297.
41. Ibid., p.296.
42. Ibid., p.298.

CHAPTER 6

1. J. Habermas, *The Theory of Communication Action*, 2 vols, i: *Reason and the Rationalization of Society* (Boston: Beacon Press, 1984) and ii: *The Critique of Functionalist Reason* (Boston: Beacon Press, 1987); M. Hollis and S. Lukes, *Rationality and Relativism* (Cambridge, Mass.: MIT Press, 1982).
2. Heller, A. *The Power of Shame* (London: Routledge & Kegan Paul, 1985), p.80.
3. Ibid., p.81.
4. Ibid., p.74.
5. Ibid., p.75.
6. Ibid., p.77.
7. Ibid., p.90.
8. Ibid., p.94.
9. Ibid., p.86.
10. Ibid., p.84.
11. Ibid., p.95.

12. Ibid., p.98.
13. Ibid., p.99.
14. Ibid., p.103.
15. Ibid.
16. Ibid., p.106.
17. Ibid., p.107.
18. Ibid., p.109.
19. Ibid.
20. Ibid., p.110. See also Heller's earlier paper 'Lukacs' Aesthetics', *New Hungarian Quarterly*, 24/7 (Budapest:1966), pp.84–94.
21. Heller, *Shame*, p.120.
22. Ibid., p.104.
23. Ibid., p.120.
24. Ibid., pp.120–1.
25. Ibid., p.123.
26. Ibid., p.131.
27. Ibid., p.134.
28. Ibid., p.124.
29. Ibid., p.128.
30. Ibid., p.129.
31. Ibid.
32. Ibid., p.131. Habermas never claimed that primary socialisation was at stake. The idea that the life-world would ultimately resist colonisation beyond a certain point was not foreign to Habermas, even in the period where he held the colonisation thesis as the central plank of his theory of modernity.
33. Ibid., p.135.
34. Ibid.
35. Ibid., p.136.
36. Ibid., p.138.
37. Ibid., p.140.
38. Ibid., p.145.
39. Ibid., p.142.
40. Ibid., p.145.
41. Ibid.
42. Ibid., p.147.
43. Ibid.
44. Ibid., p.168.
45. Ibid., p.171.
46. Ibid., p.173.
47. Ibid., p.183.
48. Ibid., p.203.
49. Ibid., p.205. See H. Arendt, *Lectures on Kant's Political Philosophy* (Sussex: Harvester Press, 1982) and C. Castoriadis, *The Imaginary Institution of Society* (Cambridge: Cambridge University Press, 1987).
50. Heller, *Shame*, pp.206–7.
51. Ibid., p.209. Again this seems to be a variation on the other pole of Habermas' diagnosis of modernity: the impoverishment of everyday life.
52. Ibid., p.214.
53. Ibid., pp.205–6.
54. Ibid., p.215.

55. Ibid., p.216.
56. Ibid., p.218.
57. Ibid., p.221.
58. Ibid.
59. Ibid., p.229.
60. Ibid.
61. Ibid., p.231.
62. Ibid., p.232.
63. Ibid., p.234.
64. Ibid., p.235.
65. Ibid., p.246.
66. Ibid., p.247.
67. Ibid.
68. Ibid., p.237.
69. Ibid., p.249.
70. Ibid., p.245.

CHAPTER 7

1. A. Heller, *Beyond Justice* (Oxford: Blackwell, 1987), p.v.
2. P. Harrison, 'Radical Philosophy and the Theory of Modernity', in J. Burnheim (ed.), *The Social Philosophy of Agnes Heller*, p.161.
3. Heller, *Beyond Justice*, p.48.
4. Ibid., p.78.
5. Ibid., p.88.
6. Ibid., p.92.
7. Ibid., p.93.
8. Ibid., p.94.
9. Ibid.
10. Ibid., p.100.
11. Ibid., p.101.
12. Ibid.
13. Ibid., p.110.
14. Ibid., p.111.
15. Ibid., p.115.
16. Ibid., p.127.
17. Ibid., p.117.
18. Ibid., p.118.
19. J. Cohen, 'Heller, Habermas and Justice', *Praxis International*, 8/4 (Oxford: Blackwell, January 1989), p.495.
20. Harrison, 'Radical Philosophy', p.156.
21. Heller, *Beyond Justice*, p.121.
22. Ibid., p.122.
23. Ibid., p.123.
24. Ibid., p.126.
25. Ibid., p.130.
26. Ibid., p.133.
27. Ibid., p.141.
28. Ibid., p.143.

29. Ibid., p.153. See J. Rawls, *A Theory of Justice* (Cambridge, Mass.: Belknap Press, 1971); R. Nozick, *Anarchy, State, Utopia* (New York: Basic Books, 1975); R. Dworkin, *Taking Rights Seriously* (London: Duckworth, 1977).
30. Heller, *Beyond Justice*.
31. Ibid., p.155.
32. Ibid.
33. Ibid., p.181.
34. Ibid., p.182.
35. Ibid.
36. Ibid., p.183.
37. Ibid
38. Ibid., p.186.
39. Ibid
40. Ibid., p.194.
41. Ibid., p.195.
42. Ibid.
43. Ibid.
44. Ibid., p.199.
45. Ibid., p.200.
46. Ibid.
47. Ibid., p.201.
48. Ibid., p.202.
49. Ibid., p.203.
50. Ibid., p.205.
51. Ibid., p.220.
52. Ibid.
53. Ibid., p.222.
54. Ibid.
55. Ibid., p.224.
56. Ibid., p.230.
57. Ibid.
58. Ibid.
59. Ibid., p.231.
60. Ibid.
61. Ibid., p.232.
62. Rawls, *Justice*, p.233.
63. Ibid., p.234. On this question, see Heller's 'Habermas and Marxism', in J.B. Thompson and D. Held (eds), *Habermas: Critical Debates* (Cambridge, Mass.: MIT Press, 1982).
64. Heller, *Beyond Justice*, p.249.
65. Ibid., p.250.
66. Ibid., p.234.
67. Ibid., p.253. As we shall see, Heller distinguishes her version of the discourse model by the emphatic assertion that the very possibility of dialogue depends on value discourse and agreement on at least one common value.
68. Ibid., p.251.
69. Ibid.
70. Ibid., p.252.
71. Ibid.
72. Ibid., p.234.

73. Ibid., p.235.
74. Ibid., p.236.
75. Ibid., p.238.
76. Ibid. Jean Cohen contests the view that in Habermas the cognitive claim rests solely in the principle of universalisation. She contends that for Habermas 'the objectivity of judgement can be rooted in the structure of argumentation itself'; that is, that the process of discursive conflict resolution that comes from outside has itself been normalised. See Cohen, 'Heller, Habermas and Justice', pp.491–7.
77. Heller, *Beyond Justice*, p.238.
78. Ibid., p.239.
79. Ibid.
80. Ibid., p.240.
81. Ibid., p.241.
82. Ibid., p.246.
83. Ibid.
84. Ibid., p.242.
85. Ibid., p.246.
86. Ibid., p.248.
87. Ibid., p.258.
88. Ibid., p.259.
89. Ibid., p.260.
90. Ibid., p.261.
91. Ibid., p.262.
92. Ibid.
93. Ibid., pp.263–4.
94. Ibid., p.266.
95. Ibid., p.267.
96. Ibid., p.268.
97. Ibid., p.269.
98. Ibid.
99. Ibid., p.270.
100. Ibid., p.272.
101. Ibid., p.273.
102. Harrison, 'Radical Philosophy', p.161.
103. Heller, *Beyond Justice*, p.277.
104. To avoid the religious connotations that still cling to the concept of righteousness, Heller prefers to speak of the decent or good person.
105. Ibid., pp.274–5.
106. Ibid., p.278.
107. Ibid.
108. Ibid., p.279.
109. Ibid. The adequacy of this definition will be considered in Chapter 9.
110. Ibid., p.290.
111. Ibid., p.289.
112. Ibid., p.290.
113. Ibid., p.291.
114. Ibid., p.301.
115. Ibid., p.308.
116. Ibid., p.309.
117. Ibid., p.304.

118. Ibid., p.305.
119. Ibid., p.313.
120. Ibid., p.312.
121. In recent times this neglect has come to attention. Note the recent major study by Martha Nussbaum, *Upheavals of Thought: The Intelligence of the Emotions* (Cambridge: Cambridge University Press, 2001).
122. Heller, *Beyond Justice*, p.320.
123. Ibid., p.319.
124. Ibid.
125. Ibid., p.318.
126. Ibid.
127. Ibid., p.323.
128. Ibid., p.313.
129. Ibid., p.325.
130. Ibid., p.327.

CHAPTER 8

1. Although *Dictatorship Over Needs* finally appeared in 1983, the latter sections, written by Fehér and Heller, had been produced somewhat earlier. The whole project had been delayed while Márkus found time to complete the very important first theoretical part of the book, which gave a comprehensive review of the competing attempts to theorise 'really existing socialism'.
2. The modernity theory that Heller developed at this time was essentially a co-production between herself and Fehér. Some of the essays towards this theory appear under Heller's name alone, while others are co-written. For the sake of brevity and elegance in regard to the latter, I will usually refer only to Heller; but this is, by no means, to disregard Fehér's essential contribution.
3. A. Heller and F. Fehér, *Eastern Left, Western Left: Totalitarianism, Freedom and Democracy* (Oxford: Blackwell, 1986), p.202.
4. Ibid., p.210.
5. Ibid.
6. Ibid., p.202.
7. Ibid., p.204.
8. Ibid., p.206.
9. Ibid., p.205. Of course, what radical action means becomes considerably more muted over time.
10. Ibid., p.213. Harrison argues, I think correctly, that they went too far in maintaining that dichotomous classes alone unified the three elements of modernity. This suggestion implies that modernity is more unified than the notion of independent logics would warrant. Heller's solution to this difficulty was to adopt a more functionalist reading of the concept of class. See P. Harrison, 'Radical Philosophy and the Theory of Modernity', in J. Burnheim (ed.), *The Social Philosophy of Agnes Heller* (Amsterdam: Rodopi, 1994), p.151.
11. Heller and Fehér, *Eastern Left, Western Left*, p.214.
12. Ibid., p.229.
13. Ibid., p.230.
14. Ibid., p.236.
15. Heller, *Theory of History*, p.283.
16. Ibid.

17. A. Heller, *A Theory of Modernity* (Oxford: Blackwell, 1999), p.66.
18. Heller, *Theory of History*, p.284. In this respect, Tormey gives the idea of the 'logics' far too strong a teleological reading when he says 'the idea of the "logic" is the teleological unfolding of a process whose end can be known and studied in advance of the process being completed'. S. Tormey, *Agnes Heller: Socialism, Autonomy and the Postmodern*, p.122.
19. Heller, *Theory of History*, p.184.
20. A. Heller, *Can Modernity Survive?* (Cambridge: Polity, 1990), p.122.
21. Even in the case of capitalism, thinkers as diverse as Karl Polanyi and the ordo-liberals have questioned the idea of a naturalistic 'logic of capital'. For the latter, see T. Lemke, 'The Birth of Bio-Politics: Michel Foucault's Lecture at the Collège de France on Neo-Liberal Governmentality', *Economy and Society*, 30/2 (London: Taylor & Francis, May 2001), pp.190–207.
22. A. Heller, *The Power of Shame* (London: Routledge & Kegan Paul, 1985), p.140.
23. Harrison, 'Radical Philosophy', p.153.
24. Heller, *Shame*, p.142.
25. Ibid.
26. Ibid., p.147.
27. Ibid., p.128.
28. Harrison, 'Radical Philosophy', p.155.
29. A. Heller, 'Modernity's Pendulum', *Thesis Eleven*, 31 (Cambridge, Mass.: MIT Press, 1992), p.4.
30. J.P. Arnason, 'Nationalism, Globalisation and Modernity', *Theory, Culture and Society* 7/2–3 (London: Sage, June 1990), p.209.
31. In general, globalisation connotes the idea of the world as a single space and system in cultural, economic, and perhaps even in political terms. Recent works by Robinson, Giddens, Habermas, Beck and Bauman, amongst others, explore its meaning and impact.
32. Heller and Fehér, *Eastern Left, Western Left*, p.235.
33. Ibid., p.210.
34. Heller, *Shame*, p.301.
35. This conceptual distinction between 'wants' and 'needs' is based on two types of orientation and their objects. Wants conform to the category of lusts, are values in quantitative measures and are ultimately incompatible with universal freedom and life as the leading value ideas of modernity. Needs, on the other hand, are orientated to these modern values, in as much as their focus is individual self-determination. See 'Can "True" and "False" Needs be Posited?', in Heller, *Shame*.
36. Heller, *Shame*, p.32.
37. This last motif is completely missing from Tormey's account of 'dissatisfaction'. Tormey, *Agnes Heller*, p.117
38. Heller, *Shame*, p.304.
39. Heller, *Can Modernity Survive?* (Cambridge: Polity, 1990), p.303.
40. Ibid., p.307.
41. Ibid., p.306.
42. A. Heller and F. Fehér, *The Postmodern Political Condition* (Cambridge: Polity, 1988), p.19.
43. Heller, *Shame*, p.307.
44. Ibid., p.309. From a contemporary standpoint this now sounds remarkably naive. As the 1980s progressed, the issue of ecological crisis became more prominent

and is reflected in Heller's work; but these issues are never at the forefront of her analysis or comprehensively addressed.

45. Heller, *Shame*, p.312.

46. It also parades the illusory belief that the First World can be quarantined from these problems without them eventually coming home to roost. Recently, increasingly large-scale movements of refugees, asylum seekers and other displaced persons between continents have demonstrated the short-sighted folly of this indifference.

47. Heller, *Shame,* p.310.

48. For an extended treatment of this issue, see the previously mentioned article, 'Can "True" and "False" Needs be Posited?'

49. Heller and Fehér, *Postmodern Political Condition*, p.33.

50. Heller, *Shame,* p.314.

51. Ibid.

52. Ibid., p.245.

53. Heller and Fehér, *Eastern Left, Western Left*, p.236.

54. For a more recent analysis along these lines, see Jürgen Habermas, *The Postnational Constellation* (Cambridge: Polity, 2001).

55. A. Heller, 'Past, Present and Future of Democracy', *Social Research*, 45/4 (New York: Winter 1978).

56. Ibid., p.867. On this point it is worthwhile to correct the misinterpretation that runs through Tormey's account of Heller's lapse into a Rousseauian republicanism during the post-Marxist radical phase. While there is always a strong communitarian moment in her thinking, this never amounts to Rousseau's democratic general will. She was always sufficiently concerned about individual rights not to ignore the crucial role that formal guarantees play in maintaining real freedom. See Tormey, *Agnes Heller*, pp. 88, 95, 158 and 160.

57. Heller, 'Past, Present and Future of Democracy', p.871.

58. Ibid., p.873.

59. Ibid.

60. Ibid., p.876.

61. Ibid., p.878.

62. Ibid., p.880. Heller never offers the precise details of how this system of socialist workers' self-management would effectively mesh with a capitalist market system; but the presupposition seems to involve a larger degree of state intervention than in the then contemporary mixed economies of liberal democratic Europe.

63. Ibid., p.883.

64. Heller, *Can Modernity Survive?* pp.4–5.

65. Ibid.

66. Ibid., pp.152–3.

67. See F. Fehér and A. Heller, *Biopolitics* (London: Avebury, 1994).

68. Heller and Fehér, *Postmodern Political Condition,* p.153.

69. Ibid., p.143.

70. Ibid., p.153.

71. Heller, *Can Modernity Survive?* p.123.

72. Ibid.

73. Ibid., p.120.

74. Heller, *Shame*, p.235.

CHAPTER 9

1. G. Márkus, 'The Politics of Morals', in J. Burnheim (ed.), *The Social Philosophy of Agnes Heller*, pp.25–58.
2. It is not surprising to find that some commentators have mistaken this strong pedagogic voice for that of a sort of prescriptive moralism.
3. A. Heller, *Der Affe auf dem Fahrrad* (Berlin: Philo, 1999), p.476.
4. A. Heller, *General Ethics* (Oxford: Blackwell, 1988), p.74.
5. Ibid., p.1.
6. Ibid., p.9.
7. Ibid., pp.5–6.
8. Ibid., p. 4. In her view, Kohlberg's moral evolutionism is a faulty realisation of this programme because its pure naturalism amounts to philosophical primitivism.
9. Ibid., p.7.
10. Ibid.
11. A. Heller, *A Philosophy of Morals* (Oxford, Blackwell, 1990), p.7.
12. Ibid., p.8. Of course, this claim is somewhat in tension with the idea of the empirical universality of certain modern value ideas, such as freedom and equal life chances. However, here Heller's emphasis is clearly on the question of the long-term historical sustainability of this project. On this question, she cannot claim knowledge.
13. Ibid.
14. Ibid.
15. Ibid., p.18.
16. Ibid., p.20.
17. Ibid., pp.21–2.
18. Ibid., p.22.
19. Ibid.
20. Ibid., pp.25–6.
21. Ibid., p.30.
22. Ibid., p.31.
23. Ibid., p.36. The elementary categories of value orientation are familiar from Chapter 4. Behind the hierarchy of norms and rules are these primary categories of value orientation that condition 'having of a world'. The distinction between 'good' and 'bad' is a human universal that allows further differentiation into the other secondary categories, such as holy/profane, right/wrong, true/false and useful/useless. These also form a hierarchy embracing all rules and norms. Rules are restrictions insofar as they lay down relatively inflexible conditions of application and fulfilment. By contrast, norms are prescriptions that are lived up to only to a certain degree and allow interpretative latitude. These are infringed by overstepping a limit but they also provide interpretative space in which the actor may develop a critical relation to rules.
24. Ibid., p.37.
25. Whether this can be counted as a 'gain without losses' seems hard to sustain given that the abandonment of conventional *Sittlichkeit* has caused untold individual suffering, even if we finally judge it to have been worthwhile on the basis of some more general accounting of historical progress.
26. Ibid., p.42.
27. Ibid., p.43.
28. Ibid., p.52.
29. Ibid.

30. Ibid., p.55.
31. Ibid., pp.58–9.
32. Ibid., p.64.
33. Ibid., pp.68–9.
34. Ibid., p.74.
35. Ibid., p.77.
36. Ibid.
37. Ibid., p.81. The greatest responsibility for collective crimes lies with the leadership, which has greater capacity to initiate and real choice of options. But some responsibility extends down the chain of command, even to those who did not participate in crimes but acquiesced with regimes that did.
38. Ibid., pp.87–8.
39. Ibid., p.92.
40. Ibid., pp.94–5.
41. Ibid., p.97.
42. Ibid., p.106.
43. Ibid., p.107.
44. Ibid., p.106.
45. Ibid., p.107.
46. Ibid., pp.111–12. A narcissistic conscience means that the individual is completely preoccupied with non-moral empirical self-reflection; a calculating conscience merges the pair good/evil with success/failure or useful/harmful; and a good conscience signifies a final thrust towards self-deification insofar as the ego becomes a superman, without gods or norms.
47. Ibid., p.113.
48. Ibid., p.132.
49. Ibid., p.134.
50. Ibid., p.137.
51. Ibid., p.143.
52. Ibid., p.144.
53. Ibid., p.153.
54. Ibid., p.155.
55. Ibid., p.156.
56. Ibid., p.159.
57. Ibid., p.161.
58. Ibid., p.163.
59. Ibid., p.164.
60. Ibid., p.170.
61. Ibid., p.174.
62. Ibid., pp.175–6.
63. Ibid., p.175.
64. Ibid., p.178.
65. Ibid., p.179.
66. Ibid., p.10.
67. Ibid., p.291.
68. Ibid., p.9.
69. Ibid., p.292.
70. For a most useful elaboration of this point, see Heller's unpublished paper 'Ethics of Personality, the Other and the Question of Responsibility' (1997), p.18.
71. Z. Bauman, *The Individualized Society* (Cambridge: Polity, 2001), p.87.

72. Heller, *Philosophy of Morals*, p.77.
73. Ibid., p.20.
74. Ibid., p.27.
75. Ibid., p.12.
76. Ibid., p.15.
77. Ibid., p.14.
78. Ibid., p.18.
79. Ibid., pp.19–20.
80. Ibid., p.21.
81. Heller, 'Ethics of Personality', p.20.
82. Ibid.
83. Heller, *Philosophy of Morals*, p.31.
84. Ibid. Whether this view is completely fair to Habermas need not detain us at this point. At that time, this was a common critique of his position. It was also before he insisted upon the merely counter-factual status of the communicative ideal of consensus.
85. Ibid.
86. Ibid., p.36.
87. Ibid., p.39.
88. Ibid., p.42.
89. Ibid., p.43.
90. Ibid., p.50.
91. Ibid., p.52.
92. Ibid., p.53.
93. Ibid., p.57.
94. Ibid., p.61.
95. Ibid., p.63.
96. Ibid.
97. Ibid., p.68.
98. Ibid., p.76.
99. Ibid., p.73.
100. Ibid., p.77.
101. Ibid., pp.78–9.
102. Ibid., p.83.
103. Ibid., p.89.
104. Ibid., p.91.
105. Ibid., p.92.
106. Ibid., p.93.
107. Ibid., p.127.
108. Ibid., p.129.
109. Ibid., p.131.
110. Ibid., p.139.
111. Ibid., p.142.
112. Ibid., p.151.
113. Ibid.
114. Ibid.
115. Ibid., p.152.
116. Ibid.
117. Ibid., p.73.
118. Ibid., p.176.

119. Ibid., p.177.
120. Ibid., pp.180–1.
121. Ibid., p 181.
122. Ibid., p.186.
123. Ibid., p.188.
124. Ibid., pp.190–1.
125. Ibid., p.193.
126. Ibid., p.207.
127. Ibid., p.217.
128. Ibid., p.222.
129. Ibid., p.223.
130. J. Habermas, 'Morality, Society and Ethics: An Interview with Torben Hviid Nielsen', *Acta Sociologica*, 33/2 (1990), p.113.
131. P. Harrison, 'Radical Philosophy and the Theory of Modernity', in J. Burnheim (ed.), *The Social Philosophy of Agnes Heller*, pp.161–2.

CHAPTER 10

1. A. Heller, 'A Reply to My Critics', in J. Burnheim (ed.), *The Social Philosophy of Agnes Heller*, p.284.
2. A. Heller, *A Philosophy of History: In Fragments* (Oxford: Blackwell, 1993).
3. Ibid., p.93.
4. Ibid., p.98.
5. Ibid., p.106.
6. Ibid., pp.108–9.
7. Ibid., p.113.
8. Ibid.
9. Ibid.
10. Ibid., p.117.
11. Ibid., p.126.
12. Ibid., p.117.
13. Ibid., p.127.
14. Ibid., p.132.
15. Ibid., p.133.
16. Ibid
17. Ibid., p.135.
18. A. Heller, *A Theory of Modernity* (Oxford: Blackwell, 1999), p.4.
19. Ibid., p.3.
20. Ibid., pp.3–4.
21. Ibid., pp.5–6.
22. Ibid., p. 5.
23. Ibid., pp.11–12.
24. Ibid., p.15.
25. Ibid.
26. Ibid., p.17.
27. Ibid.
28. Ibid., pp.17–18.
29. Heller, *Philosophy of History*, p.57.
30. Ibid., p. 60.

31. For example, see R. Bernstein, 'Agnes Heller: Philosophy, Rational Utopia and Praxis', in J. Burnheim (ed.), *The Social Philosophy of Agnes Heller*.
32. A. Heller, *A Radical Philosophy* (Oxford: Blackwell, 1984), p.134.
33. Heller, 'Reply', p.289.
34. Heller, *Theory of Modernity*, pp.1–2.
35. Heller, 'Reply', p.289.
36. Ibid., p.290.
37. Beilharz characterises this as a shift from a 'sociology of action' to a 'philosophy of experience'. P. Beilharz, 'Budapest Central: Agnes Heller's Theory of Modernity', p.111. While this formulation captures well the movement away from praxis philosophy, the impression should not be derived that Heller has returned to a contemplative conception of philosophy. Her new version of radicalism presupposes only a more mediated relation between culture and social action.
38. Ibid.
39. Ibid., p.219.
40. G. Márkus, 'Interpretations of, and Interpretations in Philosophy', *Critical Philosophy*, 1/1 (Sydney: El Faro Press, 1984), p.82.
41. G. Márkus, 'Do Ideas Have Bodies? Philosophical Content and Literary Form in Descartes', *Literature and Aesthetics*, 14/1 (Sydney: Sydney University Society of Literature and Aesthetics, June 2004); quoting from manuscript version (1998), p.24.
42. A. Heller, 'Questioning the Normative Skepticism of György Márkus', in J. Grumley, P. Crittenden and P. Johnson (eds), *Culture and Enlightenment: Essays for György Márkus* (London: Ashgate, 2002), p.9.
43. G. Márkus, 'Ten Marginalia on the Responsibility of the Philosopher', in A. Kardas et al. (eds), *Diotima Agnes Heller: Festschrift For Her Seventieth Birthday* (Budapest: Osiris-Gond, 1998), pp.343–59.
44. Heller, 'Reply', p.292.

CHAPTER 11

1. A. Heller, 'Modernity's Pendulum', *Thesis Eleven*, 31 (Clayton, Victoria: Monash University, 1992).
2. A. Heller, *A Theory of Modernity* (Oxford: Blackwell, 1999).
3. This was a mistake that I first made in an early review of Heller's development. See 'Watching the Pendulum Swing', *Thesis Eleven*, 37 (Clayton, Victoria: Monash University, 1994), pp.127–40. I then saw her new concentration on the questions of the 'dynamic' and 'social arrangement' of modernity as the abandonment of the multiple logics model and a move to a new more simplified framework. Although this was a precipitant judgement, what follows explains why it was not as far from the mark as might first appear.
4. Heller, *Theory of Modernity*, p.40.
5. Ibid.
6. Ibid., p.41.
7. Ibid., p.84.
8. Ibid., p.43.
9. Ibid., p.44.
10. Ibid., p.46.
11. Ibid., p.47.
12. Ibid., p.51.

13. Ibid., p.52.
14. Ibid., p.55.
15. Ibid., p.58.
16. Ibid., p.62.
17. Despite her strong disavowals, even close colleagues such as Mikhail Vajda have noted the systematic aspirations driving her work. M. Vajda, 'A Lover of Philosophy: A Lover of Europe', in J. Burnheim (ed.) *The Social Philosophy of Agnes Heller* (Amsterdam: Rodopi, 1994). Even Heller's postmodern turn did not completely suppress her systematic aspirations. Her aesthetics, *A Philosophy of the Beautiful* (London: Routledge, forthcoming 2004), follows a long German tradition of closing the system with aesthetics. Yet being systematic and the 'will to a system' is not necessarily the same thing.
18. Heller, *Theory of Modernity*, p.64.
19. Ibid., p.65.
20. Ibid., p.64.
21. Ibid., p.67.
22. Ibid., p.70.
23. Ibid., pp.71–2.
24. Ibid., p.72.
25. Ibid.
26. Ibid., p.74.
27. Ibid., p.76.
28. Ibid., p.78.
29. Ibid., p.79.
30. Ibid., p.82.
31. Ibid.
32. Ibid., p.84.
33. Ibid., p.85.
34. Ibid., p.93.
35. Ibid., p.91.
36. This argument ignores the Weberian thesis that associated the capitalist spirit with the Protestant religious calling and ascetic routinisation.
37. Heller, *Theory of Modernity*, pp.87–8.
38. Ibid., p.90.
39. Ibid., p.89.
40. Ibid., p.90.
41. Ibid., p.91.
42. Ibid., p.92.
43. Ibid., p.84.
44. Ibid.
45. Ibid., p.92.
46. Ibid., p.95.
47. Ibid., pp.97–8.
48. Heller, *Theory of Modernity*, pp.97–8.
49. Ibid.
50. Ibid., p.101.
51. Ibid., p.102.
52. Ibid., p.103.
53. Ibid., p.104.

54. In a paper published only after his death, Ferenc Fehér conceded that the myth of racial superiority and the establishment of the labour camps were the two most crucial factors in the Nazis project. Yet he fails to incorporate this insight into his general explanation of totalitarianism, which relies on following two of modernity's logics to their barbarous extreme. 'Imagining the West', *Thesis Eleven*, 42 (Cambridge, Mass.: MIT Press, 1995), p.63.
55. Heller, *Theory of Modernity*, p.106.
56. Ibid., p107.
57. Ibid., p.67.
58. Ibid., p.107.
59. Ibid., p.108.
60. Ibid., p.110.
61. Ibid.
62. Ibid., p.113.
63. Ibid., pp.113–14.
64. See Heller's early essay from the early 1980s, 'The Great Republic', in A. Heller and F. Fehér, *Eastern Left, Western Left: Totalitarianism, Freedom and Democracy* (Cambridge: Polity, 1987).
65. See J. Habermas, *Between Facts and Forms* (Cambridge, Mass.: MIT Press, 1996), chapters 8 and 9.
66. Heller, *Theory of Modernity*, p.114.
67. Ibid., p.114.
68. Ibid.
69. Ibid., p.24.
70. Ibid., p.33.
71. A. Heller, 'A Theory of Needs Revisited', *Thesis Eleven*, 35 (Clayton, Victoria: Monash University, 1993), p.35.
72. Ibid., p.32.
73. Ibid., p.26.
74. Ibid., p.28.
75. Ibid., p.33.
76. Ibid., p.35.
77. Ibid.
78. As we shall see, some of her ideas on the cultural exhaustion of modernity also seem to have a very Hegelian ring. While she explicitly rejects all philosophy of history, it seems to me that her idea of the 'exhaustion of culture' may also contain some residues of the earlier framework.
79. A. Heller, 'The Three Logics of Modernity and the Double Bind of Imagination', *Graduate Faculty Journal*, 21/2 (New York: New School, 1999), pp 177–93. Unpublished version, p.3.
80. Heller, *Theory of Modernity* p.63.
81. Ibid., p.66.
82. Heller, 'Three Logics', p.11.
83. Heller, *Theory of Modernity*, p.82.
84. A summary of such questions is found in my own earlier article 'The Dissatisfied Society', *New German Critique*, 58 (New York: Telos Press, Winter 1993).
85. Ibid., p.99.
86. For an early article that brings the question of globalisation explicitly into connection with debates over theories of modernity, see J.P. Arnason, 'Nationalism,

Globalisation and Modernity', *Theory, Culture and Society*, 7/2–3 (Middlesbrough: TCS, June, 1990).
87. Heller, *Theory of Modernity*, p.53
88. Ibid., p.106.
89. J P. Arnason, *The Future that Failed* (London: Routledge, 1993), p.12.
90. For an early discussion that raises the question of globalisation as a neglected dimension of contemporary sociology's theoretisation of modernity, see A. Giddens, *The Consequences of Modernity* (Cambridge: Polity, 1990).

CHAPTER 12

1. A. Heller, *A Theory of Modernity*, p.115.
2. Ibid., p.117.
3. Ibid., p.116.
4. Ibid., p.119–20.
5. Ibid., p.122.
6. Ibid.
7. Ibid., p.123.
8. Ibid., p.125.
9. Ibid., pp.125–6.
10. Heller takes over these concepts of culture from György Márkus. See his 'Antinomies of Culture', *Discussion Papers*, 38, Academy of Sciences (Budapest: Collegium Budapest, 1997). For an analysis of her appropriation, see J. Grumley, 'Exploring the Options in No Man's Land: Heller and Márkus on the Antinomies of Modern Culture', *Thesis Eleven*, 75 (London: Sage, November 2003), pp.25–38.
11. Heller, *Theory of Modernity*, p.134.
12. Ibid., p.135.
13. Ibid., p.136.
14. Ibid., pp.136–7.
15. Ibid., p.137.
16. Ibid., p.138.
17. Ibid
18. Ibid., p.139.
19. Ibid., p.140.
20. Ibid., p.134.
21. Ibid., p.129.
22. Ibid., p.132.
23. Ibid., p.130.
24. Ibid., pp.133–4.
25. Ibid., p.133.
26. Ibid., p.134.
27. Ibid., p.144.
28. Ibid.
29. Ibid.
30. Ibid.
31. Ibid., p.153.
32. Ibid., p.154.
33. Ibid., p.55.
34. Ibid., p.57.
35. Ibid., p.160.

36. Ibid., pp.162–3.
37. Ibid., p.163.
38. Ibid., pp.164–5.
39. Ibid., p.165.
40. Ibid., p.166.
41. Ibid., pp.168–9.
42. Ibid., p.170.
43. Ibid.
44. Ibid., p.172.
45. Ibid.
46. Ibid., p.186.
47. Ibid., p.189.
48. Ibid., p.191.
49. Ibid., p.193.
50. Ibid., pp.194–5.
51. Heller's claims on rising standards of living also seem to be questionable, at least in terms of some of the main indices. This suggests, again, that she may not have taken sufficiently into account the impact of globalisation on the welfare state and standards of living in Western liberal democracies in more recent times.

CHAPTER 13

1. P. Harrison, 'Radical Philosophy and the Theory of Modernity', in J. Burnheim (ed.), *The Social Philosophy of Agnes Heller*.
2. A. Heller, *An Ethics of Personality* (Oxford: Blackwell, 1996), p.2.
3. Ibid., p.3.
4. Ibid.
5. Ibid., pp.3–4.
6. M. Vajda, 'Is Moral Philosophy Possible at All?' *Thesis Eleven*, 59 (Bundoora, Victoria: Department of Sociology, La Trobe University, November 1999), p.77.
7. Heller, *Ethics of Personality*, p.69.
8. Ibid., p.48.
9. Ibid., p.71.
10. Ibid., p.72.
11. Ibid., p.74.
12. Ibid., pp.75–8.
13. Ibid., p.74.
14. Ibid., p.76.
15. Ibid., p.82.
16. Ibid., p.83.
17. Ibid.
18. Ibid., p.85.
19. Ibid., p.88.
20. Ibid., p.91.
21. Ibid., p.90.
22. Heller readily admits that the female character Fifi is a self portrait from the time before she was touched by the great tragedies of twentieth-century European history and that the grandmother is modelled on her own beloved grandmother. A. Heller, *Der Affe auf dem Fahrrad*, p.478.
23. Heller, *Ethics of Personality*, p.95.

24. Ibid., p.114.
25. Ibid., p.97.
26. Ibid., p.106.
27. Ibid., p.102.
28. Ibid.
29. Ibid., pp.109–10.
30. Ibid., p.96.
31. Ibid., p.97.
32. Ibid., p.113.
33. Ibid., p.122.
34. Ibid., pp.128–9. It is also interesting, in the light of my initial comments on Heller's relation to feminism, that she chooses a woman to present her own synthesis of Kant and the ethics of personality.
35. Ibid., p.146.
36. Ibid., p.147.
37. Ibid., p.148.
38. Ibid., p.152. In a recent interview, when asked about her life, Heller replied that 'my work is my whole life'. See 'Interview with Casba Polony', *Left Curve*, 22 (30 June 1998).
39. Heller, *Ethics of Personality*, p.153.
40. Ibid., p.164.
41. Ibid.
42. Ibid., p.165.
43. Ibid., p.181.
44. Ibid., p.168.
45. Ibid., p.165.
46. Ibid., p.195.
47. Ibid.
48. Ibid., p.210.
49. Ibid., p.214.
50. Ibid., p.215.
51. Arnason comments that Heller's preference for Stoic–Epicurean ethics sits oddly with a worldview that takes personal freedom as its highest value. J.P. Arnason, 'The Human Condition and the Modern Predicament', in J. Burnheim (ed.) *The Social Philosophy of Agnes Heller*, p.74. Yet Heller's efforts at moral synthesis are nothing new in terms of her own development; they are also just another instance of an increasing trend evident in Foucault, neo-Aristotelians and others.
52. Heller, *Ethics of Personality*, p.217.
53. Ibid., pp.218–19.
54. Ibid., p.225.
55. Ibid.
56. Ibid., p.277.
57. Ibid., p.233.
58. Ibid., p.267.
59. Ibid., p.254.
60. Ibid., p.255.
61. Ibid., p.256.
62. Ibid., p.275.
63. Ibid., p.272.
64. Ibid., p.260.

65. Ibid., p.259.
66. Ibid., p.268.
67. Ibid., p.269.
68. Ibid., p.273.
69. Ibid., p.260.
70. Ibid., p.294.
71. Ibid., p.295.
72. Ibid., p.2.
73. Vajda, 'Is Moral Philosophy Possible?' p.78.
74. A. Heller, *A General Ethics* (Oxford: Blackwell, 1988), p.1.
75. Vajda, 'Is Moral Philosophy Possible?' pp.79–80.
76. Heller, *Ethics of Personality*, p.91.

CHAPTER 14

1. W. Dilthey, *Selected Writings*, ed. H. P. Rickman (Cambridge: Cambridge University Press, 1976), p.236. Of course, even death does not close the circle of interpretation from the standpoint of historical significance, which remains open-ended.
2. A. Heller, *Der Affe auf dem Fahrrad*, p.476.
3. Ibid., p.477.
4. Ibid.
5. H. Arendt, *The Human Condition* (Chicago: Chicago University Press, 1958), p.185.
6. T. Todorov, *Hope and Memory: Lessons from the Twentieth Century* (Princeton, N.J.: Princeton University Press, 2003).
7. Ibid., pp.19–26.
8. Ibid., p.21.
9. Ibid., p.24.
10. T. Todorov, *Imperfect Garden: The Legacy of Humanism* (Princeton, N.J.: Princeton University Press, 2002), pp.231–2.
11. Ibid., p.232.
12. Todorov, *Hope and Memory*, p.39.
13. Todorov, *Imperfect Garden*, p.232.
14. R. J. Bernstein, 'Metaphysics: Critique and Utopia', *Review of Metaphysics*, 42 (Washington, D.C.: Catholic University of America, December 1988), pp.256–7.
15. A. Heller, *A Theory of Modernity* (Oxford: Blackwell, 1999), p.149.
16. J. Habermas, 'The New Obscurity: The Crisis of the Welfare State and the Exhaustion of Utopian Energies', in *The New Conservatism: Cultural Criticism and the Historians' Debate* (Cambridge Mass.: MIT Press, 1989).
17. Heller, *Theory of Modernity*, p.12.
18. L. Kolakowski, 'The Death of Utopia Reconsidered', in *Modernity on Endless Trial* (Chicago: Chicago University Press, 1990), pp.131–45; Bernstein, 'Metaphysics', p.257.
19. G. Márkus, 'After the System: Philosophy in the Age of the Sciences', in K. Gavrogly et al. (eds), *Science, Politics and Social Practice* (Kluwer Academic Publishers, 1995).
20. Ibid.
21. Ibid., p.157.
22. G. Gutting, *Pragmatic Liberalism and the Critique of Modernity* (Cambridge: Cambridge University Press, 1999).

23. Ibid., p.176.
24. Ibid., p.184.
25. S. Tormey, *Agnes Heller: Socialism, Autonomy and the Postmodern* (Manchester: Manchester University Press, 2001), p.205.
26. P. Beilharz, 'Budapest Central: Agnes Heller's Theory of Modernity', *Thesis Eleven*, 75 (London: Sage, November 2003), p.111.
27. Gutting, *Pragmatic Liberalism*, p.192.
28. G. Markus, 'After the System: Philosophy in the Age of the Sciences', p.157.
29. Gutting, *Pragmatic Liberalism*.
30. J. Grumley, 'A Family Quarrel: Márkus and Heller on Philosophy', in J. Grumley, P. Crittenden and P. Johnson (eds), *Culture and Enlightenment: Essays for György Márkus* (London: Ashgate, 2002), p.66.
31. J. Grumley, 'Exploring the Options in No Man's Land: Heller and Márkus on the Antinomies of Modern Culture', *Thesis Eleven*, 75 (London: Sage, November, 2003).

Bibliography

WORKS BY HELLER

Heller, A., 'Lukács' Aesthetics', *New Hungarian Quarterly*, 24/7 (1966), pp.84–94
—— 'Die Stellung der Ethik im Marxismus', *Praxis: Revue Philosophique Edition Internationale*, 2 (Zagreb, 1967), pp.244–52
—— 'The Moral Mission of the Philosopher', *New Hungarian Quarterly*, 13/47 (Autumn 1972)
—— 'Towards a Marxist Theory of Values', *Kinesis*, Graduate Journal in Philosophy, 5/1 (Carbondale: Southern Illinois University, Fall 1972)
—— 'Individual and Community', *Social Praxis*, 1/1 (The Hague, 1973)
—— 'Marx's Theory of Revolution and the Revolution in Everyday Life', in *The Humanisation of Socialism: Writings of the Budapest School* (London: Allison & Busby, 1976)
—— *The Theory of Needs in Marx* (London: Allison & Busby, 1976)
—— 'The Future of Relations Between the Sexes', in *The Humanisation of Socialism: Writings of the Budapest School* (London: Allison & Busby, 1976)
—— and Vajda, M., 'Communism and the Family', in *The Humanisation of Socialism: Writings of the Budapest School* (London: Allison & Busby, 1976)
—— *Renaissance Man* (London: Routledge & Kegan Paul, 1978)
—— *A Theory of Feelings* (Assen: Van Gorcum, 1978)
—— 'Past, Present and Future of Democracy', *Social Research*, 45/4 (New York: Winter 1978)
—— *On Instincts* (Assen: Van Gorcum, 1979)
—— 'The Philosophy of the Late Lukács', *Philosophy and Social Criticism*, 6/1 (1980)
—— 'The Emotional Division of Labour Between the Sexes: Perspectives on Feminism and Socialism', *Thesis Eleven*, 5–6 (Clayton, Victoria: 1982)
—— 'Habermas and Marxism', in *Habermas: Critical Debates* (Cambridge, Mass.: MIT Press, 1982)
—— *A Theory of History* (London: Routledge & Kegan Paul, 1982)
—— and Fehér, F., *Hungary 1956 Revisited* (London: George Allen & Unwin, 1983)
Fehér, F., Heller, A. and Márkus, G., *Dictatorship Over Needs* (Oxford: Blackwell, 1983)
Heller, A., *A Radical Philosophy* (Oxford: Blackwell, 1984)
—— *Everyday Life* (London: Routledge & Kegan Paul, 1984)
—— *The Power of Shame* (London: Routledge & Kegan Paul, 1985)
—— 'Can "True" and "False" Needs be Posited?' in Heller, *The Power of Shame* (London: Routledge & Kegan Paul, 1985)
—— 'The Great Republic', in Heller and Fehér, *Eastern Left, Western Left: Totalitarianism, Freedom and Democracy* (Cambridge: Polity Press, 1987)
—— *Beyond Justice* (Oxford: Blackwell, 1987)
—— and Fehér, F., *Eastern Left, Western Left: Totalitarianism, Freedom and Democracy* (Cambridge: Polity Press, 1987)

—— *General Ethics* (Oxford: Blackwell, 1988)

—— and Fehér, F., *The Postmodern Political Condition* (Cambridge: Polity Press, 1988)

—— —— 'The Gorbachev Phenomenon', in F. Fehér and A. Arato (eds), *Gorbachev: The Debate* (Cambridge: Polity Press, 1989)

—— *Can Modernity Survive?* (Cambridge: Polity Press, 1990)

—— *A Philosophy of Morals* (Oxford: Blackwell, 1990)

—— and Fehér, F., *From Yalta to Glasnost: The Dismantling of Stalin's Empire* (Oxford: Blackwell, 1990)

—— 'Modernity's Penduluum', *Thesis Eleven*, 31 (Melbourne: MIT, 1992)

—— *A Philosophy of History: In Fragments* (Oxford: Blackwell, 1993)

—— 'A Reply To My Critics', in John Burnheim (ed.), *The Social Philosophy of Agnes Heller* (Amsterdam: Rodopi, 1994)

—— and Fehér, F., *Biopolitics* (London: Avebury, 1994)

—— *An Ethics of Personality* (Oxford: Blackwell, 1996)

—— 'Interview with Casba Polony', *Left Curve*, 22 (30 June 1998)

—— 'The Three Logics of Modernity and the Double Bind of the Modern Imagination', *Graduate Faculty Journal*, 21/2 (New York: New School, 1999), pp.177–93.

—— *Der Affe auf dem Fahrrad* (Berlin: Philo, 1999)

—— *A Theory of Modernity* (Oxford: Blackwell, 1999)

—— 'Questioning the Normative Skepticism of György Márkus', in J. Grumley, P. Crittenden and P. Johnson (eds), *Culture and Enlightenment: Essays for György Márkus* (London: Ashgate, 2002)

—— *The Time is Out of Joint* (Maryland: Rowman & Littlefield, 2002)

—— *Die Auferstehung des jüdische Jesu* (Berlin: Philo, 2002)

—— '9/11, or Modernity and Terror', *Constellations*, 9/1 (Oxford: Blackwell, 2002)

—— *A Philosophy of the Beautiful* (London: Routledge, forthcoming 2004)

CITED SECONDARY WORKS

Arnason J. P., 'Nationalism, Globalisation and Modernity', *Theory, Culture and Society*, 7/2–3 (Middlesbrough: TCS, June, 1990)

—— *The Future that Failed* (London: Routledge, 1993)

—— 'The Human Condition and the Modern Predicament', in J. Burnheim (ed.), *The Social Philosophy of Agnes Heller* (Amsterdam: Rodopi, 1994), pp.57–78

Arato, A., 'Introduction: Towards a Marxist Theory of Values', *Kinesis*, Graduate Journal in Philosophy, 5/1 (Carbondale: Southern Illinois University, Fall 1972)

—— *From Neo-Marxism to Democratic Theory:* Essays in the Critical Theory of Soviet-Type Societies (Armonk, N.Y.: M.E. Sharpe, 1993)

Arendt, H., 'Ideology and Terror', in *Origins of Totalitarianism* (2nd edition, London: George Allen & Unwin, 1958)

—— *The Human Condition* (Chicago: Chicago University Press, 1958)

—— *Lectures on Kant's Political Philosophy* (Sussex: Harvester Press, 1982)

Bauman, Z., *The Individualized Society* (Cambridge: Polity Press, 2001)

Beccaria, C., *Of Crimes and Punishments* (New York: Marsilio Publishers, 1996)

Beilharz, P., 'Budapest Central: Agnes Heller's Theory of Modernity', *Thesis Eleven*, 75 (London: Sage, November 2003), pp.108–13

Benhabib, S., 'Review of *On Instincts* and *A Theory of Feelings*', *Telos*, 44 (St Louis: Telos Press, Summer 1980)

Bernstein, R. J., 'Metaphysics, Critique and Utopia', *Review of Metaphysics*, 42 (Washington, D.C.: Catholic University of America, December 1988), pp.256–7

Brown, D. M., *Towards a Radical Democracy: The Political Economy of the Budapest School* (London: Unwin & Hyman, 1988)

Burnheim, J. (ed.), *The Social Philosophy of Agnes Heller* (Amsterdam: Rodopi, 1994)

Castoriadis, C., *The Imaginary Institution of Society* (Cambridge: Polity Press, 1987)

Cohen, J., 'Heller, Habermas and Justice', *Praxis International*, 8/4 (Oxford: Blackwell, January 1989), pp.491–7

Constantinou, M., 'Agnes Heller's Ecce Homo: A Neomodern Vision of Moral Anthropology', *Thesis Eleven*, 59 (London: Sage, 1999)

Dilthey, W., *Selected Writings*, ed. H. P. Rickman (Cambridge: Cambridge University Press, 1976)

Dworkin, R., *Taking Rights Seriously* (London: Duckworth, 1977)

Fehér, F., *The Frozen Revolution: An Essay on Jacobinism* (Cambridge: Cambridge University Press, 1987)

—— 'Imagining the West', *Thesis Eleven*, 42 (Cambridge, Mass.: MIT Press, 1995)

—— (ed.), *The French Revolution and the Birth of Modernity* (Berkeley: University of California Press, 1990)

—— and Arato, A. (eds), *Gorbachev: The Debate* (Cambridge: Polity Press, 1989)

—— —— *Crisis and Reform in Eastern Europe* (New Brunswick: Transaction Books, 1990)

Giddens, A., *The Consequences of Modernity* (Cambridge: Polity Press, 1990)

Gouldner, A., *The Future of Intellectuals and the Rise of the New Class* (New York: Seabury Press, 1979)

Grumley, J., 'The Dissatisfied Society', *New German Critique*, 58 (New York: Telos Press, Winter 1993)

—— 'A Family Quarrel: Márkus and Heller on Philosophy', in J. Grumley, P. Crittenden and P. Johnson (eds), *Culture and Enlightenment: Essays for György Márkus* (London: Ashgate, 2002)

—— 'Exploring the Options in No Man's Land: Heller and Markus on the Antinomies of Modern Culture, *Thesis Eleven*, 75 (London: Sage, November 2003), pp.25–38

Gutting, G., *Pragmatic Liberalism and the Critique of Modernity* (Cambridge: Cambridge University Press, 1999)

Habermas, J., *The Theory of Communication Action*, 2 vols, i: *Reason and the Rationalization of Society* (Boston: Beacon Press, 1984) and ii: *The Critique of Functionalist Reason* (Boston: Beacon Press, 1987)

—— 'The New Obscurity: The Crisis of the Welfare State and the Exhaustion of Utopian Energies', in *The New Conservatism: Cultural Criticism and the Historians' Debate* (Cambridge, Mass.: MIT Press, 1989)

—— 'Morality, Society and Ethics: An Interview with Torben Hviid Nielsen', *Acta Sociologica*, 33/2 (1990), pp.93–114

—— 'Philosophy as Stand-in and Interpreter', in *Moral Consciousness and Communicative Action* (Cambridge, Mass.: MIT Press, 1990)

—— *Between Facts and Forms* (Cambridge, Mass.: MIT Press, 1996)

—— *The Postnational Constellation* (Cambridge: Polity Press, 2001)

Hadot, P., *Philosophy as a Way of Life* (Oxford: Blackwell, 1995)

Harrison, P., 'Radical Philosophy and the Theory of Modernity', in J. Burnheim (ed.), *The Social Philosophy of Agnes Heller* (Amsterdam: Rodopi, 1994)

Hollis, M. and Lukes, S., *Rationality and Relativism* (Cambridge, Mass.: MIT Press, 1982)

Kolakowski, L., *Main Currents in Marxism*, iii: *The Breakdown* (Oxford: Clarendon Press, 1978)
—— 'The Death of Utopia Reconsidered', in *Modernity on Endless Trial* (Chicago: Chicago University Press, 1990), pp.131–45
Lukács, G., *Die Eigenart des Äesthetischen Werke Banden*, 2 vols (Luchterland, 1963)
—— *History and Class Consciousness* (London: Merlin Press, 1971)
—— *The Ontology of Social Being*, 3 vols, i: Hegel, ii: Marx and iii: Labour (Merlin Press, 1980)
Lemke, T., 'The Birth of Bio-Politics: Michel Foucault's Lecture at the Collège de France on Neo-Liberal Governmentality', *Economy and Society*, 30/2 (London: Taylor & Francis, May 2001), pp.190–207
Márkus, G., *Marxism and Anthropology* (Assen: Van Gorcum, 1978)
—— 'Debates and Trends in Marxist Philosophy', *Communism and Eastern Europe: A Collection of Essays* (New York: Karz Publishers, 1979)
—— 'Interpretations of, and Interpretations in Philosophy', *Critical Philosophy*, 1/1 (Sydney: Fero Press, 1984)
—— 'The Politics of Morals', in J. Burnheim (ed.), *The Social Philosophy of Agnes Heller* (Amsterdam: Rodopi, 1994)
—— 'After the System: Philosophy in the Age of the Sciences', in K. Gavrogly et al. (eds), *Science, Politics and Social Practice* (Kluwer Academic Publishers, 1995)
—— 'Antinomies of Culture', *Discussion Papers*, 38, Academy of Sciences (Budapest: Collegium Budapest, 1997)
—— 'Ten Marginalia on the Responsibility of the Philosopher', in A. Kardas et al. (eds) *Diotima Agnes Heller: Festschrift for Her Seventieth Birthday* (Budapest: Osiris-Gond, 1998), pp.343–59
—— 'Do Ideas Have Bodies? Philosophical Content and Literary Form in Descartes', *Literature and Aesthetics*, 14/1 (Sydney: Sydney University Society of Literature and Aesthetics, June 2004)
Murphy, P., 'Agnes Heller's Great Society', *Thesis Eleven*, 75 (London: Sage, November 2003), pp.98–107
Nozick, R., *Anarchy, State, Utopia* (New York: Basic Books, 1975)
Nussbaum, M., *Upheavals of Thought: The Intelligence of the Emotions* (Cambridge: Cambridge University Press, 2001)
Rawls, J., *A Theory of Justice* (Cambridge, Mass.: Harvard University Press, 1972)
Szelenyi, I., Luke, T. et al., 'Review Symposium on Soviet-Type Societies', *Telos*, 6 (New York: Telos Press, Summer 1984), pp.155–92
Todorov, T., *Imperfect Garden: The Legacy of Humanism* (Princeton, N.J.: Princeton University Press, 2002)
—— *Hope and Memory: Lessons from the Twentieth Century* (Princeton, N.J.: Princeton University Press, 2003)
Tormey, S., *Agnes Heller: Socialism, Autonomy and the Postmodern* (Manchester: Manchester University Press, 2001)
Wolin. R., 'Heller's Theory of Everyday Life', in J. Burnheim (ed.), *The Social Philosophy of Agnes Heller* (Amsterdam: Rodopi, 1994)
Vajda, M., *The State and Socialism* (London: Allison & Busby, 1981)
—— 'Agnes Heller: A Lover of Philosophy, A Lover of Europe', in J. Burnheim (ed.), *The Social Philosophy of Agnes Heller* (Amsterdam: Rodopi, 1994)
—— 'Is Moral Philosophy Possible at All?' *Thesis Eleven*, 59 (London: Sage, November 1999)

Index